The China Dream

- China's obsession w/ self-sufficiency
- secrecy - lack of or inaccurate info.

The China Dream

*The Quest for the Last Great
Untapped Market on Earth*

Joe Studwell

Grove Press
New York

First published in Great Britain in 2002 by
Profile Books Ltd., London, England

Published simultaneously in Canada
Printed in the United States of America

FIRST GROVE PRESS EDITION

Library of Congress Cataloging-in-Publication Data
Studwell, Joe.
 The China dream : the quest for the last great untapped market on earth /
Joe Studwell.
  p. cm.
 Includes bibliographical references.
 ISBN 0-8021-3975-2 (pbk.)
  1. China—Economic policy—2000- 2. China—Economic conditions—
2000- 3. Economic forecasting—China. 4. China—Commercial policy.
5. Investments, Foreign—China. 6. China—Foreign economic relations.
I. Title.

HC427.95 .S78 2002
330.951—dc21   2001058996

Designed by MacGuru

Grove Press
841 Broadway
New York, NY 10003

03 04 05 06 07 10 9 8 7 6 5 4 3 2 1

For Mirri, who couldn't quite put up with me.
And for Tiffany, my wife, who strangely can.

Contents

In this paperback edition of the China Dream the last four chapters have been updated to take account of events that occurred and economic data that were released in the course of 2002. An epilogue has been added. This was written following a series of interviews with ministers in Beijing and the conclusion of the 16th Chinese Communist Party congress in November 2002.

Preface

'Nothing is required, and nothing will avail, but a little clear thinking'
John Maynard Keynes, *Collected Writings*

THIS IS A book for anyone who wonders why some developing countries become rich while others remain poor. It is also a book about why businessmen, in trying to pick between winners and losers, are mesmerised by some markets but left cold by others. For 700 years, ever since outsiders first started writing about the place, the western world has believed that there are untold riches to be garnered in China. In the thirteenth century, Marco Polo described the country with unrestrained awe; in the fifteenth century, Christopher Columbus set out from Europe to bring home its bounty; in the eighteenth century, the emergent British empire looked on China as the ultimate destination for its maritime trade routes. Over the past 150 years, with the rise of globalisation, the belief in China's unparalleled potential has taken on the order of an obsession. That obsession reached a peak in the last decade of the twentieth century, when $300 billion of foreign capital flowed into the country. The investment was of a magnitude different from anything seen previously, but it was still chasing the same end – what this book calls the 'China Dream'.

No other large developing country captures the same attention. India and Indonesia are remarked on less, and usually for their perceived disinclination to escape poverty. Brazil, courted briefly by international business in the 1970s, still has the words of former French president Charles de Gaulle ringing in its ears: 'It is,' he said, 'a country of great potential, and always will be.' Even the Japanese, who did manage to haul themselves into the ranks of the leading nations in the early twentieth century, achieved this against the expectations of most outsiders. It was only Japan's rapid growth, modernisation and naval defeat of Russia in 1905 that persuaded the Great Powers to take her seriously. China has never had this problem. The importance of her supposedly vast markets has been trumpeted for centuries. No nation in history has ever been promoted as a surer bet for investment returns.

Yet history also teaches that time and again China has failed to fulfil the promise that foreigners ascribe to her. For centuries, businessmen have gambled their capital on buying camel trains, chartering ships, building railways and financing highways in their efforts to open up the Chinese market, only to face disappointment. Perplexed by a nation that has imported only a fraction of what would be expected from such a huge, populous country, entrepreneurs have tried to sell every service or type of goods imaginable in the hope of unlocking the collective Chinese wallet. At each setback, and for each successive wave of traders – from the earliest European naval powers (Spain and Portugal), to their north European successors (Holland and Britain), to Russia, America and, in the run up to China's communist revolution of 1949, the entire developed capitalist world in unison – the China Dream has retained extraordinary potency.

The measure of this potency was put into stark relief in the 1990s. It was a decade when transnational investment flows increased by multiples. In part this reflected the development of a global financial system, allowing capital gathered in one place to be moved faster and more freely to others in search of greater profit. Cross-border investment also mushroomed because of political and technological changes, rooted in the 1980s, that opened up an unprecedented stock of investment opportunities around the world. Soviet communism collapsed, apartheid and international isolation ended in South Africa, serious moves were made towards economic liberalisation in Latin America, and in north and south-east Asia investors marvelled at the small, fast-growth countries dubbed 'Tiger economies'. In a case of complementary supply – of international capital – and demand – from deregulating emerging markets – the rich world in the 1990s had more money to invest, and more international investment choices, than ever before.

In the face of the myriad investment possibilities on offer, the world seized on two before all others. They were a new dream – the internet – and China – the oldest dream of all. The internet wowed popular imagination with technology. It promised to unite all previously known forms of communication – telephony, journalism, audio and video entertainment and commercial and market data – in a single medium. Seemingly foreshadowed by the take-off in the use of electronic mail in the mid 1990s, there was an internet gold rush to stake out territory on the world wide web. Everything, it was said – from car sales to legal services – would take place in cyberspace. Stock market capitalisations of internet companies with no revenues, let alone profits, shot past those of traditional corporations that had been around for decades. In the light of a revolutionary technology that promised, within a few years, to bring together all mankind in a single market, traditional measures of value lost their significance.

China's magnetic appeal to international capital was no less forceful. Despite all the opportunity on offer in the wake of the Cold War in eastern Europe, south-east Asia, Latin America and Africa, only the United States – the epicentre of the technology boom – managed to suck in more direct foreign investment in the course of the 1990s than the communist giant. Over $300 billion of investment inflows were recorded in the decade, into what remained one of the poorest countries on earth – an economy one-seventh the size of America's, its gross domestic product no more than that of Spain and the Netherlands combined. China had neither the youthful appeal of technology nor the post-Cold War appeal of political reform. But it did not need them. The sales pitch was the same as it had always been – the prospect of adding one quarter of the world's population to a corporation's list of potential clients in a single move, the prospect of a market with the statistical potential to become the biggest in the world. In many cases, these propositions were grasped more easily by the middle-aged executives of established multinational companies than was the theory of the internet, whose new-fangled ways were dominated by twenty- and thirty-something entrepreneurs in T-shirts and sneakers. Ultimately, however, the China Dream was the same as the internet dream – the promise of exponential market growth, delivered in short order. The fact that the latter came courtesy of a scientific breakthrough, and the former because of an opening to the outside world, was less important. What global investors were drawn to were big ideas and the chimera of fat, fat profits.

The internet dream was punctured, with a loud bang, in 2000. Despite rising numbers of internet users – young and old – investors took fright at online businesses that ate cash instead of generating it. Traditional questions were finally raised about business plans, revenue sources and returns on investment. Introspection turned to panic and, in one of the fastest acts of wealth destruction in human history, New York's Nasdaq stockmarket – barometer of the global technology sector – shed 60 per cent of its value in one year.[1] Three trillion dollars of market capitalisation – equivalent to well over a third of the annual output of the American economy – was wiped out. Companies like Yahoo! lost nine-tenths of their value. Millions of Americans and Europeans who had invested in internet stocks – either directly or indirectly through their savings and pension schemes – saw the worth of their holdings decimated.[2] Recession in the information technology economy threatened to trigger a broader global recession.

Through all this, the China Dream survived relatively unscathed. Though plagued by internet-like problems of illusory markets, high investment costs and low returns, faith in China proved more resilient than commitment to one of the most remarkable, utilitarian technologies of human history. When foreign capital inflows to China threatened to fall in the late 1990s – because of slowing growth and poor investment returns – the government promised further deregulation and negotiated to join the World Trade Organisation. At the point international investors began to dump internet stocks, there had been nothing companies could do to reassure them. China's investment commitments, by contrast, held up.

This book will grapple with the issue of how much longer the China Dream can be sustained. It is written from the perspectives of history, economics and journalism, but it is inevitable that psychology will play a major role in determining China's fate. The biggest questions today are all to do with sentiment rather than fundamentals. How long will international business fund investments that produce no return in the hope of future profit? How many times will China's government be able to escape a crisis of confidence with promises that *this time* its commitment to deregulation is real? Above all, for how long will the Chinese people keep their money in a nationalised savings system while the government drags the country towards insolvency? The complexity of these issues will become clearer in the course of the pages that follow. For now, it is enough to note that China's fate is far from certain. Like all dreams, the Chinese one could still come true, even if it is in the nature of most dreams not to do so.

Whatever the outcome, there is no denying that we are living in an era of resurgent 'Chinoiserie'. An overseas Chinese diaspora of 60 million people is energised by the hope that mainland China can break out of its historical shell.[3] Chinese culture resonates on the international stage to an extent unseen since the communist takeover. An art house fascination with Chinese cinema has grown into the mass market phenomenon of *Crouching Tiger, Hidden Dragon,* the biggest grossing non-English language movie of all time.[4] In 2000, the Chinese claimed their first Nobel Laureate in literature, Gao Xingjian. In July 2001, Beijing romped home with the nomination to host the 2008 Olympic Games. In Europe and the United States, the fashionably young are to be found tattooing themselves with Chinese characters they cannot read.[5] A tide of Chinese cultural romance is washing over the world. What remains to be seen is if this is the harbinger of a new age, or an end-of-era outpouring that is the precursor to crisis. This author suspects the latter. This book argues that the economic foundations of contemporary China have been laid on sand and constructed from the kind of hubris that drove the Soviet Union in the 1950s. Among investors, expectations and reality are grotesquely out of kilter. At the rational, reductive level at which economists operate, it is a recipe for suffering and disaster. And yet, at the less rational level at which real life operates, one can never be certain of betting against the enduring power that is the China Dream.

Cast of characters

This is a true story.

The businessmen

Robert Allen   Chairman and chief executive officer of American Telephone and Telegraph (AT&T). Retired 1997.

Barton Biggs   Chairman of Morgan Stanley Asset Management and Global Investment Strategist for Morgan Stanley Dean Witter.

John Brizendine President of McDonnell Douglas, 1973 to1982. Former chairman of the National Council on US–China Relations.

Ronnie Chan   Hong Kong billionaire and chairman of family real estate business, Hang Lung Development Company.

Christopher Columbus   An explorer and entrepreneur from Genoa, he set off west from Europe in 1492 to bring home China riches, but hit instead upon the Americas.

Carl Crow   An American journalist turned entrepreneur and advertising agency founder who lived in Shanghai through the 1920s and 1930s.

Stephen Friedman   Co-chairman with Robert Rubin, and later chairman, of Goldman Sachs, 1990–94.

Maurice Greenberg   Chairman since 1989 and chief executive officer since 1967 of American Insurance Group (AIG). Founder of the International Business Leaders Advisory Council of the mayor of Shanghai.

Hu Chengzhou   Chairman of Delishi, one of China's leading manufacturers of low voltage electrical equipment. A salesman turned multi-millionaire businessman from Liushi, near Wenzhou in China's Zhejiang province.

Louis Hughes   Executive vice-president and president of international operations at General Motors until 2000.

Li Ka-shing   Chairman of Hutchison Whampoa and Cheung Kong, Hong Kong's most famous billionaire, with a personal fortune in excess of $10 billion.

Li Xiaolin   Daughter of Chinese Communist Party number two Li Peng, she runs an energy consultancy, China Power Investment Corporation.

Frank Lo Kit-lu   Chairman and chief executive officer of Top Form, a lingerie manufacturer, until 1997. A self-made Hong Kong millionaire and the 'brassiere king' of China.

John Mack President of Morgan Stanley from 1993, president and chief operating officer of Morgan Stanley Dean Witter from 1997 to 2001.

John McDonnell Chairman and chief executive officer of McDonnell Douglas from 1988 to 1994, and chairman from 1994 to 1997, when the company was taken over by Boeing.

Minoru Mori President of Japanese real estate giant Mori Building and a multi-billionaire.

Oei Hong Leong Chairman and chief executive officer of China Strategic Holdings and one of more than 40 children of Indonesian overseas Chinese tycoon and founder of the Sinar Mas conglomerate, Eka Tjipta Widjaja.

Clifford Pang A Canadian Chinese entrepreneur who made his first fortune in China manufacturing computer disk drive heads and went on to build the country's largest private residential housing estate.

Jack Perkowski Head of investment banking at US investment bank Paine Webber in the 1980s. Founder and chairman of China investment firm ASIMCO since 1993.

Edzard Reuter Chairman of Daimler-Benz until 1995.

Mochtar Riady Chairman of Indonesia-based financial services conglomerate Lippo Group, implicated in 1997 in the campaign finance scandal surrounding Bill Clinton's Democrat administration.

Jurgen Schrempp Chairman of Daimler-Benz since 1995, successor to Edzard Reuter.

John F. ('Jack') Smith Chief executive officer of General Motors from 1992 to 2000, chairman since 1996.

Moses Tsang Chairman of Goldman Sachs Asia, 1989 to 1994.

Tsui Tsin-tong A Hong Kong businessman with close ties to mainland interests, including the People's Liberation Army, a collector of Chinese art and a man with ambitions to be Hong Kong's first chief executive prior to its return to Chinese sovereignty in 1997.

Kazuo Wada Eldest son of Katsu Wada, founder of the Japanese supermarket and department store chain Yaohan. Chairman of Yaohan until the company's bankruptcy in 1997.

Carl Walter One of the first seven American graduate students allowed to study in China after the resumption of Sino-US diplomatic relations in 1979. He went on to become an investment banker with Credit Suisse First Boston and negotiated the first direct listing of a Chinese controlled company overseas – that of Brilliance China Automotive on the New York stock exchange in October 1992.

Wei Zhonghui   Owner of the Chaoyang Button Factory in China's button capital, Qiaotou in Zhejiang province.

Jack Welch   Chairman and chief executive officer of General Electric from 1981 to 2001.

Peter Woo   Hong Kong billionaire and chairman of conglomerate Wharf Holdings until 1994. Mr Woo still controls Wharf via his family holding company Wheelock & Co. He had ambitions to be Hong Kong's first chief executive prior to its return to Chinese sovereignty in 1997.

Bill Young   North China field representative of McDonnell Douglas until 1997.

Zhao Xiyou   Chairman of Jinbei Automotive in Shenyang in north-east China until forcibly 'retired' by the central government in 1993. He conceived the first direct listing of a Chinese controlled corporation overseas – that of Jinbei holding company Brilliance China Automotive on the New York stock exchange in October 1992.

The politicians

Ron Brown   United States Commerce Secretary until his death in a plane crash in Croatia in April 1996. He was a leading critic of China's human rights record prior to the Clinton government's election. Led trade missions to China in 1994 and 1995.

Chen Shui-bian   Elected president of Taiwan in 2000. The candidate of the opposition Democratic Progressive Party, he became the first non-Kuomintang president since 1949.

Chen Yun   A Chinese revolutionary who held key economic posts in government from 1949 through the 1980s. One of the so-called Eight Immortals of the post-Mao Zedong leadership, he died in April 1995.

Chiang Kai-shek   President of China from 1928 to 1931 and 1943 to 1949 and president of the Republic of China (Taiwan) from 1950 to 1975.

Jean Chrétien   Canadian premier since 1993. Led trade missions to China in 1994 and 1996.

Deng Xiaoping   A Chinese revolutionary and paramount leader from 1978. One of the so-called Eight Immortals of the post-Mao Zedong leadership, he died in February 1997.

Eight Immortals   A name taken from characters in a famous Taoist fable to describe the key personalities in the generation of Chinese leadership that joined the Communist Party after its foundation in the 1920s and became the Party elders after the death of Mao Zedong. The two leading Immortals were Deng Xiaoping and Chen Yun. The other six are usually listed as Peng Zhen, Yang Shangkun, Bo Yibo, Li Xiannian, Madame Deng Yingchao and Wang

Zhen. Madame Deng Yingchao (no relation) is sometimes substituted by Song Renqiong. Of these possible nine immortals, only Bo Yibo was alive in 2001.

Mikhail Gorbachev General secretary of the Soviet Communist Party from 1985, and president from 1989, until the Soviet Union's dissolution at the end of 1991. Winner of the 1990 Nobel Peace Prize. He visited Beijing shortly before the June 1989 Tiananmen Square massacre.

Michael Heseltine Britain's president of the Board of Trade from 1992 to 1995 and deputy prime minister from 1995 to 1997. Led trade missions to China in 1995 and 1996.

Hu Yaobang General secretary from 1980, and chairman from 1981, of the Chinese Communist Party; he replaced Mao Zedong's chosen successor Hua Guofeng. Forced to resign in 1987 following student protests, his death in April 1989 was a catalyst for the Tiananmen Square protests of that year.

Hua Guofeng Succeeded Mao Zedong as chairman of the Chinese Communist Party in 1976 but lost out in a long power struggle with Deng Xiaoping and was stripped of his post in 1981.

Jiang Qing Wife of Mao Zedong, leader of the ultra-leftist Gang of Four during the Cultural Revolution, arrested by her political enemies one month after her husband's death, in October 1976. She allegedly committed suicide in prison in 1991.

Jiang Zemin General secretary of the Chinese Communist Party since June 1989, chairman of the Central Military Commission since 1990 and president of China since 1993. Promoted by Deng Xiaoping after the ouster of General Secretary Zhao Ziyang, who was alleged to have mishandled the 1989 Tiananmen Square protests. Previously mayor and Party secretary of Shanghai from 1985 to 1989. Jiang is expected to give up some or all of his current posts in 2002 and 2003.

Henry Kissinger United States assistant to the president for national security from 1969 to 1975 and secretary of state from 1973 to 1976. He came to prominence in 1971 when news of his secret contacts with Zhou Enlai were made public, paving the way for himself and President Nixon to visit China in 1972. In 1982, he started an international consulting firm, Kissinger Associates, that is particularly active in China.

Helmut Kohl Chancellor of West Germany from 1982, and of a reunified Germany from 1990, until 1998. Made numerous trips to China, including with trade missions in 1993 and 1995.

Lee Kuan Yew Prime minister of the Republic of Singapore from 1959 to 1990 and senior minister since 1990. Well known for his belief in the possibility of an alternative 'Asian Way' of development.

Li Peng Chinese premier from 1987 to 1998 and chairman of the National People's Congress since 1998. He rose in government through a series of ministerial jobs in the energy sector. A strong supporter of armed intervention in the protests of 1989. He is expected to retire from government in 2003.

Lord Macartney An emissary of Britain's George III who led a 700-person delegation to the Chinese emperor Qian Long in 1793 to request an opening of trade between the two countries.

Mao Zedong A founder of the Chinese Communist Party and, in 1949, the People's Republic of China. He served as chairman of the Party from 1943 until his death in September 1976 in a reign characterised by mass political campaigns including the Great Leap Forward (1958 to 1960) and the Great Proletarian Cultural Revolution (1966 to 1976).

Richard Nixon US president from 1968 to 1974, when he resigned in anticipation of proceedings to impeach him. As well as for scandal, his administration is remembered for ending US involvement in the Vietnam War and for improving relations with China.

Hazel O'Leary US energy secretary from 1993 to 1996. Led a trade mission to China in 1995 and was subsequently investigated for excessive expenditure and exaggerated claims for contracts signed on the trip.

Chris Patten Chairman of Britain's Conservative Party from 1990 to 1992 and the last governor of Hong Kong from 1992 to 1997.

Peng Zhen A Chinese revolutionary and one of the so-called Eight Immortals of the post-Mao Zedong leadership, he died in April 1997.

Robert Rubin A 26-year veteran of Goldman Sachs, and co-chairman with Stephen Friedman from 1990 to 1992, prior to joining the Clinton administration as assistant to the president for economic policy from 1993 to 1995 and treasury secretary from 1995 to 1999.

Wang Zhen A Chinese revolutionary and one of the so-called Eight Immortals of the post-Mao Zedong leadership, he died in March 1993.

Wu Yi Vice minister from 1991 to 1993, and minister from 1993 to 1998, of foreign trade and economic cooperation and a state councillor (a rank between minister and vice premier) thereafter. She led several high-profile Chinese business delegations abroad in the 1990s.

Yang Shangkun A Chinese revolutionary and one of the so-called Eight Immortals of the post-Mao Zedong leadership. Chinese president from 1988 to 1993, he died in September 1998.

Yao Yilin A Chinese revolutionary and vice premier through the 1980s, he died in December 1994.

Boris Yeltsin Russian president from 1991 to 1999.

Zhao Ziyang Premier from 1980 to 1987 and general secretary of the

Chinese Communist Party from 1987 to 1989, he was stripped of power in the wake of the June 1989 Tiananmen Square massacre.

Zhou Enlai   A founder of the Chinese Communist Party, he served as foreign minister from 1949 to 1958 and premier from 1949 until his death in January 1976. He began the negotiations with Henry Kissinger that led to Richard Nixon's visit to China in 1972.

Zhu Rongji   Vice premier with special responsibilities for the economy from 1991 to 1998, governor of the central bank from 1993 to 1995 and premier since 1998. Previously mayor of Shanghai from 1987 to 1991. He is expected to retire from government in 2003.

The economists

Milton Friedman   One of the leading lights of monetarist economics and winner of the 1976 Nobel Prize for economics. He lauded early reforms in China in the 1980s but in the 1990s became highly critical of the state's continuing role in the economy.

Albert Keidel   A consultant economist to the World Bank and senior economist at the World Bank's China mission from 1997 to 2000. In the early 1990s he challenged the accuracy of widely publicised purchasing power estimates that suggested China already had one of the largest economies in the world.

Paul Krugman   A prolific economist and author, based successively at Yale, Stanford, MIT and currently Princeton universities, and author of the highly controversial 1994 polemic, *The Myth of Asia's Miracle*.

Nicholas Lardy   A University of Washington and Brookings Institution economist and the author of key academic books in the 1990s about China's financial system and foreign trade. One of the first to raise the possibility of fiscal crisis in China.

Marco Polo   An adventurer-cum-economic commentator whose accounts of the sophistication and wealth of China in the thirteenth century influenced businessmen and politicians for hundreds of years.

Edward Steinfeld   Assistant professor of management at the MIT Sloan School and a leading authority on reform of China's state enterprises.

Larry Summers   Chief economist of the World Bank from 1991 to 1993, US under secretary of the treasury for international affairs from 1993 to 1995, US deputy secretary of the treasury under Robert Rubin from 1995 to 1999, US secretary of the treasury from 1999 to 2001. A keen supporter of purchasing power assessments of China's economic significance.

Robert Summers   The father of Larry Summers and one of the pioneers of Purchasing Power Parity theory.

Author's note

SPELLING OF CHINESE names follows local usage in the places where people are from. The names of mainlanders are rendered in the *pinyin* system of romanisation as two separate words, such as Jiang Zemin. The first names (which come last in Chinese) of Hong Kong and Taiwanese persons are hyphenated, as in the cases of Li Ka-shing and Chiang Kai-shek. South-east Asian name spellings are rendered as three words, as in Lee Kuan Yew or Liem Sioe Liong. Chinese persons who style themselves in the western manner, such as Peter Woo, are recorded in this fashion. The aim in all cases is to use the spellings that are most familiar to English language readers. All renderings of quotations and expressions in Mandarin Chinese use *pinyin*.

Some of the data in this book refer to China's gross domestic product (GDP) and some to her gross national product (GNP). The choice is usually dictated by what data are available from listed sources. A distinction is always made. However, readers need not concern themselves unduly because the difference between China's GDP and her GNP – the latter includes net income from overseas investment plus some other international transfers – is tiny. In the case of developed countries like the United States and United Kingdom, however, the difference between GDP and GNP is considerable. Cross country comparisons always compare GDP with GDP, or GNP with GNP.

China's national statistics agency used to be called the State Statistical Bureau, but changed its name in 2000 to the National Bureau of Statistics (NBS). The agency has been referred to by its new name throughout.

Measures of distance and space are the imperial ones still most familiar to Britons and Americans – miles, square feet and so on – followed by metric conversions in parentheses. All tonnages, however, are metric. This is because of the potential confusion created by the fact that there are two types of 'imperial ton'. The metric ton, which is globally most familiar, especially in modern shipping, is almost exactly the same as – 0.984 of a British imperial 'long' ton (2,240 pounds). A metric ton is about one-tenth more than – 1.102 of – a US 'short' ton (2,000 pounds). It is hoped Americans will be able to knock 10 per cent off quoted tonnages without too much difficulty.

All sums of money are expressed in US dollars as well as – where helpful – their original currencies. Exchange rates are those prevailing at the time of the transactions referred to. Further details are often provided in endnotes.

Foreign direct investment (FDI) refers to foreign investment by an outside entity – almost always a company – in a domestic Chinese entity – again, almost always a company – in pursuit of profit. It is this form of foreign investment that accounts for the vast majority of capital inflows into China because indirect foreign investment, such as that via stock markets, is closely circumscribed by the government. With rare exceptions, FDI refers to foreign companies investing directly in businesses they manage or co-manage. Data for FDI, like almost every statistic in China, are suspect. In particular, the special tax-breaks and incentives offered by the Chinese government to attract FDI have encouraged mainland businesses to route domestic investments via Hong Kong shell companies in order to receive preferential treatment. This so-called 'round tripping' of money means China's genuine FDI inflows are overstated, but there is no way of knowing by how much; estimates range around 10 to 20 per cent. At the level of FDI by country or territory of origin, investment attributed to Hong Kong tends to be further exaggerated because many Asian companies opt to route investments via the territory – Japanese ones have done this to avoid charges of exporting jobs from home; Taiwanese firms do so to avoid Taipei government restrictions on their investment in the mainland; and south-east Asian tycoons do so to avoid the charge they are exporting precious capital to China. Hong Kong, as a committed free market economy, prides itself on keeping no records of capital inflows or outflows. It is therefore impossible to know what part of reported Chinese FDI from Hong Kong actually comes from Hong Kong investors.

梦 dream *n.*, a cherished hope; ambition; aspiration.

Part 1
The making of a miracle

1

The dream through history

'Merçacciones innumeras *[an incalculable amount of trade]*'

Margin annotation by Christopter Columbus in his copy of Marco Polo's *Travels*,
an account of his time in China.[1]

THE STORY OF the western world's commercial fascination with China dates back more than 2,000 years and it began with a product that still symbolises the relationship – silk. The Chinese fabric spun into a sensual, thin gauze first became familiar in Rome around 50BC. Cleopatra, mistress of Julius Caesar and Mark Antony, and queen of Egypt, was among the first to promote a fashion for transparent dresses in the exotic fabric. Despite the outrage of sartorial conservatives – the writer Seneca railed against the wearing of such dresses in the Roman capital, 'clad in which no woman could honestly swear she is not naked' – by the end of the fourth century, silk was a universal accoutrement in civilised society throughout the empire.[2]

Silk is one of those rare traded commodities that is capable of stirring the imagination. It also gave rise to the first great myth of the China trade – the perception of the 'silk road' as the principal commercial avenue of antiquity. At the height of European colonialism in the nineteenth century, archae-ologists uncovered the flotsam of ancient trade between China and Europe along a series of routes through north-west China, central Asia and northern Persia to ports in Syria and along the Black Sea. From these discoveries derived an image of a collective silk road along which a large and regular trade was being conducted. While there is no doubt the silk routes were traversed at the time of the Roman and Han empires (which roughly coincided), more recent scholarship suggests the trade has been much exaggerated. The enormous cost of land transport in the pre-modern era (twenty to forty times that of sea freight), the thousands of miles traders had to cover, and their vulnerability to attack – both physical and fiscal – make it highly improbable that large-scale exchanges occurred.[3] Rational analysis says that most silk travelled by sea from southern China to the Malay peninsula, where it was purchased by Arab and Persian middlemen who forwarded it to Europe. The romantic image of camel trains trudging 3,000 miles through sand storms across the silk routes of central Asia is largely just that – movie material.

梦

But, if the classical silk road owes as much to imaginative fallacy as to historical fact, other aspects of China's pre-modern relationship with the outside world have been understated. Three hundred years after the fall of the Han dynasty (206BC–AD220), China produced a supremely confident civilisation of an extraordinarily cosmopolitan nature. The first, or 'golden' era[4] of the Tang dynasty (618–907) was built on a level of internationalism that was not reached again until the forced opening of China in the nineteenth century – and arguably still not then. The Tang epoch is known today for its exquisite statues and porcelain, among the most highly prized remnants of Chinese history. Less well known is that the roots of the dynasty's cultural outpouring lay in a society which combined Indian Buddhism, the courtly pastimes of Iran and a commercial inquisitiveness towards foreign goods and services with Chinese leadership in political organisation, technology and agricultural productivity. At the beginning of the Tang period, when Europe was plunged deep into the Dark Ages, China was so far ahead of the rest of the world that it needed nothing from it. Yet the dynasty remained so hungry for more that it borrowed freely from outsiders, with no apparent sense that this could ever involve a loss of national face. Tang China was too dynamic a place to care. It was, perhaps for the only time in history, just what the characters of China's name claim: the 'zhong guo', or 'middle kingdom' – the realm around which every other civilisation rotated.

In the era of the Golden Tang emperors, an estimated 25,000 foreigners lived in the capital, Xi'an, in the centre of the country. Many more, quite possibly over 100,000[5] – Moslems, Christians, Jews and Zoroastrians – were based at Guangzhou and Quanzhou at the junction of China's key southern sea routes. The foreigners were the main facilitators of an international trade in which the outside world received far more useful products and ideas than China did in return, but in which the principle of interchange was paramount. Many leading Tang dynasty figures were foreigners – Turks, Afghans, other central Asians and Koreans. Xuan Zong, one of the greatest of the Tang emperors, took a dancing girl from Tashkent, Uzbekistan, as a concubine and princess.[6]

The Golden Tang period was a true golden era. The most sophisticated and open society in the world, it bred wealth. China boasted more than two dozen cities with populations of over half a million at a time when large urban centres in Europe counted their inhabitants in the tens of thousands. Two million people lived in Xi'an. With agricultural yields up to four times the global norm, few went hungry. For the well-to-do, success brought with it an early form of the international playboy lifestyle – thoroughbred horses, hawks, polo, chess, silk, spices, aromatics and porcelain.

This cosmopolitanism, however, was not to last. For Tang China never fully overcame the xenophobic instincts of its baser subjects. In the late eighth and ninth centuries, the dynasty was weakened by rebellions, the rise of regional potentates and greater corruption, all coinciding with natural disasters that led to higher prices and increased inequality. In these more straitened times, anti-foreigner sentiment was roused. There was a massacre of foreign merchants by rebels at Yangzhou in 760. Trade recovered but, in the next century, the same latent, conservative forces built up to a greater massacre at Guangzhou, in 879. A fading regime lost confidence in cosmopolitanism and became a convert to prejudice. Foreign religions – including the Buddhism that historian Samuel Adshead believes gave Tang China 'a critical philosophy hardly surpassed in the West till Descartes' – were banned and persecuted.[7] Tolerance gave way to paranoia and fear of outsiders. When the Tang dynasty fell in 907, there ended a brief flowering of pluralism that even now, well over a thousand years later, has not been approached again.

梦

By the time the first western accounts of the country were being written in the thirteenth century, China was a civilisation past its peak. The problem was that while China had all the trappings of wealth and sophistication, it was no longer acquiring the means of further progress. The Chinese were becoming increasingly introverted and, with just a few exceptions, losing interest in what could be garnered from the wider world. Europeans, by contrast, acquired from China between the eleventh and the fourteenth centuries the critical technologies of modernisation: designs for multi-masted ships with fixed rudders; the magnetic compass; blast furnaces for the complete liquefaction and casting of iron; advanced hydraulics; gunpowder; and the 'escapement', the key component of clockwork. China took almost nothing in return that could help her retain her lead over the world. The Song dynasties (960–1279) were an era of what has been called with reference to the twilight of the British empire 'splendid isolation' – from the cultural and political life of the rest of the world.[8] China had her majesty but, in a tradition that continues to this day, her grandeur no longer indicated dynamism.

The earliest foreign commentators, most famously Marco Polo, however, had no sense of this, since China continued to enjoy a huge commercial, scientific and cultural lead over European societies. Polo, who came from Venice, Europe's largest city with 160,000 inhabitants, probably spent twenty years in China between 1275 and 1295[9]. He passed a lot of that time in Hangzhou, capital of the Southern Song dynasty, with six million inhabitants. There was no comparison. As he describes at length in his *Travels*, Europe and China were worlds apart – in terms of urbanisation, sea power, consumerism and aesthetic taste. He wrote of the Yangzi river, the great Song trade artery, that 'the amount of shipping it carries and the bulk of the merchandise that merchants transport by it, upstream and down, is so inconceivable that no one in the world who has not seen it with his own eyes could possibly credit it'. Other medieval commentators concurred. Oderic of Pordenone, also an Italian, said of Guangzhou: 'All Italy hath not the amount of craft that this one city hath.'[10] The Arab traveller Ibn-Batuta, who compared the Yangzi with the Nile, and China with the wealthiest states of Eurasia and Africa, concluded: 'Nowhere in the world are there to be found people richer than the Chinese ... porcelain in China is of about the same value as earthenware with us, or even less.'[11]

In the late thirteenth and fourteenth centuries, during the Yuan dynasty (1271–1368), China's wealth, and a series of European and Asian refugee crises created by the Mongol invasions, brought more foreigners on to Chinese shores than at any other time prior to the nineteenth century. Along its southern sea trade route, China was a huge importer of pepper and other spices from the Middle East and Africa, and foreigners were involved in this trade. Polo, who returned to Europe by the southern sea route, claimed that for every one spice ship travelling from Alexandria to Christendom there were a hundred heading for China. There were at least two established Italian trading communities with bases in the country – the Venetians and the Genoese – although the biggest commercial exchanges in terms of numbers of traders were with Moslems from central Asia.

The oceanic revolution, bad maps and unfriendly emperors

None the less, while the more adventurous fourteenth-century European merchant communities were familiar with China's thriving economy, they were not in a position to exploit it on a large scale. This could happen only with the oceanic revolution of the late fifteenth and sixteenth centuries, when, having recovered from the Black Death, European countries equipped themselves with the kind of large ships that the Chinese had been sailing for hundreds of years. Europe's maritime explosion, which began in Portugal and Spain and spread north to England and Holland, coincided with its application of another ancient Chinese technology: printing. In 1485, the first copies of Marco Polo's *Travels* appeared.[12] Christopher Columbus, the greatest of the early European adventurers, soon learned of the book's contents and decided that China was where he must go. Columbus's own copy of the *Travels* is filled with more than a hundred margin notes about the gold, silver, silk, spices, porcelain, precious stones and fine wine to be found there.[13]

Unfortunately, Columbus missed his target. Sailing west from Spain, he hit upon an unknown and unexpected continent – America. The China mission was thereby diverted as the Spanish *conquistadors* set about extracting the booty of what became Latin America. It was the Portuguese who, following Vasco da Gama's 1498 voyage eastwards round the Cape of Good Hope, arrived sooner in the Chinese orbit. But they were driven by their own get-rich-quick dream that was built around a commodity – spices – rather than a place, their interest in China being that the country was the single biggest spice buyer in the world. The Portuguese wanted to handle the business and, in 1511, seized Malacca, a key spice trade entrepôt. The plan from here was simple: go to the Chinese and negotiate trading rights. It was a plan that would fail to bear fruit for the next three centuries.

China was by now a place far removed from the cosmopolitan, mercantile empire of the Tang emperors, or even the Song dynasty described by Marco Polo. In 1368, following a long period of civil insurrection, the Ming dynasty came to power, founded by a preacher turned regional warlord, Zhu Yuanzhang.[14] The Ming state was populist and anti-capitalist. Although early Ming was also expansionist, creating an Indian ocean empire of tributaries, this was not driven by any love of trade. When the Portuguese sent a diplomatic delegation, led by Tomé Pires, to what was now the Ming capital of Beijing in 1520, they found themselves talking to an empire uninterested in doing business. Pires was told Portugal must vacate Malacca – a Chinese satellite – and forget about trading with China. When he had the temerity to suggest that Malacca now belonged to Lisbon, he was locked up in a Guangzhou jail until his death in 1524.

The Portuguese were rebuffed in further attempts to trade at Guangzhou and Ningbo, but they eventually tempted local officials, with the cash to be earned from trade, into letting them settle on the Macau peninsula. Macau became the first 'Hong Kong', an insular, isolated empire's window on the outside world. When Malacca fell to the Dutch in 1641, the more commercially aggressive Dutch East India Company thought to expand the China trade through a series of points of entry. But the Dutch navy was unable to deliver militarily, failing to take Manila in 1617 and Macau in 1622 and subsequently being kicked out of Taiwan by the Ming in 1662. Dutch diplomatic efforts to negotiate trade openings at Guangzhou and Xiamen received the same short shrift that the Portuguese had encountered.

By a curious turn of events, the single most significant route for China trade in the sixteenth century ended up in the hands of the successors of the explorer who had first set out there. After Columbus made landfall in the Americas, Spanish sailors discovered in the course of the next half century that the Pacific current and north-east trade winds would carry them from Mexico to Manila, while further north the westerlies would bring them back from Japan to California. While Mexico had silver, China had silk and other luxury goods prized by the *conquistadors* and Manila was a convenient off-shore centre from which to do business away from hostile Ming officialdom. From the mid-sixteenth to the mid-seventeenth centuries this trade was small scale but regular and profitable. Records from Manila in the 1630s show that around twenty-five large Chinese junks a year made the trip from Guangdong and Fujian provinces.[15]

European trade in the Far East via the Cape and routes originating in the eastern Mediterranean increased by a factor of about ten in the sixteenth century, but from a very low base.[16] On top of this was the Pacific trade. The mainstay of Chinese exports continued to be silk in all its guises, with the addition of more porcelain, medicinal rhubarb root and the first shipments of tea, which was originally sold as a tonic.[17] The China trade was not insignificant, but it was far less important than might be expected from a nation of 150 million people that was still unsurpassed in terms of technological and cultural sophistication, literacy and per capita income. And China bought almost nothing in return for its sales. Chinese exports had strong symbolic value – attested by the porcelain collections of Philip II of Spain and other, lesser European rulers, or the silk tents of Middle Eastern potentates – but they did not add up to much in terms of global impact. It was Spain, not China, that created the first worldwide commercial empire. The Ming rulers of the sixteenth century let their deep sea fleet rot in Nanjing, reduced the size of their army, appeased their neighbours and looked inwards, rejecting the kind of discursive reason and culture of discovery that was taking hold in Europe in favour of an ever-narrower, anti-theoretical Confucianism. China's potential as a trading partner for the west remained unfulfilled.[18]

Souls, forecast sales and Chinese diplomacy

Potential is a currency of sorts – and one that, despite repeated disappointments, has kept foreigners lined up at China's gate throughout history. The first true China interest group emerged in the Renaissance era when the prospect of a single market of 150 million souls hooked the evangelistic ambitions of the Jesuits. China, from the mid-sixteenth century, became the Society of Jesus's biggest theatre of operations. The organisation sent its best people – most famously Matteo Ricci, but many other powerful organisers and intellectuals as well. With so much of their own time and effort invested, and dependent on continued financial support from Europe, the Jesuits in China wrote enthusiastically about their experiences. Two Ricci essays published in Europe in 1616 contrasted the good order of the empire with the religious and political chaos of Europe – an argument that would recur at the end of the twentieth century as western businessmen contrasted the apparent stability of China with the chaos of the newly democratised nations of the former Soviet Union. Yet reality for the Jesuits on the ground was little different from that for their commercial counterparts. The market was nothing like as hot as they hoped – they made only a few conversions, slowly – and outside the Chinese élite they were far from welcome.

In 1644, the Ming dynasty fell and was succeeded by the Manchu house of Qing. The new, pony-tailed rulers decided to allow foreign delegations to visit Beijing, an apparent opening that led to much international diplomatic activity. The Russians sent a mission from 1653 to 1656, the Dutch in 1668 and the Portuguese in 1670. When the Chinese proved ambivalent about trade treaty requests, the Russians tried another visit from 1675 to 1678, the Portuguese in 1678 and the Dutch in 1687. Even the Papacy, stirred by Jesuit tales of souls for the saving, sent two envoys in the early eighteenth century. In every case, the leaders of the European delegations dispensed with familiar diplomatic rituals and did the nine prostrations of the kowtow – the required act of ritual abasement – before the Chinese emperor. This produced a poor return. No trade concessions were granted as a direct result of these visits. Only the Russians, whose Cossack horsemen were threatening China's northern border by the Amur river, were granted the right, in 1689, to send caravans to Beijing in order to exchange furs for silk.[19]

Although the Qing had their moments of international and intellectual curiosity – they legalised Catholicism and allowed the Jesuits to become their court technicians – the kowtowing trade ambassadors sought a liberalisation too far. Its sense of superiority reinforced by the obsequious supplications of the westerners, Qing China continued in its insular ways, leading to a gradual decline relative to a rapidly modernising world. At its peak, the dynasty was successful militarily – expanding China's borders to the north and north-west so that the empire encompassed 5 million square miles (more than in the Tang era). But size did not go hand in hand with quality. While the emperor ruled autocratically and ever more arcanely with his grand council, European governments were leveraging their power through central banks, national debt markets and more efficient taxation. There was more pluralism in Qing society than in modern communist China – with literary societies, local improvement boards and private banking networks – but it was far removed from the complexity that had evolved in Europe, with its competing churches, universities, corporations, stock exchanges, royal academies, literary, philosophical and professional societies, libraries, publishing houses, clubs and so forth. Still, the more that China sank, the more the Europeans seemed obsessed with it as a market.

In the course of the eighteenth century, the emergent global power of the era – the British empire – turned its gaze on China. With Qing expansion and a high birth rate, the Chinese population doubled from 150 million in 1600 to 300 million in 1800. To the most commercially driven power in history, this market demanded to be traded with. Relations began badly when George Anson, a British commodore, quarrelled with the authorities at Guangzhou in 1743 when his man-of-war entered the port in need of repairs and he refused to accept the Chinese demand to pay customs duties.

Five decades later, however, Britain returned with a formal, closely calculated and extremely expensive effort to develop commercial ties. The visit of George III's ambassador, Lord Macartney, to the emperor Qian Long in 1793 was the first mega western trade mission to China – he was accompanied by a 700-strong party of officials and businessmen that was not exceeded even by the jumbo jet American, French, German, Canadian and British delegations that were to follow in the 1990s. Macartney was an experienced and successful diplomat. He represented a pantheon of commercial interests and brought with him an array of modern, European technologies designed to impress an ageing emperor: telescopes, globes, barometers, lenses, clocks, airguns, swords and a complete carriage. But whereas in the 1860s the Japanese would be jolted into a political and economic revolution by the contemplation of western military and scientific prowess, Qian Long dismissed the offerings as 'amusements for children'. He told Macartney, in one of the best-known lines of modern Chinese history, that China had not 'the slightest need of your country's manufactures'.[20] Qian Long was living on hubris. He governed an empire of plummeting literacy, falling productivity, shrinking cities and scientific stultification that proposed to defend itself with war junks of one-sixth the displacement and one-sixth the armoury of the vessels that now came out of Europe.[21] But there was nothing Macartney could do. By the end of his visit, the English emissary was exhausted. He spent weeks haggling over diplomatic protocol – refusing, as a respresentative of George III, to perform the kowtow – and left China with nothing to show the investors of his mission.

Inscrutable China, drugs and the arrival of America

By the end of the eighteenth century, with the beginnings of globalisation and rising literacy, international opinion about China was far more informed than at any point previously. Yet the world was unable to arrive at a coherent view of the country. Observers divided into three camps that are still in evidence today: a sceptical minority, an unchastened, ever-hungry commercial lobby and a more culturally focused group that developed and mythologised a cult of Chinoiserie.

The early sceptics included Macartney himself, who concluded that China's efforts to overawe the world 'merely by her bulk and appearance' would come unstuck.[22] The theme of Chinese arrogance and her false sense of superiority was taken up by writers like Daniel Defoe, who wrote of 'their contempt of all the world but themselves', and Montesquieu, who concluded that the Jesuits had been hoodwinked: 'the missionaries were deceived by the appearance of order, not its reality ... China is a despotic state whose principle is fear,' he wrote. Even Voltaire, schooled by the pro-China Jesuits, observed that the emperor cared nothing for the world beyond his borders while his empire seemed fixed in time.[23]

For the commercial lobby, however, China's vast size and population – plus, perhaps, the fact that traders were constantly being spurned – convinced them there *had* to be a great market waiting to be tapped. In the course of the eighteenth century, the discovery of a new commodity export from China – tea – further whetted the appetite of global commerce. By 1800, Europe was importing more than 10,000 tons of Chinese tea a year; by 1830, more than 20,000 tons. The problem was that the Chinese still imported almost nothing in return. In order to pay for its tea, the British East India Company began shipping raw Indian cotton to China. When this did not cover the costs, it added consignments of opium.

Much that is misleading has been written about the Chinese opium trade. The drug, Middle Eastern in origin, spread from being used medicinally to becoming a social accoutrement in Qing China that symbolised the ability not to work and thereafter found a new constituency among working-class labourers attracted to a stimulant that also staves off hunger. The spread of opium use in China, predominantly in the nineteenth century, presented a mirror image to the spread of tea in Europe – from tonic to social lubricant to large-scale consumer good. Although opium was less diffused than tea, like tea, its consumption was driven not by supply but by demand.[24] By the 1830s, the China drugs trade – tea and opium – helped lift the displacement of foreign shipping entering Chinese ports to 200,000 tons – perhaps 300 ships – per year. This represents a five- to tenfold increase on trade in the Elizabethan age, though it is still far from impressive in global terms.

The biggest trading at the time took place in perceptions – informed and imagined. The Enlightenment era witnessed the rise of intellectual Sinophilia and a fashion for Chinoiserie that has never since disappeared. Late eighteenth- and early nineteenth-century Europe based its pagodas, wallpaper and decorative Rococo style on Chinese design. Production of porcelain began at Meissen, Sèvres and Plymouth. The basic ingredients of the modern European garden were also taken from China. Britain's Royal Horticultural Society was founded in 1804 and within a few years its agents were bringing Chinese plants home. Wistaria, rhododendrons, clematis and roses – all were either direct imports or Chinese hybrids. The writer Oliver Goldsmith made his name in the 1760s with a newspaper series, followed by a two-volume novel, *The Citizen of the World*, about a Chinese scholar living in London and the adventures of his son in Asia. Economic thinker Adam Smith's description of the division of labour in the *Wealth Of Nations* was influenced by what he had read of the division of labour in Chinese porcelain production. China loomed far larger in the western mind than it did in western trade – another consistency with the present. The country was popularly perceived as a living version of Ancient Egypt, although even more *laissez faire* and liberal. The reality on the ground, however, was that China's cultural decline continued while rising folk religions and rural alienation presaged the civil wars of nineteenth century.

梦

A new factor in China's external relations at the end of the eighteenth century was the arrival on the scene of the United States. The first American ship to enter Guangzhou, the *Empress of China*, docked in 1784. The commander, Major Samuel Shaw, returned home claiming a 30 per cent profit from selling New England ginseng and furs and the visit heralded a short Sino-American boomlet in fur trading, particularly of sea otter pelts. In 1805, forty-one US vessels were recorded as having come to trade at Guangzhou. With the decimation of the American sea otter by the 1820s, however, the business declined.

In the middle of the nineteenth century, geopolitical changes in the Americas began to mark out the terms of a future Sino-US relationship. Following the war with Mexico in 1848, the US annexed California and was transformed into a Pacific nation. There was a west coast land rush, a railway boom and the importation of tens of thousands of indentured labourers – particularly

Chinese – to undertake low-paid manual work. In the 1850s, Commodore Perry of the US navy sailed to Japan; in 1867 the American government purchased Alaska; and in 1898 it seized the Philippines. The nation stared out across the Pacific ocean and the biggest thing it saw on the other side was China. The first US diplomatic mission to Beijing, that of Caleb Cushing, was despatched by President John Tyler in 1843. Cushing was sent to seek a treaty to put trade on a formal footing '... so that,' in the words of a letter from the President, 'nothing may happen to disturb the peace between China and America'.[25] From the outset, US approaches to Beijing were couched in terms of friendship and mutual interest that aimed to set America apart from the increasingly aggressive European powers.

Despite this, Cushing was no more successful than European diplomats in securing trade privileges. American merchants endured the same problems as their Old World competitors. Chief among these was that the Chinese were reluctant to buy anything from them. In order to pay for the tea, silk, nankeen cloth and porcelain they wanted, the Americans found they could sell sea otter skins, seal pelts, sandalwood and certain other exotic natural products, such as New England ginseng, but the income was never enough and bills had to be made up with precious silver coins. It was to avert an excessive use of silver that Americans also began to ship opium to China. The near impossibility of selling anything but opium – and even this became more difficult as domestic production increased – sent Sino-US trade into four decades of stagnation and decline from the 1860s.[26]

Gunboats and gold rush: the limits of European patience

While Washington hoped to court Beijing with expressions of brotherliness and effusive friendship, by the mid-nineteenth century the Europeans had lost patience. Unwilling to walk away from the elusive Chinese prize altogether, but unable to persuade the Qing government to deregulate trade of its own volition, European strategy moved towards gunboat diplomacy. In the wake of the two so-called Opium Wars, four coastal cities were opened to international settlement by the treaty of Nanjing in 1842, and a further eleven by the treaty of Tianjin in 1858.[27] Britain seized the island of Hong Kong, while the Russians availed themselves of a large chunk of Manchuria, in the north-east, through the convention of Peking in 1860. By 1864, following international pressure, missionaries had been granted the right to buy land for mission stations throughout China.

From the 1860s, foreign encroachment and serious domestic rebellion did push the Qing dynasty into a belated modernisation drive. The state expanded, Beijing ministries were strengthened, the tax regime improved and tax-income increased. Trends to micro-farming and illiteracy were temporarily arrested and the populations of China's big cities increased. A more business-friendly environment saw the rebirth of Chinese private enterprise in cities like Tianjin and Shanghai. Entrepreneurs, and returned students and overseas Chinese, set up business partnerships, stock markets and chambers of commerce. A professional class, including engineers, doctors, geologists and publishers, started to emerge. There were here the beginnings of a modern China – urban-based and in communication with the outside world. But at the same time, the countryside, where the vast majority of the population lived, was being left far behind and a huge counter-élite of landlords, rural mafiosi, shamans and warlords promised trouble ahead.

International trade increased considerably in the mid nineteenth century, but still from a low base. The tonnage of foreign shipping passing through Chinese ports each year rose from 200,000 tons in the 1830s to 7 million tons in 1864.[28] In the 1860s, the China trade continued to be dominated by two commodities, tea and opium. In 1867, tea constituted 59 per cent of Chinese exports and opium 46 per cent of imports.[29] The tea trade rose to around 25,000 tons of shipped product a year. By contemporary global standards, China's trade remained paltry; it is indicative that the majority of the tea was consumed by one tiny country – England. When silk is added to tea to make up more than nine-tenths of Chinese exports, China can be seen clearly for what it still was in the 1860s: commercially, a three-product proposition.

梦

It was in the last decades of the nineteenth century that trade volumes increased to more significant levels. The opium business reached a peak in the 1870s, tea in the 1880s and China also discovered a second bulk import it was willing to pay for – Manchester cotton, a mass-market textile made affordable by the invention and application of the cotton gin.[30] By the 1890s, China was also buying grain, cigarettes, kerosene, scrap iron, coal and dyes and exporting new commodities such as soya beans, sesame and wood oil and low-grade consumer goods like matting and bristles. It began to look as if the miracle market was finally opening up. In 1905, the displacement of foreign shipping entering Chinese ports hit 72 million tons – a tenfold increase on four decades previously.

The foreign business community, with heavy backing from its various governments, scrambled to support and nurture this trade. The British navy suppressed pirates up and down the China coast. Cartographers mapped the shoreline. A joint Chinese and foreign customs service constructed lighthouses and buoys and dredged the Shanghai and Tianjin estuaries. There were joint pilotage and quarantine administrations. The Jesuits set up a typhoon warning system in Shanghai. In short, the world readied itself for a great deal of business. Between 1890 and 1930 there was the most sustained effort to unlock the China market in the pre-communist era.

By this time, there were powerful, global industrial imperatives demanding that China be brought into commercial play. In the late nineteenth century, the process of industrialisation in Europe and the United States reached a level where overseas markets were critical to further expansion. The Manchester cotton mills were but one example: there was no way that the results of their mechanised production could be consumed solely within the British Isles. As an English writer famously observed in the 1840s: 'If we could only persuade every person in China to lengthen his shirttail by a foot, we could keep the mills of Lancashire working round the clock.'[31] Surplus agricultural and manufacturing output was even more of an issue in the United States, which had led the way in mass production but had no captive imperial markets to speak of. There is the apocryphal story of James Buchanan Duke, father of the modern American tobacco industry, who, on hearing of the invention of a high-volume mechanised cigarette-rolling machine in the 1880s, ordered for an atlas to be put before him. Leafing through the population legends at the bottom of the pages, he stopped when confronted by the entry 'Pop: 430,000,000'. 'That,' he said, 'is where we are going to sell cigarettes.'[32] Henry Cabot Lodge, who represented textile interests as a senator for Massachusetts, captured the perceived urgency of the exporter's task: 'All Europe is seizing on China,' he wrote at the turn of the century, 'and if we do not establish ourselves in the east that vast trade, from which we must draw our future prosperity, and the great region in which alone we can hope to find the new markets so essential to us, will be practically closed to us for ever.'[33] Of course, the trade was still far from vast. But Mr Lodge and his mill-owning constituents were determined that if the modern Chinese was to wear a shirt made from Manchester cotton, he should also be equipped with New England underpants. Underwear, curiously, was one of the first great untapped Chinese markets to be identified by American business.

The desire for further trade with China provided the impetus for US secretary of state John Hay to ask the major powers in 1899 to declare that they would respect the country's territorial integrity and allow free use of the treaty ports in their spheres of influence. Given that the US had no territorial sphere of influence in China, this policy made sense in its own right. But behind the US government's action was a vociferous US business lobby. The New York Chamber of Commerce, terrified that the Europeans were about to grab China's riches for themselves, wrote to the State Department demanding that it take 'such proper steps ... for the prompt and energetic defence of the existing treaty rights of our citizens in China, and for the preservation and protection of their important commercial interests in that Empire'. Manufacturers and producers of textiles, cotton, steel, iron, kerosene and cigarettes all put the case for urgent action before their government, whether through open letters or congressional testimony. The pressure was reinforced by an alliance between American business and US Protestant missionaries, who numbered 3,000 in China by the 1930s. The latter could be found soliciting donations on the sidewalks of almost every big American city, and their demand was simple: free trade in souls and conversions.[34]

The China lobby was no less fierce in Europe. After 1869, the opening of the Suez Canal – contemporaneous with the development of steamships – made the Suez–Bombay–Colombo–Singapore–Shanghai route the jugular of the British empire. Not only did Manchester cotton makers and other durable goods manufacturers demand that the British government secure their market access in China, but the highly influential grandees of the City of London – blue-blooded pioneers of international financial services – insisted their turf be protected. China needed financing, and London must profit by it.

梦

The first great investment gold rush in China concerned railways. The railway investors applied John Maynard Keynes's investment 'multiplier' theory even before the British economist's career had begun. With China's modern infrastructure almost non-existent, it was reckoned that the construction of trunk rail routes would pump prime an explosion of economic growth – across trade, manufacturing and services. This was the story that players like the US Western Union Company sold to their domestic financiers. As the general turned businessman J. H. Wilson put it in a letter to the US diplomat – and later secretary of state – John W. Foster in 1884: 'If we could build for her [China] a few thousand miles of railroad, we should not only supply the steel, the locomotives, and the cars but should greatly stimulate the demand for every other article manufactured by our countrymen.'[35]

Practice was rather more testing than theory. The Chinese court was highly suspicious of railways – and their promise of unrestricted travel – and reacted to the first line, built without permission near Shanghai in 1877, by compulsorily purchasing and destroying it. The progress of the iron roads, however, was not to be stopped. Imperial consent for railway building was given, after intense pressure, in 1887. The first trunk lines were built in the

1890s, followed by countrywide construction in the first decade of the twentieth century, when 5,000 miles of track were laid. American, Russian, French, Belgian, German and British companies and entrepreneurs poured in millions of dollars of investment. The railway rush was so intense that from 1909 the financing of all projects was centralised under an international banking consortium. The US government, in particular, believed this was less likely to make railway building a trigger for the colonisation and break-up of China.

On the heels of railway money followed investment in trade and manufacturing. The sectors of activity reflected on the one hand the scale of the perceived opportunity – almost everything was tried – and on the other the kind of strategic planning that has continued to dominate foreign investment in China. Thus the American journalist turned advertising agency boss Carl Crow could write in 1937 that: 'At one time or another, almost every conceivable kind of merchandise has been shipped to China on the off chance that some use would be found for it and that a market would be built up.'[36] Equally, in a specific industry like cosmetics, foreign manufacturers seized on the predilection of a minority of urban Qing women for wearing make-up, made calculations based on the business to be had if Chinese women generally wore make-up, and flooded the market in anticipation. There were similar projections made in the pharmaceutical business. The remnants of millions of advertising posters produced by foreign drug companies in the period can still be found in the antique markets of large Chinese cities.

With inward investment came a real estate boom in coastal China. This was most impressive in Shanghai, where the years following the First World War witnessed the construction of the country's first high-rise office blocks and hotels, including the sandstone structures with Art Deco and neo-classical interiors on the Bund waterfront and Nanjing road that can still be seen, having survived the architectural ravages of the late twentieth century.[37] As is the case today, expensive new office buildings were occupied almost exclusively by foreigners. Many merchants leased grand premises as soon as they arrived in China – long before they could assess the market's potential – convinced that in such an important country their commercial 'face' was of paramount importance. Crow likened the opening of international branch offices in Shanghai between the world wars to an outbreak of measles, observing: 'It really is remarkable how much vanity there is in supposedly astute businessmen, or how much romance. It is either vanity or the romantic idea that business is like an adventure story that, in many cases, provides the urge to make them open expensive branch offices.'[38]

Vanity or not, the foreign population in China exploded in the inter-war years to 600,000 people – double the foreign population, excluding Hong

Kong and Taiwanese residents, today.[39] The largest group among the inter-war expatriates were white Russians, around a quarter of million of them. There were other refugees, including Kazhaks – also in flight from Bolshevism – and German, Austrian and Hungarian Jews who founded a community in Shanghai. But another 300,000 foreigners were in China entirely of their own volition, there to either construct or exploit the market place. There were diplomats around the country, consuls at treaty ports, flag officers, professionals in the maritime customs administration, the foreign salt gabelle and the post office, emissaries from the League of Nations, lawyers, accountants, engineers, architects, conservationists, missionaries, dentists, doctors and vets. And there were tens of thousands of businessmen and office managers, not to mention the adventurers and tricksters of popular legend.[40] With all those spacious offices, shops, bars and homes, the city in the 1930s consumed more electricity than any English metropolis except London.

Perspiration without profit

Yet, somehow, for all its bustle and excitement, late nineteenth-century and early twentieth-century China failed to make the kind of contribution to the bottom line that global corporations had predicted. Each time merchants discovered what they believed to be a jackpot commodity, the market shifted beneath their feet. Tea was a big business in the 1880s, but two decades later it was almost non-existent. In the 1860s, the British began to develop Indian tea production; they made it both mechanised and tax-free for export. Chinese producers and their government were unresponsive to this competition; tea output remained unmechanised and subject to taxation. As cheap Indian tea increased its market share, the only reaction of Chinese traders to lower international prices was to adulterate their product – thinning it down with whatever came to hand. Within a few years, China had destroyed its main avenue of international trade; in 1905, tea exports were under 4,000 tons, one-thirtieth of their peak in the 1880s.[41]

There were similar rapid declines in the key import businesses of opium and cotton. Opium sales into China peaked in 1879 at around 6,000 tons, but halved in the next twenty years as production increased in Yunnan and Sichuan, the Qing government organised an anti-opium campaign and the British government belatedly suppressed shipments from India. The mill owners of Lancashire, whose excitement knew no bounds when cotton sales boomed at the end of the nineteenth century to account for half China's annual imports, were also chastened. Chinese and Japanese producers within China moved quickly to undercut the Manchester mills and imports of manufactured cotton goods fell, at today's prices, from more than $1.3 billion a year at the turn of the century to less than $150 million in 1935.[42] In the Chinese market, price was everything and western exporters had nowhere to run once local mechanised production was ramped up. The twentieth-century Chinese consumer wore neither Manchester shirts nor New England underpants.

Trade in the period of most intense interest in the China market – from 1890 to 1930 – diversified without discovering genuinely large-scale volumes for individual products. By 1905, two-fifths of China's imports, and most of its exports, fell under the category 'miscellaneous' – and the term could not have been more appropriate.[43] Among foreign businessmen conducting regular trade were Germans from Hamburg who sold second-hand heavy horseshoes to be melted down and turned into razors.[44] There was also a steady trade in scrap iron, reject glass and other heavily discounted produce – businesses that fell under the category known as 'muck and truck'. Americans persisted in their efforts, successful in varying degrees, to sell US ginseng in China. And by 1937, foreign automobile manufacturers had sold a grand total of 50,000 lorries, buses and cars.

From a Chinese perspective, trade growth was impressive. Imports and exports as a percentage of gross national product were only 3 per cent in the 1860s, but 20 per cent by the 1910s – far more than in Maoist China later in the century. Shanghai between the World Wars was the second busiest port in the world. Yet, from an international perspective, the China experience failed to add up to much. Shanghai saw a lot of traffic, but China – a vast country with a vast coastline – had no other comparable international ports. Trade grew rapidly, but from a very low base and in an overdiversified, low-margin manner. By the 1930s, the US was China's number one trade partner, yet the China trade never exceeded 2 per cent of total US trade.[45] When Secretary of State – later President – William Taft wrote in June 1905 that 'one of the greatest commercial prizes of the world is the trade with the 400,000,000 Chinese', he had not been well briefed.[46]

The story of inward investment was even more disappointing. Carl Crow's *400 Million Customers*, a beautifully written, sardonic account of his twenty-five years in Shanghai at the height of the China gold rush, paints a picture to which it is not impossible to relate today. He writes of foreign drug manufacturers whose market calculations led them to 'rosy day-dreams in which a private yacht occupies the foreground and a country estate can be seen in the middle distance'.[47] In a nation with only 25,000 hospital beds, Crow states that his advertising and merchandising agency failed to launch a single, genuinely successful pharmaceutical product. In the 1930s, the western medicine market, at today's prices, was worth less than $30 million a year – split between hundreds of competitors. The cosmetics market was worth less than $10 million, with no less competition.[48] Crow's China is one of long receivables, rigid markets, structural inefficiency, impossible logistics and relentless, brazen copying and substitution of imported goods with cheaper fakes.

At the heart of most of the problems was the fact that the market was simply not what the foreigners believed it to be. Talking about poor countries, Crow refers to the 'theoretical customers who are interesting for statistical purposes, but valueless from a standpoint of actual sales'. There were countless examples of this in China. Some of his clients insisted on giving away free product samples as promotional ploys. In one instance this led to a near-riot and a court case as the urban poor obstructed a Shanghai thoroughfare in pursuit of free toiletries; in another, almost all the free product coupons in a Chinese newspaper were cut out by newsboys who redeemed them for thousands of dollars' worth of merchandise.[49] The soap manufacturer who funded the latter excercise fled China within six months.

It is not, as Crow stresses, that the Chinese are against spending money. The constraint, as ever, is that one can only spend what one has. When US and European export managers crossed the world in attempts to bolster China sales, local buyers placed additional orders as a means of 'giving face'. But once the managers left town, the orders were adjusted in line with market reality. 'Long before the transaction is finally closed,' wrote Crow, 'one after another of the fat orders the export manager secured will, for one good reason or another, be cancelled or cut down so that in the end the volume of business will probably be about the same as it would have been if the export manager had remained at home.'[50]

Coupled with the limitations of the market were the chaos and neurosis of China's domestic environment. Although the republican revolution of 1911 is popularly understood as a progressive event, it was in many respects a conservative backlash against the attempts by the late Qing empire to modernise China. People in the provinces did not like the anti-opium campaign, did not like efforts to nationalise and centralise domestic railway companies, and did not like the increased tax burden associated with a more developed state. Just as the Russian revolution came about partly as a reaction against serious efforts at reform in the last years of Tsarist rule, so Chinese republicans captured the support of those who saw change as unbearably painful. The country in the 1910s, 1920s and 1930s was one that proved incapable of fundamental reform but was made up – at least in the cities – of people with ever stronger individual aspirations. Crow described ambitious young Chinese desperate to work for foreign corporations. But, failed by their government and the education system, they copied English language application letters from books sold on street corners and turned up to interviews with only 'a very hazy idea' of the sentences they had transcribed.[51]

The international railway investments, the most expensive adventures of the global investment community, were victims of both economic fantasy and Chinese political reality. The most fanciful projects, despite years of planning, never got off the ground. Such was the fate of the British plan, first mooted in the 1860s, to link China with India via Burma. This would have involved the construction of a rail line across some of the most difficult terrain on the planet.[52] Many lines, however, did go ahead. In most cases the projects went over budget, sometimes prodigiously so. The planners' investment multiplier, meanwhile, failed to multiply because the Chinese hinterland was so poor. On top of this, the railways were symbols of foreign encroachment on China's sovereignty. The Boxer rebels attacked them all over the country in 1899, while the First World War, Chinese warlords and Japanese aggression were all to disrupt construction. The national government, blown back and forth by the winds of nationalism and economic aspiration, was itself ambivalent about upholding agreements – as in 1904, when it demanded that the contract to build the Canton–Hankow (today Guangzhou–Wuhan) railway be handed back because a Belgian syndicate had taken equity control of the project. If there were returns, they were meagre. In many cases, the bonds issued to finance Chinese railway construction went unpaid and are today historical curiosities bought and sold by collectors.

Reflection, amnesia, reinvestment

In the 1930s, in the wake of global depression, the China investment boom turned to bust. Fortunes were lost by real estate speculators and many of Shanghai's new offices, the ritzy shops of its Nanjing road, and buildings in other foreign concessions stood empty. Publicly traded stocks dropped to a fraction of their former values. Banks called in old loans and refused to make new ones. And whereas the depression in Europe and the United States was a temporary phenomenon, the trajectory in China was more permanently downhill. Attacked from outside by Japan, torn apart by warlordism and civil strife within, China was finally ruined by the incompetence of its central government. Hyperinflation in the 1940s was as bad as that in Weimar Germany before the rise of fascism. In something of a parallel with the German experience, such was the state of desperation among China's nascent middle class by 1949 that many of its members threw in their lot with extremism – in this case, the communists. Wiser heads, along with hundreds of thousands of disappointed foreigners, packed up what they could and headed for Hong Kong, Taiwan, Europe, Australia and North America.

For most Chinese who stayed behind, there was a brief honeymoon period with Mao Zedong's communists in the early 1950s as the stratification of society was swept away, the status of women was raised and the country basked in its freedom from foreign interference. But the Maoists also brought new forms of repression and terror. In the first years after 1949 they killed mostly landlords, but by the late 1950s there was a more general hunt for anyone – or the family of anyone – deemed to be politically incorrect by standards that changed continuously. In 1966, the country was plunged into a 10-year class war known as the Cultural Revolution. Schools and much of civilian government were closed down and persecution became the national occupation. The economy, meanwhile, was wrecked by a mix of central planning and misguided modernisation campaigns that led to famine on an unprecedented scale. The deaths by starvation of 30 million people were hidden from the outside world until the start of the 1980s, when the first census results to be published since the Cultural Revolution began revealed extraordinary loss of life.[53]

While China descended into chaos, western economic historians of the post-war era reflected at length on the pre-communist effort to open the China market. Paul Varg, highlighting the actual volume of business done in China in the period against the records of what investors said might be done, reported: 'Measured against these actualities the rhetoric concerning the China market was so wild as to suggest that it was in the nature of a myth. Indeed, the gap between the rhetoric and the actualities assumed dimensions of so great a scope as to suggest that the sheer joy of the discussion and not the facts sufficed as a propellant.'[54] Varg echoed Carl Crow's slightly subtler conclusion after his quarter century spent on the ground in Shanghai: 'It is to be hoped the manufacturers had a lot of fun out of their ventures, because they didn't make much money.'[55]

The extraordinary point about these observations, however, is not the veracity of their content, but the speed with which they were forgotten. Crow's book, published in 1937, found a widespread audience and quickly went through several imprints, in London and New York. Varg, writing in 1968 at the height of the Cultural Revolution, also spoke to a receptive academic audience. But four years later, in the wake of Richard Nixon and Henry Kissinger's historic and unexpected 1972 visit to China, a short-lived market for scepticism was blown away. The Nixon trip resulted in Washington recognising the Beijing government over that of the Kuomintang (Nationalist Party) on Taiwan. After a hiatus of only twenty years, the mainland market was re-opened for business. From spring 1972, American traders could visit the bi-annual Canton (Guangzhou) Trade Fair.[56] The National Council for US–China Trade was founded. Though it limited its membership to American corporations with revenues of more than $50 million annually, it signed up 136 companies in its first year.[57]

From 1972, the China game was on again – for some hardy European and Japanese traders it had never ended – and it was accompanied by a resurgence, started in America and picked up in Europe, of Chinoiserie and cultural Sinophilia. In the Cold War context, Russia was bad, China was suddenly good, and things Chinese were hip. The same month her husband went to Beijing, First Lady Pat Nixon posed for the cover of *Ladies Home Journal* in a Chinese-style evening gown.[58] 'Opulent Chinoiserie for grand evenings', ran the text, as husband Dick sipped *maotai* in Beijing. The Chinese government started 'friendship tours' for small groups of selected foreign friends who were bussed around Maoist model villages. This was to great effect. David Rockefeller, CEO and chairman of the board of Chase Manhattan bank, was one of the first to travel. He came back in 1973 and reported in *The New York Times*: 'The social experiment in China under Chairman Mao's leadership is one of the most important and successful in human history.'[59] Far from having destroyed the wonder market, he suggested, the communists had improved it.

In a love fest atmosphere, it was not long before global capitalism hit on the next big Chinese thing: oil. The reopening of China coincided with a global energy crisis. The oil majors, along with Chinese engineers, guessed that the application of modern technology might reveal the existence of large on- and off-shore oil deposits. Possibility was soon being reported as inevitability. *Newsweek* wrote in 1975 that 'the only sure thing is that China's oil reserves are vast ... more oil than is contained in the North Sea and Alaska's North Slope combined'.[60] In the late 1970s and early 1980s, there was a black gold rush in which the oil majors spent $1.7 billion. But they found no worthwhile oil deposits, just a little gas, in the South China Sea.[61]

If the oil rush was another bust, it put China projects back on the map. Waves of foreign investment interest began to crash again on Chinese shores. After the oil men came the bankers. There were fifty-seven international banking delegations to China in 1978 alone.[62] The bankers, in turn, roused the politicians. Ronald Reagan, François Mitterrand and Helmut Kohl travelled to China in 1983 and 1984. Queen Elizabeth II visited in 1986, sailing aboard the royal yacht *Britannia* into Shanghai harbour, where the façades of the 1930s foreign office blocks on the Bund had been sandblasted for her benefit.[63] American state and city politicians discovered their own vehicle to express enthusiasm for the China trade: twinning. By 1984, a dozen American states, and many large cities, paired off with Chinese provinces and cities. Ohio became twinned with Hubei province, New York with Beijing, St Louis with Nanjing, San Francisco with Shanghai, Los Angeles with Guangzhou.

The dance hotted up and the music of commercial possibility played to a rising tempo. In the mid 1980s Armand Hammer, chairman of Occidental Petroleum and self-styled bad boy of American capitalism, strolled on to the stage. Hammer had traded with Lenin's Russia and was welcomed to China by the most senior leadership, with permission to fly his private jet into the country and a fleet of black limousines with which to transport his party around Beijing. It was an early expression of what one historian called the 'techniques of hospitality', used and refined by the Chinese government to massage the egos of visiting executives.[64] Mr Hammer signed four investment agreements, for coal mining and other projects, and recalled his oft-quoted 1932 remark that 'Business is business, but Russia is romance'. 'The same,' he added, 'goes for China.'[65] Romantic or otherwise, the familiar refrains of an earlier generation of China investor began to be heard again. Ralph A. Pfeiffer Jr, chairman of IBM, mused to the American press in early 1984: 'With their labor force, their resources, and their market, anything could happen. If we could just sell one IBM PC for every hundred people in China, or every 1,000, or even every 10,000 ...'[66] He left the sentence unfinished. American Motors Corporation (AMC) – later to become part of Chrysler – succeeded after four years of negotiation in forming the first automotive manufacturing joint venture. The US company, which was posting heavy losses, saw its share price jump 40 per cent on the news that a deal was signed in 1983. The *Detroit Free Press* enthused: 'American Motors' plan to join with the Chinese in auto manufacture could well turn out to be one of the shrewdest industrial strokes of the decade.'[67]

Both AMC and Occidental Petroleum ran into problems as soon as their staff began to operate in China, however. The first Chinese-made AMC Cherokee jeep, assembled in 1985, had to be pushed off its Beijing production line because it could not be driven. Armand Hammer's coal project was invested in and then abandoned. Yet the pressures of market interest and expectation kept rising. The first joint venture hotels opened in Beijing in the early 1980s and China began to grant group and individual travel visas more freely. A generation of China 'consultants' was born. The most colourful were Americans. Harned Hoose, the son of China missionaries, ran a consultancy out of a Los Angeles mansion formerly owned by Greta Garbo and filled with Chinese knick-knacks and musical instruments. Replete with a waxed moustache, he became a darling of the American business press. James Ryan, later linked to China deals in which US financial services firms were defrauded, claimed to have a hot line to Chinese leaders from his work as a USAF pilot in Asia during the Second World War. Charles Abrams, a former New York real estate agent, was so much in demand he was able to undertake a public listing of his China consultancy.

By the late 1980s, there was plenty of circumstantial evidence that something big was going to happen in terms of foreign investment in China. The loosening of communism's economic shackles had produced an immediate consumption boom. For the first time in a generation, farmers were producing more food than they could eat, urbanites were looking a little less down at heel. Chief executives of Fortune 500 companies were making visits and noting change. As had been the case in the inter-war period, the China proposition was so big that they were not about to leave investment decisions in the hands of regional managers. China needed to be strategised, forecasted, handled from the top down. The rewards of victory in this battle might be so great that only the chief of staff could lead the assault.

Big capital perked up. The market proposition that had been 150 million buyers in the sixteenth century, 300 million in 1800 and 400 million prior to the hiatus of 1949, was now a catchment of more than a billion people. The refrain '1.2 billion consumers' was to become the commercial poetry of the 1990s. Yet multinational business needed something more. It needed a further rationalisation for a grand adventure and a reason for why the market was going to be different this time. China obliged. Anyone who asked who turned on the ignition of the Chinese economy was told it was a small man called Deng Xiaoping. He was the missing link, the difference between the bad old days of disappointment and a future filled with riches. As Mao Zedong was to political revolution, so – the world was informed – Mr Deng would be to economic revolution.

2

A man called Deng

'The people are happy and we have captured the attention of the world'
Deng Xiaoping, January 1992.[1]

THE EVENTS IN China of the past twenty years cannot be understood without an appraisal of the phenomenon of Deng Xiaoping. Or, at least, what Deng stands for in the popular imagination. Between the myth and the reality, there is a large gap. Often presented as a proactive moderniser and original thinker, Deng's real contribution to China was not so much what he did as what he left alone. In most instances, where he tried to make policy, Deng acted with all the ham-handedness and unintended consequence for which Marxists are renowned. The price of his 'Southern Tour' – a Mao-like political campaign for breakneck growth in the wake of the Tiananmen Square massacre of 1989 – has probably still to be paid. But, in other instances, after he came to power as the victor in a protracted succession struggle in 1978, he proved to be the first leader since before either Mao Zedong or Chiang Kai-shek who was willing to allow people a little freedom in their economic lives. He was also less xenophobic than most of his peers. While this hardly qualifies as a contribution to economic theory, it has had enormous repercussions for China and the world.

梦

The 1980s – Deng's real decade of power – were an era of genuine, deep-rooted and under-reported change in China. There was considerable growth in the domestic economy, much of it in rural areas and unexpected by government. After the deprivation of Maoism came an end to rationing and the appearance of goods in the shops. Ordinary people could seek bourgeois solace in their first fish, a badly made wristwatch or a semi-reliable bicycle. It was as if a war had ended. In many respects a war *had* ended – the cultural and class war unleashed by Mao. Deng earned the credit for a decade of recovery. Demand and output were unleashed where previously they had been suppressed. Foreigners, eyeing up an expanding economy for the business they might one day seize for themselves, came back where previously they had been spurned. This was not a revolution. It was a return to what in most countries would be called normality. But in the world of the China Dream and communist propaganda, spin said otherwise. According to official history, the 1980s was not just a period of recuperation after Maoism, it represented the inception of an economic miracle. The supposed instigator of that miracle was a little-known character with whom the West fell into deep and instant love. Whatever the differences are between the China of today and China at the death of Mao, Deng Xiaoping's name has been used as shorthand for them.

Like Trotsky, Lenin and Marx himself, Deng was an archetypally middle-class communist. He grew up in an attractive, 22-room house in Paifang, in rural Sichuan province in south-west China. It was (and remains) the biggest house in the village, large enough to accommodate fourteen families, and more than fifty people, after the communists introduced land reform in 1949 and dispossessed the Deng family.[2] Deng Wenming, Deng Xiaoping's father, was a landlord with 25 acres (10 hectares) – not enough to make him genuinely rich, but it was a significant holding in a country where cultivable land is scarce but productive.[3]

That many communist leaders have a middle-class background is almost inevitable, given that in the poor, feudal societies in which Marxism took hold in the twentieth century, the social mobility required to rise to political power was usually beyond those who did not already possess money and education. But Deng's story also bears out a more telling point: that the most middle class communists have tended to be the most internationalist in outlook. This was certainly the case with Deng, whose father was wealthy enough to send him to spend his formative years, aged 16 to 21, studying and working in France.[4] It was in France that Deng Xiaoping met and befriended Zhou Enlai, his mentor and the one other ranking communist leader to survive the Cultural Revolution who consistently envisaged China returning to the international fold.[5] Mao Zedong, who could not afford to study abroad but was, from an early age, an avid reader of imperial Chinese history, never saw the country's future in international terms. In the first years of communist rule Mao had pursued progress with Russian assistance, but he soon jettisoned this in favour of an isolationist policy of economic development through mass political mobilisation – the campaigns known as the Great Leap Forward (1958–60) and the Great Proletarian Cultural Revolution (1966–76). Eventually, in 1972, Mao did welcome Richard Nixon and Henry Kissinger to Beijing, but only as part of a geopolitical manoeuvre against the Russians, whom he believed had betrayed both communism and himself. When Deng restored diplomatic relations with the US in December 1978, by contrast, it was out of the nationalist conviction that in order to be strong China had to be more open to the world.[6]

It would be easy to overstate the extent to which Deng Xiaoping was a cosmopolitan person, but by comparison with Mao he was. De-purged by Mao at the end of the Cultural Revolution and sent to speak at the United Nations in New York in 1974 (after the communists had assumed China's seat in place of the Nationalist Party of Taiwan), he was given the chance to see the might of capitalist America for himself. In the wake of the worst of China's Maoist deprivations, the visit cannot have failed to have made an impression. On the return leg, Deng used a stopover in Paris to buy croissants, which he shared with a now ailing Zhou Enlai. At the end of January 1979, three years after the deaths of both Zhou and Mao, and four weeks after the resumption of China's diplomatic relations with the US, Deng spent a full week in America. The trip is best remembered by Americans for the diminutive Chinese leader's donning of a 10-gallon hat at a rodeo in Texas; he also met the Harlem Globetrotters, drove through a Ford plant in Atlanta and took the controls of a space shuttle simulator at the Johnson Space Center in Houston. Chinese tend to remember the trip for the extraordinary height difference between Mr Deng and his hosts – the formal handshakes shown on Chinese television were done at an angle of about 45 degrees. The important point, however, was that, whatever his size, China's new leader received the respect of his American peers.

The trip enjoyed extended media coverage around the world. Not publicised at the time, but known to the US government, were the movements of other members of the Deng family. In 1980, Deng Xiaoping's eldest son, Deng Pufang, was flown to Canada, where he underwent a series of operations to relieve partially his paralysis, caused by his being thrown out of a window by Red Guards at Beijing University during the Cultural Revolution. Mr Deng's youngest son, meanwhile, headed off to post-graduate studies at the University of Rochester in New York and his three daughters started to make forays to the United States and Hong Kong. The run for the international airport by China's first family was one of the earliest signs of the opening that was about to occur.

When the bamboo curtain parted, Deng Xiaoping became the western world's most loved communist. He was *Time* magazine Man of the Year in both 1978 and 1985. His profile in Asia was raised enormously in 1979 by a tour of south-east Asian countries and Japan. After Deng's US trip, overseas travel was curtailed, but his international profile was maintained through repeated meetings with those who had participated in China's diplomatic rapprochement with the west – Richard Nixon, Henry Kissinger, Jimmy Carter and Edward Heath – as well as with the earliest of the US and European entrepreneurs to be smitten by China, among the latter Armand Hammer, who first met Deng in 1979 after Hammer bluffed his way past Secret Service agents to attend the patriarch's post-rodeo dinner at Simonton, Texas.[7] In the wake of Mao and the Gang of Four, the Deng media image in the west was benign: he was the 5-foot (many who met him believed him smaller) Chinese reformer wearing sandals who received foreign guests in the Great Hall of the People in overstuffed armchairs; if he leaned too far to one side his feet left the ground.[8] The contrast with the sullen, Cold War features of Leonid Brezhnev, who continued to rule Russia until 1982, could not have been greater.

Mr Deng was presented by China's domestic media and, almost always, by the international media and academic community as the person who created Chinese reform. A term often used to describe him was '*architect*', as if reform were a structure and Deng had designed it. Given the performance of China's economy in the 1980s, much of the kudos associated with double-digit economic growth was bound to rub off on the most powerful person in the country. Yet the reality of the origins of the reform process was far more complex. Indeed, hard evidence shows that reform in China began, not with a modernisation plan put together by Deng Xiaoping, but with a Marxist economic crisis which he helped to create.

Don't mention the fifties, the sixties, or the seventies

Towards the end of the Cultural Revolution, in March 1973, Deng had returned to government in Beijing after a long period of internal exile in southern China – the price he had paid for so-called 'rightist deviation'. Even by Maoist standards, the next three years were a disjointed and chaotic period in Deng's life in Zhongnanhai (the walled ex-imperial home of China's senior leadership), as Mao's health declined and politicians jockeyed for position. Deng went into self-imposed exile in southern China again for several months in 1976 after the death of premier Zhou Enlai in January.[9] It was only on 6 October 1976, with the arrest following the death of Mao of his wife and the other members of the Gang of Four, that a degree of normality returned to government. And it took a further two years before Deng managed to outmanoeuvre Mao's chosen successor, Hua Guofeng, to emerge the winner of a power struggle that had lasted nearly a decade.

During the periods in the 1970s when he was not on the run, Deng had important responsibilities for managing the economy. In the aftermath of the Cultural Revolution, his approach to his work was to re-establish the

1950s bureaucracy which had been torn down in the anarchy of the late 1960s. It was a central planning bureaucracy with which Deng was familiar because he had helped to create it in the 1950s as a vice-premier (the same rank he held after his rehabilitation in 1973). In a process that peaked in 1978, China's banking, finance and tax systems were recentralised and the country's largest state-owned enterprises returned to the direct control of central government ministries; this happened with 1,000 of the biggest state companies in 1978 alone.[10]

With central authority and the government's planning apparatus restored, the issue was how to create growth in the economy. The solution sought was the same as that pursued in the 1950s – construction of heavy industrial projects of the type which communists believe distinguish modern countries from backward ones. In 1975, when Deng held overall responsibility for the economy, a 'Ten-Year Plan for Economic Development' was drawn up. The plan was delayed repeatedly because of political circumstances in Beijing, but by the time it was finished, in February 1978, it had become a list of 120 large-scale investment projects, the biggest of which were in the energy and petrochemicals sectors. The plan version approved in 1978 required the importation of twenty-two complete industrial production units at an average cost of more than $500 million each – a total of more than $12 billion. The necessary foreign exchange (equivalent to the value of fifteen months of Chinese exports in 1978) was supposed to come from increased oil exports.

The Ten-Year Plan was interesting because it echoed the Great Leap Forward. Most obviously, the plan promised to catapult China to a new level of industrial activity. It also emulated the Great Leap by relying on budget numbers which had no basis in reality – in this case, figures that assumed China had oil reserves equivalent to another 10 million barrels of production a day, or ten times the output of Daqing, the country's biggest oilfield. Where the Ten-Year Plan appeared to refine the approach of the Great Leap was in its insistence on importation of industrial units from the developed world, particularly Japan. In the late 1950s, Deng Xiaoping's only stated doubt about the efficacy of the Great Leap, which he supported in opposition to other senior government ministers[11] – and which led to the worst famine of the twentieth century – was that the technical standards of the tiny backyard steel furnaces set up around the country could be improved. Deng suggested, after an inspection tour in the autumn of 1958, that perhaps the steel furnaces would benefit from imported technology. The Ten-Year Plan of the late 1970s promised to remedy such deficiencies.

In 1978, central planners and the bosses of China's energy ministries, under the auspices of Mr Deng, set to work ordering the fanciest heavy industrial equipment that money could buy. One project that was particularly closely associated with Deng was the Baoshan steel works outside Shanghai, a vast production complex imported in toto from Japan and West Germany, whose budget was $1.4 billion. In the course of the spending spree, China committed to purchase $10 billion of imported industrial lines that it did not have the foreign exchange to pay for. Chinese engineers – enthusiastically assisted by foreign oil companies – were sinking test drills all over the country looking for the oil which the planners said would pay for the imports. But no significant oil deposit was found.

By the end of 1978, China faced a balance of payments crisis. As is so often the case in the reform of developing countries, it was the sudden reality of large and unpayable bills that provided the impetus for a shift in policy. This is not to say that Deng was anti-reform; his determination to open China to the world was a critical theme of the era. But he was from a part-socialist, part-Chinese tradition of economic management that showed, at best, a very limited grasp of economic fundamentals. Deng loved to leap; he believed a combination of foreign industrial technology and socialist mobilisation was nine-tenths of what China needed. He looked at the outside world with the same nationalist vision as those in the late nineteenth century who had coined the expression 'zhong xue wei ti, xi xue wei yong' – or, 'the essence from China, the practical from the west'. He did not for one moment doubt that socialism was better than capitalism, or that China's development trajectory was unique. As much as any of his colleagues, Deng had to have his eyes opened to the undogmatic, transnational realities of the market place by experiences not of his making.

The accidental miracle

Fortunately for Deng and the others who led China into the crisis of 1978, a seasoned damage limitation expert was on hand. Chen Yun, a dour technocrat not given to the sort of fantasy economics that possessed Mao most of the time and Deng in his more excited moments, had made a career out of undoing their excesses. He tamed Chinese inflation after the communist victory in 1949, reined it in again in the second half of the 1950s, and undid some of the damage wrought during the Great Leap Forward (which, unlike Deng Xiaoping, he always opposed) in the early 1960s. Chen Yun had an uncanny knack of disappearing in periods of ideological extremism – he avoided being purged during the Cultural Revolution – only to reappear when his services were needed. At the Third Plenum of the eleventh Central Party Committee in December 1978 – the meeting at which Deng Xiaoping won not his final but a key victory in his power struggle with Hua Guofeng – Chen Yun returned to the forefront of government once more; he was promoted to the standing committee of the Politburo. Soon after, he became head of the government's Economics Leading Group, a position which gave him ultimate control of the economy.

Chen's prescription for rectification was simple enough: an end to most of the mega-projects (although Deng's beloved Baoshan steel plant survived), an increase in the price the government paid for agricultural produce, and more investment in sectors – such as light industry and services – which create jobs more cheaply than heavy industry. This last consideration was driven in part by the fact that as many as 7 million people, who had been sent by Mao to work in the countryside and 'learn from peasants' during the Cultural Revolution, returned to China's towns and cities in 1978 and 1979. Several million more were either declassified as 'rightists' or 'capitalists', or were released from prison and were also supposed to be given jobs.

With regard to the countryside, there was a general government consensus that the communes established by Mao should be disbanded. (Mao himself knew how much the peasants disliked sharing common facilities – particularly the commune canteens – from visits to Shaoshan, his home village in Hunan.)[12] With Mao gone, the communes could go too. In their place the leadership decreed that from 1979 land could be divided and farmed on the basis of smaller 'work groups'. But these work groups had to remain socialist: the principle of common ownership was inviolable.

Neither Chen Yun nor Deng Xiaoping was planning to end socialist agriculture, yet this is what happened – by accident. Chen's view was that the agricultural sector, which employed more than 700 million of China's 1 billion people, had been squeezed too hard with low procurement prices to cross-subsidise urban industrialisation. He wanted to give the peasants a break, even to allow them to indulge in some marginal private buying and selling of crops outside the state plan. Chen did not believe, however, that the agricultural sector had much room to grow. The communists had long since swallowed their own propaganda about Chinese farming – that with one of the lowest per capita endowments of cultivable land in the world,[13] Chinese agriculture had a very limited upside. In the twenty-three years from 1955 to 1978, grain production per person rose only 5 per cent.

Fortunately for the great mass of Chinese, the country's leadership turned out to be both incompetent in its agronomy and unable to predict what its plans for managed decollectivisation would mean in practice. China's per capita cultivable land may be less than half that of India, but it is of a generally high quality. Self-renewing loess soils in the north never have to lay fallow; in the south, land quality has sustained two, or even three, plantings of rice a year since the third century. Moreover, the communists had failed to reap the economic benefits of the biggest and most violent campaign against feudal farming in human history. Fifteen million landlords were displaced in the two years following the passage of China's agrarian reform law in June 1950.[14] But instead of releasing China's potential for increased yields through this bloody revolution, the communists simply substituted their own inefficiencies – banning the growing of most non-grain crops and insisting on regional self-sufficiency. This meant that many parts of China grew crops that were ill-suited to the area. Left alone, Chinese agriculture should have blossomed after land reform. But it was not left alone.

Ideology was still a potent force in 1978. Chen and Deng not only backed socialist agriculture at the Third Plenum meeting, they specifically outlawed family farming. In practice, however, their planned switch from large collectives to smaller ones was undermined at local level. Offered an inch by a totalitarian government's partial retreat from an untenable policy, the masses took a mile. As soon as the new work group policy for agriculture was introduced in 1979, farmers started to make their work groups their families. The process occurred fastest in provinces such as Sichuan and Guangdong, far from Beijing, where reform-minded leaders lent tacit, and later explicit, support. The pace at which the re-parcelling of land into family plots took place increased month by month. In 1980 household farming accounted for 14 per cent of agricultural output, in 1981 it was 45 per cent and in 1983 it was 98 percent.[15]

There was an immediate impact on output. China's grain harvest was 305 million tons in 1978, 355 million in 1982, and 407 million in 1984. Per capita grain production, which had risen 5 per cent in the three decades prior to 1978, went up 20 per cent in the next four years. But this was only part of the story. China's grain harvest took off at the same time as the sown area of grain was being reduced. Farmers were starting to plant other crops and raise more animals – activities which had been forbidden by the plan. Between 1978 and 1985, output of oil-bearing crops such as rape and sesame tripled, that of sugar cane increased 2.5 times, and fruit production went up 1.75 times. Whereas in 1978 a Chinese person consumed the equivalent of a quarter pound ration of meat every four and a half days, by 1983 it was the same every 2.7 days.[16] In a country where rationing of staples as basic as tofu and eggs persisted right through the 1970s, ordinary people could now buy citrus fruit, fresh fish and toffee apples on street corners.

The absolute increase in individual income was, of course, very low by most countries' standards. But because it affected the vast majority of the

Chinese population it had a huge effect on the economy. As farm households earned more money, they wanted more electricity and more fertiliser. The richest and boldest – or those with co-operative extended families – began to eye mini tractors or even the cheapest of China's light trucks. Everybody was in the market for basic consumer goods, from clothing to washing powder. It is a fair rule of thumb to say that consumption of anything widely affordable tripled in China's countryside between 1978 and 1990. Fertiliser consumption increased from 8 million tons to 26 million tons a year. Rural electricity consumption went from 25 billion kilowatt hours in 1978 to 84 billion in 1990. Ownership of bigger ticket items increased even faster, although this was partly a function of China's extreme poverty in 1978. At that point, the country had only 74,000 agricultural trucks, a number which increased to more than 600,000 in the course of the 1980s. Ownership of three-wheel mini tractors increased five-fold in the period, from less than 1.5 million to 7 million.

All the fertiliser, agricultural machinery and consumer goods – not to mention bricks and cement which were in demand everywhere as peasants showed off their new prosperity by extending their homes – had to be made by somebody. This was the origin of an extraordinarily virtuous economic circle that dominated life through the 1980s. In the course of the decade, non-farm employment in the countryside increased from 30 million people to 93 million,[17] representing more than one in three of all the manufacturing and service jobs in China; 16 million new rural businesses were created. The rural share of industrial output almost tripled, from 10 per cent to nearly 30 per cent of the national total. Millions of young men and women – the products of a Maoist baby boom in the 1960s – had been kicking their heels at home as a result of chronic agricultural underemployment; within a short period of time they all had jobs. After the misery of the Cultural Revolution, the early 1980s were a golden age, with harvests setting new records and rural industrial output rising 30 per cent a year. At a macro level, what was happening was a massive transfer of wealth, from a government which had monopolised society's savings to pay for urban industrial development to the majority, non-urban population. While China's total savings (those of government, enterprises and households) remained constant at around 35 per cent of national income, the rural household savings share of national income leapt from 4 per cent in 1978 to 15 per cent in 1984.

梦

There are few places that illustrate the best of what happened to China in the 1980s as well as Wenzhou. Located 225 miles (360 kilometres) south of

Shanghai, in Zhejiang province, Wenzhou is the most isolated big city on China's coast. It is surrounded on three sides by mountains and rivers and on the fourth by the sea. Throughout the 1980s, Wenzhou had no airport and no rail connection. The trip to the provincial capital, Hangzhou, took twelve hours over unpaved mountain roads; '*Qiche tiao, Wenzhou dao*', ran a local ditty – 'When your vehicle jumps, you're on the way to Wenzhou.' The city was also one of the few places in the 1980s where China's shortage of cultivable land was an immediate constraint – the 6 million people living in Wenzhou and its surrounding counties shared an average of one-tenth of an acre (0.04 hectares) of farmland per head, half the national average. Local fish stocks had been decimated during the Cultural Revolution in an effort to avoid starvation. In 1978, the output of Wenzhou's economy, measured in the local currency of renminbi, was Rmb1.3 billion,[18] equivalent to $10 per person per month at an exchange rate which was artificially overvalued and almost certainly made the place sound richer than it really was.[19]

When Mao died and it became clear that the political winds were blowing in a new direction, however, Wenzhou's isolation became its greatest asset. Central government wanted marginal, incremental change to the way the economy was run, but in a place like Wenzhou it was impossible to enforce such diktats. Senior governmental officials rarely made inspection tours from the provincial capital, let alone from Beijing. After the end of the communes was announced in December 1978, the return to household farming in the area was immediate. By 1984, records of what is now the Wenzhou branch of the State Administration of Industry and Commerce also show that 30,000 new family businesses had been registered.[20] This is certainly an underestimate; many families, remembering how previous periods of political relaxation had been followed by 'rectification' campaigns, preferred not to register their activities. According to the Wenzhou Association of Self-employed Labour,[21] a semi-official organisation set up locally to help family businesses, there were already 100,000 family businesses by 1984 and 190,000 by 1987. Most of these businesses were of the type the Chinese call '*qian dian, hou chang*', or 'shop in front, factory behind'. In this arrangement a family lives in the upstairs part of its home while downstairs a back room is used for manufacturing and a front room as a retail outlet. With tens of thousands of mini factories like this, Wenzhou became one of the earliest non-state producers of affordable consumer goods in China – pens, lighters, clothing, shoes and, ironically, badges and other paraphernalia which sustained the personality cult of Mao Zedong.

It was not long, however, before local entrepreneurs ran up against the limitations of the government's family enterprise reforms. Household businesses were supposed to employ no more than seven people from one extended family – it was forbidden to 'exploit' (which is to say, employ) third-party labour, the hallmark of capitalism. Wenzhou entrepreneurs needed a way around this constraint. So, in 1984, a group of family clothing businesses in Cang Nan, one of Wenzhou's subsidiary counties, persuaded local officials to register a new form of enterprise. They called it a 'stockholding co-operative'. Unlike family businesses, which were the only form of private company tolerated at this juncture, the stockholding co-operative was presented as a new form of socialist enterprise; its designers claimed it was a derivative of the collective businesses promoted by Mao. The reality, of course, was no such thing. Mao's collectives had been wholly state-owned; those promoted in Wenzhou were invested by private equity partners. Their sop to socialism was a promise to give a quarter of annual profits to all the workers in the co-operative. In return for this, the companies claimed the right to expand without limitation.

Within a few years, the stockholding co-operatives spread out from Cang Nan county and became the dominant form of ownership in Wenzhou; by the end of the decade, 20,000 co-operatives accounted for two-fifths of Wenzhou's industrial output.[22] The city government was so nervous about Beijing's reaction to this new form of ownership that it dared not, until 1987, promulgate regulations governing the co-operatives' activities. Whenever the local branch of the National Bureau of Statistics was required to file returns to Beijing it marked the output from the co-operatives in the owner-ship column labelled 'collective' on standard reporting forms. As a result, the average 16 per cent growth in Wenzhou's economy each year during the 1980s was passed off as a socialist triumph. The locals referred to this ruse as '*dai hong maozi*' – or 'donning the red hat'.

If the socialism was not for real, then at least – imperfect Chinese statistics aside – most of the growth was. In 1990, Wenzhou's gross domestic product was Rmb7.8 billion ($1.5 billion), six times what it had been in 1978. In a meta-morphosis that was mirrored in other fast-growing areas of southern China in the 1980s, the very appearance of Wenzhou and its environs changed. The city itself experienced a rash of construction, but far more striking was what happened outside the urban centre. Villages agglomerated into townships, as local farmers' children – and several hundred thousand migrants from farther afield – took up jobs in manufacturing. In 1978, Wenzhou had eighteen town-ships of more than 20,000 inhabitants; in 1990 it had 110. Two million people lived in these new towns, which accounted for more than half of Wenzhou's industrial output. It was an extreme example of what happened in the coun-tryside all over China: in 1978 the country had 4,000 townships; in 1990 it had more than 10,000 – at a time when overall population growth was slowing. As had been the case in the industrial revolution in Europe, many of the towns specialised in the manufacture of a single product.

梦

Liushi, thirty miles (45 km) north of Wenzhou, began the 1970s as seventy-seven separate villages; it ended the decade as Wenzhou's largest and most prosperous satellite. Liushi's speciality is low-voltage electrical switches. As early as the late 1970s, scores of local families were making electrical components in their homes. When other families saw there was a market for the products, they entered the business. Savings were accumulated and local entrepreneurs learned how to make complete electrical switching units used to control power supply in industrial plants, particularly state-owned ones making steel and cement. In the mid 1980s, family businesses reinvented themselves as shareholding co-operatives and expanded. By the early 1990s, Liushi had its first millionaires.

Hu Chengzhou – distinguished by an enormous diamond ring on his left hand – is one such millionaire. He started out in 1978 as a teenager selling electrical products made by local families. Almost all his income was commission, and he made lots of it. By 1984 he had enough money to buy a motorbike – rare even in cities at the time; he was also able to put down $21,000[23] with a friend and his younger brother to start their own business. The partners began by making components on the ground floor of Mr Hu's home. It took them three years to gain the wherewithal to make complete industrial switches needed by large companies. Once they could, they found themselves in a lucrative market, selling to state companies with long credit lines. 'The state-owned enterprises used to look down on us,' said Mr Hu. 'We were hicks. But they still bought our stuff.' By 1990 Mr Hu was driving one of the first privately owned cars in Liushi, travelling to Hong Kong and preparing a deal to import German equipment that would help his company obtain the global quality certification known as ISO 9000. Mr Hu and his friend, Nan Sunhui, broke their partnership in 1990, but it did not stop either of them from becoming multimillionaires in the course of the next decade. By the end of the 1990s, the two men's businesses would claim combined revenues of over $1 billion a year.

Mr Hu and and Mr Nan became the richest people in Liushi, but there were plenty of other successful entrepreneurs. From 1985, the town, which has now grown to a population of 96,000 residents and 50,000 migrant labourers, controlled one-third of the market for all the low-voltage electrical equipment sold in China. Specialisation in other townships around Wenzhou made the area the supplier of more than half of all the ball pens, buttons and lighters used in the country and the single biggest supplier of footwear to the domestic market.[24] The environment in which this happened was capitalistic in the extreme. In the space of a few years, life around Wenzhou changed from a communal farming existence, in which reward was unrelated to endeavour, to a largely urban experience in which people were not paid if they did not work. From the outset, manufacturing workers were remunerated on piece rates, salesmen on commission. In an area where many people had grown up living below the poverty line, no one complained.

Qiaotou township, not far from Liushi, became the button capital of China. The local government claims the town makes 70 per cent of all the buttons used in the country. It is impossible to know if this is true, but Qiaotou certainly makes hundreds of millions of buttons a year. Each day on Market Street a mass of wives and daughters of factory owners gather with bags of samples to do business with traders from around the country. Capitalism in Qiaotou is particularly raw. In the Chaoyang button factory which Wei Zhonghui started in 1982, the stench of plastic-making is asphyxiating. Resin is dried in rods which are cut into buttons and dyed in vats in the courtyard outside Mr Wei's small factory. Vividly coloured toxic waste runs off into drains which in turn run down to the long-dead river on which Qiaotou is built. The upstairs of the factory contains imported Italian machines that grind and shape the buttons and fill the air with plastic dust. No one wears a mask. Ultimately, the buttons return to the courtyard to be spun in vats containing small stones and chemicals which give them a sheen. This waste too ends up in the Qiaotou river, where the only signs of local life are the polystyrene lunchboxes cast down from the market place.

The fierceness of the entrepreneurialism which took off in places like Qiaotou in the 1980s was shocking to many people in the Communist Party. But with the economy growing at an average 9 per cent[25] a year – much the best performance since 1949 – and change being driven by the 700 million people who lived outside China's cities, there was a new limit to what the government could do. Liushi is a case in point. In 1990, China's State Council, the country's cabinet, issued a circular[26] to the Wenzhou and Liushi governments insisting that local manufacturers stop producing switching equipment for use in industry. The stated reason was safety and trademark concerns; the unstated reason was that six publicly owned switch makers in other parts of the country were not able to compete. The Wenzhou and Liushi townships governments simply ignored the ruling; Beijing was unable, or unwilling, to force the issue.

Outside the biggest cities, where its grip remained relatively strong, the

Chinese government spent the 1980s playing catch-up. Household farming was sanctioned for officially designated 'backward areas' in September 1980, but by this time one in seven of all households – many not in backward areas – had already made the transition. The central government gave its general support to household farming in 1983; at that point the phenomenon was already all but universal and the summer harvest was suggesting the country was in for a record full-year grain yield. After five more years, in 1988, the central government legitimised the non-family private businesses that had sprung up all over China.[27] Inevitably, in the official propaganda of the period, everything good turned out to have been the Communist Party's idea. It is a credit to Deng Xiaoping that he was honest enough in later years to admit that this was not the case: 'It was the peasants who invented the household contract responsibility system with remuneration linked to output,' he wrote, in typically turgid fashion, in his third volume of collected works, published in 1994.[28] 'Many of the good ideas in rural reform came from people at the grass roots.' None the less, Deng could not resist a paternalistic addendum. The Communist Party, he added, had 'processed' the people's good ideas and 'raised them to the level of guidelines for the whole country'.

Big city socialism

History, as opposed to the Chinese Communist Party, will more likely concern itself with the contrast between the startling success of what Deng did not foresee or intend in the countryside in the 1980s and the general failure of much of what his government did promote in China's cities. As early as July 1979,[29] before the rural revolution took hold, China's State Council laid out plans for the reform of state-owned enterprises concentrated in the country's biggest urban centres. The objective was to introduce more market- and profit-oriented behaviour into state companies in order to improve their performance; this was to be done within the framework of centralised planning.

The means employed were essentially those which had been tried out in eastern European countries from the 1960s, and later – and to a lesser extent – in the Soviet Union. The measures are often referred to by economists as 'rationalising reforms', because they sought to rationalise the more egregious distortions inherent in planned economies. Three basic reform initiatives were introduced in China in the course of the 1980s. First, state enterprises could sell output beyond that which the state plan required from them at higher, more market-driven prices (by the end of the decade, most enterprise managers were left to make their own production plans instead of depending on ones handed down by the central government). Second, enterprises were allowed to retain a share of their profits; from the mid 1980s, this policy became one based on contracts whereby enterprise managers agreed to deliver fixed sums to the Ministry of Finance and in return retained all other net income. Third, there were labour reforms: wages were supposed to be linked to profits, Communist Party officials were instructed not to interfere in the day-to-day running of enterprises; and managers were given some latitude as to which of their staff to promote.

Such changes failed to improve the performance of socialism in eastern Europe before the fall of communism, and early indications in Deng Xiaoping's China were not promising. This was not for lack of interest on the part of state companies. Indeed, all state managers were keen to sell at market prices and retain profits, and all workers wanted bonuses. Most large state enterprises signed up for profit-retention schemes within six months of their introduction in 1979 and bonuses rose to 10 per cent of the state wage bill within a year.[30] The problem was that, while grabbing at the benefits of reform, state enterprises were adept at avoiding the costs – a task facilitated by the central government's ideological unwillingness to contemplate root and branch reform.

The opportunity to sell above-quota production at higher prices was particularly attractive because state-owned companies could still buy many raw materials and utilities at artificially low cost under the state plan. Profit retention was attractive because it gave state managers control of investment funds. A ministry in Beijing was unlikely to sanction the construction of new offices or the importation of luxury cars; but managers could do what they wanted with their retained income. The managers argued that the fiscal guarantees they had to give the government in return for profit retention involved great risk. In reality, that risk was minimal. As well as buying cheap and selling dear as a result of fixed input prices, state enterprises successfully resisted the Ministry of Finance's demands that they pay interest on funds allocated to them in the national budget.

Cheap inputs and free money made it hard to lose. Between 1980 and 1988, the amount of profit retained by China's state-owned enterprises quadrupled. However, the overall profits of the enterprises increased only marginally (and actually fell in dollar terms).[31] The big winner was not the state but the enterprise manager, who became a powerful player in the economy, rewarding his constituency – himself and his workers – with better housing, hospitals and schools, all of them controlled by his company. At the same time, government revenue as a share of GNP fell from 35 per cent in 1978 to 20 per cent in 1990.

On the shop floor, state sector workers expected, and usually received, the maximum bonuses allowed. There was nothing in the tradition of state enterprise management to encourage wide salary disparities; indeed, managers were loath to do anything to rock the boat of industrial relations. It remained impossible to sack state workers (unless they were found guilty of a gross misdemeanor) and the main incentive to productivity improvements continued to be workplace banners imploring the masses to strive in the name of socialist modernisation. Regulations promulgated in 1984[32] allowed managers to promote a maximum of 3 per cent of their workforce each year without external government and Communist Party review; senior management appointments still required outside approval. Despite the employment opportunities provided by a fast-growing economy, the pro-portion of people leaving the state sector for reasons other than retirement peaked at 0.25 per cent in 1989; workers were seven times more likely to leave a state sector job through death than because they quit or were fired. Total employment in the public sector, meanwhile, increased from 80 million in 1980 to 103 million in 1990.[33]

Despite all this, there were trends working in the state sector's favour in the 1980s. Most obviously, the government's investment policy became more rational – or at least less irrational. Under Mao, huge sums of money had been wasted on heavy industrial projects begun on a whim, often in remote areas of the country, many of which had never been completed. After Deng Xiaoping – temporarily chastened by the unfinancibility of his own heavy industrial leap forward – put day-to-day control of economic planning in the hands of Chen Yun, the latter switched the investment emphasis to consumer goods, services and housing. As a result, heavy industrial output declined between 1979 and 1981, but light industrial output shot up by a third. The change made sense for two reasons. First, there was tremendous pent-up demand for basic items such as bicycles and sewing machines, whose distribution depended on pos-session of special coupons even in the late 1970s. At the same time, China's greatest endowment – massive amounts of cheap, unskilled labour – was far better suited to making bicycles than heavy industrial machinery. Although all available data are based on local samples, it seems certain that there was some improvement in the state sector's total factor productivity in the 1980s – in other words, more came out for every dollar that went in.[34]

Between 1980 and 1985, as disposable incomes rose, the Chinese people bought more than 150 million bicycles, 250 million wristwatches and 100 million (mostly black and white) television sets. From 1985 to 1990, China consumed another 120 million bicycles, 130 million electric fans, 50 million washing machines, 40 million refrigerators and 120 million (increasingly colour) television sets.[35] Even state enterprise managers found it hard to miss the economic opportunity. A former state military factory called Changhong became the country's biggest producer of television sets (China was making 25 million a year by the end of the 1980s). Many state firms created new collective enterprises – which paid lower taxes and were easier to register and control without central government interference – to move into new business lines. This occurred across services like restaurants, hotels and trading – which were no longer state monopolies – as well as in manufacturing.

There was a handful of mainland Chinese economists in the 1980s who questioned this trend. They argued that many collectives – which already accounted for a fifth of industrial output at the end of the 1970s – were simply using state connections to secure credit and turn a fast buck. The heart of the critique was that the local government leaders behind most collectives did not face personal liability for their businesses and were much less accountable to central government – which financed them – than state enterprise managers. If investments fared well, managers of collectives rewarded themselves with large cars, homes and salaries, not to mention foreign travel. If a business went badly, it was the state and the nationalised banks that would carry the can.

In the 1980s, however, it was difficult to make the case that the collectives were a bad thing. The industrial output of rural township and village collectives was reported to have risen an average 34 per cent a year from 1980 to 1995.[36] The total number of enterprises with a collective registration rose exponentially; after the agricultural revolution, they were hailed as the second great driver of the reforming economy. The collectives' share of industrial output rose from 22 per cent in 1978 to 36 per cent in 1990.

In hindsight, the reality of the collective sector was that no one knew with any clarity what was going on. Chinese statistics divided the non-farm economy into state, collective and 'other' (including, from the late 1980s, foreign-invested). The meaning of state-owned was clear enough and 'other' was a small slither of mostly private family business. But 'collective' ownership covered everything from private businesses – like those in Wenzhou – masquerading as collectives, to businesses set up by local governments, to subsidiaries of state-owned companies, to the large number of old urban collectives and Maoist 'commune and brigade industries' left over from the 1970s. The government learned to describe this eclectic mix as need arose: from an ideological point of view it was all collectively owned and therefore socialist; when speaking the language of reform, however, the collective sector was non-state business of 'mixed ownership'. Throughout the 1980s and 1990s, the Chinese government reported a rapid decline in the state-owned share of the economy, based on the presumption that all collective enterprises are non-state.[37] In 1992, the government announced that industrial output in the non-state sector had exceeded that of the state sector for the first time – a conclusion reached by aggregating collective output with the small but growing private and foreign-invested sectors. The subtext was that the bulk of the Chinese economy was now privatised. The official analysis went unchallenged, at home and abroad.

Hello Deng, hello world

In contrast to many state sector reforms, one area of the economy where it was obvious in the 1980s that real progress was being made was in foreign trade and investment. Here Deng Xiaoping deserves real credit; his determination to reintegrate China into the international economy is a matter of record. As early as 1975 Deng wrote an internal Party report advocating accelerated exports from China, as well as the acceptance of foreign loans, in order to promote growth.[38] At the time, rumours of the content of the report spurred a vicious counterattack by leftists and, in the spring of 1976, Deng was temporarily stripped of all his Party and government posts. But within a couple of years, with Mao dead and the Gang of Four in prison, he was able to pursue his most un-Maoist economic conviction – that China would never become a modern economy in isolation from the rest of the world.

In the twenty years prior to 1978, China had created one of the most self-defeating foreign trade systems ever invented, built on the twin pillars of an overvalued currency and the destruction of all incentives to export. The latter was guaranteed by the fact that the state paid producers an equal renminbi price for a product regardless of whether it was sold at home or abroad. The effect of an overvalued currency – standard socialist practice in the Cold War era – was to deliver a double whammy. When goods were exported, the exchange rate usually meant that their international price was lower than the domestic cost of production, leading to a loss which then had to be subsidised by the government. In its worst year, 1962, China lost $1.5 for every dollar of goods it sold abroad.[39] Still more perversely, most exports tended to be raw materials and energy resources, because the state plan made them artificially cheap at home in order to help domestic manufacturers. China, a country whose comparative advantage is in cheap labour, was selling precious coal abroad because the plan priced it domestically at 25 per cent of the world level. Unsurprisingly, having rigged the terms of trade against itself, China found that it had a quarter of the share of world trade at the end of the 1970s that it had had at the end of the 1920s.[40]

The mess was not easily undone. Throughout the 1980s, China continued to export large volumes of mostly primary goods, on which the government took hefty losses. However, the foreign trade system was slowly rationalised. The renminbi was gradually devalued, from an average 1.5 to the dollar in 1980 to 2.9 in 1985, 4.7 at the end of 1989 and 5.2 at the end of 1990. When

judged in terms of demand for foreign exchange or the need for export subsidies, the currency was still overvalued at the end of the decade, but much
less so than in 1980. The government also allowed exporters – dependent on
location and sector of business – to retain a portion of their export earnings,
introducing the first real incentive to sell abroad. The incentive became
greater in the late 1980s, when firms could swap their retained foreign
exchange into renminbi in embryonic currency markets. These produced
foreign exchange rates at a premium to the official rate – a premium as high
as two-thirds in, for example, 1988. Finally, the government began to rebate
a portion of sales taxes on exports and stopped taxing imported components
of exports.

The effect of these changes, combined with innumerable opportunities for
state firms and state officials to exploit loopholes in a part-reformed system,
led to a rapid run-up in foreign trade. China moved from being the world's
thirty-second exporter in 1978 to the number thirteen spot by 1990, when
exports totalled $62 billion. Total trade – imports plus exports – expanded 15
per cent a year through the 1980s, three times the world average. Some of
this growth was not of the sort the government liked, as when, in the mid
1980s, officials on Hainan island in the south abused foreign currency privileges to import and resell a billion dollars worth of foreign automobiles and
household consumer goods. None the less, most of the increased trade was
positive for China. Exports by township and village enterprises – one of the
more market-driven subcategories in China's collective sector – leapt from $5
billion in 1987 to $12.5 billion in 1990, as a falling currency, foreign exchange
retention and tax rebates encouraged them to sell abroad. Non-urban enterprises, along with the foreign-invested exporters who began to arrive in significant numbers in the late 1980s, were the biggest drivers of increased
exports. These two groups accounted for a third of all China's exports in
1990 but, more importantly, produced half of all the export growth through
the preceding decade.

梦

Foreign trade and investment made the late 1980s and early 1990s the era of
Guangdong, the province abutting Hong Kong in southern China. When the
Chinese government opened four experimental Special Economic Zones
(SEZs) for foreign investors in 1980, three of them were located in Guangdong and one in neighbouring Fujian province. Zhao Ziyang, the Chinese
premier from 1980 to 1987, was a former governor of Guangdong. As
premier, Mr Zhao gave the province the highest foreign exchange retention

rates in the country and cut a tax deal which meant a province of 60 million people paid to the central government one tenth as much money as the city of Shanghai, population 13 million.[41] These privileges, combined with Cantonese entrepreneurialism and the extraordinary cost-cutting opportunities that the opening up of the mainland presented to Hong Kong manufacturers, set off a foreign trade explosion.

Guangdong's exports increased from $2.9 billion in 1985 to $50 billion in 1994. From 1986, the province overtook Liaoning, through which most of China's foreign oil shipments passed, and Shanghai, the country's traditional industrial centre, as the number one exporter. By the late 1980s Guangdong was manufacturing most of China's toy exports, its cotton textile exports and its exports of plastic goods. In 1990, China, in turn, became the world's biggest textile exporter, with $13.5 billion of goods sold overseas. By the early 1990s, Guangdong accounted for 40 per cent of all China's exports.

The most forceful drivers of this growth were Hong Kong manufacturers. According to the former British colony's Trade Development Council, 25,000 Hong Kong factories were already operating in Guangdong in 1991, employing 3 million workers. The Federation of Hong Kong Industries, a local manufacturers' association, reported in 1993 that 90 per cent of its members had opened a factory in China. The reason was simple enough: the average manufacturing wage in Hong Kong in 1990 was almost $4 an hour; in mainland China it was less than 50 cents an hour. At just the moment when rising labour rates in Hong Kong threatened to force local manufacturers out of low value-added businesses, some of the lowest labour rates in the world had become abundantly available to them.

Many multimillionaires made their fortunes as a result. Frank Lo Kit-lu's was made in brassières. Mr Lo, the son of a small-time Hong Kong trader, opened his first factory in the British colony in 1962. Through the 1960s and 1970s he and his father employed immigrant labourers who had escaped from China to make tennis shoes, gloves and underwear. But by the end of the 1970s the business was being squeezed by rising labour rates. Mr Lo was among the first Hong Kong businessmen to take advantage of China's 1979 foreign investment law. In 1980, he opened two mainland factories, in a village called Yimpo[42] in Guangdong, and in Dalian, a port city in the northeast. In the first year of production 2,000 workers made 14 million brassières, more than 12 million of which were shipped to the United States. Under the so-called Multi-Fibre Agreement which governs the international trade in garments, Mr Lo thereby triggered the imposition of a United States quota for the importation of Chinese brassières. 'They created the lingerie quota because of me,' says Mr Lo proudly.[43]

By 1990 he was operating eleven lingerie factories with the capacity to make 48 million brassières a year, as well as other, specialist lingerie items. He began with simple, cheap products. But after five years of quality improvements Mr Lo was making some of the best bras in the world and was supplying the leading luxury brand, Italy's La Perla – 'the king of bras', as he calls it. Chinese silk, having been sent to Hong Kong for dyeing, was combined with high-quality imported elastics and underwiring and hand-sewn by young girls recruited to Mr Lo's factories from the countryside and housed in all-female dormitories. Like most export manufacturers, he found that migrant labour worked harder than the local population. By the end of the 1980s, Mr Lo's company, Top Form, controlled 4 per cent of the US bra market. More important to Top Form's bottom line, it controlled 10 per cent of the Japanese market. In the bubble economy of the late 1980s, Japanese women were paying the highest bra prices in the world. By 1990 Mr Lo's company was making profits of $10 million a year. Yimpo village, where most of Top Form's production was concentrated, became the bra capital of China. As well as Mr Lo's five factories, local entrepreneurs set up another 110 of their own.

A few miles away from Yimpo, still on the south side of Guangdong's Pearl river, Clifford Pang's arduous road to riches was a reminder of both the trials that faced early investors and the rewards available to those who persevered. At the start of the decade Mr Pang, a successful civil engineer in Hong Kong, was persuaded by an American Chinese computer engineer friend to invest in a computer components factory in a small town called Panyu, best known as a smuggling centre. In 1982 Mr Pang put up a million dollars of his own money and $4 million of borrowed money to build a plant to manufacture computer heads, the instruments which write and erase information on hard and floppy disk drives. Although the heads are quite sophisticated items, requiring precision assembly and a clean manufacturing environment, their production is highly labour intensive. It was this consideration which made the Guangdong investment a money spinner. Mr Pang came up with the capital, his friend was supposed to manage the plant.

Unfortunately, soon after the plant became operational, in 1983, Mr Pang's friend took off. According to Mr Pang he had enriched himself with kickbacks from the factory's constructors. Mr Pang, who had never worked in the computer industry, was left with a $5-million factory in rural China and no customers. So he gave up his civil engineering work, bought every book he could find on computer electronics and took over the factory management. After six months of touting for business, he was given a tiny order for 5,000 heads by Control Data Corp. (CDC), one of the biggest disk drive makers in the US, which had been let down by an existing supplier. Mr Pang made sure the order was delivered on time and to specification. As to the invoice, he noted: 'The buyer could not believe the price.'

CDC became Mr Pang's first bulk customer. Over the next few years his factory started to supply IBM, Wang Computer, Digital and Siemens. By the late 1980s, Mr Pang was one of the three biggest computer head makers in the world. His factory was employing 6,000 people, turning over $100 million a year and making profits of more than $15 million a year. In 1989, he exited the business – one he had only ever intended to be a sleeping partner in – selling out for $60 million. Armed with his cash, Mr Pang decided to do what he had been trained to do – build buildings. In the course of the 1990s he would develop the biggest private housing estate in China – the eponymous Clifford Estates – grossing well over a billion dollars.[44]

The take-off in Guangdong's exports in the late 1980s, led by men like Mr Lo and Mr Pang, started to transform not only Guangdong itself, but neighbouring Hong Kong as well. The British colony in the early 1980s was a rather parochial place, a shadow of what Shanghai had been in the 1920s. But by the end of the decade, it was on its way to becoming what it would be known as in the late 1990s, an international city and a world financial centre. Hong Kong had always been an important port for China – through the 1980s, the city handled most of the mainland's foreign trade. But as the years went by, Hong Kong businesses learned how to do far more than just transportation and manufacturing. Professional firms mushroomed as they moved into marketing and exhibitions, design, advertising and quality control. International law practices and the trade departments of financial institutions burgeoned. Such firms gobbled up the so-called value chain, linking globalised manufacturing to international consumers. The biggest trading firm in Hong Kong, Li & Fung, increased its turnover from US$36 million in 1980 to $200 million in 1990 and over $1 billion in the course of the next decade. To achieve this, it offered value-added services – putting US and European buyers in touch with its network of make-to-order Hong Kong manufacturers in Guangdong and overseeing everything from quality to packaging to delivery schedules. Add the money made from selling into China at a time when Chinese purchasers were often naïve about world prices and markets, and business in the late 1980s was lucrative. 'Li & Fung is a very good reflection of what happened in China,' says Victor Fung, the company's chairman and former head of the Hong Kong Trade Development Council. 'From about 1985 people were making money hand over fist.'[45]

Murder, mayhem and a communist let-off

The bonanza was temporarily interrupted in 1989. The events of April and

May of that year, leading up to the shooting of several hundred people[46] in Beijing during and after 4 June and the detention of thousands more around the country, came as a surprise to almost all foreign investors. Even as student demonstrations had grown in size in May 1989, staff at the British embassy in Beijing told foreign visitors there was no serious cause for concern. American diplomats gave a similar reading of the situation. There was no precedent for what was about to occur. In 1986, smaller student protests in Shanghai, Hefei and Beijing had ended without bloodshed. The government's suppression of dissidents in the winter of 1978–9 – the so-called Democracy Wall movement that greeted Deng Xiaoping's victory over Hua Guofeng – occurred at a time when there were very few foreigners in China. The beatings meted out to those who mourned or protested after Zhou Enlai's death in 1976 were practically unheard of abroad. Most important, the 1989 protests in China preceded, rather than followed, the fall of the Berlin Wall and communist governments in eastern Europe. In April and May 1989, no one knew that the world was entering of one of the most tumultuous periods of political upheaval in the twentieth century.

The Beijing protests date from 15 April and the death of Hu Yaobang, the former general secretary of the Communist Party, who had carried the political can for the demonstrations of 1986. Hu was no liberal, but in the Chinese context he was a clear-cut reformer. His funeral on 22 April drew a crowd of 100,000 people to Tiananmen Square, Beijing's equivalent of Moscow's Red Square, in defiance of police orders. It was the quick arrival of two more important dates on the political calendar that sustained and enlarged the protests over a period of seven weeks. The first was 4 May, the anniversary of the marches in 1919 when Chinese students protested the decision at the Versailles peace conference to hand over German colonies in China to Japan. The Chinese Communist Party has long made this anniversary its own, but in 1989 it could not. The most important date turned out to be 15 May, the day Mikhail Gorbachev arrived in Beijing for the first Sino-Soviet summit in thirty years. Mr Gorbachev was a communist who was opening the door to political as well as economic reform; the contrast with Deng Xiaoping was stark. It was during Mr Gorbachev's visit that more than a million people a day joined processions and protests in Tiananmen Square and elsewhere in the capital. After Mr Gorbachev left, the Chinese premier, Li Peng, signed an order declaring martial law on 20 May. Two weeks later, after several false starts, soldiers chosen from Chinese army units around the country – in order to tie the whole military into the operation – shot their way into Beijing. The killing began just before midnight on 3 June and continued until 7 June.

The economic context in which the Tiananmen shootings occurred is important to understand. Although exports were rising rapidly by 1989 and $30 billion of foreign investment had been contracted (half of it already delivered), the situation in the domestic economy was less rosy. In the second half of the 1980s, the government's deteriorating fiscal position began to catch up with it. Budgetary revenues as a proportion of national income fell by more than a half during the decade, as state enterprises handed over an ever smaller share of their earnings to the Ministry of Finance without becoming more profitable. At the same time the government began to spend heavily on major infrastructure and investment projects and to tolerate a much looser monetary policy. There was a sustained investment boom, paid for by state bank loans. Where total credit in China had grown an average 13.5 per cent a year from 1977 to 1985, the rate of expansion leapt to 27 per cent from 1984 to 1988.[47] State enterprises hummed and their rate of output growth increased sharply as their bank debt as a share of book value quadrupled in the 1980s.[48]

Inflation was brewing in the last years of the decade. However, because China held on to price controls for many goods, any increase in prices was artificially restrained. The grain harvest peaked in 1984, but while the supply of money increased substantially, prices of staple foodstuffs remained fixed. Most raw materials and industrial goods had two prices – a state-planned one for approved state sector buyers and a higher, more market-driven one for buyers outside the official plan. Apart from requiring considerable state subsidies, the situation was a recipe for corruption. Everything from vehicles to construction steel could be bought by state enterprises at planned prices and sold on, illegally, for as much as double. During the Tiananmen protests the most sought-after student poster pasted up in Beijing universities was one which listed the family trees of twenty-seven senior officials whose relatives allegedly made fortunes from nepotism and graft.

The families of Zhao Ziyang, the ex-premier who replaced Hu Yaobang as general secretary of the Communist Party, and Deng Xiaoping, were both featured. None the less it was Mr Zhao, the government's leading reformer after the forced exit of Mr Hu in early 1987, who recognised most clearly that China could not square its commitment to marketisation with the retention of price controls. By 1988, despite his patchy record with economic theory, Deng supported Zhao's diagnosis; he too wanted to press ahead with price reform. Unfortunately, the manner in which the two men set about price deregulation was inept in the extreme.

First, Deng let it be known within government that he supported rapid price liberalisation. This was a blunder because it tipped off the entire state sector to what was about to happen. Next, both Deng and Zhao made the policy public, via the official media, promising that price reform would go ahead 'despite all risks'. Mr Deng was so enthusiastic that in May 1988 he lectured a visiting North Korean military delegation on 'the law of value', reiterating to his bemused Stalinist guests that: 'We have no choice but to carry out price reform, and we must do so despite all risks and difficulties.'[49] Such public comments were ill timed and ill advised. Inflationary expectations were already running high. Instead of simply proceeding with price liberalisation, the leadership forewarned the population it was about to happen. The result was chaos. Panic buying spread through Chinese cities. Hoarding and speculation became endemic – often led by government agencies. State enterprises ignored government price controls and sold their goods to the highest bidder. By the summer of 1988, inflation was running at an annual rate of 50 per cent. Most of the price rises were for staple foods, thereby causing the maximum economic pain to the maximum number of people.

China's price reform big bang was a fiasco. In the autumn of 1988, many price controls were reimposed, which brought some hoarded goods back on to the market. The inflation rate for the year as a whole dropped to 19 per cent, but the political damage was done. Mr Zhao's influence in matters economic waned; communist conservatives, led by premier Li Peng and Party elder Yao Yilin, two of five members of the Standing Committee of the Politburo, wrested control of economic management and introduced a policy of austerity. Deng Xiaoping watched from the sidelines as his protégé Zhao Ziyang was politically emasculated by his enemies. The patriarch's own support for price reform, critical to its introduction, was not mentioned.

As China entered 1989 the two government leaders identified by the population as genuine reformers in the 1980s, Zhao Ziyang and Hu Yaobang, were politically finished. At the same time, the summer of 1988 saw the worst inflation in a generation, corruption was rampant and a group of unpopular hardliners were imposing an austerity programme. This was the background to the June 1989 protests and killings. The economic context was not in itself enough to explain what happened, but it was a factor. The combination of a succession of protest 'hooks' with the fact that in China people are always waiting to protest, while the government's security apparatus is always suppressing them, meant there was ample tinder for the fires of dissent. What was unique about 1989 was that the government – galvanised by Deng Xiaoping in his capacity as chairman of the Central Military Commission – used heavy-calibre machine-guns and semi-automatic rifles to kill its opponents.

梦

The situation in the aftermath of the killings appeared to almost every observer to be extremely grim. The world was awoken to the brutal streak in Deng Xiaoping's character, China's reformers were ousted – Zhao Ziyang lost his posts immediately after the shootings, scores of senior and middle-ranking officials affiliated with him lost their jobs subsequently – and economic growth turned negative. In eastern Europe at the end of the year, by contrast, freedom triumphed as a succession of totalitarian regimes were toppled, ending with Nicolae Ceausescu's in Romania on Christmas Day. The sun went down on China but it appeared to be rising elsewhere in the world.

At least this was contemporary perception. Reality proved to be more complex. For, even as people were being shot, luck, market forces and underlying trends in China's external economy were conspiring to rescue Deng and his government. A first stroke of good fortune was that fine weather in 1989 helped produce a record grain harvest; at 408 million tons, the crop just beat the previous record of 1984. Increased grain supply immediately tempered inflation (the price of foodstuffs accounts for more than half of China's retail price index). The weather was helpful again in 1990, but when it was reported that the grain harvest had leapt to 446 million tons – 52 million tons ahead of 1988 – it was clear that more than just the sun and rain were at work. China's farmers, the one part of the economy that had been truly privatised, were reacting to higher food prices by planting more crops. In the countryside, the market was working. Food became abundant, prices fell and grain output held steady at a higher level from 1991.

A second, and particularly perverse, effect of the aftermath of the Tiananmen killings was that the government was able to see through its austerity programme – reining in the inflationary pressure it created in the late 1980s – without a murmur of dissent. The population was too terrified to object. Credit growth was cut to 10 per cent in 1989, versus an average 27 per cent a year in the four years prior to 1988. Urban wages were held down and the urban unemployment rate reached its highest level since the start of the decade. Investment was reduced and more of what remained was focused on energy production – which had become seriously overstretched. The government's dampening of demand, combined with increased grain output, saw inflation drop to just 3 per cent in 1990. By the time that austerity officially ended in 1992, demand and supply were broadly in balance in the economy. The government was then able to quietly and gradually remove price controls without creating panic. The task which had appeared so daunting in 1988 ultimately went off without incident.

Finally, the trend of rapid growth in foreign trade and investment continued across the 4 June period. The Tiananmen killings did not stop either exports or foreign direct investment from rising. Many US and European companies backed off, temporarily, but they were not yet significant players in the Chinese economy. In the late 1980s it was Hong Kong investors who were providing two-thirds of China's total direct foreign investment.[50] By the time of Tiananmen, export-oriented entrepreneurs like Frank Lo and Clifford Pang had seen enough to know that, for their businesses, the economics of mainland production were irresistible. As a consequence, the rush of Hong Kong manufacturers into Guangdong – a province 1,250 miles (2,000 kilometres) from Beijing which saw little violence in 1989 – was barely interrupted. Foreign investment in China rose from the $3.2 billion recorded in the boom year of 1988 to $3.4 billion in 1989 and $3.5 billion in 1990. Similarly, China's exports rose from $48 billion in 1988 to $53 billion in 1989 and $62 billion in 1990, with a large part of the increase accounted for by Hong Kong manufacturers.

In the capital, underlying trends in the economy put China's hardliners in a difficult ideological position. From the summer of 1989 they demanded, and sometimes achieved, a return to familiar means of economic control: Communist Party activists were given back management authority in many state enterprises; regulations governing private enterprise were tightened; the government's investment focus was shifted to heavy industry. But as recession set in, the conservatives had nothing new to offer, no vision of their own beyond the discredited Maoist one. While Li Peng and Yao Yilin spouted Marxist rhetoric, it was the unintended rural free market that was increasing food supply and bringing down prices. In 1990 foreign trade – a product of reformist policies – amounted to 30 per cent of gross national product.

If China's hardliners wanted to curtail foreign investment and market reforms, they needed new sources of growth. On the other side of the world, in Europe, the people of former socialist countries had by now deposed – and in the Romanian case, executed – communist leaders who for decades failed to deliver better living standards. East German leader Egon Krenz may have been a guest of honour at the celebrations for the fortieth anniversary of the founding of communist China on 1 October 1989, but by the end of the year he was out of a job and facing trial for the manslaughter of former East German citizens killed trying to flee to the west.[51] The only countries other than China which officially subscribed to Marxist economic theory by 1992 were Cuba, Vietnam and North Korea. It was not an enviable club of which to be a member.

梦

In the end it was Deng Xiaoping who decided the direction in which China should be going. He had no intention of letting the country return to its central planning past. Throughout the 1980s Deng supported Hu Yaobang and Zhao Ziyang as economic reformers. He ditched them not because he had turned against reform but because they had allowed the authority of the Communist Party to be challenged. In the wake of the Tiananmen killings, Deng brought Jiang Zemin – the politically neutral Party boss of Shanghai – to Beijing to replace Zhao Ziyang as general secretary of the Communist Party and called for a two-year freeze on the promotion of senior government personnel. Well before that period was ended, however, Mr Deng was looking to advance cadres who could move the process of reform forward. In particular, he needed someone to replace the golf-playing Mr Zhao as the internationally acceptable face of Chinese communism. This was not a role to which the incumbent premier, Li Peng, was suited.

Eighteen months after the Tiananmen shootings, Deng made his move. He travelled to Shanghai during the lunar new year – China's main annual holiday – in late January and early February 1991. There he spent three weeks meeting with local government leaders, letting it be known that he believed it was time to push economic growth again. The mayor of Shanghai was Zhu Rongji, an English-speaking intellectual who had impressed early foreign investors in the city, including influential US businessmen like Maurice 'Hank' Greenberg, the chairman of the insurance company American International Group. Zhu and Deng found a common focus for their reform proposals – both men wanted to accelerate the development of Pudong, the vast marshland to the east of the city, and restore Shanghai as China's financial centre.

As Mao had done decades before, Deng started a propaganda campaign from the provinces. The national press in Beijing was in the hands of leftists in the wake of 1989. So Deng's calls for another round of faster growth began in the pages of the *Liberation Daily*, the official mouthpiece of the Shanghai government. In March 1991, the *Liberation Daily* carried a commentary signed by Huang Puping – a combination of a surname almost identical to the character for the river on which Shanghai stands, the Huangpu, and a first name the same as the *ping* of Deng Xiaoping – calling for 'faster, better, deeper' economic reform. Through the rest of the year, the *Liberation Daily* set the tone for China's regional press in putting rapid growth back on the agenda. The Deng-friendly media hammered two themes: that markets could somehow be socialist (and therefore not an ideological problem), and that government officials should start taking risks.

The timing of Mr Deng's offensive was carefully orchestrated. At the end of March 1991 the annual meeting of China's rubber-stamp parliament, the National People's Congress (NPC), was due. As Party elders and senior officials met to decide what, if anything, should happen at the NPC, Deng suggested the elevation of Zhu Rongji to the position of vice-premier. In the tradition of China's palace politics, he was willing to compromise over the promotion of a known reformer by similarly promoting a more orthodox socialist, Zou Jiahua, a Soviet-trained military industrialist born of first-generation revolutionary parents.[52] Moreover, Deng agreed to shunt the governor of southern Guangdong province, Ye Xuanping, who conservatives said was not sufficiently loyal to the centre, into an inconsequential job in a parliamentary advisory body. The trades were lined up and, shortly before the NPC began, a deal was done which delegates endorsed.

The elevation of Zhu Rongji was a master stroke. It provided evidence of something positive in China for foreign proponents of re-engagement in the wake of the Tiananmen killings. It also put the prime minister, Li Peng, on the back foot. When Yao Yilin became seriously ill in early 1991, Li found himself the standard bearer of the conservative camp in government. But Li's job was up for renewal in 1992 and reformers inside China and sinologists outside started talking of Zhu as a possible new premier. Lastly, the government reshuffle sent a signal back to the provinces that the reform process was on the move.

This had an immediate effect in the more progressive coastal regions. Other than in quinquennial election years, many of China's provinces hold their own local People's Congress meetings immediately after the national one. In 1991, the congresses of Tianjin (the port city near Beijing), Shanghai and Fujian each announced accelerated reform programmes, involving measures from the creation of free trade zones and the expansion of existing foreign investment areas to the licensing of more foreign bank branches. In December 1990, even before the NPC, Shenzhen – the city that had grown out of the rice paddies on the border with Hong Kong in the 1980s – opened a stock exchange without formal central government approval.

By the summer of 1991, life was moving inexorably in the direction prescribed by Deng. Li Peng, though not generally regarded as a clever man, had been in Chinese politics long enough to read the writing on the wall. His adoptive father – Zhou Enlai – had survived as premier throughout Mao's reign by agreeing with every substantive position the Great Helmsman took. Li, who had been at one with Deng over the need to use the army to crush the protests in 1989, followed the same tack. He began to distance himself from the ideological left and in June was quoted in the official press as saying that China should 'broaden and hasten' economic reform. As of this moment, there was consensus among China's leaders about the need to reignite the reform process.

Deng Xiaoping, however, was not satisfied. In late 1992 the Communist Party would meet in Beijing for a full congress, the first since 1987. The meeting was designed to establish the political and economic agenda for the next five years. After the setback of 1989, it was the moment for Deng to re-stamp his imprimatur on China's future. He was 87 years old in 1991 and unlikely to be in day-to-day control of the country when the next congress took place in 1997. For a person who had shown impetuous instincts throughout his career, time was running short; Mr Deng was an old man in a hurry. Urged on by his closest relatives, he decided it was time for more holiday diplomacy.[53] He resolved to put his cause before the nation – once more echoing Mao, who had toured the provinces when rallying support for his fateful political campaigns. On what became known as his 'Nan Xun', or 'Southern Tour', Deng chose the founding father's preferred form of trans-port – a specially equipped private train. He set off, however, for a city that had not existed in Mao's lifetime and which would have been a source of socialist scandal if it had. Deng's destination was Shenzhen, the frontier boom town on Guangdong's border with Hong Kong.

Deng's last leap

The arrival date – already taught to Chinese school children for its historical importance – was 19 January 1992. It was on that morning that Mr Deng arrived at Shenzhen's newly completed railway station. His visit was billed as the private vacation of a retired leader (he had not held any formal civilian post since 1987 and had given up the chairmanship of the Central Military Commission in November 1989 even though in practice he still wielded enor-mous power). The Southern Tour was sanctioned neither by the government in Beijing nor by the so-called 'Eight Immortals', the surviving Party elders – of whom Mr Deng was but one – who remained the ultimate arbiters of policy. This was an individual enterprise. Supported by his two middle-aged daughters, Deng Rong and Deng Lin, a smiling Mr Deng disembarked from the train and wrote a calligraphic inscription for the entrance to the station.

The patriarch had with him his wife, Zhuo Lin, as well as his children and an old friend, the then president Yang Shangkun, also accompanied by his children and grandchildren. On Tuesday 21 January, the group took in the leading sights of Shenzhen. They toured the Splendid China amusement park, which features replicas of China's best-known tourist sites – from the Great Wall to Tibet's Potala Palace – remade in jarring plastic and cement miniature. Mr Deng cruised around in a golf buggy. The entourage also visited the Botanical Gardens, where boats in the shape of swans bob up and down on an artificial lake. Here Mr Deng planted an alpine banyan tree.

This, however, was the limit of Deng's efforts to maintain the fiction of a vacation. He had started making political speeches even before he had left

Shenzhen station. Addressing the assembled ranks of the Guangdong leadership, he announced that, without development both China and the Communist Party were finished. The theme was similar to that hammered home in Shanghai a year earlier, but the tone was more robust. Over the course of the next week, Deng gave a series talks in which he confronted every one of what he perceived to be the criticisms of the reform agenda. Reform and the opening of China to the outside world had not caused the Tiananmen protests, he said. In fact, it was economic growth and higher living standards which meant the protests could be contained. He referred to those who opposed reform as like 'women with bound feet'[54] – an expression Mao had used against his enemies. There had always been those in the Party and government who opposed change, he said, but the 1980s had proved them wrong. It was time to take risks in the cause of progress and to reassert the policies that had created fast growth prior to 1989.[55]

Most of the stop-offs that Mr Deng made were far from vacation fare. He toured Shenzhen's main port facilities at Shekou, reviewed the construction of a foreign-invested expressway linking Shenzhen to the provincial capital, Guangzhou, took in the embryonic – and initially illegal – stock exchange; and dined at high-rise revolving restaurants overlooking the foreign colonies of Hong Kong and Macau. On a visit to a foreign-invested factory making compact audio and video discs and players, Deng pronounced that 'foreign-funded enterprises ... are good for socialism'. Furthermore, he claimed: 'Special Economic Zones are socialist, not capitalist.'[56]

The logic of Deng's pronouncements was sometimes elusive, but this was unimportant. He had not come to Guangdong to debate with his followers. Two thousand years before, China's first dynasty, the Qin, tested the loyalty of government officials by putting before them an animal which their eyes told them was a deer but which the senior imperial civil servant in Beijing told them was a horse. Those who stated that the animal was a deer were executed; those who called it a horse were rewarded. Likewise, Mr Deng was inviting government officials to 'biaotai' – to 'declare their stand'. The response from Guangdong was unequivocal. The province had gained more than any other from the policies of the 1980s. The provincial Party secretary, Xie Fei, told the patriarch that, given the right policies, Guangdong could catch up with Asia's 'little dragons' – Hong Kong, Taiwan, Singapore and South Korea – by 2010. This was just the sort of thing Deng Xiaoping wanted to hear.[57]

It was the patriarch's intention that others should hear the message, too. This was ensured – at every turn of the Southern Tour – by the presence of television and newspaper cameras and notetakers. The latter included Deng Rong, Deng Xiaoping's youngest daughter, who doubled as his official biographer. No sooner had the holiday party arrived in Guangdong than cameramen started shooting the footage for the official Southern Tour video, *The Choice of History*, to be released later in the year.[58] Photographs of the tour would emblazon the pages of the official media and pro-Deng propaganda material for the next two years. Deng Xiaoping's every word was being recorded for inclusion in Communist Party circulars, newspaper reports and a new volume of his *Collected Works*. Even the spade he used to push a bit of soil around the alpine banyan tree in the Botanical Gardens was destined for a Shenzhen museum.

Deng could not directly court international publicity, but even here he and his acolytes conspired to grab the headlines. On Monday 20 January, the day after Mr Deng arrived in Shenzhen, the Hong Kong paper *Ming Pao* was tipped off to his presence across the border. On Tuesday, at the Splendid China amusement park, security was markedly less tight than it would normally be for a Deng outing. Ordinarily, the whole park would have been cleared, but on this occasion locals as well as Hong Kong and foreign tourists were able to see the old man scooting around on his golf cart. When Hong Kong-based journalists called the Shenzhen government for information, spokesmen confirmed Mr Deng's presence in the city and identified themselves by name; information, let alone names, would never have been given without the Deng group's sanction. By Thursday, the Hong Kong media had obtained photographs of the entourage at Splendid China from Chinese state media photographers, and by Friday these photographs were splashed all over the British colony's newspapers.

Mr Deng was squaring up for a global media offensive. And what the press picked up on was just what he wanted – his choice of Shenzhen as a destination. A trip to Shenzhen was not like the visit to politically correct Shanghai the year before. It signalled Mr Deng's support not only for growth, but for the fastest possible growth, even at the expense of a little of what Chinese communists call '*jingshen wuran*', or 'spiritual pollution'. For, in China, Shenzhen's name was synonymous with not only internationalism and making money, but vice and corruption as well. In the early 1990s, the city was a filthy, chaotic construction site where Hong Kong businessmen bought condominiums in which to house their mainland mistresses and the streets were plied by luxury cars with right-hand drive – a sure sign that they had been stolen from the British colony (where, in contrast to the mainland, traffic travels on the left side of the road). Shenzhen was morally suspect, but it was also a place where gross domestic product had grown by 50 per cent a year since 1980, and its exports by more – reaching $3.5 billion in 1991. By 1992, 4,000 foreign-invested enterprises – mostly Hong Kong-backed – were present in the city. There was little doubt which side of Shenzhen's character – its frenetic economy or its questionable ethics – was more important to the patriarch, the man with a 35-year weakness for great economic leaps forward. His message was loud and clear: maximum growth, immediately, and don't worry unduly about the side effects.

梦

Back in Beijing, some of Deng's gerontocrat colleagues did worry. The patriarch's antics were reported to them via Internal Reference News,[59] the limited-circulation press service which allows Chinese leaders – but not the general public – to read foreign newspapers. Deng was out on the stump in Guangdong, breaching not only the rule of collective leadership enforced since Mao's death[60] but also challenging the political consensus reached among the Party elders in the wake of the Tiananmen protests. The ideological verdict on Tiananmen was that the country's political problems had been created by too much 'rightism', communist code for anything from free markets to foreign cultural influences. Yet in Shenzhen, one of the first statements Deng Xiaoping made to his hosts – and subsequently the most widely quoted – was 'Watch out for the right, but the main thing is to defend against the left' ('Yao jingti you, dan zhuyao shi fangzhi zuo'). In communist speak, this was a straightforward attack on the conservative left of the Party.

Chen Yun, another of the Immortals, turned down an offer from Deng to accompany him to Shenzhen. He was painted by the Hong Kong and foreign press as a hardliner, but his opposition to the patriarch was far less one-dimensional. As a competent, if Marxist, economist, Chen knew that growth in China had already reached a rate in 1991 – 9 per cent and rising – which threatened higher inflation.[61] Exports were up 16 per cent to $72 billion, foreign direct investment up 25 per cent to $4.2 billion. In these conditions, Chen regarded the patriarch's demand for faster growth as irresponsible. He argued that it was the government-driven investment boom of 1984–8 which had been responsible for both endemic corruption in the country and the Tiananmen protests – a point Deng went out of his way in Shenzhen to deny.[62] Chen opposed the Dengist call to arms on the basis that it would lead to uncontrolled credit expansion, more official corruption and ultimately more instability. His supporters pointed out that, although Chen was labelled a conservative, he opposed armed suppression of the 1989 protests; by contrast it was Deng who, having created a Party-threatening mess, used the army to shoot his way out of it.

Given the divisions at the top of the Party, it is not surprising that Mr Deng's trip south was not reported in the Beijing-controlled media for more than three weeks.[63] Those who tried to oppose the Deng campaign, however, were fighting a losing battle. Without any hint of irony, Deng dismissed his colleagues – including Chen – as old-timers holding up China's progress. Travelling on to Shanghai from Guangdong in late January, the patriarch made his attack on his fellow veterans explicit: 'Don't put your trust only in old age,' he told local leaders, in one of several indirect but unmistakable references to his peers. 'More young people must be chosen.'[64] In the battle of the geriatrics, Mr Deng's remarks were particularly timely. Although he himself had been ill in the summer of 1991, during his Southern Tour it was other Immortals who were threatening to defy their sobriquets. Three veterans – Peng Zhen, Vice-president Wang Zhen and Chinese People's Consultative Conference chairman Li Xiannian – were all hospitalised between December 1991 and March 1992; within a year, Wang Zhen and Li Xiannian would both be dead.

The other Party elders and their allies were no match for Deng. The senior members of the formal Party and government apparatus owed their allegiance to the patriarch. General Secretary of the Communist Party Jiang Zemin – brought to Beijing from Shanghai by Deng in 1989 – rallied support for his benefactor in Shanghai before Deng's three-week sojourn there in February. Qiao Shi, the security chief, performed a similar role in Guangdong, convening a national security conference in Zhuhai in January to coincide with the patriarch's visit. Even Prime Minister Li Peng, always dubbed a hardliner but in reality prone to agreeing with anyone who was nice or senior to him, made speeches in favour of accelerated reform before and during the Southern Tour.

On 11 February, while Deng Xiaoping was still in Shanghai, Jiang Zemin circulated extracts from the patriarch's Guangdong speeches to members of the Politburo. Simultaneously, pro-reform commentaries appeared in Shanghai's *Liberation Daily* and *Wenhui Daily*. The Deng group wheedled away and the national propaganda machine succumbed. A week after the Shanghai reports, second-tier Beijing newspapers – *Economic Information Daily*, *Workers' Daily* and *Youth Reference* – ran stories paraphrasing Deng's remarks. Li Ruihuan, another Deng acolyte and the Politburo member responsible for propaganda, had the hardliners in day-to-day charge of propaganda work on the defensive.[65] On the weekend of 23–4 February the conservative national Party paper, the *People's Daily*, relented, running articles in support of accelerated reform. On 1 March, the Politburo, led by Jiang Zemin, released Internal Document Number 2, containing transcripts of the Southern Tour speeches for dissemination to 50 million Communist Party members around the country. At another meeting of the Politburo the following week, Deng's argument that leftism was the chief obstacle to progress was formally endorsed and this position was broadcast by the state news agency, Xinhua.

By March Deng's opponents were in retreat and the patriarch was still holding his trump card – support from the provinces. All down the China coast in 1992, local officials were concentrated on the foreign investment wave that had begun to roll in to the country in 1991. That year China contracted twice as much foreign investment – $12 billion – as in any previous year. The money started to arrive well before the Southern Tour, but support for Deng promised riches of a new magnitude. When the annual meeting of the National People's Congress convened in Beijing on 20 March, the provinces had an opportunity to show their hand. It fell to the unpopular premier Li Peng – despite his recent public support for reform – to be the delegates' whipping boy.

According to tradition, Mr Li presented his official 'Work Report' to the Congress on its first day for ratification – meaning, in the Chinese parliament, automatic approval. In 1992 this did not happen. Instead, delegates tabled 150 amendments. Among these were clauses that lifted text verbatim from Deng's recent speeches – including his line about focusing political struggle against the left. Party and government delegates, from inland provinces as much as coastal ones, called press conferences during the Congress at which they made uncharacterisically strident criticisms of leftists for holding up China's development. The chairman of the Provincial People's Congress in impoverished Shaanxi, Li Xipu, told the *People's Daily* that the reason his province was still poor was because of 'people who look left, right, front and back but who are afraid to experiment boldly and to breach forbidden zones'. This was classic Deng speak. The NPC turned the patriarch's fight with the conservatives into a national referendum. The provinces voted with their newspapers. On 26 March, in the first week of the Congress, the *Shenzhen Special Zone Daily* ran the complete, 10,000-character text of Deng Xiaoping's speeches as included in Party Document Number 2. Media coverage of the speeches multiplied until, on the early evening news on 30 March, extracts were recited to the nation by a Central Television newsreader in a report that lasted eight minutes. By the time the Congress in Beijing voted on a revised Work Report on 3 April, its whole tone had been changed.

梦

Chen Yun was dismayed. Yet to understand the irresistible force of the Dengist campaign, he need have looked no farther than his and his fellow Immortals' children. As of 1992, three sons of the hot-tempered general 'Big Cannon' Wang Zhen – Wang Jun, Wang Bing and Wang Zhi – were, respectively: executive director of China International Trust and Investment Corp., the country's leading investment company; chairman of South China Oil Joint Service Corp., as well as of an airforce helicopter company – both of which made millions of dollars from foreign oil companies; and general manager of the Great Wall Computer Corp. Two of Peng Zhen's three children – son Fu Yang and daughter Fu Yan – had also gone into business, as director of a law firm and director of China Fuli, a trade-to-real estate conglomerate run by the General Staff Department of the People's Liberation Army. Even Chen Yun's family was commercially active. One of his two daughters, Chen Weili, consulting for international investment banks and multinational companies as deputy general manager of Venturetech, another state investment firm.

The establishment's snout was deep in the commercial trough. The Deng family set the standard. Elder son Pufang already had one conglomerate, Kangua Development, closed in 1988 for what the state media called 'financial irregularities'; younger son Zhifang was building a real estate business in Shanghai; youngest daughter Deng Rong was moving into consultancy. Almost every important family had members involved in state business. What happened in 1992 was that the whole nation made money its mantra. The Southern Tour was in fact a misnomer for a far bigger and longer political campaign, centred on the personality of one man and calling for all-out growth. On his way to Guangdong in January Deng Xiaoping had stopped to lecture provincial leaders in Hubei province and in Changsha, in Mao's home province of Hunan, about the need for faster development. From Shanghai in February he ventured out to Nanjing, capital of Jiangsu province, to chide local leaders for their conservatism. After he returned to Beijing, Deng went with his daughter Deng Rong on a highly publicised trip to Capital Iron & Steel works in the west of the city in May, lauding its diversification plans. In June, he toured the traditional industrial heartland of north-east China calling for bold experiments. Deng's aim was to set the whole country alight.

He did so. The cult of personality surrounding Deng Xiaoping grew week by week. In April, Central Television screened a documentary entitled *New Call: Inspiration from Deng Xiaoping's Southern Visit*. In June, Shenzhen unveiled a 3,200 square foot billboard in the Special Economic Zone featuring a beaming Mr Deng in front of the city skyline.[66] In August, China's most important indoctrination centre, the Central Party Training School,[67] published *Mao Zedong and Deng Xiaoping on the Chinese Condition*; tellingly, it contained sixty-four articles by Deng and only twenty-four by Mao. By the time of the quinquennial Party Congress in October, there was a giant poster of Mr Deng at the north-east entrance to Tiananmen Square; beneath it a floral display spelled out the message that the Party line – which was to say, Deng's line – 'must not change for a hundred years'. In the course of the next year, Party leaders and academics attended Deng Xiaoping conferences, the second volume of his *Collected Works* was published and a 1.8 million-word, 6-volume *Almanac on Deng Xiaoping's Works, Thoughts and Life* was produced.

For fifteen years Deng Xiaoping had railed against the cult of personality built up by Mao Zedong. He had refused to let his home in Sichuan be turned into an official tourist site and banned the manufacture of anything bearing his image. But in 1992, at the age of 88, Mr Deng became obsessed by his own place in history. At the Party Congress in October the keynote address – 'Speed Up the Pace of Reform, Opening and Modernisation and Strive for Even Greater Victories in the Cause of Building Socialism with Chinese Characteristics' – was a Deng script from cover to cover. The patriarch personally supervised the editing of the document which referred, *inter alia*, to his 'brilliant thesis' of the 'socialist market economy'. After General Secretary Jiang Zemin presented the report to the congress – Deng did not attend – delegates voted overwhelmingly to revise the Party charter to make Deng's 'socialism with Chinese characteristics' its core objective. When the National People's Congress met in March 1993, the nation's constitution was amended in the same manner. Deng Xiaoping Theory, and not Mao Zedong Thought, was now the guiding ideology of the nation. Within weeks, *Selections of Comrade Deng Xiaoping's Theories of Building Socialism with Chinese Characteristics* was rolled off the presses of the Central Committee's Propaganda Department to become mandatory reading at the Central Party School in Beijing. The stage had been set. The biggest foreign investment gold rush in the history of the world could now begin.

3

Frenzy

'Before the year 2000, China will have become one of the world's biggest markets for automobiles. This is not a dream and it is going to happen.'
Jerry C. Wang, managing director for Asia, General Motors,
quoted in the *China Daily* in May 1992

DENG XIAOPING could not have guessed at the scale of the forces he was to unleash in 1992. He probably believed that domestic public and bureaucratic opinion would rise to his clarion. Probably, too, he calculated he could whip up a storm in the provinces by using the tactics of Mao – an imperial peregrination that appealed over the heads of government. Yet even if Deng foresaw the domestic reaction to his Southern Tour – from the birth of his own cult of personality to the changing of the Chinese constitution in homage to his hazy economic ideas to an orgy of domestic speculation – he was aware of only half of what was going to happen. The rest of the story was being written overseas.

Deng Xiaoping's 1992 speeches, writings and perambulations played to two main audiences outside mainland China. The first was the overseas Chinese, 30 million of whom live beyond what the Beijing government claims as its rightful frontiers, mostly in south-east Asia but also in sizeable numbers in the United States and western Europe; another 30 million live in Hong Kong, Macau and Taiwan. This wealthy diaspora was energised, not to say mesmerised, by Mr Deng's sudden drive for national rejuvenation. After a wait measured in generations, all the promise of a once-great nation seemed as if it might come to pass. Emotions ran high and the investable riches of the overseas Chinese were readied for a great commercial adventure.

The second overseas audience was multinational business. The 1990s had arrived and 're-engineering' and 'downsizing' were no longer the key themes of corporate life. A new mantra had arisen – 'globalisation'. Business theorists and worldwide services firms – investment banks, legal practices and logistics enterprises – were singing the praises of global endeavour and telling multinationals they could and should move capital, technology and ideas around the world at a previously undreamt of velocity. Rising growth in Asia encouraged a sense of optimism – verging on exuberance – among the institutions of world economics and development. In the mid 1980s, the World Bank had forecast that China's disposable income per capita in 2000 would be a paltry $200.[1] That kind of thinking was changing. Even though the developed world was still in recession in 1992, its hunger for an international investment proposition was already keen. When Deng Xiaoping offered up the China Dream, not only the mainland Chinese, but the whole world, arose in frenzy.

梦

The bedrock of Deng's support, and naturally the first to react to his Southern Tour, was his domestic constituency – the provinces. In the south of the country, even as Deng was still touring about, the Special Economic Zones (SEZ) pressed ahead with investments that had been held up in the wake of the 1989 retrenchment. Everywhere else, the patriarch's visits to three of China's four original SEZs – Shenzhen, Zhuhai and Shantou – were taken as the signal to mimic these successful experiments. No longer were towns – and even villages – that had been left out of 'reform and opening' in the 1980s willing to let development be the preserve of a small number of fenced-in sites, most of them in southern China. The whole country demanded its share of the fruits of the socialist market economy, and set itself up to woo foreign investors.

Nineteen ninety-two became the year of 'investment zone fever'. At the start of the year, there were around a hundred foreign investment zones in China; by the end of the year there were 8,700.[2] Some of the new investment areas were licensed by the Special Economic Zones Office (SEZO) of the State Council, the central agency responsible for their management. In June, SEZO announced that every one of China's thirty provincial capitals was open to foreign investors.[3] The approval of other new zones, the office said, would be based on a strategy called the 'three alongs' – more zones along the coast, new zones along the Yangzi river and new zones along the Chinese–Russian border in the north-east. In the event, strategy had little to do with what happened. Most zones were opened not by the central government but by provincial governments and – in the case of as many as 6,000 of them – by China's 2,142 counties.

All over the country, townships and villages erected hoardings declaiming new foreign investment areas. After a free port was approved by the central government at the northern tip of Hainan island in the far south of the country in March 1992, local peasants decided to compete with a score of their own investment zones along the rural road between the port and the provincial capital Haikou. The zones were given international-sounding names like 'American Village'.[4] On inspection, Hainan's village leaders had little of substance to offer companies – they proposed to build utility supplies only after cash had been received – but their enthusiasm was unbridled. A few rural locations were more attuned to investor expectations, and these were reported in the press as national models. For instance, outside Fuzhou, the provincial capital of Fujian province, farmers in a township called Gushan formed a collective enterprise, pooled their capital with that of the town government and opened a zone which contracted $250 million of investment by the end of 1992. The zone initially attracted Taiwanese manufacturers with its low costs and reduced bureaucracy, and these investors in turn recommended other investors. In the course of 1992 the local farmers who ran the zone received approving visits from Vice-premier Zhu Rongji as well as from China's most famous movie director, Zhang Yimou, and its leading actress, Gong Li.[5]

Almost anything seemed, and often was, possible in 1992 and 1993. Along with Deng's exhortation that 'to get rich is glorious' came sweeping personnel changes in the provinces. The spring Provincial People's Congresses – normally rubber-stamp meetings – voted for new mayors in major cities including Shenzhen, Xiamen, Hangzhou and Tianjin. Each of the new men was younger and more strongly identified with the Dengist camp than his predecessor. Under the direction of Deng Xiaoping himself, conservative provincial governors and Party secretaries were eased out in several provinces including Sichuan and Hebei. The new incumbents gained their jobs on the expectation of faster growth and more openness towards the outside world.

As 1992 progressed, Chinese people spoke of not just one investment fever – development zones – but of five fevers, the 'wu re'. The others were stock market fever, real estate fever, government-cadres-getting-into-business fever and fast growth fever. In Shanghai, the stock market index rose 1,200 per cent in the first half of the year; the Shenzhen index put on 170 per cent. The combined turnover on the exchanges increased from $8 billion in 1991 to $124 billion in 1992 and $637 billion in 1993.[6] In Hong Kong, the Hang Seng index posted record closes for four days immediately before Mr Deng's January visit to neighbouring Shenzhen and on each of the four days during it. Hong Kong's biggest gains would come in 1993, when foreign money flooded its market, but for domestically driven

Shanghai and Shenzhen the fever rose with every Dengist statement about 'reform'.

Despite price earnings ratios of 80 times in Shenzhen and 300 times in Shanghai, demand for stocks was such that the Shenzhen exchange stopped selling actual shares. Instead, the exchange sold 'share purchase certificates' for Rmb30 ($5.50) each. These entitled holders to enter a lottery in which the winners were allocated whatever stocks became available. Half a million people queued for a sale of certificates in Shenzhen on 8 and 9 August 1992. When the certificates ran out, and rumours spread that government officials had helped themselves to many of them, rioting ensued. Despite heavy corrections in the Shenzhen and Shanghai markets at the end of summer, overall gains were considerable and other Chinese cities applied to open their own stock markets. Wuhan and Tianjin reckoned themselves frontrunners. Hainan island, taking a leaf from Shenzhen's book, ignored the requirement for central government approval and opened its own exchange in March. This time, however, after months of bureaucratic wrangling and a personal visit by Zhu Rongji, the central government shut the bourse down.

Hainan caught every fever that was going in 1992. The tropical island was the scene of the most frenzied real estate speculation in the country; it also set all standards for government-cadres-getting-into-business fever. Hainan had unique attractions. As China's fifth SEZ, the island was granted special privileges that made it the only place in the country where companies could retain 100 per cent of hard currency export earnings and, when desired, exchange the full amount for renminbi at a market exchange rate rather than the official government rate. Hainan also offered 15 per cent corporate income tax, compared with rates of between 30 per cent and 55 per cent on the mainland.

With foreign trade booming, exporting state enterprises from across the country set up shell companies in Hainan and processed exports through them. Much of this activity was illegal, but all of it was profitable. Other state companies and government ministries and agencies set up companies to invest in Hainan. The biggest players were the army and navy, for whom the island is the base of operations in the South China Sea. They controlled valuable land, including the site of the capital's airport.[7] The next biggest investors were companies representing government ministries in Beijing, followed by the enterprises of state units from inland, northern and northeastern China.

Most people bought the same thing: real estate. China had no capital gains tax in 1992 and investors stood to reap huge gains in a fast-rising market. The price of the best commercial land in Haikou rose from Rmb90 per square foot (Rmb1,000 per square metre) in 1989 to Rmb1,300 per square foot (Rmb14,000 per square metre) in early 1993. As prices surged, hundreds of high-rises were under construction in 1992. Offices and apartments within the blocks changed hands two, three or more times while they were still being built. Each time the price went up. Those who played the market well became millionaires. Feng Lun, a graduate of the Central Party School in Beijing and a former employee of the Communist Party's Propaganda Department, formed a real estate business with five partners that made each of them multimillionaires within two years. Four of the partners were still in their twenties. The group later moved back to Beijing and turned their company, Vantone, into the biggest private real estate business in the capital, with assets of over $120 million.[8]

Hainan government officials spoke privately of Rmb20 billion ($3.7bn) of mainland money being invested on the island, the bulk of it in property.[9] With Hainan's economy growing at well over 20 per cent a year this was not implausible. One sign of the times was the brand new stretch Cadillac parked each morning outside Haikou's best hotel, the Haikou International Commercial Centre. It belonged to the army. The vehicle had no number plates – it did not need them – and the chauffeur and passengers dressed in casual shirts and sunglasses, the new uniform of military–industrial business. The army, however, had no monopoly on brazen behaviour. In 1992, the Haikou government drew up plans to build a casino on a small island in the Haikou river. This despite the fact that gambling remained the Communist Party's biggest social taboo.[10]

Some of the money spent in Hainan came from exports. But most of it was bank loans and the working capital of state enterprises. The central government lost all control of bank credit in 1992. After Deng Xiaoping's tour, provincial leaders demanded state banks take up the call for faster growth by lending more money. In many cases the banks needed little encouragement. As the five fevers gripped China, enterprising bank managers and local political leaders formed subsidiary real estate and investment companies. These, and scores of 'trust and investment corporations' (TICs) set up in the 1980s to invest in local infrastructure, were used to take equity positions in real estate projects which the banks financed. As the sources of more than 90 per cent of all the credit in the economy, China's four biggest state banks got a look at almost every investment opportunity going. Their appetite was considerable. In the first half of 1992, new loans amounted to more than twice the credit ceiling set by the government. Fixed asset investment, which includes new real estate development, was reported to have risen a nominal

33 per cent in 1992 and 47 per cent in 1993; the figures were later revised to 44 per cent and 62 per cent respectively.[11]

Fast growth fever spread through China, and the statistics were there to prove it. The Chinese economy expanded more than 12 per cent in 1992 and more than 13 per cent in 1993, becoming the fastest growing economy in the world. Heavy industry grew faster than light industry, as banks pumped credit into traditional state companies. But the real star performers were held up as the township and village enterprises (TVEs), the rural mixed ownership businesses that were presented as China's unique contribution to economic development theory. Their output was reported to have grown by 40 per cent in real terms in both 1992 and 1993, creating 6 million new jobs a year and doubling TVE exports to $36 billion in twenty-four months. At a National Working Conference on Rural Enterprises in September 1993, vice-minister of the State Planning Commission Chen Yaobang declared the performance of the TVEs to be 'a miracle'. A national plan was published whereby rural industrial output would rise another 1.6 times by 2000 and create 50 million more jobs.[12]

The overseas Chinese: big money comes home

The provinces hailed Deng Xiaoping – and his call for all-out growth – as their deliverer. But the patriarch had another, equally important, constituency. The overseas Chinese, recently unnerved by the events of 1989, and still unsure how far and how fast reform would proceed, were offered in the Southern Tour and the fourteenth Party Congress an unequivocal commitment to economic development. As a result, small and medium-sized manufacturers from Hong Kong and Taiwan who had not already started mainland manufacturing did so in 1992 and 1993. Foreign investment actually delivered in Guangdong and Fujian – the provinces closest to Hong Kong and Taiwan – more than doubled in 1992, to $5 billion, and doubled again in 1993, to $10.4 billion. Much of the investment came from export manufacturers – combined exports from Guangdong and Fujian more than doubled in two years, from under $16 billion in 1991 to over $33 billion in 1993.

There was another, huge chunk of overseas Chinese investment, however, which was not of the traditional export manufacturing variety. The cash came from the most élite club in Asia – the ethnic Chinese tycoons who account for two-thirds of all the multibillionaires in the region and dominate the economies of not just Hong Kong, Taiwan and Singapore, but Indonesia, Malaysia and Thailand as well.[13] For the first time on a large scale, they targeted their money at the domestic economy, particularly real estate and infrastructure. Galvanised by the patriarch's rallying cry, China's plutocratic diaspora returned with a vengeance.

One of the first to burst on to the scene was Oei Hong Leong. Mr Oei is the son of Eka Tjipta Widjaja, the founder of Sinar Mas Group, the third biggest business conglomerate in Indonesia and the largest pulp and paper producer in south-east Asia. Like his polygamous father,[14] he is a colourful character. In 1960 he was sent to study in mainland China, only to be caught up in the Cultural Revolution at a time when most schools shut down. Mr Oei's education from 1966 until 1969 (when he managed to leave China) consisted of Cultural Revolution songs and the writings of Chairman Mao, learned whilst he was labouring in the countryside. The repertoire proved unexpectedly useful when he began to woo provincial Chinese leaders in the 1990s. He kept the comrades alternately commiserating and laughing with tales of how his Cultural Revolution girlfriend had been forced to drop him because he had a capitalist background and how a fellow villager offered him instead the hand of an old widow.

Like many wealthy overseas Chinese, Mr Oei had looked at investment opportunities in China in the 1980s. He had toured hundreds of factories, all of them state-owned, in 1984 and 1985, but had found it impossible to negotiate with the bureaucrats he met. When Deng Xiaoping went south at the start of 1992, the situation changed. Reformist cadres were being promoted around the country. Where once it had been impossible to do any deals, suddenly everything was for sale. In the sixteen months following Deng Xiaoping's trip, Mr Oei made headlines around the region by committing $452 million to buying up 196 Chinese state companies.[15] He picked up fourteen in Shanxi province, where he had laboured and been a Red Guard during the Cultural Revolution; he bought all but one – forty-one – of the state factories in his father's home town, Quanzhou, in southern Fujian province; he acquired thirty-four in the port city of Ningbo, south of Shanghai; and he signed up to buy 101 firms in Dalian in northern China.

Mr Oei bought into basic industries – tyres, beer and paper. A year after acquisition, with the global appetite for China equities insatiable, he listed his tyre companies on the New York stock exchange as China Tire Holding. He sold paper mills to his father and was packaging his breweries for a possible public offering or sale to a multinational. As the mainland investment environment heated up, Oei Hong Leong became one of its hottest names. Other powerful tycoons snapped up shares in his holding company, China Strategic Investment. Li Ka-shing, Hong Kong's most famous billionaire, took 8 per cent and an option for more. The US investment bank Goldman Sachs also acquired equity.

There was a great deal of Barnum about Mr Oei. But his determination to do very big projects in China – while buying up state companies he signed other deals to build roads and a $2 billion power plant project in Shanxi province – was not unusual. In fact, it became the norm among the tycoon fraternity to do megadeals. The ethnic Chinese billionaires, almost all of them over sixty, had only lived in China as children. Returning as old men to the land they had fled, they acted as if only the biggest undertakings could make up for lost time.

Mochtar Riady, the ethnic Chinese head of Indonesian financial services conglomerate Lippo Group – later to become infamous for his family's political involvement with President Clinton – spent eight months driving around China in 1990 to acquaint himself with the motherland. He still ended up, like so many of his peers, investing in his family's ancestral home, a grubby little town called Putian in Fujian province. In November 1992, Mr Riady signed a lease on 25 square miles (64 square kilometres) of land south of Putian, naming it Dadi ('Big Land') Industrial Park. He also took a 60 per cent interest in a venture to develop nearby Meizhou island, the legendary home of the Chinese sea goddess Mazu, as a tourist, retirement and convention centre. The price tag to complete Lippo's undertakings – requiring port, power and road infrastructure as well as commercial construction – was $10 billion. Mr Riady was unflustered; he would find co-investors: 'With 5,000 years of history and millions of overseas Chinese wanting to retrace their cultural heritage, I thought it was the right time to invest,' he declared. 'We [the overseas Chinese] are the dealmakers, the ones that will provide investment and financing advice to a country in the throes of economic transformation.'[16]

It was the era of the big plan. While Mr Riady believed direct links would soon be restored between the mainland and Taiwan – turning adjacent Fujian province into a gold mine – another businessman, Peter Woo, decided that the most strategic location in China was bang in the middle. The chairman of Hong Kong conglomerate Wharf Holdings invited local journalists to his office in Kowloon, spread maps on a boardroom table, and with the aid of a ruler demonstrated how the city of Wuhan was the logisticial hub of the nation, approximately 750 miles (1,200km) from each of Beijing, Shanghai and Hong Kong. Mr Woo said he would turn Wuhan, located on the Yangzi river, into 'the Chicago of the east'. In fact, he went on: 'It's really Chicago, Kansas City and Dallas all rolled into one. There is air, rail, road and waterways. There is a 350 million population in this region, which is the size of the European Community.'[17]

On 27 August 1992, Wharf signed a deal with the Wuhan government to build what Mr Woo called 'a megacontainerisation centre', capable of handling a million 20-foot containers a year. The company also committed to expand an existing power station, build an air cargo centre and a new light rail line and invest in numerous real estate projects. The price tag was put at $1.8 billion over ten years. Mr Woo had first called the project 'Hong Kong Plus'; in the end he decided to call it 'Hong Kong Plus Plus'.

If an overseas Chinese tycoon had not carved out a chunk of several square miles of China by 1993, and promised to invest billions on it, he was not on the map. It was an exercise reminiscent of the Great Powers' rush for concessions at the end of the nineteenth century, except that this time the claimants were ethnic Chinese and paying top dollar. While Mochtar Riady grabbed Putian and Peter Woo signed up Wuhan, other tycoons hoisted their corporate and familial flags around the country. Henry Fok, co-partner with Stanley Ho in the Macau gambling monopoly, acquired 9 square miles (22 square kilometres) of rural Guangdong on which to build a new town for 70,000 people in a place called Nansha. The son of a fisherman, Mr Fok had been born nearby on a boat.[18] Bangkok Land, the biggest listed company in Thailand, controlled by the ethnic Chinese Kanjanapas family, leased 24 square miles (62 square kilometres) near Guangzhou also to build a new town.[19] Kumagai Gumi, a company controlled by mainland and Hong Kong investors, leased 12 square miles (30 square kilometres) to create China's first free port on Hainan island and promised to invest more than $2 billion over fifteen years.[20] Liem Sioe Liong, also known as Sudono Salim and the richest man in Indonesia, leased 20 square miles (50 square kilometres) of land in his birthplace, Fuqing in Fujian province, and promised an initial $185 million of basic infrastructure;[21] he also built a four-star hotel for his three sons to stay in on the family's annual pilgrimage to the ancestral home, an impoverished township.

The biggest project of all was undertaken by the Singaporean government. Lee Kuan Yew, senior minister and longtime leading proponent of the 'Asian way' of development, was determined to stamp his mark on China's progress. After scouting several possible sites, his advisers settled on Suzhou, 50 miles (80 kilometres) west of Shanghai and one of the most historic locations of the old Chinese empire, to construct a city in their image. A 21-member consortium, led by companies and agencies owned by the Singaporean government, signed a letter of intent to lease 27 square miles (70 square kilometres) of land outside Suzhou in May 1992. As final terms were hammered out over the next twelve months, the Singaporeans sought not only development rights but an agreement whereby they would train the new town's entire bureaucracy. As Lee Kuan Yew told the *Business Times* of Singapore in 1993: 'We propose to work with them in planning, implementation and administration not only of industrial estates but also commercial centres and residential housing. In other words, how to plan, implement and administer a little township with industrial, commercial and residential sectors integrated.'[22] The project was not so little as the senior minister indicated. The Singaporean Suzhou town had a proposed population of 600,000 and a tentative budget of $20 billion.

Between Deng Xiaoping's Southern Tour in January 1992 and the end of the year, half a dozen overseas Chinese tycoons and the Singapore government leased 117 square miles (299 square kilometres) of sovereign Chinese territory and announced developments requiring $40 billion. And these were only the biggest residential and industrial park projects. Other overseas Chinese billionaires piled into different businesses. Robert Kuok, the Malaysian commodities-to-real-estate tycoon, undertook to build the largest luxury hotel chain in China, calling it Shangri-La, invested in huge commercial real estate projects in Shanghai and Beijing and poured tens of millions of dollars into edible oil refineries. Hong Kong's Li Ka-shing entered a fifty–fifty joint venture to run and expand Shanghai's container port, the biggest in the country.[23] The Thai–Chinese Chearavanont family, which dominates Thailand's agribusiness sector, stepped up investments in feed mills, property, golf courses, motorcycle manufacturing and food and brewing. The management of the family's closely held businesses gave out few financial details, but the Chearavanonts were widely reckoned by 1993 to have committed more money to China than anyone else – around $1 billion and rising, in about a hundred projects.

Most of the overseas Chinese investments were made via Hong Kong subsidiaries. This was not only because the British colony offered a liquid stock market and low taxes. Malaysian, Indonesian and Thai Chinese were also keen to conceal the scale of their mainland activities from their home governments in south-east Asia, which were becoming concerned that vast amounts of investment capital were being diverted to China. It was difficult, however, to hide entirely what was going on. When, in early 1993, Credit Lyonnais Securities Asia, a stockbroker, decided to tally up publicly announced mainland investments by Hong Kong-listed businesses, those of non-resident Chinese tycoons were prominent among them.

Credit Lyonnais's survey results were difficult to comprehend, then or now. The firm identified 802 mainland projects of Hong Kong-quoted companies with pledged investment of $67 billion (HK$521bn). This was equivalent to more than half of Hong Kong's GNP[24] and most of the investments had been announced in a period of less than one year. Hong Kong-based companies had already acquired a mainland land bank of 2.37 billion square feet, or three times the size of Hong Kong island, with $27 billion committed to real estate projects. One company alone, New World, proposed to build ten times the annual residential property uptake of Hong Kong in China[25] – 200 million square feet (18.6 million square metres) of gross floor area. The seven biggest Hong Kong real estate companies had between them forty-nine projects of over a million square feet of construction space (a million square feet being roughly equivalent to a 50-storey tower). The scale of their proposed construction was matched only by their optimism.

Enter the cavalry: multinational business rides in

The developed world's first big bites at the Chinese cherry took the form of frenzied grabs at any China-related equity offerings and the desperate efforts of multinationals to close investment deals. In the boardrooms of corporations in New York, London, Paris and Frankfurt, it was not long before chief executives convinced themselves they must sign contracts or lose out in the miracle market. There was no emotional, ethnic attachment between the average global corporation and China, yet many multinationals were no more sober in their approach to investment opportunities than either domestic players or the overseas Chinese.

If proof were needed that the appeal of the China Dream was universal, it came on 9 October 1992. That day, the first Chinese-controlled company to gain a direct listing overseas began trading on the New York stock exchange. A billion dollars of orders were placed for the $80-million offering of Brilliance China Automotive, a Bermuda-based holding company with a majority interest in a state minibus maker. In its first day's trading, Brilliance was the second most actively traded stock in America, surpassed only by Ford, which had posted a major profit warning. The Chinese president, Jiang Zemin, celebrated the capitalist triumph with a communist encomium: 'Brilliance has connected the finance line with the United States and the world,' he pronounced.[26] As a token of their gratitude for a successful offering, Brilliance's Chinese managers presented the New York exchange with a painting. The canvas, 'One Hundred Birds Worshipping the Phoenix', they explained, represented the scores of other Chinese state enterprises that would now seek listings in America.

Four months later, in February 1993, a second Chinese-controlled holding company with automotive interests had its initial public offering in Hong Kong. Denway Investment, the lead partner in a car-making joint venture with France's Peugeot, was billed as the first mainland Chinese industrial play in the Hong Kong market. When the company's offer closed, it was 657 times oversubscribed. Thirty-one billion dollars of application funds were received for a $52 million offering. Mainland-controlled banks in the British colony provided loans to apply for the issue in return for a 5 per cent deposit; a local reporter walked into a bank branch on Hong Kong island and was offered $2.6 million.[27] By the time trading began on 22 February, the equivalent of two-fifths of Hong Kong's gross domestic product was tied up in Denway's hands. The company received $17 million in interest, equivalent to more than half its net income in the previous twelve months, in the few days it held the subscription monies. The squeeze on Hong Kong's liquidity drove up overnight interbank lending rates by 40 percent.

In July 1993, encouraged by the success of these first two offerings, the Chinese government began to list a batch of nine mainland-incorporated state companies on the Hong Kong exchange. Six companies – five of them industrial and one a brewer, completed their listings before the end of 1993. They sought to raise a combined total of just over $1 billion; they attracted application funds of more than $62 billion.[28] Other, Hong Kong-incorporated subsidiaries of mainland interests like Denway – dubbed 'red chips' – raced to complete initial public offerings and were chased by still more money. Denway and three other red chips asked investors for $225 million in late 1992 and 1993; they received subscription funds of $67 billion,[29] that is, $298 for every dollar of equity available.

The Hong Kong market was in frenzy. The only other phenomenon in the late twentieth century that would cause such stockmarket excitement was the internet – a concept that was then barely known about. By late May, Hong Kong's Hang Seng index was up 35 per cent on the year. Then, in the third quarter, American institutional money began to pour into the market; news had crossed the Pacific that something extraordinary and, from an investor's perspective, profitable, was happening. In the second half of September, some of the most powerful capital allocators on Wall Street arrived for an 8-day tour of mainland China.

David Roche was the global strategist for Morgan Stanley, Wall Street's biggest investment bank. With him was Barton Biggs, the founder and chairman of Morgan Stanley Asset Management, and a group of client money managers with $400 billion under their control. After a week on the mainland, Mr Biggs had seen enough. He and Mr Roche filed a report entitled simply *China!*, recommending that Hong Kong – as the financial window on the mainland – be upgraded from 11 per cent to 16 per cent of emerging market portfolios and from 0.2 per cent to 3 per cent of global portfolios.

'Over the years,' wrote Barton Biggs, 'I have heard a lot of developing country macro stories and a couple of times even been present at the creation of bull markets, but the China story is the best and brightest ... Sometimes you have to spend time in a country to get really focused on the investment case. After eight days in China I'm tuned in, over-fed and maximum bullish.'

The phrase 'maximum bullish' already had a counterpart in the Chinese lexicon. The expression '*chao gupiao*', or 'stir-fried stocks', had been coined to describe the speculative frenzy. Hong Kong's Hang Seng index responded to the Morgan Stanley report by reaching a record high of 7,676 on 30 September 1993; it rose another 55 per cent in the next three months, driven by $2 billion of foreign money. By year end, the Hang Seng index had gained 115 per cent in twelve months, the best performance among of any of the world's big markets. The bourse's capitalisation stood at $374 billion, 3.5 times Hong Kong's gross domestic product, and the highest such multiple in the world.[30] Barton Biggs was investigated and, in December, cleared of market manipulation by the Hong Kong Securities and Futures Commission.

梦

The world was ready for its China good news story in 1993. The previous year had been a truly awful one, when all that had looked possible after the collapse of Soviet communism appeared to have come to nought. It was the year the Yugoslav war started to count its kill in thousands of lives per week and half a million refugees fled to western Europe. The Czechs and the Slovaks, once hailed for their velvet revolution, went to the polls and demanded divorce; the Russian parliament ousted Yegor Gaidar, architect of Russian reform; and the Romanians voted overwhelmingly for an ex-communist as president.

In western Europe, the antidote to division was supposed to be economic and social integration. But in June 1992 the Danes rejected the Maastricht treaty. The European exchange rate mechanism fell apart and George Soros became a household name as a harbinger of doom. The FTSE 100 ended 1992 at 2,846, the Frankfurt Dax at 1,545. In Britain, three million people were unemployed. In Germany, not only were another three million people out of work but public borrowing was at a record high. The *Treuhand*, the agency set up to privatise the former East German state sector, announced that the net value of everything the state owned was less than zero.

The economic mood in the United States in 1992 was, if anything, bleaker. After gross domestic product in 1991 shrank for three quarters in a row, Americans became obsessed with the idea of the relative decline of their country. President George Bush was deemed by the media to confirm American weakness when he vomited during a banquet in Japan – it went without saying that the Japanese who came to the United States to buy movie studios did not throw up at parties. America's figures were indeed depressing. The budget deficit was at $300 billion a year and forecast to rise by half again, unemployment was around 8 per cent, the trade deficit was at $10 billion a month and nobody would spend money despite the lowest interest rates for thirty years.[31] The mean-spiritedness of the times was symbolised by the pop star Madonna, who published a book called *Sex* sealed in a plastic bag; she wanted $49.95 for a peek at the contents. The Dow Jones Industrial Average ended the year at 3,301. The Nasdaq closed at under 800.

Most of Asia was in no better shape. Of the three countries that define the region – Japan, India and China – two were a mess. Japan's Nikkei stock market index, which had peaked at nearly 40,000 in 1989, was trading at around 14,000. The banking system was barely solvent, real estate prices were plummeting and the government was in denial. In India, the growth prospects touted as a result of IMF-led economic reforms in 1991 gave way in 1992 to a murderous confrontation between Muslims and Hindus at a mosque in Ayodhya. The sectarian killings of 1,500 people around the country in December capped a year of chaos.

That same month, Russia's president, Boris Yeltsin, travelled to Beijing. The last time a Russian leader had been in the Chinese capital – Mikhail Gorbachev, as president of the Soviet Union, in May 1989 – had been just before the government had turned its army on the Tiananmen Square protesters and suppressed what it dubbed a counter-revolutionary rebellion. In 1992, the campuses were quiet, the communists were still in power and the economy was growing at more than 12 per cent a year. The economy of Mr Yeltsin's now-democratic country was shrinking. He came to China not to lecture on the merits of political reform, but instead to ask the Chinese leadership to swap Russian artillery, Sukhoi-27 fighter planes and a nuclear power station for clothing, footwear and tinned food.[32] Only the power station deal was signed before Mr Yeltsin's trip was cut short by a political crisis at home; in his absence, his democratically elected parliament was trying to oust his reform-oriented cabinet.

In a world of chaos, China was suddenly a bright and fixed star. Its government spoke the language of economic, not political, reform. China would make money first and address other issues later. In the context of 1992, the question to international business was what did it prefer? The chaos of Russia and eastern Europe? Or the orderly, disciplined progress of a nation of 1.2 billion industrious souls? In the press and academia this was an oft-repeated juxtaposition. In the capital markets, investors were already placing their bets on China. Multinational companies were starting to do so on the ground.

From Russian nightmare to Chinese dream

Amid the domestic battle to woo foreign investment funds, the north-eastern city of Shenyang, home of Brilliance China Automotive's minibus plant, was billing itself as the gateway to China's traditional industrial heartland. It was here, 400 miles (650 kilometres) north-east of Beijing and 220 miles (350 kilometres) north-west of the North Korean capital of Pyongyang, in the long stub of Chinese territory which extends up into Siberia, that Russian planners had directed the construction of 'New China's' most advanced heavy industrial facilities in the 1950s – including key weapons, machine tool and non-ferrous metal installations. The grand endeavour was the brainchild of Joseph Stalin and Mao Zedong. The best talent in China had been harnessed in the rebuilding of Shenyang which, as 'Mukden', was the capital of the Japanese puppet state of Manchukuo until 1945. The country's two premiers of the 1990s – Zhu Rongji and Li Peng – and many other senior members of the current leadership had all worked in Shenyang early in their careers. The Russian love affair, however, was short-lived.

In 1953 Stalin died. Mao reviled what he regarded as the weak-kneed liberalism of his successor, Nikita Khrushchev. The two men's relationship deteriorated to a point where, in one of the great set pieces of Marxist history,[33] Mao received Khrushchev on a state visit to Beijing at the side of his swimming pool, inviting the Soviet leader to hop in wearing a pair of borrowed trunks. Khrushchev, who could not swim, floated around in a rubber ring. A few weeks later, in 1958, the Sino-Soviet axis collapsed and the Soviet technicians left Shenyang, taking with them everything they could carry: blue prints, technical specifications, specialist equipment.[34] The Chinese were left to stew in their Maoist juices.

For more than twenty years they did so, but in 1992 it was the Russians who were doing the stewing. That year Russia's industrial output contracted by 23 per cent; China's increased by 25 per cent. While the industrial cities the Russians had built in their own country were being asset-stripped and closed down, the one they had helped build in China was booming. Japanese, American and European businessmen were scouring Shenyang for investment deals. The municipal government said that by 1993 it had over $1 billion of direct foreign investment under contract, boasting the country's first New York-listed company as proof of its stature.

The city became the temporary or permanent home of a handful of pioneering expatriates, each with a story to tell. The Brilliance listing was put together by Carl Walter, one of the first group of seven American graduate students allowed to study in China after diplomatic relations were restored in 1979. By 1992 he was an investment banker with Credit Suisse First Boston, using a rare talent and fluency in Chinese to put together a pathfinding deal. The Brilliance listing was completed at a time when China had no securities commission and no securities law. 'It was an under the table deal at a time there was no table,' he remembers.[35] Carl Walter met the players behind Brilliance through a New York law firm they had retained. The prime mover was Zhao Xiyou, chairman of Jinbei Automotive in Shenyang, and one of eight model managers selected and publicised by the national government as exemplars of state enterprise reform. Mr Zhao was extremely ambitious. He wanted to steal the march on rival automotive manufacturers by cornering the market for luxury minibuses, which were enjoying a boom in popularity among businessmen and government officials. Mr Zhao already had a licensing agreement to assemble Toyota vehicles from kits; what he needed was hard currency to import production lines.

The difficulty was that only central government could sanction direct listings of state enterprises overseas, but had never done this. So, with a resourcefulness more normally associated with Hong Kong businessmen, Mr Zhao arranged the sale of a majority interest in the Shenyang minibus maker to a Bermuda-incorporated holding company, Brilliance. It was just the sort of original thinking that Deng Xiaoping appeared to sanction. Mr Zhao's principal allies in the affair were Shenyang's mayor, Wu Disheng, and Li Guixian, chairman of China's central bank as well as former Party secretary of the province of which Shenyang is the capital. In the period before China set up a securities commission in the mid 1990s, the central bank was the *de facto* arbiter of anything relating to equities.

Zhao Xiyou, Li Guixian and their friends used a front organisation called the Chinese Financial Education Development Foundation to retain majority control of Brilliance after listing. Brilliance's official prospectus said only that the Foundation's owners were the central bank and its 'affiliates and associates'. But investors in New York and London, gripped by the underlying investment proposition, showed little interest in the ownership details. The Chinese economy was growing faster than any in the world, and throughout the 1980s the automotive market had grown faster than the overall economy.

Working from the Zhongshan guesthouse, close by a 20 foot high red statue of Mao Zedong which looks and feels like an Edam cheese, and dominates central Shenyang, Carl Walter laboured for several months on the listing documents and due diligence procedures for the Brilliance offering. The government-run Zhongshan was a dirty, noisy place complete with karaoke bar and prostitutes (unknown in China for the past forty years). Also featuring a restaurant at whose entrance were kept cages of exotic wild animals, to facilitate individual selection by diners, the Zhongshan was the best Shenyang had to offer while foreign investors built new hotels.

By the time work on the Brilliance prospectus was finished, it told how the number of passenger cars in China in 1990 was 5.5 times what it had been in 1980.[36] The demand for luxury minibuses, used to shuttle groups of businessmen and government officials between meetings in a frenetic economy, was set to explode. Brilliance claimed 40 per cent of the market for 11- to 15-seat minibuses; more important, it was the sole producer of luxury minibuses. The government agency responsible for the automotive industry[37] was quoted in the prospectus as predicting that sales of domestically manufactured minibuses would increase five-fold to 150,000 units within four years; it added that Brilliance would enjoy a market share of not less than 25 per cent. The company sought funds to double output by 1995 and raise production of its $50,000 luxury minibus seven-fold.

In New York, Credit Suisse First Boston analyst Nick Colas forecast that earnings per share at Brilliance would more than triple in its first full year of trading in 1993 and rise by another 20 per cent in 1994.[38] Brilliance's stock rose 117 per cent on the New York exchange within three months of listing. Carl Walter, after much drinking – for which north-eastern China claims to hold all national records – innumerable banquets, countless hours of karaoke and many, many thousands of cigarettes, was the envy of every investment banker in China.[39] He had done the first deal.

梦

Among Shenyang's foreign pioneers in 1992, the longest-standing resident was Bill Young, a large, affable engineer from Oklahoma. Bill had come to China because McDonnell Douglas, his employer, said it would double his salary if he went. He packed his bags, arriving in Dalian, a port city to the south of Shenyang, in 1985, and moved to Shenyang itself in 1987. In the beginning, most people still wore Mao suits and the foreigner was followed around by two government employees. He rarely went out; there was nowhere to go. But by the early 1990s, life had improved a great deal. A local entrepreneur, tapping a closed society's fascination with the unusual, opened a traditional hotpot restaurant in which all the waiters were dwarves. Another Shenyang native came back from the US with a green card and opened a burger restaurant. Meanwhile, China's booming economy drew in many more expatriates, among them representatives of Boeing, Lockheed, Pratt & Whitney and Airbus, and Russian military and civilian aircraft makers, all looking for business in the city which had launched China's first jet aircraft.

Bill Young was glad of the company, but had to be careful what he said to his new colleagues. The reason was that Douglas, the commercial aircraft wing of McDonnell Douglas, was working on the biggest foreign business deal that China had ever seen. The project was known to competitors in outline, but its details were a closely held secret. Shenyang, in Douglas's grand design, was part of a plan to put a stranglehold on the Chinese market for the narrow-bodied single aisle aircraft that make up nearly two-thirds of all the planes that China buys.

It was no flash in the pan idea; the strategy had been nearly two decades in the making, the bold gamble of a visionary Douglas chairman taken at a time when most American businessmen could not place Beijing on a map. John Brizendine, an engineer who had risen through the ranks at Douglas to take the top job, planned to use China to help reclose the gap on the parvenu leader in commercial aircraft manufacturing, Boeing. Douglas had been the dominant US aircraft maker with its DC-class planes until the late 1960s, when Boeing's leadership bet the future of the company on the development of the 747 and came up trumps.

By the time Richard Nixon and Henry Kissinger came to China in 1972, they were flying on a Boeing 707. It was a potent symbol of Douglas's decline. After the leaders of the free world were whisked off in a motorcade to meet Mao Zedong, a group of Chinese air force officers went out on to the tarmac to take a look at the plane. The US pilots and secret service agents, under instruction to be as obliging as possible during a critical diplomatic mission, invited the men into the cockpit. A discussion ensued about the aircraft and its performance. Asked how he rated the plane, one of the pilots replied that since the President of the United States flew in it, it could be assumed it was the best commercial aircraft available.[40] Shortly after Mr Nixon left Beijing, the Chinese ordered ten.

In 1972, in the midst of the Cultural Revolution, China presented a very limited selling opportunity for commercial aircraft manufacturers. But towards the end of the decade, as the country returned to a sort of normality, there was a real prospect of further sales. Unfortunately for Douglas's sales people, when they made approaches to the department of the Chinese air force which sanctioned civilian aircraft purchases, it became clear that Boeing had already cemented its relationships with the agency's key decision-makers. The Chinese, to whom the idea of competitive tendering was both alien and politically incorrect, preferred to deal with their existing, single supplier.

So John Brizendine started to look for a different point of entry to the market. He became chairman of the National Council on US–China Relations, the key conduit for bilateral business exchanges in the period before diplomatic relations were restored. He travelled to China in 1975. He brainstormed with other managers about both the potential of the market and the way in which socialist China operated. A continent-size country divided by mountain ranges and three enormous rivers – the Pearl, the Yangzi and the Yellow – across whose deltas bridges could not yet be built, suggested enormous potential for short-haul air travel. Equally apparent, however, was that the Chinese wanted to build their own aircraft. The Third Machine Building Ministry, in charge of aviation, had already invested in lines producing Chinese derivatives of small, 1950s Soviet turboprop aircraft called Y-7s and Y-12s. In 1970, Mao's wife Jiang Qing demanded China prove its industrial credentials by building a much bigger plane, in Shanghai. Codenamed 'Project 708', the aircraft design incorporated features of several US and European aircraft. Some years after Boeing sold its first ten 707s to China, the company discovered why the order included an unusually large number of spare Pratt & Whitney engines. They were being used to power the Project 708 planes, or Y-10s as they were known.[41]

The Y-10 proved three things to Brizendine: that China was determined to build aircraft; that China had some engineering skill (it is no easy thing for a third world country to make a 170-seat jet aircraft); and that China had no commercial understanding of the aircraft business. None of the Y-series planes achieved commercial success; a Y-10 was test flown from Shanghai to Lhasa and back, but it was monstrously heavy and fuel-inefficient and only three were ever made.

What Mr Brizendine seized on was the potential to pull capitalist success from the jaws of socialist failure. By the late 1970s, he was already concerned that the labour-intensive nature of aircraft body building – thousands of hours of riveting and sheet metal beating – made the industry susceptible to the pressures affecting ship building; the whole of that industry was following lower labour costs to Asia. He thought of using China's under-utilised aircraft factories to outsource construction of aircraft body parts. This involved a degree of technology transfer – precisely what socialist countries craved – and could be leveraged to encourage the Chinese to buy Douglas planes. If the outsourcing went well, China could be licensed to assemble entire Douglas aircraft from knock-down kits. The Chinese would be happy because they would be making aircraft; Douglas would be happy because the cashflow on knock-down kits is far better than on finished airplanes as the money arrives in the corporate coffers that much more quickly.

A plan was put into action. In 1979, Douglas signed a first licensing deal for the manufacture of landing gear doors in Shanghai. Government support at the highest level was evinced when the new Chinese patriarch, Deng Xiaoping, granted the company an audience in 1980. It was an apparent victory over Boeing, which had not been entertained by Mr Deng. The patriarch asked for the Americans' appraisal of China's technical standards, stated that his country's opening to the world was irreversible and smoked his way furiously through a 45-minute meeting. Douglas executives were delighted. A dozen more outsourcing deals followed, culminating in orders for complete nose sections. By 1985, Douglas and its partners were ready with a 400-page contract to license assembly of complete, 147-seat MD-80 planes in Shanghai. Manufacturing started in a former bus factory; the first of an eventual thirty-nine MD-80s flew in 1987.

The Shanghai project was a huge undertaking. Douglas trained a Chinese workforce to assemble its aircraft from scratch; the Federal Aviation Authority was brought in to certify the process. At the peak, 150 Douglas expatriates were living in Shanghai, most of them in the Hilton hotel. The kit pricing – 90 per cent of the components were imported – gave the company a good margin, but this was quickly eroded by unforeseen costs. Additional expatriate engineers, huge amounts of cross-Pacific travel and millions of dollars of breakages later, it was clear that Douglas would be lucky to break even. This, however, was not a problem so long as the programme continued and expanded. John Brizendine, and his ex-General Electric successor James Worsham, knew they were playing a long game. Their partners at what became in the 1980s Aviation Industries of China (AVIC) began to discuss a second deal, involving increased localisation and 150 aircraft.

The Chinese called the project 'Trunkliner' because the aircraft manufactured would form the backbone of the domestic fleet for the forseeable future. At 150 planes, the deal was worth about $6 billion. In the spring of 1991, the Chinese government indicated to Douglas that so long as terms could be agreed, it was the favoured partner for the operation. Furthermore, China signed a memorandum of understanding to look at the possibility of producing a smaller, 100-seat aircraft. Douglas had such an aircraft – the MD-95 – in development. This would add billions of dollars more business. There was even talk of co-production of Douglas's C-117 transport plane.

Douglas had learned enough about China to know that genuine local manufacturing – as opposed to kit assembly – would present formidable logistical problems. All Chinese aircraft manufacturing facilities are joint military–civilian affairs, and the key plants had been hidden away by Mao Zedong in the 1950s and 1960s in the far recesses of the country in the belief that this would make them more difficult targets in the event of war with Taiwan, the United States or the Soviet Union. There was no way that Douglas would be awarded Trunkliner without co-operation from the military, and there was no way that the military would tolerate the closure of existing facilities. The American company would have to utilise the existing factories and bring different parts of its aircraft to Shanghai for final assembly. The Trunkliner plan, which was finalised in 1991, meant that wings and fuselages would come from Xi'an, 800 miles (1,300 kilometres) to the northwest of Shanghai, nose cones would continue to come from Chengdu, 1,100 miles (1,700 kilometres) to the south-west, and tail sections and electrics would come from Shenyang, 1,000 miles (1,600 kilometres) to the north. This involved extraordinary logistics – not to mention the bizarre sight of huge pieces of aircraft riding through the Chinese countryside on trains – but for $6 billion or more of business it was well worth it. The prospect for Bill Young, Douglas's lone field representative in north-east China, was that he was about to be joined by forty to fifty more Douglas expatriates. He was soon helping personnel managers from headquarters to scout for accommodation. In 1992, company chairman John McDonnell also paid a visit to Shenyang to show his support. The limousine provided by his Chinese hosts broke down before it reached the airport perimeter, and Bill Young had to drive his boss to town himself, but McDonnell's confidence in the great China project was unshakeable.

梦

John McDonnell was not the only American to feel this way. Just before him, John F. Smith Jr – better known as Jack Smith – had also passed through Shenyang's Tongxian airport. His corporation, General Motors (GM), was on the brink of bankruptcy; it posted a loss of $4.5 billion in 1991, and by the end of 1992 would have lost $12 billion in its North American operations in the previous 36 months – a global, if dubious, record. However, Jack Smith's part of GM's business, international operations, was doing relatively well. Under his leadership in the late 1980s, GM had substantially increased its market share in Europe and Latin America. Profits from these markets were the only thing keeping the company alive. Jack Smith's star was rising fast, and he came to Shenyang in the bitter Siberian winter at the end of 1991 to open up a new front in his empire – a pick-up truck joint venture with Jinbei Automotive, the same company that was about to list its minibus unit via Brilliance China Automotive in New York.

The joint venture was a foot in the door to what Smith saw as the last great automotive market in the world. He had first come to China in 1984, hosting an incentive trip for GM dealers from Canada; the place was drab, poor, sombre and had just 5,600 privately owned vehicles for a billion people. But when he returned in 1991, and stayed in the same hotel in Beijing, he was struck by how much construction had taken place. Volkswagen, GM's main

European rival, had in 1985 moved a production line for a failed European car called the Santana to Shanghai; sales were miserable at first, but in 1991 they doubled to 35,000 cars. Jack Smith smelled money. He wanted GM to pursue a bigger presence in China immediately. The company's chairman, John Smale, whose previous company, Procter & Gamble, was already an early and aggressive entrant in China, agreed. GM's first toe in the water was to take 30 per cent of a $100 million venture to make a pick-up truck called the S-10. A no-nonsense truck division manager from Detroit called Robert Stramy was sent to Shenyang to manage the operation.

Just as Stramy was settling into his new and alien life in a villa in a foreigners' compound in Shenyang, equally big changes started to affect his boss at international operations. In April of 1992, GM chairman John Smale and non-executive board members turned against the company's chief executive officer, Robert Stempel, demanding he relinquish much of his day-to-day control of the corporation. The directors thought that Stempel was too soft to push through the 74,000 redundancies deemed necessary to save GM from bankruptcy. A majority of the board wanted, and elected, Jack Smith as GM's new chief operating officer and president. Mr Stempel held on for another six months, but when he came under attack again in October, he resigned. Within days Jack Smith was the chief executive officer of the company with the largest revenues in America.

Jack Smith had to give up international operations in order to play the role of grim reaper in the United States as GM slashed its costs and its payroll. But he knew the perfect replacement for himself in the overseas market. Louis Hughes had worked with him since the 1970s, in the finance office in New York and later in Europe. The two men were lifetime GM employees with a shared vision of why their company was apparently in perpetual decline. GM was flabby at home but, more than anything, it was behind the curve in emerging markets. The two GM loyalists were determined to make their lumbering company work.

The basis of Jack Smith's alliance with Louis Hughes was simple. Smith would ruthlessly cut costs and restructure in North America and return the core GM operation to profitability. Hughes would establish an enlarged international operations headquarters in Zurich, at the geographical centre of his business world, and make his already profitable division bigger and more profitable. The men were as one about where new investment should go: one more plant in South America, one new plant in eastern Europe, one full plant, plus additional kit assembly, in south-east Asia, and an as yet to be decided investment in China.

The more the two looked at China through 1993 – the year when Smith did return GM to profitability in North America – the more convinced they became to take their biggest punt there. In Shanghai, Volkswagen had set a sales target of 100,000 units for 1993, and it was soon clear the German company would achieve this. Volkswagen would be the first auto maker to achieve real economies of scale in China and in a heavily tariff-protected market its 1970s vintage sedans were selling for nearly $30,000 a piece; VW was starting to make real money. Even GM had a little windfall in early 1993. In April, the Chinese government, worried by US president Bill Clinton's threat to stop 'coddling dictators', put in an order for 4,600 GM vehicles worth $50 million. Just prior to this, state-controlled Capital Iron and Steel in Beijing purchased the unwanted foundry operations used for making autoparts of GM Canada. In a competitive world, these vehicle and machinery sales were easy money at good prices. GM wanted more of the same.

The company rushed to open five new sales dealerships in southern China in spring 1993 through its own agents and signed up Denway Investment, fresh from its listing success in Hong Kong, as an additional distributor. Louis Hughes arrived in China in July, predicting GM would sell 40,000 imported vehicles by the end of the year. His local manufacturing strategy had been decided in outline before he arrived and agreed by Jack Smith. In essence, the men determined that GM needed to make a full product range in China, and rip the initiative away from Volkswagen and Peugeot–Citröen. The plant in Shenyang could be expanded to manufacture sport–utility vehicles as well as pick-ups; another plant was needed to manufacture small cars under the Adam Opel marque and another to make next generation minivans, or multi-purpose vehicles (MPVs), which were experiencing rapid import growth. In all, GM wanted three Chinese car plants, able to make up to a million vehicles a year. Louis Hughes came to China to confer on where to build what.

Hughes's sources of local intelligence were Jerry Wang, GM's managing director for Asia, who was handling imports, and Richard Swando, a veteran China expatriate who had joined GM from Chrysler. Wang's belief in the market potential was total. Even limited vehicle penetration in China would make it one of the world's biggest automotive markets. As he told reporters in 1992: 'China has 250 million families – just say 10 per cent of them own a car – that's 25 million already.' It was the same logic employed by Manchester shirt makers and New England underpants salesmen in the nineteenth century, but with an explosion in vehicle imports in the first half of 1993, to 125,000, and Volkswagen's shoddy Santana unable to meet demand, Wang appeared to be in the money. Richard Swando, whose experience of China began at the troubled AMC Jeep joint venture in Beijing in the mid 1980s, was more circumspect. Beijing Jeep was widely perceived to have been a failure. Swando knew better that the Americans had covered their costs through kit sales, but he was a realist about the difficulty of operating in China. He believed in the market, but was nervous about finding the right partners. For minivan production, he wanted to work with Volkswagen's existing partner in Shanghai. For compact cars, there were only two manufacturers and one of those, in Tianjin near Beijing, was already tied into a licensing deal with Daihatsu, an affiliate of Toyota, GM's greatest international rival. The other option was China North Industries – or Norinco – a military industrial company whose interests ran from retailing to gun making. Norinco had a licensing deal making small numbers of tiny Suzuki Altos in western Sichuan province. GM happened to own a strategic 3 per cent stake in Suzuki.

Louis Hughes was unfazed during his week-long visit to China that Adam Opel was reported in the Chinese press as 'Adam Open', or that Chinese translators invariably introduced him as 'Mr Loose Shoes'. Hughes shared Wang's enthusiasm and Swando's strategic perspective. Swando was told to press ahead with negotiations as quickly as possible; most important was Shanghai – 'Whatever it takes,' Jack Smith told him, adding only: 'Just don't lose money.'[42] GM and Richard Swando set to work, started serious talks with Shanghai Automotive Industry Corp., and signed a memorandum of understanding for a joint venture with Norinco. By late 1993, Louis Hughes was letting it slip in Detroit that GM was on the point of doing the deals that would make it the number one automotive player in China.

From Xanadu to Shanghai

GM's decision to make Shanghai its core investment was an easy one. Not only did the city have China's only proven automotive manufacturer but, as a prelude and a complement to his Southern Tour, Deng Xiaoping had launched a campaign to restore the metropolis to its former commercial glory. A reborn Shanghai was to be his monument. For forty years, government policy had been to contain Shanghai's ambitions, not encourage them. However, the logic of China's 'reform and opening' now made necessary a grand project the like of which the country had not seen since Mao's time. Deng had decided to build a second Shanghai, bigger and better than the old one – a new financial capital invested by foreign business but modelled and controlled by Chinese minds. It would make the old foreign concessions pale by comparison. The construct was to be called the Pudong New Area and it became the epicentre of the 1992–3 investment frenzy. It was here that companies like GM were told to build their factories.

The communists' traditional distaste for Shanghai was the product of history. When they took over the city, in May 1949, it epitomised three bad things: capitalism, colonialism and Chiang Kai-shek's Nationalist Party. Their response was swift and uncompromising. Out went the Hong Kong and Shanghai Bank from its huge, domed headquarters – the city's dominant structure and most potent symbol – and in went the new People's government. Shanghai's great hotels – the Cathay, the Park (at twenty-two storeys, the tallest in the country), the Palace and others – its snobbish expatriate clubs, its huge department stores, its churches, synagogues and merchant's houses were seized and transformed into a mix of government offices, Communist Party guest houses and apartments for the masses. Before long, where once the general manager of the Hong Kong and Shanghai Bank had watched junks and sampans go by from his panelled office suite on the Bund, now the Party secretary and mayor did so. The difference was there was much less traffic. The beautiful neoclassical mosaic on the underside of the bank's dome, depicting the world's financial capitals – London, Paris, New York, Calcutta, Bangkok, Tokyo, Hong Kong and, in a bygone era, Shanghai – was plasterboarded over. The communists announced the nature of their business by mounting a red star on the outside of the dome instead.

But Shanghai's economy was too important to the cash-strapped government to destroy completely, so for four decades it was milked. The city's nationalised factories were made to pay the whole of their operating surplus to Beijing, contributing 15 per cent of national fiscal revenues. Mao Zedong took the money and spent it elsewhere – in Shenyang and north-east China on Soviet industrialisation projects in the early 1950s; in Beijing, which was an industrial backwater in 1949; and in the later 1950s and 1960s on grandiose military–industrial projects in the west and south-west of the country. Shanghai was squeezed. No new infrastructure project of any significance was commissioned in the city. Like imperial China in its last several hundred years, the place was stuck in time. The grandeur of the great colonial buildings frayed and they became a surreal setting for the antics of China's most leftist politicians. Ke Qingshi, one of Mao's most steadfast supporters, was Party secretary.[43] During his tenure in the city he turned the luxurious Cathay Mansions and the former French Club opposite into a private palace, frequented by both Mao and the Gang of Four[44] who, headed by Mao's neurotic wife Jiang Qing, made Shanghai their base of operations for the Cultural Revolution.

At the start of the 1980s, when capitalists were allowed back into China, it was to the far south. Shanghai remained off limits. But as Guangdong – a laboratory for economic reform – became the country's fastest-growing region, it presented a new problem. Guangdong was 1,200 miles from Beijing and difficult to control. In 1984, the British government agreed to return to Chinese sovereignty neighbouring Hong Kong. This was a diplomatic triumph, but it brought into focus a worrying prospect: that the future commercial life of

China, a northern-run country, might be dominated by the south – specifically, by the Cantonese of Guangdong and Hong Kong, who have their own language and their own culture. Deng Xiaoping had no intention of letting this happen. His solution was to reinstate Shanghai as quickly as possible as the nation's commercial capital under Beijing's supervision.

The vehicle for the renaissance of Shanghai was an idea first mooted by the founder of the Chinese republic, Dr Sun Yat-sen,[45] and planned in some detail by the Nationalist government before 1949, but never acted on. It was the development of Pudong, an island of 202 square miles (522 square kilometres) – roughly the same area as Singapore – on the east side of the Huangpu river, which divides it from old Shanghai. The land in Pudong is naturally waterlogged and the river itself several hundred yards wide. The costs of bridging the Huangpu, draining marshes and building a new city had always made the Pudong plan a pipedream. But not for Mr Deng. For the diminutive commissar, Pudong was to be the showpiece of his long career; he would find the money to make it happen. In military style, he had a master plan drawn up for required infrastructure: three bridges, seven vehicle and pedestrian tunnels across the Huangpu; an inner ringroad and an outer ringroad; north–south and east–west elevated flyovers; two underground metro lines; a 4-runway international airport in the east of Pudong; new rail and light rail lines, new sewerage, new power stations. All of the above to be completed before the end of the millennium.

Foreign consultants were brought in after Deng announced his plans. They said the schedule was impracticable. Ken Rippin, an Australian engineer recruited to advise on the construction of the elevated inner ringroad, told the government that it was impossible to complete the work as planned. He reckoned, however, without 24-hour construction and demolition teams that forcibly cleared recalcitrant property owners from thousands of homes in the path of the expressway. This was Mr Deng's personal project. The inner ringroad was finished in thirteen months – the World Bank, which financed part of the project, had forecast three years.[46] Other infrastructure work forged ahead. It was said by 1993, though no one was quite sure where the statistic came from, that half the cranes in Asia were operating in Shanghai.[47] Looking out from the then highest point in the city, the bar of the Shanghai Hilton, it seemed not entirely fanciful to believe this.

The Chinese knew better than to question Mr Deng's willpower. They realised that once the patriarch had put his name to the project, central government would spend whatever was necessary to make the Pudong New Area happen. In 1991, Shanghai was handed back control of its tax revenues for the first time in a generation.[48] Sixteen billion dollars (Rmb125 billion) was budgeted for Pudong's infrastructure up to 2000. State banks were told to lend to local projects as a national duty. Hong Kong's billionaire real estate barons arrived on the scene and, in one year, 1992, the Shanghai government leased out more than 200 million square feet (19 million square metres) of urban land for development – about the same as it leased in the previous decade. Over the next two years, the seven biggest Hong Kong property firms committed to build 20 million square feet (1.9 million square metres) of grade A commercial and residential property in the city.[49] A total of 50 million square feet (4.6 million square metres) of office space alone began construction in the three years from 1993, all due for completion within five years. London and Tokyo, in post-war building booms that replaced property lost in the Second World War, each took a decade to build the same volume.[50]

At the heart of the Shanghai government's plan for Pudong was a new financial district called Little Lujiazui. In 1992, the world's leading architects were invited to present their ideas. They rushed to do so, with a dozen including the Richard Rogers Partnership from Britain, Dominique Perrault Associates from France, Massimiano Fuksas Associates from Italy and Toyo Ito and Associates from Japan putting forward formal proposals. The architects' models are still displayed in an office of the Lujiazui Finance and Trade Zone Development Company. The Shanghai government, however, after reviewing the submissions, decided to go ahead with its own, hybrid design, albeit one which closely resembles the proposal of the Rogers practice. The plan contained sixty-nine high-rise buildings, with 42 million square feet (3.9 million square metres) of floor space – or more than the entire grade A office stock of Singapore.[51] Among the buildings was a new stock exchange and a series of new headquarters, of thirty to forty storeys, for each of China's five biggest state banks. But the essence of the financial district plan was to have much taller buildings than these – ones which would announce the resurgence of Shanghai in the same way Manhattan's skycrapers told the world in the 1920s that New York had become the financial capital of the world.

The government kicked off the development itself with the construction in 1992 of the Oriental Pearl Television Tower, a futuristic, 1,535 foot (468 metre) tubular structure supporting two giant spheres and overlooking the Huangpu river; it was to be the tallest communications tower in Asia.[52] Soon afterwards, the Ministry of Foreign Trade and Economic Co-operation turned to the Chicago firm Skidmore Owings Merrill to design an 88-storey hotel and office tower drawing on the architectural tradition of the Chinese pagoda. The Shanghai Golden Trade Building, the official press noted approvingly, would be ten storeys higher than the tallest building in Hong Kong. The skyscraper would still be 70 feet (25 metres) shorter than the tallest building in the world, the Sears Tower in Chicago (which Skidmore Owings Merrill had designed), but not for long.[53] The Pudong masterplan envisioned two other towers of around a hundred storeys – taller than anything ever built. They were to be paid for by foreign investors.

The issue was, which investors? Hong Kong's real estate magnates were already massively committed – to the tune of billions of dollars – to redeveloping sites in old Shanghai, where some of them had been born. They preferred to wait on Pudong projects until the area's basic infrastructure was complete. But the Pudong adventure was not about waiting. Deng Xiaoping and the Shanghai government wanted big money backers who shared their sense of urgency and their vision immediately. They found them. They were Japanese.

梦

Minoru Mori was reckoned in the Forbes list of wealthy individuals in the early 1990s to be one of the ten richest people in the world, worth $8 billion. He and his father had made their money building and leasing out high-rises in Tokyo and Osaka. It was an uphill struggle, since both Japanese planners and public opinion have historically opposed high-rise living – a 'legacy of conservatism', as Mr Mori told the *Australian* in 1998. Mr Mori came to Shanghai as a long-time frustrated modernist, a collector of the designs of Le Corbusier, the French architect who proposed the razing and high-rise rebuilding of large parts of Paris, and someone who had lobbied persistently for the creation of more efficient 'vertical cities' in Japan. But where the recalcitrant Japanese held out for vegetable plots and little detached houses, Mori faced no such conservative opposition in China. In the cause of the new Shanghai, the city authorities had already shown themselves willing to demolish anything in old Shanghai that stood in their way.[54] Mr Mori was of the belief that the twenty-first century would be dominated by city states, and in Pudong he saw the opportunity to create an exemplar. In 1994 he bought the land to build a 96-storey tower. The Shanghai World Financial Tower would be the tallest building in the world, costing $630 million. Mr Mori gave the design job to the New York firm Kohn Pederson Fox Associates. While the plans were being laid he bought another plot of land nearby and began construction of a 46-storey tower.

Mr Mori's enthusiasm for Shanghai was measured by comparison with that of Kazuo Wada. Mr Wada is the eldest son of Katsu Wada, the woman who created the Japanese supermarket and department store business Yaohan, which by the early 1990s boasted more than a hundred outlets and $3 billion in annual turnover. As his mother became infirm in the late 1980s and early 1990s – she would die in 1993 – Mr Wada looked around for a way to stamp his own mark on the family company. His view, as he repeatedly told colleagues and speaking audiences, was that the twenty-first century would be the 'era of China'. In May 1990, at a time when many foreign investors were pulling back from Hong Kong in the wake of the Tiananmen massacre, Mr Wada moved Yaohan's global headquarters to the city. He reinforced the point by buying Sky High, the 12,000 square foot home of William Purves, chairman of the British colony's most powerful company, the Hong Kong and Shanghai Banking Corporation, located at the top of The Peak overlooking Hong Kong island. Mr Wada said Sky High, a symbol of British colonial and commercial dominance, would become Yaohan's 'worldwide strategic headquarters'. He suggested Deng Xiaoping might like to stay there when Hong Kong reverted to Chinese sovereignty in July 1997.

Mr Wada bought retailing and entertainment businesses in Hong Kong and began to build relationships with both local Hong Kong players and influential mainlanders. He hooked up with Venturetech, the mainland investment company run by members of some of China's most powerful families. The principals – known euphemistically in China as 'princelings' – were Chen Weili, Zhang Xiaobin and Lao Yuanyi, the children of elder statesman Chen Yun, of a former health minister and of the country's intelligence chief respectively.[55] Venturetech brokered influence, able to avail its partners – for a cut – of land and licences controlled by the Chinese state. Mr Wada entered a spate of deals with the firm, including several manufacturing ventures to make Yaohan-branded consumer products and a joint venture department store in Beijing, which opened in 1992. But the big prize was Shanghai. Mr Wada talked with the management of the No.1 Department Store, the biggest in the country, whose bland socialist name disguised a different past – as the *Da Xin*, the Grand Contemporary Department Store, one of the four great emporia of pre-revolutionary Shanghai.[56] The two sides agreed to build the biggest department store in Asia – exceeded in size worldwide only by Macy's in New York – in the marshland of Pudong.

NextAge was the name given to the store. It would comprise 1.1 million square feet (100,000 square metres) of retail space and another 450,000 square feet of offices above.[57] The retail area was equivalent to five times that of the No.1 Department Store; at its centre would be a 2,200-seat food court, which Mr Wada said would be the biggest restaurant in the world. He set targets of 100 million visitors in the first year – an average of 274,000 a day – and $200 million revenue, leading to a payback on NextAge's $235 million investment in just over five years. At the same time, Mr Wada announced his intention to open 1,000 supermarkets and 3,000 burger restaurants in China by 2010; the date was subsequently brought forward to 2005. China, said Mr Wada, would soon account for half of Yaohan's revenues, which would double by 1997. The Shanghai government was delighted with both Mr Wada and Mr Mori. Their vision meant that, within three years of completing the Pudong master plan, new Shanghai was set to have the world's tallest building, the world's tallest hotel, the biggest department store in Asia and the tallest communications tower in Asia. The Pacific century was coming, and China and Shanghai would lead it.

In search of gold

Down in Hong Kong, Moses Tsang, a partner at Goldman Sachs, was preparing his company to dominate the financing of China's future. Mr Tsang, a Goldman staffer since 1978, was the first Hong Kong Chinese to have made general partner in a major US investment house. He returned to Hong Kong, after a career in bond trading in London, New York and Tokyo, in October 1989 as chairman of Asian operations outside Japan. In the wake of the Tiananmen massacre, the firm maintained a Hong Kong office of just a dozen people. But as investment sentiment began to recover from the shock of Tiananmen in the early 1990s, Goldman rolled out a plan for an unprecedented strategic commitment to China.

The firm was perceived on Wall Street as the most conservative of the big American investment houses. But at the start of the decade, with Goldman's profits swelling from astute proprietary trading in Europe and North America, its partners were hungry for new lines of high-yield business outside traditional markets. Goldman's management committee had been eyeing Asia since the late 1980s. The firm's co-chairmen (Stephen Friedman and future Treasury Secretary Robert Rubin) as well as two chairmen-to-be (future US senator Jon Corzine and Henry 'Hank' Paulson), all agreed that Asia represented an opportunity they were failing to exploit. Mr Tsang in turn argued that any expansion into Asia must place Hong Kong and China at its centre and that the *modus operandi* in the region should be unusually aggressive; instead of simply trading and making commissions in secondary markets, Goldman needed to be a player on its own account – a direct investor. To make his case Mr Tsang gave Mr Friedman and Mr Rubin a tour around Hong Kong, mainland China and Taiwan – so-called Greater China. He pointed out that his and his (originally Shanghainese) family's connections in Hong Kong with some of the best-known members of the local business élite could deliver a unique advantage, putting Goldman ahead of the Wall Street pack, which lacked the personal relationships that drive Chinese deal making.

The attack on China and Asia became two-pronged. First, Goldman's New York headquarters assembled a team of economists and researchers to quantify, model, analyse and scenario-plan the region. It was the classic, top down approach that made the firm's senior partners the most revered investment bankers in the world. Confronted with the problem of how to tackle the Asian markets, Goldman hired the best brain power it could buy. Janice Wallace, a veteran China watcher from the British investment bank Baring, and Jan Lee, a China specialist, economist and currency strategist with Union Bank of Switzerland, were recruited to lead the research. The team was joined by Donald Hanna from the World Bank, Dr Sun Bae Kim, a north Asia specialist from the San Francisco office of the Federal Reserve Board, Tom Barkett, a foreign exchange and interest rate expert from the London School of Economics, Dora Hung and Rebecca Wu, two top-rated analysts from Hong Kong, and Shan Li, the best young mainland Chinese economist Goldman could find, signed up as he was completing his doctorate at the Massachusetts Institute of Technology. In terms of reputation – both in academia and the markets – Goldman put together the China research dream team.

The second manoeuvre in the firm's strategy was for Mr Tsang quickly to establish Goldman as a player in the Hong Kong markets, and thereafter in direct investment in China. He announced the firm's arrival by leasing three floors of the Asia Finance Tower, the most prestigious new block in the territory's Central business district. When local contractors tried to fit wood panelling not of the same hue as that in Goldman's headquarters in New York, they were told to stop, and office furnishings for 400 people were shipped over from the US. The only items that were allowed to distinguish the Hong Kong office from Goldman's headquarters were antique Chinese porcelain and art works, some bought, others – priceless pieces that not even Goldman money could buy – leased from museums and housed in specially air-conditioned casing. To this style Mr Tsang added the substance of some of Hong Kong's top traders, led, on the equities side, by Nick Harbinson, who in his previous job at W. I. Carr had been reckoned by peers to be the best in the market. As China and Hong Kong exploded into the world's investment consciousness in 1993, Harbinson soon proved his worth. Trading activity at Goldman's office boomed. The firm added futures, foreign exchange, asset management and proprietary trading desks. In the course of 1993, its staff overran three floors of the Asia Finance Tower and Mr Tsang leased parts of another two; the head count rose to more than 500, up ten-fold in two years.

Mr Tsang made it his own priority to develop Goldman's proprietary direct investment strategy for China. He hired Liu Erfei, the son of a Chinese provincial vice-governor and one of the first mainlanders to graduate from

Harvard Business School, to identify and win investment banking deals on the mainland. Mr Liu in turn hired a group of other mainland graduates of foreign universities to work with him. Meanwhile, Mr Tsang set to work to realise his comparative advantage by cultivating old friends in the Hong business community.

Chief among these was Tsui Tsin-tong, or T. T. Tsui. Mr Tsui was best known in Hong Kong for his personal $600 million collection of Chinese antiques, most of which are kept on public display in the old Bank of China building in Central. The location was convenient for Mr Tsui because the building was also home to Hong Kong's 1920s Shanghai-style China Club, the drinking, dining and cigar establishment that he and Mr Tsang both frequented.

As well as enjoying cigars and being a philanthropist – in 1991 he gave £1.25 million ($2.2 million) to create the T. T. Tsui Gallery of Chinese Art at London's Victoria & Albert Museum – Mr Tsui was also known as a hard-nosed businessman with long-standing ties to mainland China. He was involved with at least one of China's military–industrial conglomerates, though no journalist has ever quite uncovered what he did. More important to Mr Tsui's friends was the quality of his political connections on the mainland, something confirmed in 1992 when he was chosen as one of a group of Hong Kong tycoons appointed by Beijing to advise on the colony's return to mainland sovereignty. (He was known to have designs on the job of first post-British governor, or 'chief executive', as the position was to be called). In the autumn of 1992, Mr Tsui set the China Club buzzing when he let it be known that the Chinese premier, Li Peng, and foreign trade minister, Li Lanqing, were encouraging him to form an investment partnership with other wealthy overseas Chinese. The inevitable rumour that followed was that some juicy deals were already in the offing from Beijing.

Within a few months, the promptly incorporated New China Hong Kong Group, as Mr Tsui called the partnership, signed up a roster of billionaires. Li Ka-shing, widely believed to be the wealthiest person in Hong Kong, Stanley Ho, the Macau casino magnate, Charles Lee, chairman of the Hong Kong stock exchange, the Riadys, among the most powerful ethnic Chinese families in Indonesia, the Singapore Trade Development Board (a Singaporean minister telephoned Mr Tsui personally to ensure the island state would have a share) and a major Taiwanese securities firm were some of the forty overseas Chinese partners. Thirteen others were mainland Chinese state companies, mostly controlled by ministries, with one a direct subsidiary of the State Council, China's cabinet. Only one non-Chinese partner was invited to join: Goldman Sachs – thanks to the good offices of Mr Tsang. The management committee in New York had no hesitation in taking up the offer.

It was a triumph for Mr Tsang, and made Goldman the envy of every investment bank in Asia. Mr Tsang was gaining something of a reputation with the local press, which dubbed him 'The Invisible Man' on account of his ability to be everywhere and yet never be seen. And he was everywhere. In 1993, Goldman teamed up directly with Li Ka-shing and took a minority stake in the biggest grade A property development in China, Oriental Plaza, a colossal 9 million square foot (840,000 square metre) office, apartment and retail complex at the north-eastern corner of Tiananmen Square in the heart of Beijing. The planned floor area was five times that of Macy's in New York and ten times that of Harrods in London. Goldman's direct investment team called it 'the project from Jupiter', after the largest planet in the solar system; it would cost $2 billion. Mr Tsang took the firm into another big property development in Shanghai through his ties to the Kwoks, a family of Hong Kong multibillionaires who control a company called Sun Hung Kai. He encouraged his investment team to seek out manufacturing plays, ranging from a Shanghai ice-cream maker to a factory producing diesel engines that Goldman targeted for listing in New York. It was not long before the firm was committed to a billion dollars of proprietary investment deals.

The real estate investments would take years to produce a return; Oriental Plaza was so huge its completion was at least five years away. So Mr Tsang looked for other, quicker return deals as well. He wanted to target infrastructure financing. The world's fastest economic growth was causing power cuts all over China; the country needed more electricity plants and the financing to pay for them. But the bureaucratic obstacles put up by Beijing's State Planning Commission and power ministry were daunting. So Mr Tsang turned to Venturetech, the mainland's hottest dealmaker and partner to Yaohan's Kazuo Wada. With Venturetech's relationships at the highest levels of Chinese government he believed Goldman could cut through the red tape that had so far emeshed other bankers. Through 1993 Goldman and Venturetech worked to structure a $180 million private placement of shares in electricity plants in northern China's Shandong province. It was the boldest move in Chinese infrastructure financing that anyone had made. By the autumn, the word in Hong Kong was that the deal was all but done.

Goldman obtained pre-sale commitments from investors around the world, many of them American independent power producers (IPPs) eager for an entrée to the market, to purchase the entire $180 million share issue. The Chinese were impressed. The Shandong government confirmed it was ready to go to contract. Goldman staffers travelled to the Great Hall of the People in Beijing and completed the signing. It was another first, and a tribute to the firm's application. Moreover, the investment banking team already had a second Chinese province – Guangdong – in advanced negotiations for another $200 million power station placement.[58] The Shandong deal could become a model for the whole country. Goldman's senior investment bankers decided they must leverage their initial success as fast as possible. They put together a reception and seminar for provincial power bureaus from around China in order to spread the message that they too could raise capital from international investors. The meeting was hosted by Liu Erfei and attended by representatives of many of China's thirty provinces. If a third of provincial governments raised capital for power plants using the Goldman strategy, there was $2 billion of business in the offing in the electricity sector alone. This did not seem impossible given that excess demand for power was causing black-outs and brown-outs almost everywhere in China. Moreover, the same or similar financing techniques could be used to raise money for much-needed roads, ports and airports – almost any kind of infrastructure imaginable in the world's biggest infrastructure market. The Shandong contract was the start of what investment bankers call 'dealflow' – the conveyor belt of riches that makes tricky first deals worth doing.[59]

4

All roads lead to Beijing

'When the barbarians manifest sincerity and respect, I shall unfailingly treat them with kindness. When they are full of themselves, they do not merit the enjoyment of my favours.'
Emperor Qian Long to Lord Macartney on the latter's trade mission to Beijing in 1793

THE EUPHORIC ATMOSPHERE of 1992 and 1993 had an effect above and beyond the immediate gold rush in the provinces. It made the Chinese capital, Beijing, a site of commercial pilgrimage for both businessmen and foreign government leaders seeking an audience with China's rulers. The central leadership retained for itself the right to approve all large-scale foreign investments, thereby drawing a constant stream of supplicants to its court.[1] There were similarities of style with the long series of delegations – including the 700-person party of Lord Macartney – that had pleaded for market access with the Qing emperors of the seventeenth and eighteenth centuries. In their hunger for deals, the business and diplomatic leaders of the international community showed a tendency to perform a virtual kowtow, the ritual prostrations before the Chinese seat of power. Visits were heavily choreographed. Senior representatives of the world's developed nations – sometimes heads of state – and the leaders of the most powerful corporations on earth, with revenues the size of small countries, acted out an idiosyncratically Chinese script in pursuit of their cut of the China Dream.

There was the brief meeting with the senior officers of the Chinese government – President Jiang Zemin, Prime Minister Li Peng or Senior Vice-premier Zhu Rongji. (An increasingly frail Deng Xiaoping, confident that China was at last leaping forward, withdrew from public life in 1994.) It was deemed important to arrive at these meetings with maximum fanfare, thereby symbolising recognition of the importance of the market. There was the ceremonial opening of a new office to demonstrate actual commitment. If an office had already been opened – as was often the case – it was necessary to theatrically restage a ribbon cutting. Most important of all was the public signing of memoranda of understanding – the all-important initial commitments to China investments. In an environment such as Shanghai where it was said that only an investment of more than $10 million could secure the attendance of the mayor at its signing, it was essential to think and act big. Government delegations, which brought with them scores, if not hundreds, of representatives of large companies, were best placed to do this. They could pull together signings that ran to billions of dollars.

By 1994, when trade missions to China were rolling in from month to month, the China Dream was at the peak of its efficacy. It was able to change world politics, redefine the manner in which developing countries are measured by economists and reshape global perceptions. The latter feat was achieved through the medium of the international press. Millions of column inches around the world were written on the subject of China's economic miracle. But what did more than anything to propagandise China's claims to the world's attention were three long cover stories in the most important international news weeklies. They came late – at the end of 1992 and the beginning of 1993 – by the standards of Asian reporting. At that point, Hong Kong's English language daily, the *South China Morning Post*, was already relegating mainland investment projects under HK$100 million ($13m) to the inside pages of its business section. But the international press took the China story to a global audience and played a critical role in communicating new academic ideas about the real scope and prospects of the Chinese economy.

梦

On 28 November 1992, what was probably the most influential piece of China journalism of the era appeared in the *Economist*. The 16-page survey – 'The Titan Stirs' – was penned by Jim Rohwer, the *Economist*'s senior Asia correspondent. It was an article whose time had come, and one which is often still cited. American diplomats at the US embassy in Beijing faxed photocopies of the piece back to government leaders in Washington to make doubly sure they read it.[2] A year later, the Chinese foreign minister, Qian Qichen, was still referring to the survey in his year end review published in the *People's Daily*, noting: 'When the Western economy is bogged down in a prolonged recession, the potential of the huge Chinese market is being turned into a reality.'[3]

What made Jim Rohwer's article so compelling was that it drew on interviews with World Bank staff in which they explained the support of the agency's chief economist, Larry Summers, for a non-traditional measure of economies that could better express the significance of a country like China. Mr Summers' father, Robert, had been instrumental in developing the alternative benchmark, called 'purchasing power parity' (PPP),[4] which first appeared in the 1960s as a little-known academic model. It dispenses with gross national product figures converted into American dollars and looks instead at what money buys in different countries. The idea is to take the dollar exchange rate out of calculations of a country's economic strength. The *Economist* explained how China had devalued its currency repeatedly in the 1980s. Largely as a result of this, the country's dollar-denominated GNP had risen only from $290 per capita in 1980 to $370 per capita in 1990, according to World Bank figures. It was a still lower $330 by Chinese numbers.[5] But China's economic growth rate in the 1980s implied that GNP per capita, after inflation, should have more than doubled. The official figures, Larry Summers argued, had been grossly distorted by the renminbi–dollar exchange rate. Using the purchasing power methodology, and China price data collected by another economist, Irving Kravis, Robert Summers had calculated the strength of the Chinese economy at as much as seven times the official dollar figure – equivalent to a GNP per capita of $2,300–$2,700.

At this level China was catapulted instantaneously into the ranks of the great economic powers; the country had an economy worth around $3 trillion a year, similar to the GNP of Germany, two-thirds that of Japan and two-fifths that of the US. And China was growing far faster than any of these countries. The *Economist* stated starkly: 'China is already the world's third – or fourth – biggest economy, behind only America, Japan and maybe Germany. The official figures belie this ... The official figures about China are gibberish.'

Larry Summers was not the only authority cited. The *Economist* quoted other researchers who had concluded that a purchasing power reassessment of China was overdue. Furthermore, the magazine melded the idea of purchasing power – which in China could be characterised as the country having relatively little money, but that money buying much more than elsewhere because of a legacy of price controls – with another powerful concept, that of China's unredeemed greatness.

This latter argument – popular among Chinese academics, especially those connected with government – posits that China has fallen from grace in recent history (500 years out of the last 5,000) but is ripe, because of its intrinsic qualities as a nation, for renaissance. Greatness in antiquity, in short, will beget greatness in modernity. As the opening lines of the *Economist* survey put it: 'As far as anyone can guess, it was around 1500 that Europe overtook China as the world's most advanced civilisation. For centuries – maybe always – before then, Chinese science and technology and Chinese productivity and incomes were the world's best.'

The combination of China's unrecognised purchasing power and the idea, expressed most famously by Napoleon, of the country as a great sleeping dragon ready to awaken ('Let it sleep,' he advised) made for potent writing. The conclusion was apocalyptic: 'Just a generation from now,' wrote Rohwer, 'one of the world's weightiest questions may well be how to handle a self-confident nuclear-armed China presiding over the biggest economy on earth.'

By the time *Newsweek* came out with a China cover on 15 February 1993, Larry Summers had spoken publicly about his conviction that only PPP could capture the magnitude of the China opportunity. He had also moved on to a new job at the US Treasury, with responsibility for international affairs.[6] 'Many economists believe a standard estimate of China's per capita gross national product is already two or three times too low,' the magazine reported. 'Former World Bank chief economist Larry Summers recently argued that China could surpass both Japan and the United States to become the world's largest economy by 2020.' *Newsweek*'s feature, entitled 'Long March. China's Push toward Prosperity: What Does It Mean for the Rest of Us?' focused on Jiangsu, a province of 71 million people west of Shanghai whose GDP was reported to have grown by 26 per cent in the previous year. At this clip, China was catching up with the developed world at a prodigious rate. And if the country's economy was already far bigger than regular data suggested, the trend was doubly significant. *Newsweek*'s China coverage stood in stark contrast to the publication's lead story the previous September, when the words 'America's Gloom' were overlaid on a photograph of the locked gates of a redundant North American factory. Where the earlier article dwelt on an economy that had grown at 1 per cent a year over the previous four years – less than the rate of US population growth – the China piece celebrated an economy growing at 13 per cent a year. Below the words 'The World's Latest, Greatest Economy', the contents page introduced the story as follows: 'The old conventional wisdom is giving way to predictions that China could emerge as the world's dominant economy by early in the twenty-first century. Yes, that means bigger than Japan, and, say some, bigger than the United States.'

The last of the China covers was the longest and most heavily flagged. On 10 May 1993, *Time*, the largest circulation news weekly in the world, ran a 32-page cover story entitled simply *'The Next Superpower'*. Making up for tardiness with enthusiasm, the magazine pronounced that China's economy was 'highballing'. The introduction to its survey started off in the dramatic tone in which it continued: 'For the first time in history, an ancient, proud civilisation is stepping forth decisively from its intermittent isolation to claim an important place in the sun.' It was the end of China's being pigeon-holed among the poorest countries on earth.

The hugeness of the market, of course, depended on an acceptance of a high purchasing power multiplier for China. But in 1993, the PPP methodology gained wide currency. In May, the International Monetary Fund (IMF) published an assessment of Chinese purchasing power at $1,460 per capita for 1991 in its *World Economic Outlook*. This was lower than Robert Summers' figure, but still nearly five times China's GNP per capita when converted at the prevailing exchange rate. The report, combined with off-the-record interviews given by Fund officials, gave rise to daily news stories around the world. On 30 May, *The New York Times* carried a front page article giving a Chinese per capita purchasing power of $1,600 for 1992, based on IMF information.[7] Since Japan's purchasing power was reckoned by the IMF and the World Bank to be less than its dollar GNP, the *Times* noted, China's economy was already as important as Japan's.

The World Bank itself had never given a purchasing power estimate for China, but in 1993 it published two. The first, based on price data, was $1,680 per capita for 1991; the second, implied from educational enrolment statistics, was $2,200,[8] also for 1991. When adjusted for 1992's growth, the Bank was reckoning China's purchasing power significantly higher than the IMF. The organisation also decided in 1993 to substantially increase its standard dollar GNP figure for China, upping it from $370 per capita in 1991 to $470 per capita for 1992 on the basis that China was underreporting the size of its economy and pricing many goods and services below market levels. Nineteen ninety-three was also the year in which China became the World Bank's biggest borrowing client, a position it has retained.

Perceptions of China changed rapidly and dramatically. In the past, the country had been regarded by an informed few as a poor economy growing quite fast. By the end of 1993, China was seen by almost anybody who read a newspaper as a very big economy growing by leaps and bounds. The zeitgeist book of the time was *China: The Next Economic Superpower* by William Overholt, managing director of Bankers Trust in Hong Kong.[9] The title's assertion about China's prospects was based squarely on the foundations of purchasing power analysis. Mr Overholt quoted the IMF's purchasing power report, an unidentified Australian study, unnamed foreign investors and the ubiquitous Larry Summers:

> Some companies marketing consumer goods in coastal China have noticed that purchasing patterns are typical of people with about four times the income that Chinese statistics show these customers to have ... Based on extensive travel in

China and other Pacific Asian countries, my impression is that average Chinese
living standards are about as high as Thai living standards, although Thailand's
statistics show a per capita income four times higher ... Such a view of the
Chinese economy has become widely accepted by analysts. In fact, this figure
[$1,500] is far less than the estimate of $2,500 provided by Lawrence Summers,
formerly World Bank chief economist ... If Summers' calculation is correct, China's
economy will pass the US economy in sheer size within eleven years.[10]

Despite some curious assertions – the second paragraph of *China: The Next
Economic Superpower* claims that 40 million of the 105 million people in
China's north-east still live in caves[11] – the book was widely read and praised.
Sir Charles Powell, long-time adviser to Margaret Thatcher, echoed other
reviewers when he wrote in Britain's *Sunday Telegraph*: 'I am sure that Mr
Overholt is right ... Great shifts in the world balance occur rarely. But as Mr
Overholt perceives we are witnessing one now.' In Washington, a 'senior
Treasury official' quoted in *Business Week* in October 1993 was thinking precisely like Sir Charles. Explaining why the Clinton administration had to
retreat from its pre-1992 election pledge not to 'coddle dictators', the official
stated matter-of-factly: 'China will soon have the world's second biggest
economy. The administration has no alternative but to be constructively
engaged with China.'[12]

They came from afar, in private jets ...

The Chinese economic miracle arrived, via the media, on the breakfast tables
of the developed world. When leaders of governments and multinational
businesses in the United States and Europe read the news, they all reached
the same conclusion: it was time to go to Beijing. There is no easy way to
characterise the politicians and business executives who made the pilgrimage to the Chinese capital. They represented every shade of political opinion
– from theoretically liberal democrats to straight-talking right wingers who
sympathised with China's authoritarianism – and every sector of commercial
activity. The only thing they had in common was that they were drawn inexorably onwards by the force of the China Dream.

Among them were men of a strategic disposition. Robert Allen, chief executive officer of American Telephone & Telegraph (AT&T), made repeated lobbying trips to Beijing during the period, becoming a familiar face among the
Chinese leadership. Mr Allen saw in China an answer to his company's quest
for a new direction in the face of deregulation and increased competition in
the US. He needed licences from the Chinese government in order to fulfil his
aims. AT&T spent $500 million on consultants between 1989 and 1994,[13] not

a small part of which went to people advising on entry to the Chinese market. On one visit to see the central government, the chief executive gave away the scale of his ambitions when he told the *South China Morning Post* that China would be worth $10 billion a year to AT&T by 1997[14] – equivalent to 15 per cent of his company's 1992 revenues.

Other visitors were famously hard-headed, like Jack Welch of General Electric (GE), who flew into China in 1992 with his vice-chairman Paolo Fresca and a posse of his most senior executives. The group toured Deng Xiaoping's commercial capital, Shanghai, and hosted a party aboard a boat on the Huangpu river for government leaders and members of the American Chamber of Commerce. Welch, not normally one to jump into a deal head first, was taken with what he saw. He contrasted China's frenetic construction activity with the recessionary economies of western Europe and a now sluggish recovery in the US. At a debriefing session on the corporate jet on his way home, America's most respected business leader told staff he wanted every one of GE's twelve business units to look for China investment opportunities. Within weeks, business development officers from headquarters were scouring the country. Welch said the company should consider 'getting a billion dollars invested'.[15]

Other business executives moved on China in packs. After initial foraging in 1993, the leading lights of Wall Street and the City of London descended on Beijing in the spring of 1994. In ten weeks between March and May, chairmen or CEOs including John Mack of Morgan Stanley, Daniel Tully of Merrill Lynch, John Chalsty of Donaldson, Lufkin & Jenrette, Sir Evelyn de Rothschild of N. M. Rothschild and Peter Baring of Baring all made trips to China, as did delegations from the London and New York stock exchanges. For three months, one of the chief occupations of Chinese premier Li Peng – a Soviet-schooled engineer with little understanding of financial markets – was to receive the high priests of global capitalism.

Irrespective of who came to Beijing, the visiting game was played according to a set of unwritten but apparently unbreachable rules. These required the visitor to present as much 'face' as possible in order to attract the attention of the Chinese leadership, to meet with the highest government officials possible, to hold an office-opening ceremony and to sign some sort of agreement. For almost everybody, there were only two places to stay. The first was the China World Hotel on Jianguomenwai Avenue, which is half-owned by the Ministry of Foreign Trade and Economic Co-operation. The second was the central government's state guest house, Diaoyutai, which opened its villas, set amid lakes and parkland on the west side of town, to the best-heeled of the foreign visitors. The rack rate for the most basic room at the China World promptly rose to $240, while a night in a villa at Diaoyutai for a small group cost as much as $30,000.

The standards for 'face' were set by Wall Street. Both Morgan Stanley's John Mack and Goldman Sachs' Stephen Friedman chartered private jets. Upon landing, anyone wishing to be taken seriously had the Public Security Bureau (PSB) – via its agents at five-star hotels and government ministries – provide a lead car and uniformed officers to escort them about town. The flashing lights and sirens of the PSB's black limousines became a daily torment for the citizens of the Chinese capital. The cars carry not only the regular police siren but also those of the fire, ambulance, emergency power services and civil engineering departments, as well as megaphones. The burly officers in the front passenger seat bellowing '*Rang-a-Rang-a*' – 'Get out of the way! Get out of the way!' – and frequently more obscene lines, soon learned that the violent hoot of the civil engineers' emergency service was the most effective at intimidating the general public. Even CEOs habituated to slavish obsequiousness found it hard not to be impressed, especially if, like John Mack, their subordinates had paid for the PSB's full treatment including motorcycle outriders.

Meetings between chief executives and senior leaders were couched in formulaic terms with pronouncements about the need to work from positions of 'mutual respect' and for 'mutual benefit'. In a typical encounter with Li Peng, Donaldson, Lufkin & Jenrette's John Chalsty suggested that two great nations 'should strengthen co-operation on the basis of mutual respect, which will be beneficial to both sides'. 'It is our common interest and in accord with the will of the people,' replied the prime minister, 'to see that Sino-US relations continue to improve.'[16]

The essential adjunct to the formal meeting was the formal banquet, at which foreign corporations aimed to secure the attendance of mayors and vice-mayors and senior ministerial officials. Such people were also in demand for the opening of representative offices and the signing of the all-imporant memoranda of understanding. These agreements, although not legally binding, were the trophies of a successful visit. The most ambitious memorandum of the early gold rush period was that between AT&T and China's State Planning Commission, signed in February 1993 and paraded during a week-long tour in August by CEO Robert Allen. The American telecoms giant said the document covered investment in telephone switching, microelectronics and network management, the setting up of a Bell Laboratories research and development centre and assistance for China with 'training'. The full content of the memorandum was never made public, but Robert Allen assured both the press and shareholders it meant 'multibillions' of revenue for his company.[17] After showing 'face', Mr Allen gave it. He made AT&T (China) the only one of twenty divisions in the world to be based on geography rather than product or service line and the only one to report directly to him. William Warwick, taken from the leadership of AT&T's global microelectronic division to run the China operation, explained: 'China is the largest telecom infrastructure market in the world, and it will likely be that for maybe the next thirty years.'[18]

... and chartered jumbos

In November 1993, western commercial engagement with China took a dramatic new turn, as a visit by German chancellor Helmut Kohl, an old friend of China who had first visited the country in 1974 and returned twice as chancellor in the 1980s, heralded the era of the diplomatic trade mission.[19] Mr Kohl arrived in Beijing accompanied by forty of his country's most senior businessmen. The chairmen of Germany's biggest industrial conglomerates – Daimler–Benz, Siemens, Volkswagen–Audi, BMW – and the heads of the three biggest German banks and leading insurer, all now embarked on a collective business sortie.

German expectations were high. In the run-up to the visit, Chinese premier Li Peng made a pointed remark in the official press that the Kohl delegation was 'sure to go home with packed suitcases'.[20] The Chinese did not disappoint. On 19 November, the German business leaders, together with 250 Chinese and German government officials, gathered in the Grand Eastern Room of the Great Hall of the People in Tiananmen Square. A dozen rows of armchairs spread back from the centre of the room where Li Peng sat with Helmut Kohl. The press were let in to hear the Chinese premier joking with the chairman of Siemens that he would sell back to the company a still-functioning pre-1949 Siemens fan that he had at home. In this jovial atmosphere the businessmen signed twenty contracts and memoranda of understanding worth at least DM3 billion ($1.8bn). This was the value of the sales orders – including six Airbus planes, a subway system for the southern city of Guangzhou, two power stations, ships, rail cars and industrial equipment – itemised by the German government. Mr Kohl himself claimed the total value of business secured on his trip was more like DM7 billion ($4.1bn). Whatever, the sum at stake was enormous.

The Kohl visit set the standard for a wave of international trade missions that followed. Between the German chancellor's trip at the end of 1993 and the middle of 1996, ten trade delegations from the world's richest countries came to China. Mr Kohl visited twice, as did US commerce secretary Ron Brown and British trade minister (and subsequently deputy prime minister)

Michael Heseltine. French premier Edouard Balladur, Canadian premier Jean Chrétien and US Energy Secretary Hazel O'Leary each came once. The missions were accompanied by 1,050 businessmen, among them the chief executives and chairmen of the world's most powerful companies; no systematic count has been completed, but it is probable that an absolute majority of the businesses listed in the Fortune 500 index of multinational conglomerates were represented.

Announced on these visits were contracts with a face value of $27–29 billion,[21] depending on who made the announcements. Furthermore, the missions to China led to reciprocal visits to western countries by Jiang Zemin, Li Peng and Chinese foreign trade minister Wu Yi. In less than two years, from July 1994 to April 1996, five such visits produced reported business deals totalling $12–15 billion.[22] On paper fifteen international exchanges had produced contracts worth at least $40 billion – or nearly $3 billion per trip.

It was international commerce the likes of which the world had never seen. Helmut Kohl established the pace and others increased it. The peak of activity was between August of 1994 and July of 1995, when three visits by Jiang Zemin and Li Peng to Europe and three trips to China from North America and one each from France and Britain produced $32 billion of signings. This was more than the previous year's combined exports of the US, Canada, Germany, Britain and France to the People's Republic.

Contracts and memoranda covered everything from sales of aircraft and more than a dozen power stations to joint venture investments to build car and petrochemical plants. Hardware sales involving exports to China formed by far the biggest component. Ron Brown, en route to Beijing on 27 August 1994, told US journalists travelling on his plane that his list of potential sales was $25 billion long: 'We will be advocating $25 billion in deals and I expect several billion to come to fruition while we're on the ground,' he announced.[23]

Sure enough, on his third day in the Chinese capital, Mr Brown was able to declare to the assembled press: 'I stand before you exhilarated by the results of our first two and a half days in Peking. As of this afternoon we have already signed agreements with a total value of almost $5 billion.' Mr Brown went on to become the first of three $6 billion men and women in terms of signings on a single visit. He was equalled by Canadian prime minister Jean Chrétien in November 1994 and US energy secretary Hazel O'Leary in February 1995. Between them they secured $18 billion of business, including at least seven complete power plants, large numbers of ancillary power equipment deals and hundreds of millions of dollars of telecommunications and aircraft sales. If it seemed like a lot of money, the politicians pointed out, it was only the beginning. Ron Brown told chief executives from Chrysler, Salomon, Federal

Express, Westinghouse, McDonnell Douglas and twenty others who were accompanying him – as well as the assembled membership of the American Chamber of Commerce in Beijing – that China had 'a quarter of a trillion dollars of infrastructure projects in the pipeline'.[24]

These sorts of prospects had grown businessmen straining at the leash of respectable behaviour. When Michael Heseltine brought sixteen senior insurance and banking executives from Britain – among 130 businessmen on his trip to Beijing in May 1995 – there was a near breakdown of order over who should sit at the senior table at the official banquet. There were thirty places for the top representatives of British business at a table featuring forty Chinese ministers and vice-ministers. The insurance companies, which believed a single licence was in the offing for a British firm, were all determined to take their seats. But there was not enough space. When the British Chamber of Commerce decided the only fair resolution was not to allow any insurers to sit at the top table, the Chamber's chairman, Peter Batey, was screamed at by infuriated executives. They were exiled, distinctly nonplussed, to a special insurance industry table. Mr Heseltine returned a year later with 280 more British businessmen and the banqueting arrangements were no less contentious. On this occasion executives tried to bypass the unhelpful Chamber authorities, surreptitiously swapping place names at the senior table. This was discovered and, after more opprobrium, the original seating plan was restored.

China realpolitik

The antics of normally reserved international executives reflected what they believed to be at stake. Ben Chapman,[25] the head of the UK's Department of Trade and Industry in Manchester, told his local newspaper when he returned from Mr Heseltine's first visit: 'China will offer a market as big as the European single market. To put its scale in context, it has one-quarter of the world's population and each of its thirty provinces has a geographical size and economic potential of a European country.' The *Manchester Evening News* added: 'Having grown at nearly 10 per cent since 1978, analysts reckon that if this rate continues it [China] will be the world's biggest economy by the year 2004. There are markets for virtually everything, but especially power, transport and communications, agriculture, infrastructure and chemicals.'[26]

During Ron Brown's trip in August 1994, Joe Gorman, the chairman of TRW Inc., the US's biggest manufacturer of auto parts, told journalists it was quite possible that China would have 500 million cars by 2020. 'I can envision the day when over half the automobiles sold in the world are sold in Asia and perhaps even in China. If China were by the year 2010 or 2020 to have as many autos as the current per capita auto population of Germany today, there would be 500 million autos,' Mr Gorman said. He pointed out that, even if his calculations were wrong by a factor of two to four, China would still see massive sales: 'Even if I am only half right or a quarter right, China is a huge market.'[27]

The strength of such convictions among businessmen and politicians explains the extraordinary international politics of the period. At one level, Sino-foreign relations could take on an air of farce. It was revealed after Michael Heseltine's second China mission that the deputy prime minister had pressured the England football team to travel to China in support of his commercial efforts. At the time, British sports journalists were flummoxed as to why, a few weeks before enjoying the home advantage in the four-yearly European championships, the England team should travel 5,000 miles to play on a dangerous pitch against an unrated team. Only a year earlier, the England goalkeeper, David Seaman, had broken a foot during a club match at the decaying Workers' Stadium in Beijing. The Chinese, however, were keen to play and Mr Heseltine was keen to have the England team oblige. A senior English Football Association official later explained to Britain's *Sunday Times*: 'We were told to go to China. It was repeatedly suggested by people in Heseltine's office that to ignore the Peking bid would harm the national interest.'[28] A trip that the soccer official was told had 'advantages beyond football' went ahead, featuring a bizarre joint press conference between Michael Heseltine and England's cockney football coach, Terry Venables, on the lawn of the British ambassador's residence.[29] As it turned out, England easily beat China 3–0 in a game which ended with 50,000 Chinese spectators chanting unprintable obscenities at their national team. It was unclear whether this was a gain for British business.

Beyond the Heseltine soccer manouevre, however, reaction to the China market opportunity had effects which reshaped global diplomacy. As of 1993, three of the world's most powerful countries – France, the United States and Britain – were in a state of diplomatic conflict with China. France had sold sixty Mirage fighter jets to Taiwan in 1992, leading to the closure of its Guangzhou consulate. Outgoing US president George Bush had sanctioned the sale of F-16s to the Taiwanese the same year. Despite, this Mr Bush was lambasted throughout the 1992 presidential campaign for being soft on Beijing. Bill Clinton, the man who went on to beat Mr Bush, accepted the Democratic nomination in July 1992 with the stirring words that if elected president he would run 'an America that will not coddle dictators from Baghdad to Beijing'.[30] Upon election, Mr Clinton signed an executive order making China's normal trade tariff structure with the US – its so-called Most Favoured Nation (MFN) status – dependent on progress in seven areas of human rights. Henceforth, Mr Clinton declared, the US would have a relationship with China based on principle.

British premier John Major made a similar determination. In September 1991, he had been forced into a humiliating visit to Beijing – making him the first western premier to visit China since Tiananmen – in order to secure a memorandum of understanding for a new Hong Kong airport. Mr Major returned to London deeply disenchanted with the Foreign Office China specialists who had organised his trip. Having narrowly won the general election in 1992, he decided to replace David Wilson, the Foreign Office sinologist who was then governor of Hong Kong, with someone more combative. Former minister Chris Patten accepted the post. Within weeks of arriving in Hong Kong, Patten made it clear that the last five years of British colonial rule would not be like the previous 150. In 1993, he used a loophole in the Basic Law, the agreement governing Hong Kong's return to Chinese sovereignty in 1997, to create a far broader franchise for subsequent elections to Hong Kong's Legislative Council than the Chinese had envisaged. The prospect was that China would inherit a near-democracy in Hong Kong. The government in Beijing was livid.

At face value, the developed world was involved in a series of intractable disputes with China. Taiwan, Hong Kong and human rights were not issues over which the Chinese Communist Party could afford to back down. Taiwan was the government's most potent propaganda tool – a living reminder of the communist victory over the corrupt Nationalist regime in a civil war that has never formally ended. Hong Kong represented both the iniquitous legacy of European colonialism and the unnerving possibility of political insurrection from within China's borders. Human rights was, in propaganda terms, the latest western conspiracy to impose foreign standards on developing countries. In practical terms, rights for the individual so obviously undermined the collective fear needed to keep the communists in power that they were beyond contemplation.

Despite all this, the political differences between China and western governments in the period ended up as nothing more than a sideshow. The main force was commercial engagement, whose powers were so many and so strong that they co-opted many of the politicians who had previously rounded on China's repressive regime. The Clinton administration was one of many cases in point. By the time the US president signed the order linking China's trade status to human rights improvements, there were already doubts about the prudence of the policy among his key aides, including the chairman of the National Economic Council Robert Rubin (formerly Goldman Sachs co-chairman) and Larry Summers, now deputy treasury secretary. Even those who had chanted the get-tough-with-China mantra most loudly during the election changed their tune within months of being in office. Commerce secretary Ron Brown was the most outspoken China critic during the Clinton campaign, referring to President Bush's policy of unconditionally renewing China's MFN status as an example of 'More Failed Notions' of the Republican Party. When the winds of multibillion dollar business began to blow across mainland China, however, it was Mr Brown who led the about turn on MFN policy; unconditional renewal, he decided, was a matter of US 'economic security'.[31]

For their part, the Chinese played a good political hand, although, given the blind exuberance of multinational executives, they could just as well have played a bad one. The signing of $2 billion of deals with Helmut Kohl's first trade group in November 1993 neatly coincided with President Jiang Zemin's visit to an Asia Pacific Economic Co-operation (APEC) forum in Seattle. A first meeting between Mr Jiang and Mr Clinton took place on the fringes of the conference with newspaper headlines shouting out Mr Kohl's success. Television crews, meanwhile, followed Mr Jiang on a visit to the nearby Boeing factory. The world's leading aircraft maker was going through a bad patch. Commercial airplane orders had been falling since 1990 and were set, in 1994, to reach their lowest level for more than thirty years.[32] The Chinese, however, were buying – they took delivery of thirty-three aircraft, 8 per cent of Boeing's annual order book – in 1993.[33] So when Mr Jiang indicated he was interested in visiting the factory, Boeing went the whole hog, even laying on an encounter with a model Boeing family. Cameras rolling, the Chinese president sat in an American living room and pulled photographs of his grandchildren from his wallet. Was China so bad? Boeing chief executive Frank Strontz said pointedly that China was 'a very important sustaining market for us'.[34] The subtext of the word 'sustaining' was clear: in a period when Boeing was shedding jobs, China was a force for protecting jobs.

Mr Clinton's get-tough-with-China policy lasted less than three months. It began with his signing of the executive order linking trade to human rights on 28 May 1993, and ended with the drafting of a joint White House and State Department paper on the merits of a less confrontational China policy in July. This supposedly secret policy document was agreed by Mr Clinton's cabinet in September, well before Mr Kohl travelled to China or Mr Jiang went to Seattle in November, and was promptly leaked, in outline, to the press.[35] The US government then spent seven months prior to the renewal of China's MFN status in June 1994 negotiating with no credibility. The Chinese knew there was no real commitment to confrontation. Deputy foreign minister Liu Huaqing, meeting Robert Rubin in Washington in January 1994, taunted him with the Kohl export deals. The hapless US secretary of state, Warren Christopher, despatched to Beijing to obtain some sop to human rights in March, was told by Li Peng that he did not represent the views of his own government; Mr Li said he knew full well that China's MFN status was going to be renewed.[36] The only party to remain nervous about MFN was US business, which, in the form of the American Chamber of Commerce in Beijing, barred the press from a breakfast meeting with Mr Christopher and tore into him for trying to wreck their market. The excoriation was led by the local respresentatives of AT&T and General Motors. Back home, the heads of 800 US businesses and trade associations wrote to President Clinton urging him not to put US commercial interests in peril. Hand-picked, English-speaking employees of American firms in China were flown to Washington and toured around the political circuit to make the case that economic growth alone was changing the nature of China. In June 1994, China's MFN status was de-linked from human rights and renewed unconditionally.

梦

The French climbdown over its weapons sales to Taiwan was more straightforward, involved less soul-searching and was more immediately remunerative than the Clinton experience. In the run-up to the Kohl visit to Beijing, the government of Edouard Balladur had already decided it must get back on terms with China. French business, led by state-invested multinationals in the nuclear and non-nuclear power, telecommunications and infrastructure sectors, were telling politicians they had been frozen out of China ever since the Taiwan fighter jet sale was announced. The government's response was to send an envoy, Jacques Friedmann, to Beijing to atone for the Mirage deal, explaining it was the short-sighted decision of a previous government.[37] The Chinese were receptive. In January 1994, foreign minister Qian Qichen concluded an agreement in Paris under which the French promised to block further weapons sales to Taiwan. In the course of the next twelve months Mr Balladur, minister of posts and telecommunications and foreign trade Gerard Longuet and industry minister Jose Rossi travelled to Beijing to sign deals valued at nearly $4 billion.

The French newspaper Le Monde later reported that the Sino-French rapprochement included a promise by the Chinese to deliver a total of $10 billion of business. There were editorials in the French press talking of a sell-out, but French politicians and businessmen were in no doubt of the justification for the course they followed. Even before the ink was dry on the Paris deal, foreign minister Alain Juppé spoke candidly about his view of the relative importance of Taiwan and China: 'Where is France's interest?' he asked a Reuters journalist in an interview at the end of November. 'Is it betting on a country with 20 million people or on a country of 1 billion 300 million people and which is perhaps already the world's third leading economic power? For me, the choice is perfectly clear.'[38] The interview revealed that Mr Juppé, like so many of his peers, was in touch with the latest in purchasing power theory.

In Britain, what Chris Patten described as 'these great, fat carrots' hung before trade delegations to China had the effect of splitting the government. On the one side was Mr Major, a prime minister who was indebted to him for managing an unexpected election victory in 1992 as Conservative campaign manager, and foreign secretary Douglas Hurd who, like Mr Major, had been forced by Hong Kong's airport saga to visit Beijing when the developed world still considered it impolitic to do so. On the other side of what became an embittered argument stood the representatives of the Conservative Party's traditional links to British business. Aligned with these commercial interests were the so-called 'mandarins' of the British Foreign Office.

By the time Michael Heseltine brought his first trade mission to China in 1995, Mr Patten had already experienced two years of vituperation from former and current colleagues over his Hong Kong democratisation strategy. Lord Young, a stalwart of Margaret Thatcher's administration of the 1980s and now chairman of Cable & Wireless, paid repeated visits to the Hong Kong governor urging him to change course. Cable & Wireless owned a controlling interest in Hongkong Telecom and, Lord Young believed, was therefore uniquely positioned to profit from the China market. As he put it in an interview with Patten's biographer Jonathan Dimbleby: 'I think a number of us saw there were opportunities in China on a heroic scale. That we could go back and reclaim markets that were ours in the last century.'[39] The view that Mr Patten was preventing this was less surprising coming from Lord Young, a hard-nosed businessman, than it was from Lord Prior, another former Conservative colleague of Mr Patten's who had resurfaced in business. Yet Mr Patten found that as chairman of GEC, Lord Prior, a close political ally from the Thatcher era, was no less critical of his handling of China. The pressure from British big business gave no quarter. After a visit from the chairman of Shell, Mr Patten remarked that the executive employed 'the sort of crudeness which I don't think the Mafia would show'.[40]

Michael Heseltine's visit to China in 1995 took the tension to a new level, pitting Chris Patten against a serving minister and his allies in the same government. At issue in Hong Kong at the time was the creation of a local Court of Final Appeal over whose composition Beijing and Hong Kong legislators differed. Prior to his trip, Mr Heseltine, the Foreign Ministry's China experts and the Department of Trade and Industry successfully lobbied Mr Patten to put off tabling legislation on the issue. Once the trip was over, Mr Heseltine – with $1.6 billion of orders in his pocket – began trying to change Hong Kong policy from within the cabinet in London. Mr Patten was not best pleased to discover that, while in Guangzhou, Mr Heseltine and the British ambassador, Len Appleyard, had held a meeting in a People's Liberation Army-owned hotel to discuss what they referred to as 'the Patten problem'.[41] After Heseltine returned to London, Appleyard wrote a despatch to the government claiming that, apart from the $1.6 billion of business secured during the trip, another $8 billion of deals were now in play for UK companies. However, he noted, Li Peng had told Mr Heseltine that this level of bilateral business could only be sustained if the issue of Hong Kong was dealt with in a manner more acceptable to Beijing.

The affair ended with Mr Patten putting a 'Back me or sack me' ultimatum before the British cabinet. The government did back the Hong Kong governor at the time, but the in-fighting and recriminations reverberated all the way to the Conservative electoral defeat and the return of Hong Kong to Chinese rule in 1997. The promise of the China market proved too much even for the longest-serving Conservative government of the twentieth century. This was par for the international diplomatic course. China turned the Clinton administration, which on other foreign policy issues achieved comfortable unanimity, inside out. The French, who had taken in scores of Chinese dissidents after the Tiananmen massacre, and who had briefly claimed to be the most principled country in Europe for supporting Taiwan's self-defence, ended up in a show of grovelling obeisance before the Chinese Communist Party.

The momentum of the China gold rush carried the whole world before it. In 1993, the country contracted $111 billion of direct foreign investment, more than any other nation on earth and equivalent to half the actual global flows of cross-border investment that year.[42] Over $27 billion of capital was delivered in 1993, a figure that would increase each year for the next five years until China had absorbed $300 billion of foreign investment – the equivalent of 70 per cent of its 1993 GNP – by the end of the decade. It was a striking performance for a nation with a GNP per capita of $370.[43] Only the United States, with a GNP per capita around $25,000, could attract more money in the 1990s – and before the global mergers and acquisitions boom at the end of the decade, the margin was not enormous. China's utilised foreign direct investment in the four years after 1993 was almost two-thirds of America's. In terms of cash investment and investment in new capacity – as opposed to stock swaps and acquisition of existing capacity – inward flows into China almost certainly exceeded those into the United States. When compared to other developing countries, China was in a different league, accounting for one-third of their total direct cross-border investment in the mid 1990s, half of that in Asia, more than all of that in Latin America and the Caribbean and three times the investment in central and eastern Europe.[44] The sums involved were more than enough to bend political wills. And their economic effects were exactly what the text books predicted.

5

Demand and supply

'Love is blind, and greed is insatiable'

C HINA IN THE mid 1990s became a place of long and agitated queues as a surge of would-be international investors competed for a limited supply of licences and investment opportunities. There were ferocious bidding wars between multinational companies. As a result, market entry costs rose exponentially. Almost no one questioned the prices being paid.

In the wake of Deng Xiaoping's Southern Tour, the government had promised to expand investment opportunities to include an array of new businesses that targeted China's domestic economy. It was the prospect of investing in retailing, transportation, power generation, banking, insurance and other services that precipitated the biggest flood of money into the country. While overall investment rose each year, the proportion registered as manufacturing – which dominated the 1980s because of the predominance of export processing – went into relative decline, from more than three-quarters of the total to less than half. Instead of exports, the greater part of the $300 billion invested in China by the turn of the century was chasing new businesses focused on local consumers.[1]

A flurry of 'experimental' contracts following Mr Deng's tour – including Hong Kong joint ventures for the management of ports in Shanghai, Shenzhen and Zhuhai, department stores such as Yaohan's in Pudong and the first foreign insurance licence since 1949 (granted to American International Group) – suggested the investment environment was indeed changing. Yet every deal required its own operating licence and, as foreign companies piled into the country, demand for licences ran far ahead of the pace of approvals. Investors were backed up in the queue to become invested, spending money to launch operations rather than actually running them, and global capitalism was driven to the limits of its ingenuity in its efforts to get business off the ground. When there were not enough listed shares for financial investors to buy, they created direct investment funds instead. Communist cadres and the children of senior leaders who appeared able to influence the granting of contracts and operating licences were hired on salaries that ran to hundreds of thousands, occasionally millions, of dollars a year. Retired political leaders from around the globe who had past dealings with China were called in for lobbying work. The likes of former international statesmen George Bush and Henry Kissinger were among those who benefited.

Investors were ready to do and spend almost anything to jump the line in their dream market. But the amount of capital committed always outstripped the supply of deals. Foreign companies opened 2,200 representative offices in Beijing alone in 1993 – most of them the first step in the application for a business licence. By the end of 1995, foreign banks had opened over 400 representative offices around the country and foreign insurers more than 150 in their quests for licences; the numbers continued to rise every month. At this stage, 150 international power projects were pending approval at the State Planning Commission. Every major US, European and Japanese automotive maker had applied for a production licence. Companies like Shell and Elf Aquitaine were lobbying to start construction of multibillion dollar integrated petrochemical sites. In this environment, it was not only the price of the deals themselves that sky-rocketed. International investors wanted modern offices for their staff, shopping malls in which to sell their goods, comfortable homes for their expatriates, schools for their managers' children, and so on. But China did not have the infrastructure to cope. Costs therefore followed demand – rapidly upwards.

The cash bonanza

Among the most impatient players awaiting their turn were those from the financial services industry – fund managers, investment banks and privately wealthy individuals looking to take a punt on the China Dream and thereby add to their riches. More than fifty open-ended investment funds targeting Chinese stocks were launched by 1996 and fund managers and retail investors were desperate to buy into them. But the funds all faced the same problem – there were not enough listed shares to go round. Buyers were restricted by the Chinese government to investment in a tiny number of Hong Kong dollar- and US dollar-denominated stocks sold through the Shenzhen and Shanghai exchanges. At the end of 1994, the total value of dollar-denominated stocks on the Shanghai bourse was just $200 million.[2] The only alternative to mainland shares was to purchase those in listed companies in Hong Kong and elsewhere with exposure to China's market. But this indirect route into the China opportunity was not enough to slake the thirst of global capitalism. So many institutional players, and high net worth individuals, decided to skirt around the problem and invest directly in the country.

There was a rush of what is called 'private equity financing' – capital pooled into funds for direct investment in businesses and infrastructure projects. According to a database maintained by the *Asia–Pacific Private Equity Bulletin*, an industry journal, the accumulated inflow into such funds reached $5.6 billion in 1995[3] and involved sixty-two investment vehicles. For two years from the autumn of 1993, insurance companies, investment bankers and entrepreneurs raised over $200 million a month for private equity investment in China – something unprecedented in the history of venture capital. Not until the internet phenomenon at the very end of the 1990s would such sums of money again be committed to a single proposition.

While some funds were opened to retail investors via listings on the Hong Kong, Singapore, New York, London, Dublin and other stock exchanges, the appetite for them was such that around two-thirds were unlisted – they raised all the capital they needed from private and institutional investors. American Insurance Group (AIG) set the pace in early 1994 when it pulled in $1.09 billion for its Asian Infrastructure Fund from only twenty-four backers. Proxies of the Singaporean government committed $250 million for the fund, whose prospectus promised to sink up to $500 million into China.[4] Peregrine Investment Holdings, whose chairman, Philip Tose, was famed as the most aggressive China bull in Hong Kong, launched a similarly named $1 billion Asia Infrastructure Fund in 1994, raising an initial $500 million. Peregrine's fund was lent credibility by a sponsoring group – all of whom invested – that included the International Finance Corp. (the private sector lending arm of the World Bank), the Asian Development Bank and affiliates of the financier George Soros. Other private funds were the brainchildren of charismatic individuals. Ronnie Chan, the billionaire controlling shareholder of Hong Kong property developer Hang Lung, started his China Renaissance Fund with $40 million of his own money; he attracted $160 million from other investors. Mr Chan told friends he was in the habit of dressing up in peasant garb when scouting investment opportunities on the mainland because this avoided unwanted attention.[5]

Jack Perkowski, a 15-year veteran of US investment bank Paine Webber, raised $418 million for direct investment in China. Mr Perkowski had already quit his Wall Street job to set up a hedge fund in Hong Kong in 1991 and was well placed to tap former investment banking associates when the China private equity boom began. He started his fund raising in New York in December 1993 and the process was easier than he expected: 'I raised $150 million in six weeks over the Christmas holidays,' he said. 'I started after Thanksgiving on 1 December and had nearly half the money from individuals by Christmas. After Christmas I saw one institutional investor which came up with $15 million. Once the others heard about that, the rest of the money came very fast.'[6] The final tally from the first round was $158 million; it was followed by further successful cash calls of $100 million in February 1995 and $160 million in June 1995. As a former head of investment banking at Paine Webber, Mr Perkowski knew how to press Wall Street's buttons. His fundraising roadshows featured charts extrapolating China's growth at 10 per cent per year far into the future. He highlighted potentially limitless demand from a quarter of the world's population for the products in which his company, ASIMCO, was investing: automotive components and beer. There were, he contended, no surer routes to profit in the world's fastest growing emerging market than alcohol and cars.

Participants in the private equity bonanza competed to set records. Jack Perkowski believed he had raised more money than any other individual and more money than anyone else for a specific industry – automotive. AIG said its infrastructure fund was 'the largest ever direct investment fund for emerging markets'.[7] Mark Mobius, whose Yul Brynner-lookalike shaven head – featured in his own television advertising campaign – came to symbolise emerging markets investment in the 1990s, claimed of his firm Templeton: 'We raised the largest ever single country closed-end fund. $800 million for China.'[8] Mr Mobius, whose firm solicited only $300 million, had long been known for his opposition to single country funds in emerging markets, believing them to be too risky.[9] But in the context of 1994, not even the godfather of emerging markets, the man who travels the world in an iguana skin-upholstered private jet, could swim against the Chinese tide. At exactly the moment Mobius's Templeton Dragon Fund was launched on the New York and Osaka stock exchanges, in September 1994, no fewer than three other big China funds were being touted to investors. Norinco, a commercial subsidiary of the People's Liberation Army, was sponsoring a fund that raised $185 million.[10] San Francisco-based investment bank Hambrecht & Quist was raising $80 million for its China Dynamic Growth Fund, which already contained $70 million. And Singaporean conglomerate Keppel announced the launch of a $100 million fund. With the right presentation, a fund could raise cash for almost anything – a group of investment banks including Baring and Oppenheimer pulled together $200 million for China Cement Corp., a fund investing only in cement plants.

The catwalk
The rush to mobilise capital went hand in hand with a rush to lock in critical local talent – a limited number of individuals whom investors perceived as able to make deals happen. Investment funds sought investment advisers.

ING, the Dutch financial services group, launched a $70 million private equity fund, ING Beijing Investment, with the deputy director of Beijing's municipal planning commission as chairman and Wang Baosen, executive vice-mayor of the capital, as a special adviser. Investment banks sought out the foreign-educated children of China's senior leaders. Bear Stearns hired Margaret Ren, daughter-in-law of former premier Zhao Ziyang. Ms Ren had interviews with all the major US investment banks in 1993; most were worried that her connection to her father, who had been thrown out of government in the wake of the 1989 Tiananmen massacre, was a liability. But when Ms Ren started to win Bear Stearns mandates for Chinese companies doing initial public offerings, other 'princelings' like her became even hotter commodities.

Lehman Brothers recruited Huang Bin, the son of Huang Hua, trusted foreign minister to both Mao Zedong and Deng Xiaoping. Goldman Sachs had built its China team around Liu Erfei, the Harvard-trained son of a deputy provincial governor, although when, in late 1993, Smith Barney offered Mr Liu a guaranteed minimum $1 million a year to start its China practice, he jumped ship. Smith Barney also recruited a daughter of Vice-premier Zou Jiahua. CS First Boston picked up the daughter of Ding Guanggen, Communist Party propaganda chief and former minister of railways, even though she was barely past her twentieth birthday. The hire appeared to give the bank the inside track on an early listing – that of Guangshen Railway, the operator of the key Hong Kong–mainland rail link. Bear Stearns, however, managed to trump First Boston. It hired the big-hitting Ms Ren and it took on the propaganda chief's son. It won the mandate.

Some princelings formed their own consultancy companies to peddle their connections. Chen Xiaopo, the son of the revolutionary marshal Chen Yi, started Standard International, offering multinational companies access to senior government figures.[11] Liu Ting, the daughter of Liu Shaoqi, the former head of state who died in a prison cell during the Cultural Revolution, created Asia Link, a firm with more credibility than most in what was often a straight cash-for-access business. Ms Liu's ability to negotiate workable deals won her a client roster that includes the likes of GE Capital, Morgan Stanley, Prudential and Raytheon. Other princelings were less sophisticated: they simply demanded an equity position in any business with which they were involved. Venturetech, the government-backed and princeling-led investment firm that assisted Yaohan's Kazuo Wada and Goldman Sachs, typically extracted a 10 per cent share of a business as the price of its involvement.[12]

American multinationals made ready use of local fixers, but they were also able to tap a long tradition of ex-Washington politicians working as China consultants.[13] Jimmy Carter's assistant secretary of state Richard Holbrooke (later Bill Clinton's special envoy to Yugoslavia and UN ambassador), energy secretary James Schlesinger, Treasury secretary Michael Blumenthal and agriculture secretary Bob Bergland had been some of the first to offer their services to American companies in China in the 1980s. Ronald Reagan's secretary of state Alexander Haig followed suit as a highly active China consultant after he left office in 1982.[14] In the 1990s, however, the money available to former US politicians willing to use their China connections for profit reached a new level. After the defeat of the Republican administration in 1992, George Bush himself, his national security adviser Brent Scowcroft and his trade representative Carla Hills were the most senior of a raft of Bush administration officials who began to offer themselves to corporate America as China specialists.[15]

Former president Bush, at $250,000 per project,[16] did not come cheap, and nor did his peers. Yet many US firms were so determined to jump the queue in China that no cost seemed unreasonable. The determination of Chubb insurance CEO Dean O'Hare to win an operating licence was such that his firm paid for Mr Bush to visit Beijing twice, Mr Scowcroft six times and former under-secretary of state Arnold Kantor many more times; the insurance firm also hired Brant Free, former deputy assistant secretary of commerce under President Reagan, to work on its China project on staff.[17] Since Mr Bush's father had been on the Chubb board, it was believed he would provide unique value for the company in his lobbying efforts. The calculation proved naive. A few months after his first visit for Chubb in 1996, Mr Bush reappeared in Beijing as the paid representative of John Hancock, another US insurer.[18]

But when it came to China lobbying, no one held a candle to Henry Kissinger. The man who crafted the American rapprochement with the Chinese communists started an opaque consultancy firm, Kissinger Associates, in 1982; China was very much Mr Kissinger's turf. As commercial opportunities opened up, he was frequently sighted in the capital in the 1990s. His ability to access senior leaders was second to none, and multinational companies paid handsomely for the service. A typical Kissinger Associates contract for a corporate client in China begins with a retainer of $200,000–250,000 per year. To this base is added Mr Kissinger's *per diem* when he travels to China – high if he brings two or three chairmen or CEOs in a group; extremely high if he travels with only one, giving him his undivided attention. Where investment projects are involved, Kissinger Associates receives 'milestone' payments for meeting specific objectives – such as the signing of an initial memorandum. Upon successful conclusion of a project, a 'success fee' is paid. This is likely to be around 5 per cent of a project's value. Since Kissinger Associates has worked in China on projects involving hundreds of millions of dollars, Mr Kissinger's firm can secure closing fees of tens of millions of dollars; in one deal for a US oil company, which failed to come to fruition, he stood to reap $40 million.[19] One of the few publicly acknowledged Kissinger clients in China is AIG, which obtained the first foreign insurance licence since the Communist take-over, in 1992. Mr Kissinger became a member of the AIG board.

The uses of shareholder funds

The sums of money deployed to try to jump the line for access to the China market were big by any standards. AIG, as one example, used Kissinger Associates as but a small part of its lobbying strategy. The firm also invested $200 million in the Portman Centre, a bell-wether real estate development in Shanghai, prior to its obtaining a licence, which was limited to that city. AIG sweetened its name by raising hundreds of millions of dollars for private equity investment. It flew scores of Chinese officials on 'inspection tours' of its businesses around the world. Maurice Greenberg, AIG's chairman, formed an 'International Business Leaders Advisory Council' for the mayor of Shanghai, a billionaires' support club which other CEOs were soon scrambling to join. When Mr Greenberg located a set of brass windows looted from the imperial Summer Palace in Beijing at the end of the nineteenth century, he bought them from a French collector and handed them back to the Chinese government.[20] By the time Chubb entered the fray for a licence, the cost of ingratiation had increased. The firm seemed to employ every consultant it could find. It paid $3 million to set up a Chubb School of Insurance in Shanghai, placed large advertisements in the official *China Daily* when it had no business to advertise, paid for Chubb billboards to be erected close by the central bank (at the time, China's insurance industry's regulator), sponsored an international football match, held large conferences and donated several million dollars for the restoration of a house in the old Legation Quarter of Beijing for the use of the city government. Other insurers started their own educational foundations, opened offices that had no business, toured Chinese apparatchiks around the world, flew in foreign orchestras, ballet troupes and theatre groups and invited senior leaders to attend the performances.[21] By the end of 1995, in the insurance sector alone, seventy-six international firms with 129 representative offices were probably spending in excess of $200 million a year in the pursuit of operating licences; the Chinese government had so far issued only two.[22]

When limitless cash chases an investment proposition, the effect is inevitable. Between 1993 and 1995 the prices of everything from staff to real estate sky-rocketed. As expatriates poured into the country, the cost of apartments licensed for foreign occupation increased by thousands of dollars per month. Frantic real estate construction was under way, but little was completed – only 625 foreigner apartments came on the market in Beijing in 1993 and 1994.[23] Developers with property to offer could name their prices. The first to complete a villa project outside Beijing, in 1993, was a joint venture between the Poly Group, an arms trading subsidiary of the People's Liberation Army, and a Hong Kong investor. Legend Garden Villas, sixteen miles from Beijing city centre, consists of 150 hastily finished homes set around an artificial lake. Most were sold before completion, for $650,000–$750,000 each. Buyers with smaller budgets fought it out for small one- and two-bedroom apartments at $170,000 to $300,000 apiece.[24]

Most foreign companies chose to rent. Rental prices for 'villas' outside the capital – in reality cookie-cutter homes that would sell for about $100,000 in the suburbs of a large American city – rose to $10,000–$13,000 a month. In downtown Beijing, even the smallest apartments commanded $3,000 a month, with modest two-bedroom apartments around $7,000. The situation in Shanghai was the same. The Portman Shanghai Centre, the most prestigious address in the city, raised its rental prices seven times in 1993 and 1994. The American consul general in 1995, Joseph J. Borich, wanted to live somewhere more homely than a newly built apartment block and instructed a property agent to find a pre-liberation Shanghai town house. Thousands of such houses were built before 1949, each with its own small garden. The one identified for the consul general, in Hongqiao district, on the way to the airport, had an asking price of $28,000 a month. Mr Borich balked at the cost, settling instead for a new property at a more modest $20,000 a month. Five US marines, meanwhile, who had to be located close to the consulate for security purposes, were installed in adjoining rooms of the Shanghai Centre at a combined rental of $25,000 a month.[25]

Offices became even more expensive than apartments. By the end of 1993, Hong Kong office rentals, driven by investor fervour for mainland China, rose to over $10 per square foot ($110 per square metre) per month in the city's Central district, Hong Kong thereby displacing Tokyo as the world's most expensive city for commercial real estate. Beijing and Shanghai were not far behind with monthly rates in new buildings running at $7.40–$8.40 per square foot ($80–$90 per square metre). To this base cost was added an array of fees for services which in most markets would be included in the rent: everything from phone lines to air-conditioning and parking. In some cases such charges made Beijing and Shanghai more expensive than Hong Kong. At a typical 40 square feet (12 square metres) of required space per person, foreign firms in China were paying up to $1,000 per employee per month just to rent their offices.

Demand for offices was so high that any space attractive to a foreign business was turned to this use. The top – thirty-seventh – floor of the China World Trade Centre in Beijing had been home to an English-style pub until management cleared out the bar in 1994 and leased it as offices at $9.30 per square foot ($100 per square metre) per month. In Shanghai, the city government shut down the Shanghai Museum in 1993 put the exhibits into storage, and leased out the space to the likes of Credit Lyonnais and Motorola. The blue-domed Russian Mission Church, on the corner of Xin Le and Xiang Yang Streets, became a securities exchange and a karaoke bar. At the Shanghai Centre, the only way to jump a waiting list more than a hundred companies long was to be imaginative. The Reuters news agency took a converted janitor's closet as its office. Morgan Stanley, with a bigger budget, had an office built on the hotel tennis court and then rebuilt the tennis court on top of the office.

By 1994, Beijing and Shanghai office rentals were multiples of those in capital cities of other Asian developing countries – three times Bangkok, four times Kuala Lumpur or Jakarta. The Chinese prices were also three times more than in Sydney, over twice the price of midtown Manhattan and 50 per cent more than prime space in London.[26] And property prices were only the most obvious of the costs that entrants into the China market faced. A combination of restrictive regulations and insatiable demand meant that many other expenses – from employment costs to air tickets – were at world-beating levels.

The thousands of representative offices opened by foreign companies were not supposed to conduct business – regulations restricted them to liaison work or preparation for investments – but their expenditures were still taxed. All Chinese staff in such offices had to be hired through one of a handful of approved state agencies, the biggest of which was the Foreign Enterprise Service Corp (FESCO). FESCO charged the equivalent of 67 per cent of each employee's salary per month, for which it claimed to provide basic welfare insurance.[27] But FESCO also required foreign companies to take out personal accident and medical insurance policies for local employees with the People's Insurance Company of China. While the theory was that a foreign company could hire an English-speaking secretary for $250 a month, the reality was that associated mandatory fees at the very least doubled the cost of employing anybody. When China unified what had been a dual exchange rate system, with one currency for locals and another one for foreigners, on 1 January 1994 – effectively a devaluation – FESCO raised all its prices by 50 per cent overnight. The American Chamber of Commerce was among a vociferous group of complainants, but the state agency took no notice. Its one concession to foreign companies which did not like its service was to agree to charge them only $100–$200 per employee per month as a fee to forego its monopoly rights. In such cases foreign firms were liable for all welfare costs themselves.

As well as for staff, China set dual prices for everything from telephone and fax lines to advertising space, hotel rooms, air tickets and car hire. The first question a secretary in an office would be asked when calling to book an air ticket was whether the ticket was for a foreigner or a local. On arrival at the airport, passengers were confronted with two windows for payment of departure tax: one for locals and another, with a higher charge, for everybody else. The cost of the premium pricing for foreigners added up. As of 1994 in Beijing, where some 6,000 representative offices had been opened by foreign companies, the operating costs of a small outfit with only one expatriate were running at around $700,000 per year.[28]

Expatriates cost more than anything else. Surveys by human resource firms suggested a typical salary, including hardship allowance and home leave, was around $120,000 in Beijing or Shanghai. But this was only the starting point for real employment costs. The price of expatriate 'perks' – such as children's schooling and company car – pushed the figure up much higher. At the International School of Beijing, which had a waiting list of 500 in spring 1994, annual fees were $14,000–$15,000 per child per year.[29] If a foreign manager required an imported car – and many did – tariffs increased the cost to two to three times that in Europe or North America. A Lexus LS-400 sedan sold in Beijing in 1994 for $152,000, as against less than $50,000 in the United States.

The most astonishing cost differential, however, between China and the developed world was the price of industrial land. Many foreign companies were prepared for high living costs for their expatriates; commercial office prices came as a shock. But the price of industrial development land on which to build factories was without precedent. Many poor countries make such land available for nominal sums to attract multinational investors. Not so China. With billions of dollars of foreign investment pouring into the country, the national and local governments set out to maximise revenue from land leases. They did so by restricting most foreign investment to approved zones where prices were set not by auction but by fiat. The only way for a market mechanism to work would be if large numbers of investors walked away. They never did, and prices were ratcheted up month by month.

Many Hong Kong and Taiwanese investors in southern China managed to cut costs by moving into illegal local investment zones not licensed by the central government. But multinational companies were almost invariably ushered into the most expensive Beijing-approved industrial parks. The biggest of these were called Economic and Technological Development Zones, or ETDZs. Fifty-year land leases – purchase was not allowed – in major cities like Dalian, Beijing and Guangzhou rose to over $6.50 per square foot ($70 per square metre) in 1993. This compared with purchase costs in the United States of, for instance, $2.80–$3.70 ($30–$40 per square metre) in Chicago or $1.80–$2.80 ($20–$30 per square metre) in Dallas, Atlanta or Detroit. Even in New Jersey, the most expensive traditional manufacturing centre in America, land was readily available for under $6.50 per square foot ($70 per square metre). And for this price land was bought, not leased. Even New Jersey's premium, suburban industrial land – at as much as $9 per square foot ($100 per square metre) – was a giveaway compared with Shanghai, which commanded China's highest rates. In October 1993, Shanghai's municipal government raised industrial land prices in the Pudong New Area to between $14 and $17 per square foot ($150–$185 per square metre). Seven years later, in 2000, at the height of the California high-tech boom, investors were paying these prices for commercial real estate in downtown Los Angeles.[30]

梦

Extraordinary prices were rarely a deterrent in China. When Henry Fok, the overseas Chinese billionaire and long-time friend of the Chinese leadership, leased 9 square miles (22 square kilometres) of development land near his birthplace in Guangdong, one of his sons, Ben Fok, made a cost comparison with Canada. His conclusion, which took into account the price of the land plus the price of 270 million cubic feet (13 million cubic metres) of land reclamation and basic infrastructure needed to make the area serviceable, was that his father could have bought the equivalent area of completed commercial real estate in downtown Calgary for the same price.[31]

Henry Fok told his son he was missing the point. This was China and a project in China was not to be judged by standards prevailing elsewhere. Other investors agreed. High prices seemed only to confirm the scale of the opportunity. If land was expensive, anything built on it should be still more expensive, and from this profit would derive. The key was to beat other companies to market. It became normal for construction crews to work 24 hours a day in the early 1990s, a habit they maintained for the rest of the decade. Building work and construction noise were the most obvious signs of China's new prosperity, ones frequently cited by visiting CEOs as evidence of the importance of the market. Real estate investment became the consuming passion not just of established mainland and Hong Kong property companies but of any business with cash to spare. The more prices went up, the more people who were not in the market became convinced they had to invest or risk being priced out for ever.

By 1995, the biggest listed Hong Kong real estate firms had signed deals for mainland projects involving some 300 million square feet (28 million square metres) of construction space.[32] At a construction cost of $40–$100 per square foot ($430–$1,100 per square metre), these companies – fewer than a dozen in total – would have to invest at least $20 billion to complete their deals. This was the single biggest chunk of the $55 billion of overseas real estate investment in the 1990s. The rest came from developers from Taiwan, Singapore, Japan and elsewhere, as well as manufacturers who had made fortunes in the 1980s from low-cost export processing in China. Self-made Hong Kong millionaires in businesses like textiles, shoes and toys took their companies' profits and ploughed them into property on the mainland.

For those who got in early, the real estate boom was a bonanza. Clifford Pang, who had already made one fortune manufacturing computer disk drive heads in Guangdong, sold his factory in 1989 for $60 million, took part of the proceeds and signed a 51:49 real estate joint venture with the township government of Panyu. A trained civil engineer, it was his life's ambition to design his own residential housing project. In 1991 he began construction of what would become the biggest private housing estate in China – the eponymous Clifford Estates. The local government provided the land, Mr Pang the money. The original plan was to build and sell 3,500 homes over ten years.

Clifford Pang had a clear vision: he set out in chaotic Guangdong province to create a haven of efficient, tranquil living. Clifford Estates was fenced off from the outside world. Hundreds of security guards were set to work patrolling its perimeter; the guards saluted Mr Pang and Mr Pang occasionally saluted them back. The estate was designed to radiate out from a lake with an 18-hole golf putting course on an island at its centre. The master plan included a school, a 24-hour medical centre, a police station, a bank, a heliport, a supermarket, several children's playgrounds, an aviary, trekking trails and – the *sine qua non* of Guangdong cuisine – a large store selling live fish. Residents' rules were rigorously enforced from the outset: no chickens to be kept, no laundry hung from windows, no parking outside other people's houses, only one dog or cat per home. Bedroom and kitchen units were pre-fitted; in larger houses, everything from saunas to steam rooms to snooker tables and cinema projectors were pre-fitted. Prospective purchasers had only to pay – everything else was done for them.

It was a winning combination. Mr Pang sold his first house in 1992 for $38,000.[33] As the real estate boom took off, the price quickly doubled, tripled, then quadrupled. An initial 500 units were snapped up by Hong Kong speculators. By the end of 1995, Mr Pang had sold not the 3,500 units he planned to market over a decade, but 6,000 homes, grossing more than $500 million; and the number of sales was increasing each month. On a hillside nearby, a makeshift town of 15,000 construction workers grew up. Mr Pang's partners in the local government increased the size of his site to more than 1,000 acres (435 hectares) – enough space for 60,000 houses. At the best vantage point overlooking Clifford Estates, Mr Pang took a large piece of land, shrouded by trees, for himself. Here he would build his own dream home, able to survey, but not be surveyed by, all that he was creating.

Most investors got into mainland property later than Mr Pang. The real estate ambitions of Frank Lo, the brassière king of China, lay in the retail field. His lingerie company, Top Form, raised $17 million through a small initial public offering in Hong Kong in December 1991 and, with corporate profits running at $10 million a year, Mr Lo started to think beyond the dilapidated Kowloon office that was still the official headquarters of his business. Eleven mainland brassière factories had made his fortune, but Mr Lo – like many of his peers – was determined to diversify away from the unglamorous world of manufacturing. He wished to do this with some style and, in October 1993, he signed a franchise agreement with Printemps, the famous French department store chain. Top Form was given exclusive rights to the Printemps trademark in China and immediately announced that it would open three large department stores in Shanghai, Chengdu and Dalian. The latter two developments were joint ventures in which Top Form had a minority interest. Shanghai was the big investment, a wholly owned, six-storey, 180,000 square foot (17,000 square metre) designer shopping centre in the most expensive area of the city. Top form was to invest $26 million.

The store was not the first to bring European and American designer labels to Shanghai, but it offered a bigger range than had been seen before. When Printemps opened in June 1995, Mr Lo claimed to have recreated the ambience of the Champs-Elysées, home of the chicest shopping in Paris. He brought in designers like Christian Lacroix, Gianfranco Ferre and Jacques Leonard. Dresses on sale at the Leonard boutique were priced at between $2,100 and $3,571 – thirty to fifty times Shanghai's average monthly disposable income.[34] Printemps also secured the first Chinese installation of the English ceramics specialist Wedgwood, a company which almost exactly 200 years before had sent a representative to Beijing as part of Lord Macartney's trade mission. Mr Lo, something of a *bon viveur*, was soon enjoying his new life as Shanghai's most sophisticated retailer. He threw parties for the well connected, held banquets for lonely college students and even opened Printemps after midnight for the benefit of karaoke hostesses. Mr Lo told reporters the store needed to turn over a million renminbi a day – $119,000 – to break even. This, he promised, it would do in its first year of operations. Top Form, meanwhile, would open three more stores in Shanghai.

The greatest race on Earth

The atmosphere of the mid 1990s was such that competitors egged each other on. Foreign investors raced against one another and they raced against a government that was seen to be limiting the number of investment opportunities in each sector through its licensing regime. Nowhere was this felt more keenly than in the automotive industry. In February 1994, China's State Planning Commission issued a policy paper which said that the government would consolidate the nation's automotive sector into just three or four main producers.[35] No new foreign car plants had been licensed since 1992 and officials at the Ministry of Machine Industry (MMI), in charge of the automotive sector, indicated there would be at most three foreign car factories licensed before 2000. There would be a licence for a luxury car and a licence for a joint venture to make multi purpose vehicles (MPVs) or 'people carriers'. China was also interested in a sub-compact, mass market car but had not yet decided how to proceed.

With two dozen foreign car makers wanting to enter the market, the message that there could be at most three winners set up an intense bidding war. Louis Hughes, the head of international operations at General Motors, already believed his company was close to clinching deals to manufacture both luxury and compact cars at the end of 1993, but nothing had happened. The deals were not signed and every day the competition became fiercer. By 1994, Mr Hughes and his CEO Jack Smith were no longer unusual in being besotted with China. Chrysler, which had acquired China's first Sino-foreign auto joint venture – Beijing Jeep – when it took over American Motor Corp. in 1987, believed that troubled venture was about to pay off and wanted to enter the regular car market.[36] Ford, under chairman Alex Trotman, had become fixated on China; Mr Trotman lectured his board and journalists alike that 80 per cent of the world's population lived outside western Europe, the US and Japan but accounted for only 8 per cent of world car and truck sales. This was about to change, he said, in countries like China. Even Japanese car makers, which had spurned the idea of production in China in the 1980s, were excited by official projections of 1.3 million car sales in 2000,[37] more than four times the level of 1993. Toyota, Nissan, Honda, Mitsubishi and Subaru were all seeking licences.

What interested manufacturers most was the outlook beyond the end of the century. In Stuttgart, Edzard Reuter, the strategically minded chairman of Daimler–Benz, Europe's biggest industrial company, set a group of twenty people to work on a project he called 'Megatrends'.[38] The work led to an internal report on the world's emerging markets looking forward to 2010; no country shone so brightly from its pages as China. One after another, charts and tables extolled the demand that would flow from the country's huge but young population as the Chinese economy expanded. The widely publicised take-off in sales at the Shanghai car plant of Volkswagen, which entered the China market in 1985, to 115,000 vehicles in 1994, made Mr Reuter and others dream. The regional business magazine *Asia Inc.* pointed out that at a German level of car ownership – one vehicle for every two people – the 571 million cars in China would be enough to fill a seven-lane highway stretching from the earth to the moon.[39] Hisashi Nakada, the China manufacturing representative of Nissan, encapsulated how high the stakes appeared to be when he said: 'We see China as the last big market in the world – one that is roughly tripling every ten years.'[40]

In the end, the bidding for licences came down to who would pay the most. And the most turned out to be a lot. Although Ford and Toyota were keenly interested in building a luxury car in Shanghai, and Daimler–Benz had been the early front runner, GM's Jack Smith was simply unwilling to lose. The GM CEO and his head of international operations concluded that a partnership with Shanghai Automotive Industry Corp. was so valuable that they should pay whatever was required. China's 1994 national automotive policy said that component manufacture was the number one priority for developing the industry. So GM's components subsidiary, Delphi, started an investment process whereby it would commit $350 million to fifteen factories over four years. China wanted to learn how to design cars as well as assemble them. Toyota was unwilling to teach a Chinese company how to compete with it and dropped out, but GM committed $40 million for a Joint Venture Technical Development Centre for automotive design; the US company also financed the GM Technology Institute at Beijing's Qinghua University and the GM–Shanghai Jiaotong Powertrain Technology Institute at Shanghai's Jiaotong University. 'Through our joint venture, China is going to learn how to design and build a car,' said Rudy Schlais, GM's president of China operations.[41] GM spent so heavily on public relations, charitable donations, seminars and the like that in a poll which appeared in the *Beijing Youth Daily* newspaper the company was ranked the best-known foreign auto-maker in China.[42] This despite the fact the market was dominated by two existing car plants belonging to Volkswagen and two others belonging to Peugeot–Citroën.

..thing was too much trouble for Mr Smith and Mr Hughes. They personally showed Chinese automotive officials around GM's top secret research and development facilities in Detroit. When they wanted to give presents from Tiffany's, the New York jeweller, they made sure that its signature white ribbons – the colour of mourning in China – were thoughtfully switched for red. When it came to cash, GM offered $750 million for 50 per cent of a joint venture with a capacity of only 100,000 vehicles. This was as much as double what GM paid to own 100 per cent of equivalent manufacturing plants in other developing countries in the 1990s; on a price-for-equity measure, the cost was quadruple.[43] Asked why Ford, which had also spent millions on its lobbying campaign, always lagged behind GM in the bidding, a senior Chinese auto industry official told one journalist: 'Jack Smith gave his personal promise that GM would provide China with whatever it wants.'[44]

Edzard Reuter was no less determined. Outbid by GM for the Shanghai luxury car licence, Daimler–Benz refocused on the deal to build MPVs. Despite the fact that Chinese bureaucrats wanted the venture split inefficiently between two factories in two different provinces – one making the bodies and engines, the other the chassis – Chrysler and Ford were also aggressively interested. Chrysler thought it had the deal sewn up. But when Mr Reuter's company said it was willing to meet all of China's technology transfer requirements and pay $490 million for just 45 per cent of the deal – a minority position – victory went the German company's way. Mr Reuter backed his bid with political support from German chancellor Helmut Kohl, outmanoeuvring Chrysler's attempts at closing the contract through the lobbying efforts of commerce secretary Ron Brown.

It was high stakes poker and the companies had to believe that what they were playing for was worth the ante. When, in the summer of 1994, the Chinese government started to seek out opinions on a suitable mini car for China – presenting the possibility of a third licence for a sub-compact vehicle – it was clear the auto multinationals had no doubts about the value of the prizes they were chasing. A compact car for China conjured images of postwar bestsellers like the Mini in Britain, the Fiat 500 in Italy and the Beetle in Germany, on a massively bigger scale. A people's car in China might, in a few years, be manufactured in millions of units a year. If the government offered a single licence to a foreign partner in the project, then that licence could be extraordinarily valuable.

The Ministry of Machine Industry (MMI) dubbed the vehicle the 'family car' and set up a special department to plan its future. Whereas almost all cars in the mid 1990s were bought by state companies or government departments, the Strategic Development Research Team of China's Family Car predicted that two-thirds of all vehicles would be bought by individuals by 2010 and most of those would be economy vehicles; China's annual car production was forecast to be at least 3.5 million units. Other government projections said car production in 2010 would be as high as 8 million units, while 270 million Chinese households would become potential car buyers as soon as 2000.[45] Peregrine, the Hong Kong investment bank that had won more business than any other in mainland China, forecast 180 million Chinese households would own cars by 2010. China would be the first or second biggest car market in the world within fifteen years.

When the MMI invited international car firms to present their ideas for the family car at an exhibition in Beijing in November 1994, the response was overwhelming.[46] Twenty-two multinational auto companies applied to stage exhibits involving more than eighty vehicles. Some proposed existing, or modified versions of existing, cars. Other contenders for a manufacturing licence, knowing how China liked to be treated differently, brought specially designed prototypes. Daimler–Benz spent tens of million of dollars on a prototype of a mini car which it called the 'Family Car China' (FCC).[47] The company announced it was willing to invest $800 million immediately to build a plant with a capacity of 250,000 units. Porsche, the German sports car and auto design firm that produced the blueprints for the original Beetle, showed a 1.1 litre, 5-seat prototype called the C88. The backdrop to the company's stand was a huge Chinese flag with 'Porsche' written across it; the stylised 'P' of Porsche was centred on the largest of the symbolic communist stars. Among the Japanese auto companies, Mitsubishi showed a China prototype called the X-Concept.

With 400 executives and virtually every major international auto company in attendance, it was not easy to garner attention. Ford took one of the largest stands, shipped over a 1907 Model-T, the first mass market car, and displayed it suspended in mid-air. Daimler–Benz added an historical dimension to its display with the world's first automobile, built by Gottlieb Daimler and Karl Benz in 1886. General Motors set up a separate stand for its European subsidiary Opel, as vice-president for Asia-Pacific operations Thomas McDaniel told journalists that GM was already in advanced negotiations for small car production in southern China.[48] Every company sought the angle that would make it look unique or particularly well connected in the eyes of the media and Chinese government officials. None the less, each company was granted just a single, brief audience at which to present its case. There were so many supplicants that the MMI split them into two groups and had them present simultaneously in different meeting rooms. Only a dozen companies were allowed to make their presentations direct to the MMI minister, He Guangyuan.

The curiosity of the week-long family car meeting was that the Chinese government never once confirmed that a production licence was on offer. Still more curious was that the international firms did not press the issue. It appeared the foreigners were afraid of asking a question which might be deemed to be too forward. Any company that upset the MMI was bound not to be picked, and being picked was the whole point of the exercise. Effusive friendliness was the order of the day. 'It was crazy, absolutely crazy – a feeding frenzy,' remembers Gerald Kania, then one of Ford's representatives in Beijing.[49] At the end of the week, the auto companies packed up their cars, went home and waited to hear who had won.

梦

By 1995, China was the epicentre of global foreign direct investment in emerging economies. It was joked that western CEOs could not face their peers at the country club if they did not have at least one business there; the average multinational had many. At the end of the year, there were already 234,000 registered foreign investments in China, triple the number at the end of 1992. Thirty-four billion dollars of corporate money arrived in 1995; over the next four years the amount would rise to $45 billion a year, as tens of thousands of contracted investments were paid up.

The money went everywhere. Already in 1995, more than a billion dollars was invested in 1,500 pharmaceutical joint ventures, up from a dozen at the end of the 1980s. Five thousand joint ventures had been formed in the chemicals sector, sucking in $5.1 billion of foreign money. Two billion dollars were invested in the automotive sector, with more capital arriving every week. Wherever China allowed foreign investment – and often in sectors where the government did not allow it – money poured in, paying for factories to make everything from telecommunications equipment to consumer goods to building materials.[50]

The world of cross-border investment was a phenomenon of the 1990s and China was its magnetic pole. In 1985, transnational investment in the whole world was less than $60 billion; in developing countries it only exceeded $35 billion for the first time in 1990. Yet five years later China was pulling in more foreign investment in a year than all the developing nations of Asia, Latin America, Africa and central and eastern Europe combined had managed in 1990.[51]

If the price of investment in China was higher than anything seen previously in an emerging market, then so were the promised rewards. According to the National Bureau of Statistics, retail sales grew by an extraordinary

22 per cent a year in the decade from 1985 to 1995. Although many were uncertain quite what the expression meant, businessmen and journalists thrilled to the refrain that China had a world-beating 'savings rate' of 40 per cent; whatever the detail, it had to mean that banks and mattresses alike were stuffed with cash. This was the promised land that Marco Polo, Columbus, Macartney and the buccaneers of inter-war Shanghai had striven for but never quite grasped. At last it was within reach. As big deals were closed, the most powerful leaders in the world made time to attend the signing ceremonies. Daimler–Benz beat out its rivals to make MPVs in south China and the contract was inked in the presence of President Jiang Zemin and Chancellor Helmut Kohl in July 1995. Soon after, General Motors closed the deal for the Shanghai car plant that had obsessed the company's CEO, Jack Smith, for more than three years. A special, retrospective signing ceremony was laid on in the Great Hall of the People when Vice-president Al Gore visited China in March 1997. These were investments which promised old companies a foothold in potentially the greatest market of them all. It was time for the likes of Daimler–Benz and General Motors to celebrate. And then, as everywhere in the world, it would be time to get on with the business of doing business.

Part 2
Miracle deconstructed

6

The mornings after

'Oh no. China's a graveyard for us all. We've all fucked up China'
A British businessman, overheard in conversation by the author in the lobby of the
Mandarin Oriental hotel in Hong Kong, September 1997

IN NOVEMBER 1994, at the height of the rush into China, the most pre-
scient piece of Asian economic journalism of the 1990s appeared in the
highbrow American bi-monthly *Foreign Affairs*. 'The Myth of Asia's Miracle'[1]
was written by the then Stanford economist Paul Krugman. The article –
unexpected in every quarter – argued that the high growth rates associated
with many Asian economies were unsustainable. 'The future prospects for
that [Asian] growth,' wrote Professor Krugman, 'are more limited than almost
anyone now imagines.'

Professor Krugman's argument likened growth in developing Asian countries in the 1980s and 1990s to that of the Soviet Union in the late 1950s and
early 1960s. In that period the Soviet economy had grown 6–7 per cent a year
– twice the rate of the United States – leading many in the west to conclude
that communist planners had discovered a short cut to prosperity. In a prog-
nosis reminiscent of the purchasing power predictions for China in the
1990s, Calvin Hoover, a US government adviser and president of the American Economic Association, forecast that the Soviet economy might outstrip
America's by the 1970s. Likewise, the Russian leader Nikita Khrushchev
promised the capitalist world that: 'We will bury you'. Neither man was right.
Soviet growth rates slumped in the mid 1960s and stagnated for a further
quarter of a century, until the collapse of the Soviet empire.[2]

A handful of American economists, working in a field called 'growth accounting', had predicted this. Growth accountants add up each year's inputs
into an economy – labour, investment, and so on – and compare them with the
total size of that economy. The aim is to separate out what part of economic
growth derives from increases in productivity and what part simply from increased expenditure of time and money. Although working longer hours and
spending savings expands economic activity, it is only rising productivity that

promotes sustainable growth. In the case of the Soviet Union, economists showed that rapid growth was based almost entirely on more inputs of labour and capital, rather than greater efficiency.[3] Eventually, the Soviets were going to run out of hours to work and cash to spend. In his article, Professor Krugman revealed as yet unpublished growth accounting analysis for Asia that pointed to a similar trajectory.[4]

Three years before the Asian financial crisis of 1997, Krugman drew a parallel between the Cold War fear of the Soviet economy when it was outpacing capitalist countries and the current obsession with Asia's new 'tiger' economies of the 1980s and 1990s. He recalled America's panic over the Russian launch of the Sputnik spacecraft – which put communism ahead in the space race – and likened it to the rhetoric of contemporary pundits who forecast Asian economies would soon dominate the world. The pundits, he said, were missing the point again; they were focusing on growth rates without asking what was driving them and, therefore, how long they could last.

Although Asian economies had posted world-beating growth in the 1970s and 1980s, Professor Krugman asserted that they too were over-reliant on increased inputs. The countries had expanded the size of their working populations and made big strides in education – important but one-off gains. The main cause of their rapid growth, however, was vastly increased levels of investment – much of it state-derived. The growth accountants showed that in countries like South Korea, Thailand and even Singapore, the contribution of investment to total output had risen from as little as one-tenth in the 1960s to around two-fifths in 1990. Neither such a rapid increase in, nor such a high level of, investment was sustainable. The more these countries invested, the lower the returns were becoming. What Asian nations needed was rapidly rising productivity. But, according to the analysis contained in 'The Myth of Asia's Miracle', despite ostensibly booming economies, productivity gains were behind those of the US. Asian growth rates were therefore heading for a slow-down. 'Current projections of Asian supremacy extrapolated from recent trends,' concluded Professor Krugman, 'may well look almost as silly as 1960s-vintage forecasts of Soviet industrial supremacy did from the perspective of the Brezhnev years.'

The comparison with the 'fake' growth of the former Soviet Union riled Asian business leaders and governments alike. Singapore's Lee Kuan Yew was one voice among many, from Jakarta to Seoul, who decried 'The Myth of Asia's Miracle' as variously anti-Asian and ill-informed.[5] It was such denunciations that ensured an otherwise academic article a worldwide readership. More surprising than the righteous indignation of the likes of Mr Lee, however, was that the one Asian country that escaped the attention of both the economists whose work led to 'The Myth of Asia's Miracle' and Krugman himself was the one that would most clearly validate ment. China, whose economic growth in 1993 was nearly 14 per barely mentioned. Yet the country – though it could in the short term insulate itself from the kind of external financial shock that precipitated the Asian crisis – offered the world the perfect case study of how growth driven by state-mandated spending is fleeting.

The growth accountants showed that the 'miracles' of south-east Asia and South Korea were suspect, but China's economic miracle was open to a far more complete form of deconstruction. The country was afflicted not just by the Asian disease of over-reliance on investment. It faced other, deeper structural maladies as well. China had a communist government more obsessed with interference in the economic process than any in Asia. It had a bureaucracy unrivalled in its stubbornness, its corruption or its capacity to mismanage public finances. And it had the power to continue to make mistakes without fear of criticism or accountability. Other Asian nations depended in part for their financing on external creditors; in 1997, they were pulled up short when faith in their capacity to repay evaporated. But authoritarian China, in total control of a nationalised financial system, and with a non-convertible currency, could rely on and spend the accumulated savings of a nation until they were exhausted – many years hence.

After Deng Xiaoping's Southern Tour at the beginning of 1992, China had embarked on an investment binge of unparalleled proportions. Fixed asset investment – covering everything from factory construction to machinery purchases to real estate development – shot up 44 per cent in 1992 and a further 60 per cent in 1993,[6] the fastest increase since Mao Zedong's Great Leap Forward in the late 1950s. State- and collectively-owned enterprises led the way. The latter, supposedly the magic force in China's drive to prosperity, increased investment more than 90 per cent in 1992 and more than 70 per cent the next year. Most of the money came from the state-owned banking system, which responded to Deng Xiaoping's call for accelerated growth by opening its credit spigot. In addition to traditional lenders, provincial governments around the country issued high interest bonds and sanctioned hundreds of new deposit-taking institutions which re-lent depositors' money as fast as they could take it in – almost always for state-controlled investments.

China had the potential for a crisis out of all proportion to those seen elsewhere in the region. In the mid 1990s, however, when the gap between market perceptions and Chinese reality was as wide as at any point in history, this was far from apparent. Foreign investors began to be aware of the bureaucratic nature of the operating environment. A pattern of delay, obfuscation

and outright cancellation of deals previously signed pointed to problems beyond those of credit. But in most instances Chinese bureaucracy was shrugged
off as an issue typical of emerging markets. Indeed, in many cases, foreign
companies blamed their own governments for upsetting China's sensitive
politicians. There was almost no public debate as to whether the market war-
ranted the attention it was receiving, and multinationals that were in turmoil
on the ground were at pains to present a façade of success. The immediate
concern in 1994 was not the validity of the China Dream, but that the country
was entering a period of forced monetary contraction because its economy
was overheating. It was the pain of this temporary withdrawal from the
steroids of public expenditure that captured businessmen's attention. The
rest of the story would unravel much more slowly.

Aspirin, please

The initial hangover was augured by inflation. Rising expenditure caused
China's economy, like those of other Asian nations, to grow faster, but it also
brought higher prices. By mid 1992, with credit mushrooming in the weeks
after Deng Xiaoping's Southern Tour, the cost of living in major cities was
already rising at more than 10 per cent a year on an annualised basis.[7] Inflation in 1991 had been less than 3 per cent. The central government glibly
forecast an inflation rate of 5 per cent for 1993. Three months later, the
national statistics agency reported the cost of living index in China's thirty-
five biggest cities was up 16 per cent in the first quarter of the year. Inflation
was rising at 20 per cent a year by May, approaching the levels that had
caused panic buying in 1988. As still more credit was pumped into the
economy, the renminbi began to slide, trading as low as eleven to the dollar
on the black market by the summer of 1993[8] – a depreciation of more than a
quarter in the space of a few months.

The government's reaction was skittish. Vice-premier Zhu Rongji, taking on
the mantle of the veteran fire fighter Chen Yun, announced a 16-point austerity plan in July that included tighter credit, higher interest rates and the calling
in of loans to speculative projects. He promised to send inspection teams
from the Auditing Administration to the provinces to uncover unsanctioned
lending and illegal local bond issues. But provincial governors and their supporters in central government resisted Mr Zhu's attempts at a forced economic slow-down. Many politicians, bureaucrats and bank managers, dabbling
directly or indirectly in business, had a vested interest in seeing the boom
continue. Furthermore, the patriarch himself had called for a period of very
fast growth that would catapult China to a new stage of economic development. The senior leadership was divided and, after bank credit was withheld

for a couple of months in the summer, there was a further infusion of credit in the autumn. Inflation in large cities promptly moved towards 30 per cent.

Only in the last months of 1993, after its annual sojourn at the seaside resort town of Beidaihe, did the central leadership reach a consensus that an austerity programme must be sustained. In the New Year, the government rallied around Zhu Rongji's plan to tame inflation. Fixed asset investment growth for 1994 was targeted at 14 per cent – less than a quarter of the level of 1993. A State Council circular published in the *People's Daily* announced the cabinet would not approve any new investment projects during 1994.[9] To his 16-point programme of the previous summer, Zhu added what were quickly known as his 'Three Regulations': no lending in breach of central bank guidelines; no unauthorised higher interest rates to draw money into local financial institutions; and, critically, a demand that all financial entities sever ties with businesses they had established. As of 1 January 1994, the government imposed a capital gains tax on real estate transactions and overhauled the rest of the tax system, including introducing new value-added taxes. From a situation in which the state was throwing money at the economy, credit was suddenly almost impossible to obtain. The spending boom of 1992 and 1993 had been a wild party, but on New Year's Day 1994 China woke up with what was to prove an enduring headache.

Internationally, the significance of the austerity measures was perceived only gradually. Excitement about China among the global CEO fraternity was still rising. But on the ground the effect was immediate. The first businesses to notice the change were those which depended most heavily on direct state purchases. Despite the theoretical promise of a massive private market, China's automotive sector was such a business, with nine out of ten cars being bought by units controlled by the state. In 1994, the central government not only cut its spending, it banned the importation of foreign cars by government units and ended a long-standing concession which allowed some foreign enterprises to import vehicles duty free.

The impact was profound. Denway Investment, whose Hong Kong listing in February 1993 set a world record for oversubscription – 657 times, involving $31 billion of subscription funds – saw its orders dry up. Denway's joint venture with the French firm Peugeot sold 20,000 cars in 1992 and was on target at mid-year 1993 to sell 30,000. But after state units and taxi companies stopped buying in the third quarter, the venture was able to sell only 21,000 vehicles by year end. With twelve months of reduced government credit in 1994, sales plummeted. That year, the joint venture sold just 5,726 cars, against a forecast of 48,000. Denway and Peugeot began to lose money and Denway's share price shed 80 per cent of its value.

Brilliance China Automotive, the New York-listed company which controls the minibus-making interests of Chinese auto company Jinbei, fared only slightly better. The company sold 10,000 minibuses in both 1994 and 1995, marginally less than it sold before listing in 1991. But Brilliance's prospectus contained official projections from China's automotive ministry that the company would sell at least 37,500 vehicles a year by 1996. Chairman Zhao Xiyou had predicted double that figure.[10] In the event, where Credit Suisse First Boston, the American investment bank that took Brilliance to market, forecast earnings per share of $1.50 by 1994, the company returned only 20 cents.[11] In New York, Brilliance shares lost three-quarters of their value between 1993 and 1995 and, like the stock of Denway, came to trade at less than half their listing price.

Jinbei's unlisted pick-up truck joint venture with General Motors was in a worse state still. By the end of 1993 the factory suspended production. Unpacked boxes of parts, with their distinctive red GM labels, littered the shopfloor. In the year since the first S-10 pick-up was assembled in August 1992, the new line had put together just 300 vehicles, and sold far fewer. It was only partly a problem of austerity. The joint venture picked the wrong product; it was assembling a two-door pick-up truck for which there was little demand even when government credit was abundant. In China, almost all trucks have four doors. Labour is cheap and jobs are closely defined – drivers do not load or unload, they travel around with a group of more lowly co-workers who do that for them. A two-door truck, with only one row of seats, lacks the necessary space for four or five passengers; government work units did not want it.

Six months after launch, the Chinese and Americans were at each other's throats over who was to blame for the fiasco. The Chinese said publicly that it was all GM's fault, GM insisted that at least part of the problem was Jinbei's inability to market products and its unprofessional management. Relations between chairman Zhao and GM's senior manager, Robert Stramy, became so embittered that in the summer of 1993 Mr Stramy left the joint venture. Mr Zhao's career was soon at an end as well. In July 1993, Li Guixian, the central bank governor who had sanctioned the Brilliance listing, was fired from his post in Beijing for allowing the economy to run out of control. Zhu Rongji, highly suspicious of the circumstances surrounding the Brilliance offering, forced Mr Zhao into early retirement and ordered an enquiry into how the Jinbei automotive plant was being run.[12] In the short term this did not help GM. With the central government investigating its partner, the American company was unable to restart its joint venture.

In Guangzhou, Peugeot's relationship with its partner also began to fall apart under the strain of falling sales. The two sides had never been close – Denway did not even bother to inform the French about its listing in 1993[13] – but during the government-engineered boom, rising revenues and the belief that mass volume car production was around the corner created a degree of harmony. With the slide in the renminbi's value in the spring of 1993 and the beginnings of austerity, that goodwill disappeared. As the exchange rate fell, a bitter dispute broke out about how much of the cost of car kits imported from Peugeot should be paid in renminbi and how much in hard currency. The French insisted on sticking by prior agreements. The Chinese demurred and – as the sole distributor for the finished Peugeot sedans – refused to take delivery of any more vehicles. Only four months after Denway's extraordinary listing in Hong Kong, and when its share price was still riding high, the fields around the Guangzhou Peugeot factory were filling up with unsold cars.[14] By the time the dispute was resolved in the summer, Zhu Rongji's austerity programme meant that demand had dissipated. The working relationship never recovered.

In another market, the sorts of problems that were affecting the Peugeot and GM operations by 1994 would have caused their parent companies to rethink their strategies. But not so in China. Despite all the difficulties, the boards of Peugeot Citroën, Peugeot's parent company, and GM remained geared to expansion. The obstacles in China were regarded as short term. Peugeot Citroën was determined to build one more full-scale car plant, GM two. Operational teething problems were not to interfere with strategy. In April 1992, Peugeot Citroën had signed financial and technical agreements committing it to a second, much larger joint venture in Wuhan in central China. By 1994, Dongfeng–Citroën Automobiles was halfway through construction of a state of the art factory with the capacity to make 150,000 Citroën ZX cars a year, four times the maximum volume of the Peugeot plant. The venture was due to begin production in 1995, with investment of $1.25 billion. Company president Jacques Calvet expressed confidence that by the time cars were rolling off the lines, China's auto market would be growing at the same pace it had in 1992. On a trip to Beijing in December 1995, he predicted China would account for a combined 200,000 Peugeot and Citroën car sales by 2000.[15]

GM's president of international operations Louis Hughes also took the sanguine view that bumps were to be expected on Chinese roads. He spared his shareholders the details of GM's Shenyang pothole. At the company's May 1994 annual general meeting Mr Hughes told attendees only that pick-up truck manufacturing was 'in place' in China and that the company was in final negotiations to make MPVs and Opel Corsas. He pointed to 'near-explosive growth in Asia'[16] although he did not revisit his previous year's forecast that GM would sell 40,000 vehicles in China in 1993;[17] the company actually sold 9,000. Mr Hughes' and chief executive Jack Smith's commitment to opening three car plants was unshakeable and, as part of their lobbying efforts to the win the necessary licences, GM's components divisions began its $350 million investment programme in 1994. With the Shenyang plant out of production, the company's negotiators finally tied up a second vehicle manufacturing deal, to make the Buick, in Shanghai in October 1995. The Opel mini car deal was more elusive – despite several moments in 1993 and 1994 when the GM negotiators reported they were close to signing, the company failed to complete a contract with any of China's state auto makers. There was also no news from the Chinese side as to who had been chosen to build China's 'family car'. Mr Hughes urged his executives to persevere.

梦

In Hong Kong, at Goldman Sachs' regional headquarters, Moses Tsang was learning his own lessons about patience. Goldman's seminar to explain to other provincial power bureaus the details of its planned $180 million placement of shares in a Shandong power company had definitely been a mistake. One of the VIP guests invited to the gathering was Li Xiaolin, daughter of then premier Li Peng, who had listened intently as Goldman staffers explained a deal in which the return on equity for investors would be around 17 per cent per year.[18] Ms Li subsequently conveyed the content of the seminar to her father, most of whose career had been spent as a senior apparatchik in China's electricity industry. He was not happy. From Goldman's perspective the projected return – which had been set by the market – was modest because of the risk of investment in China and the fact that power station financing provided no easy exit strategy. But Mr Li thought otherwise. Profits for foreigners, in his conservative and xenophobic view, were bad enough, but 17 per cent suggested China was being taken for a ride by a bunch of sharp Americans. At Mr Li's urging, the State Council cancelled the Shandong placement. A similar Goldman deal close to completion in Guangdon province was also called off.

Goldman turned to its 'princeling' partners at Venturetech to help it out of a fix. But in a crisis situation, the designer-clad children of Party luminaries turned out to be powerless. The placement was finished. The only positive news was that the Shandong provincial government still wanted to proceed with fund raising of some sort and came up with a proposal to change the exercise into a public listing. The central government said it was willing in principle to support this.[19] The exercise would raise not the $180 million in equity and $180 million in bank loans originally envisaged, but more than $700 million. A new carrot dangled. After eighteen months and more than $2 million of Goldman time wasted on the first deal, the investment bank began to structure the initial public offering of a company named Shandong International Power Development (SIPD).

But as Goldman staffers worked on the listing through 1994, the market environment took a turn for the worse. In February, the US Federal Reserve made the first of several increases in American interest rates. With most Asian currencies connected to – and the Hong Kong dollar pegged to – the US currency, regional stock markets became bearish. Turnover on the Hong Kong bourse fell to half its 1993 level. It emerged that Morgan Stanley guru Barton Biggs had touted the China miracle to his investors just three months before the Hong Kong bull run ended. The outlook for new listings darkened. Two Chinese power companies the government sanctioned for offerings in New York in the autumn of 1994 barely achieved their subscriptions, despite pricing which would have seemed unduly generous a year earlier.[20] In November, Goldman was forced into the first of a series of postponements of SIPD's listing that would last until 1999.[21]

Goldman's 500 staffers, sitting in Hong Kong's most pricey office block, began to look extremely expensive. By 1994 the chatter in the champagne bars of the Central financial district was that China fever was costing America's most revered investment bank millions of dollars a month. Despite heavy spending on an equities team, Goldman failed to become one of Hong Kong's top ten brokerages. Nothing had gone to plan and key employees were bailing out. Mainland rainmaker Liu Erfei was poached by Smith Barney at the end of 1993 – not that he had made much rain – and many of his acolytes left with him. The China research dream team was frustrated and demoralised. Tasked with mapping out investment areas for the next decade, they had found China an impossible challenge. In some cases the economists discovered data about the mainland economy were unavailable, more often they were available but of such doubtful quality as to be unusable. 'We couldn't populate the spreadsheet,' lamented Jan Lee, Goldman's co-head of investment research.[22] The firm's New York formula – super-rational, top down analysis – was failing to produce the goods and headquarters wanted to know why.

Moses Tsang had hoped that big deals would flow from his tie-up with Tsui Tsin-tong's New China Hong Kong Group (NCHK), the investment bank of the Chinese rich and famous. But here, too, nothing happened. Though the shareholders were a who's who of Hong Kong and mainland big business, there were too many – fifty-four – for anyone to take a serious interest in the firm's business. In the mid 1990s the activities of Mr Tsui and NCHK brought

Goldman only ugly publicity. There was a failed mainland advertising agency in which Hong Kong's head of immigration was sold shares, creating a scandal over conflict of interest. There was an investigation into Mr Tsui – long rumoured to be involved in the arms trade – by Hong Kong customs with respect to a shipment of specialist tubing from China to Iran. And one of the directors of NCHK, Zhou Beifang – son of the head of Capital Iron & Steel in Beijing – was arrested for corruption on the mainland in February 1995, tried and given a suspended death sentence.

This was not the big opportunity that Stephen Friedman and Robert Rubin had expected. At the end of 1994, after a year of bear Asian markets, even the 9 million square foot (840,000 square metre) bell-wether Beijing property project in which Goldman had taken a stake hit the skids. A breaking corruption scandal in the capital and a dispute over planning rights brought site preparation for Oriental Plaza to a halt. Not even Li Ka-shing, the most powerful tycoon in Hong Kong and Goldman's partner in this, appeared able to get a mainland deal done. The firm's New York central management committee had had enough. In November 1994, after consultation with New York, Moses Tsang resigned as partner in charge of the Asian operation. Goldman cut its Hong Kong staff from a peak of over 500 in 1993 to under 200 in 1995. It was a humiliating retreat. Most of the huge Hong Kong office stood empty.

梦

If Moses Tsang regretted his investment seminar, then so must John Wolf have rued his behaviour at the 1991 Paris Air Show. It was there that the executive vice-president of McDonnell Douglas waved in front of fellow delegates a memorandum of understanding for what he believed was a 150-aircraft co-manufacturing deal with China. Douglas – the civil aircraft arm of McDonnell Douglas – he declared to attendees, was 'second to none' in globalisation.[23]

The bravura was understandable. Douglas had been working since 1975 to crack the Chinese market. The company assembled thirty-nine aircraft in Shanghai at no profit to itself, holding out for a bigger reward down the line. The 'Trunkliner' programme looked like the pay-off Douglas had been waiting for. When the company was confirmed as China's partner for the project in April 1991, management was ecstatic.

As the details of Trunkliner were negotiated in 1991 and 1992, however, the deal became rather less sweet than Douglas imagined. In a contract signed in June 1992, China's aviation trading arm, China National Aero-Technology Import Export Corp. (CATIC), guaranteed to buy not 150 China-made aircraft worth $6 billion, as Douglas had been led to believe, but forty. It was a reduction reminiscent of those observed by Carl Crow in the 1930s: 'Long before the transaction is finally closed,' he had noted, 'one after another of the fat orders the export manager secured will, for one good reason or another, be cancelled or cut down.' In this case the Americans were told that if all went well the order would increase subsequently. But CATIC insisted on a high level of local content immediately – over 50 per cent, compared with just 10 per cent for the aircraft Douglas assembled in Shanghai in the 1980s. For an order of only forty planes it was unlikely the company would achieve the economies of scale necessary to make local manufacturing profitable. If it was to go forward, it had to believe the Chinese would not tool up factories to make MD-80 and MD-90 aircraft only to stop production after forty units. After much soul searching, Douglas decided to proceed and began work with different military-controlled facilities around China to localise production of its aircraft.

A year after signing the Trunkliner deal, Douglas had still not received any money from its Chinese partner, which was also hit by the austerity programme. Instead, in 1993 CATIC focused its energies on persuading the Americans to sell it dual military and civilian use machine tools from a factory it was closing down in the US and obtain a necessary export permit from the Commerce Department in Washington. Douglas did so; a permit was granted on the basis that the Chinese would keep all seventeen of the machine tools they wanted in one civilian factory in Beijing. A leaked 1993 letter from CATIC's executive vice-president, Tang Xiaoping, to Douglas promised that the sale 'shall have a big influence on the Trunkliner program and long-term co-operation'.[24] Yet even with the sale made, Douglas did not receive any of its partner's money.

In August 1994, commerce secretary Ron Brown, travelling to China on his first trade mission, was asked to intervene. Mr Brown's visit, coinciding as it did with the ending of annual congressional renewal of China's Most Favoured Nation trade status, was of great political significance to Beijing. With this impetus, Douglas was offered a renegotiated forty aircraft contract whereby twenty MD-90s would be made at the company's headquarters at Long Beach, California, and twenty more would be co-manufactured in China.[25] Co-production in Shanghai finally began in the fall of 1995 – just when the first deliveries of finished aircraft had originally been scheduled. By this point, with the project so truncated, there were those at Douglas who believed the company was being led on an endless dance. But with so much time and money invested, it was almost impossible to quit. The Americans hoped, despite increasing evidence to the contrary, that Trunkliner would one day become the huge project that had been formerly envisioned. Furthermore, the Chinese still held out the prospect of basing their plans to build a small 100-seat aircraft around Douglas's MD-95.

A policy of non-discrimination ...

Many American and European investors, if their projects were delayed, refused to face up to the problems on the ground in China and instead saw themselves as victims of international politics. American companies were infuriated by the annual congressional debates over China's normal trade relations status. US business groups spent hundreds of thousands of dollars schooling their most presentable Chinese employees before sending them to Washington to plead with senators and congressmen for a more compliant China policy. British corporations railed against the democratic reform initiatives of governor Chris Patten in Hong Kong which, they claimed, cost them huge infrastructure projects such as the Guangzhou metro. German captains of industry were horrified in 1996 when their parliament passed a resolution condemning Chinese behaviour in Tibet. Yet there was scant evidence, as overseas Chinese investors would testify, to suggest that there was really any form of systematic preferential treatment being meted out.

Projects of all descriptions and all origins failed to materialise – as Peter Woo, chairman of Hong Kong's Wharf Holdings, discovered. Mr Woo was among the most vocal of the China bulls in the early 1990s and reckoned himself close enough to Beijing to be a candidate for the post of Hong Kong's first post-colonial chief executive. But his plans to turn the Yangzi river city of Wuhan into 'the Chicago of the east' came to nought. He signed fifteen letters of intent to rebuild the city's entire infrastructure. His company toured Chinese central government officials around Frankfurt and Washington to look at urban rail systems (unwise, since they subsequently insisted the budget for Wuhan's light rail system be increased from $65 million to $413 million). But the Wuhan government, also feeling China's cash crunch, offered no money of its own, while demanding a controlling interest in every project. 'They wanted 51 per cent and they had no cash,' said Bennie Wu, a Wharf director. 'They wanted us to lend them the money to pay for 51 per cent.'[26] When Wharf hesitated, the projects were offered to New World, one of its main Hong Kong competitors. What Mr Woo claimed to be his 'special connection' with the mayor turned out to be not so special. His British director for mainland China, John Hung, who is a quarter Chinese, had even gone so far as to change his Anglo-Saxon surname to blend in with the locals. But that produced no dividend either. The whole exercise became a costly embarrassment. 'We spent millions of dollars,' recalled Bennie Wu. Wharf was so strung out in China by 1995 that it omitted to mention the country in its annual report.

Oei Hong Leong, the Indonesian-Chinese entrepreneur who spent time on the mainland during the Cultural Revolution, was nimbler and less naïve than Peter Woo. Mr Oei had sewn up deals to buy 196 Chinese state companies within months of Deng Xiaoping's Southern Tour, when the economic environment was at its most gung-ho. He quickly repackaged tyre companies into a New York listing and sold off breweries he had acquired to Japanese beer maker Asahi. This work yielded Mr Oei some profit and considerably more fame, but the long hand of Chinese bureaucracy eventually caught up with him. The contracts of Mr Oei's Hong Kong-listed company China Strategic Investment to purchase 101 factories in Dalian were torn up after central government intervention. A $2 billion power project and an $887 million coal slurry pipeline – in which Goldman Sachs had taken an interest – came to nothing. China's official press attacked Mr Oei for making money at the country's expense. There were strikes and law suits at his factories. By 1996, he was saying he would buy no more industrial state enterprises because the work was not worth the trouble.

... even among nations

The best *guanxi* – as the Chinese term personal connections – in the world seemed to be over-rated by the mid 1990s. Mr Oei had spent the Cultural Revolution getting to know future leaders of China. Still more impressively, the government of Singapore had been praised in the *Collected Works* of Deng Xiaoping. The island state was said to provide a future political role model for the mainland. It was with this kind of recognition that the Singaporean government undertook to build its $20 billion satellite business town outside the central Chinese city of Suzhou. Singapore's senior minister, Lee Kuan Yew, personally led the negotiations. Soon after the deal was signed in 1992, however, it emerged that the local government was creating an alternative, wholly Chinese owned industrial zone itself which would undercut Mr Lee's township. The Singaporeans, who thought they were doing their poor mainland cousins a favour, were exasperated. 'Obviously we are not happy,' Lee told CNN, 'because we are not getting the kind of attention we were assured that we would get – special attention. Indeed, what we are getting now is competition.'[27] With higher overheads and industrial and commercial land costs set above those in the locally run zone, the China–Singapore township failed to meet any of its revenue targets. It lost money every year through the 1990s until, in 2001, the Singaporeans gave up the game and sold out their majority position to the Chinese at an undisclosed price. Goh Chok Tong, the Singaporean prime minister, said pointedly that his country would not be undertaking any more state-to-state projects with China. The overseas

Chinese, who had been wooed by Mr Deng as a unique constituency, turned out to be more dispensable than they had imagined.

China punctured the expectations of companies and nations alike. It was in 1994, just as the ambitions of existing corporate investors were being called into question, that the enthusiasm of the world's political leaders for the Chinese market reached its zenith. That summer was the peak of the trade mission craze, during which $40 billion of export and investment deals were signed in fifteen visits to and from China. More than $13 billion of deals were signed in July, August and September 1994 alone, as Li Peng travelled to Germany, Ron Brown came to Beijing and Jiang Zemin went to France. The exchanges were deemed so successful that the leaders of the western world raced to book their next trips. Helmut Kohl, Michael Heseltine and Ron Brown all scheduled return visits for 1995 and 1996. The only problem with going back to China was that questions were beginning to be asked about how all the deals signed on the first trips were progressing.

On inspection, most deals turned out not to be progressing at all. Ron Brown was the first to experience the negative public relations value of unconsummated Chinese memoranda of understanding when he landed in Beijing for a second time in October 1995. Before leaving Washington, Mr Brown insisted that almost all the $6 billion of business he trumpeted a year earlier was going ahead. 'With the exception of one project, all the projects announced are on track,' he told a press conference.[28] A few days later, in Beijing, he was forced to concede that more than $5 billion of projects for which he had witnessed signings were going nowhere. None of the three $1 billion power stations was being built and nor was anything happening with other major projects, including one for Waste Management International to build five $100 million waste reprocessing plants.[29] Faced with undeniable and uncomfortable fact, Mr Brown resorted to politicians' bluff; he insisted that project delays were temporary and that the China market was more important than ever. 'The centrality of this relationship and our absolute commitment to making it work is often easy to lose amid the stories about week-to-week problems,' he told a meeting of the American Chamber of Commerce.[30] China's minister of foreign trade, Wu Yi, assured Mr Brown that the projects would go ahead and Mr Brown stated publicly his confidence in her assurances. The commerce secretary left Beijing saying he had discussed another $20 billion of deals on the trip and laying down a new but entirely unsubstantiated claim that, since the de-linking of China's normal trade relations status from its human rights record in 1994, work had begun on $3.5 billion of American business supported by US government advocacy.[31]

The US companies which had signed deals, and their representatives in

China, waited. Still nothing happened. It was the same story with the projects agreed during the visit of energy secretary Hazel O'Leary in February 1995. The one difference was that Ms O'Leary never made it back to Beijing; the expenditure on her first trip had been so high that it had triggered an investigation by the General Accounting Office of Congress. Ms O'Leary sent two advance parties of forty bureaucrats each to Beijing before she left Washington – an expense normally incurred only for a trip by the secretary of state or president. She spent $1 million on her visit, on which she took sixty corporate executives – nearly $17,000 per businessman. The energy secretary's lavish presentational arrangements were described by one embassy official as the political equivalent of *The Oprah Winfrey Show*.[32] At a meeting with the State Planning Commission her communications team had equipped her with a special cordless microphone system so she could leave the speakers' platform and wander in and out of a bemused audience of po-faced planning apparatchiks, talk show style. There were no complaints from the American side at the time because Ms O'Leary announced the signing of three complete power plants deals and over twenty other memoranda for fertiliser plants, oil and gas projects, renewable energy investments, and so on. Had these deals – worth $6 billion according to the Department of Energy – come through, Ms O'Leary would have been justified in her claim that the trip produced a return on expenditure of 'one thousand times'.[33] However, the General Accounting Office found otherwise. Almost every piece of paper signed on the visit proved worthless.

Michael Heseltine came back to China in May 1996 as British deputy prime minister, oblivious to a high tide of evidence that billions of dollars of China projects agreed before mid 1995 either were not happening or were turning sour. He tasked the Department of Trade and Industry (DTI) with outdoing his first visit by rounding up more British businessmen than had ever been on a trade delegation before. 'I am delighted,' he wrote in the official tour brochure, 'to be leading to China and Hong Kong the largest ever British trade mission.' This assertion – Mr Heseltine brought 270 businessmen to China – was only true if Lord Macartney's 700-man mission of 1793 was not included. The British government left Lord Macartney out, but British journalists drew an unattractive parallel. The country's exports to China had fallen after Mr Heseltine's first visit while it was pointed out that the government never substantiated the £1 billion ($1.6bn) deal total claimed by the former trade minister. DTI press officers proffered somewhat lamely that British companies were too press shy to want their (by implication large) business transactions itemised. All but one of the projects that were named turned out to have been sealed well before Mr Heseltine's arrival. The only genuinely new contract from the first trip was a £25 million ($40m) brewery joint venture by Bass which, a DTI press release assured in May 1995, 'is expected to become one of the top three brewers in China within five years'. In the event, the brewery began operating at a fraction of capacity and losing large sums of money, a situation it never improved on. Journalists who questioned Mr Heseltine face to face about the status of projects signed on his missions were excoriated for doing Britain down.[34]

The only western leader who managed to return to China in some comfort was German chancellor Helmut Kohl. At least some – though by no means all – of the $1.8 billion of projects he announced in November 1993 had gone ahead. This was because they were backed by concessionary government finance. In 1993, at the time of his trendsetting trip, Chancellor Kohl had been unpopular at home over the weak condition of the economy and the costs of German reunification. He faced re-election in 1994. His government looked at export opportunities in China as a means of maintaining jobs – particularly in former East Germany – and was willing to use government subsidies to this end. The $300 million Guangzhou subway deal signed by the chancellor in 1993 was underwritten by DM350 million ($220m) of long-term concessionary finance, with loan rates as low as 0.75 per cent. A $92 million purchase of rail rolling stock was paid for with German development aid on condition the wagons came from the Deutsche Waggonbau plant in Ammendorf in the east; German development aid was also used to finance Chinese purchases of subway rolling stock.[35] These business deals were not really business at all.

With German taxpayers footing much of the bill for the country's China 'exports', Mr Kohl's deals were the ones that stuck. Ron Brown and Hazel O'Leary had no concessionary finance to offer; the US Export–Import Bank was not even willing to guarantee commercial credits to China. The only trading lever the American ministers wielded was the importance of their country; because of this, Chinese government negotiators signed non-binding memoranda of understanding with abandon. Also, there were additional, short-term imperatives to produce lucrative-sounding letters of intent. Ms O'Leary's trip coincided with a dispute over intellectual property rights, in which Washington was on the brink of imposing punitive tariffs on $1 billion of Chinese exports. Deals signed in such an environment did not last. Concessionary finance was the link between almost all the big China projects from the mission era that went ahead. French and Canadian state companies closed nuclear power plant deals which were heavily subsidised by their governments. Canadian prime minister Jean Chrétien announced the sale of two Candu nuclear reactors as part of the $6 billion in business he claimed from his first China mission in November 1994; the sale was backed by the biggest federal export loan in Canadian history – $1.5 billion over twenty-two years – for which the credit terms were never published. It still took the Canadians a further two years and another trip by Mr Chrétien to finalise the arrangements. The French offered similarly soft terms to provide a second nuclear reactor at China's Daya Bay plant in Guangdong in January 1995. A representative of the French state nuclear company Framatome conceded in the *Financial Times* that the price had dropped 20 per cent since the first phase of Daya Bay and that China was buying the 'least expensive' nuclear reactors in the world.[36]

Even with state-supported exports at fire sale prices, it is unlikely that a quarter of the $40 billion of deals signed on government-to-government trade missions in China in the mid 1990s ever went ahead. The only significant sales on a commercial basis were those of aircraft, and these were not a direct result of political visits. Chinese airlines in the early 1990s were desperately short of aircraft and took options – often not binding – on scores of new planes. Beyond aircraft, there were whole rosters of deals that came to nothing. Conspicuous at a country level were the $12 billion of memoranda signed by the missions of Ron Brown and Hazel O'Leary. Not a single one of their major deals bore fruit;[37] an officer at the American embassy in Beijing calculated the actual business resulting from Mr Brown's first trip was as low as $10 million.[38] The figure may have been higher, but not enough to close a fraction of the gap on the $6 billion claimed by the commerce secretary.

By the time that world leaders made their second trips to China in 1995 and 1996, it was clear that demand in some sectors of the economy was collapsing. Moreover, the stalling of so many deals pointed to systemic, rather than merely cyclical, weaknesses in the market. Despite this, investor confidence was far from broken. Quite the opposite. Foreign money poured into China at an ever increasing rate, setting records for direct investment of $42 billion in 1996 and $45 billion in 1997. If it were true that smart investors follow the money, there could be little to worry about. International chambers of commerce continued to host seminars for new arrivals about the scale of the opportunity, not the apparent difficulty of harnessing that opportunity. There was little discussion of the problems of ongoing investments – beyond the attacks on unhelpful foreign governments – and the Chinese state media pumped out its hyperbolic propaganda with established reliability. Where there were difficulties, denial was the order of the day. The psychology of the moment was that the China Dream would come to pass if only enough people believed in it.

7

Suspect numbers and the perils of projection

'The daily news bulletin was read by Mr T. T. Li: "Of seven planes brought down by Chinese ground forces, fifteen were destroyed by infantry." Nobody bothered to question the arithmetic.'

W. H. Auden and Christopher Isherwood, quoting from a Chinese government press conference in 1938 during the war with Japan.[1]

THE SECOND HALF of the 1990s was reminiscent of Samuel Beckett's play *Waiting For Godot*, except that the business world was waiting not for God but for the Chinese market. Almost all investors believed that once China's austerity programme ended, its 1.2 billion consumers would re-emerge and their businesses would forge ahead. Almost all investors believed other operating difficulties were temporary. They were wrong. In the course of 1994 and 1995 inflation was tamed, the government removed price controls it had reintroduced for staple foods and exports grew strongly. But the domestic economy failed to reignite. Each year growth was a little slower than the last, going from 14 per cent in 1992 to 10 per cent in 1995 and 7 per cent by the end of the decade. And this was according to China's official statistics, which became more opaque the closer analysts looked. For an increasing number of people, it became apparent that there was more amiss with the Chinese economy than just a reduction in government credit. The most inquisitive observers began to wrestle with an unspeakable prospect: that the world might have fundamentally misread the market.

In the second half of the decade, the level of China's commitment to deregulating its economy would to be called into question. The sustainability of its finances would be raised. But the most immediate concern for businessmen was how realistic they had been in the forecasts they made in their China business plans. For it was here that corporate headquarters might one day have to answer to investors and shareholders. There began a slow, and often reluctant, re-examination of the assumptions that had been made about the Chinese market place. It turned out to be the opening of a statistical Pandora's Box. The first question raised in this investigation was, what had happened to the burgeoning consumer demand that China was supposed to deliver?

Multinational business bet billions of dollars in the 1990s on the emergence of a Chinese middle class with the disposable income to pay for anything from designer clothing to cars. It was this consumption that in the second half of the decade was most palpably missing. Retail sales growth fell from on average 25 per cent a year from 1985 to 1995 to less than 7 per cent in 1999 – and still off a small base.[2]

Kazuo Wada, the Japanese head of Yaohan, opened his mammoth NextAge department store in Shanghai's Pudong New Area in December 1995 to heavy operating losses. His confidence in the future was such that six months later he brought forward his target date for opening 1,000 Chinese supermarkets from 2010 to 2005, declaring: 'It is now harvesting time.'[3] But a year after that remark, Yaohan Japan was filing for court protection, ruined by Mr Wada's profitless expansion. He had amassed the biggest retailing debt in post-war Japanese history – ¥161 billion ($1.3 billion). Mr Wada's explanation of the débâcle in China was as bland as his earlier promises had been colourful. 'We failed to get returns on investments and loans,' he said. 'We made overly optimistic projections of markets.'[4] Yaohan started only twenty-seven of its 1,000 planned Chinese supermarkets before being forced out of business. These outlets were bought by the European retail chain Royal Dutch Ahold, which in turn posted perennial losses in China before pulling out of the country at the end of the decade. Yaohan's Shanghai department store – the biggest in Asia – was taken over by its Chinese partners.

Frank Lo, the brassière millionaire, cut the ribbon at his luxury Printemps department store in Shanghai in June 1995 to equally disappointing sales; turnover was half what Mr Lo had predicted. Yet he, too, remembering the boom of 1993, was confident of a powerful economic recovery. Three months after opening, Mr Lo showed his determination to stand by an upmarket sales strategy by putting on an exhibition of eighteenth century timepieces by the Swiss watchmaker Blancpain. Business languished. By 1997, the debt incurred to build the $26 million Printemps store, and the operating losses it was suffering, threatened the very survival of Mr Lo's Hong Kong-listed company, Top Form. Since the department store had been Mr Lo's idea, he decided the buck must stop with him. In a debt restructuring exercise in May 1997, he used a large part of his personal fortune to buy the loss-making Shanghai store from its struggling parent. He handed over Top Form's management to former subordinates and installed himself in an office on the top floor of the Printemps shop on Shanghai's Huaihai Road. Mr Lo was determined to make the business work. Two years later, despite continuing losses, he was still insisting: 'Sooner or later this sort of expensive shop will be in demand.'[5]

It was not just luxury retailers who were baffled by the absence of demand. Foreign investors seeking more broad-based consumer markets were in at least as much trouble. International brewers had arrived in China like stampeding wildebeest. They were driven by numbers which showed that in 1993 the country was already the world's second biggest beer market – one that had grown 20 per cent a year for over a decade. By the mid 1990s, global drinks makers had opened sixty breweries in China and were operating another thirty via licensing agreements. The investments were not small. Fosters, the world's fourth biggest beer producer, put down $150 million for three production facilities around China and planned a fourth 'mega-brewery' in Shanghai's Pudong New Area. Bass, Britain's biggest brewer, spent $40 million on a deal signed before Michael Heseltine. Jack Perkowski, the Wall Street investment banker who had raised $415 million for China deals, acquired two breweries in partnership with America's Miller for more than $80 million. By the end of the decade each of these investments had gone to the wall.

For brewers, as for retailers, China's millions-strong middle class failed to materialise. The premium segment of the beer market – on which the foreign investors depended – turned out to be not even one-tenth of the total. They had not researched their market properly: most of the beer which China said made it second to the United States in overall consumption turned out to be beer in name only. It was low-grade, low-cost alcohol, retailing for less than the price of bottled water. The efforts of multinationals to have the Chinese pay up to five times as much for their brands came to nought, despite huge advertising expenditure. Bass promoted its Scottish lager with advertisements featuring the Loch Ness monster and product launches backed by bagpipe-playing Scotsmen, but created more bemusement than revenue. Fosters tried a different tack, cutting prices to loss-making levels to build market share. This strategy enjoyed some early success, but when management at the company's brewery in Tianjin decided to push up the price of a bottle of beer by four fen – half a US cent – the company lost half its market share in six months and never regained it.[6] Such was the price sensitivity of consumers. Jack Perkowski's frustration led him to change his general manager at the Beijing Five-Star brewery three times in four years – trying both local Chinese and expatriates – but he never made a penny.

Fosters was the first to fold. After losses of $17 million in its first year, $19 million in the second and more than $20 million in the third, the company wrote off the whole of its $150 million investment and pulled out of two of its three breweries. The third was still losing money and expected to close at the end of the decade. Soon after, Bass sold out of its China operations, writing off almost all its $40 million investment. Relations with the Chinese partner were so bad prior to closure that Bass managers needed bodyguards in order to visit their own plant. Jack Perkowski sold his two breweries to Tsingtao, China's biggest domestic brewer, for $22.5 million in August 2000 – $60 million less than he had paid for them five years earlier. Investors, who were lured with talk of returns of up to 40 per cent a year, were expected to receive a maximum of 25 cents on the dollar. Mr Perkowski's Asimco tried to reassure the backers of its other, automotive investments that their businesses were in better shape.[7] In the beer industry, consolidation became a rout as other international brewers – including Britain's Guinness, Denmark's Carlsberg and New Zealand's Lion Nathan – decided to cut their losses and run. Even America's biggest brewer, Budweiser, which had spent wildly to convince thousands of bars around China to stock its beer, was negotiating in 2000 to lease space at its Wuhan brewery to a domestic beer maker to cut losses.

Beer was not exceptional. By the second half of the 1990s, there were many industries where it was a challenge to find more than one or two profitable foreign companies, despite billions of dollars of investment. Not one of the ninety foreign breweries was believed by peers to have turned a profit. In 1998, a survey of 229 foreign-invested businesses by management consultants A. T. Kearney showed that only 38 per cent of all manufacturers were covering their operating costs.[8] Had the companies' price of capital – the borrowing expenses of the money they employed – been taken into account, fewer still could have claimed to be breaking even. And, as with other surveys of this nature, the results were further skewed by a widespread tendency among multinationals to bill part of their expatriate costs in China to headquarters rather than to the ventures themselves. With most companies failing to meet their targets, this was one way for besieged country managers to make their accounts look better. When General Motors began production of the Buick in December 1998, the auto maker had sixty temporarily assigned foreigners at its Shanghai plant and twenty permanent expatriates at an office in Shanghai, all working for a joint venture of which it owned only half, but being paid on the Detroit payroll.[9] GM's Chinese partner said it was unable to contribute to the costs of these staff, which were of the order of $20 million a year. Jack Smith's GM was an extreme example, but the tendency to bury China losses through accounting sleight of hand is common.[10] The returns from surveys like A. T. Kearney's, which showed that in the worst ctors – such as consumer goods and pharmaceuticals – less than a third of businesses were turning an operating profit, were almost certainly optimistic.

Sum trouble

With the first bankruptcies and pull-outs by foreign investors, a small constituency of economists, management consultants and businessmen began to ask what had gone wrong with projections about China. Part of the problem, it was quickly apparent, was down to mathematics. The country's growth – as chief executives persistently reminded their boards – was still world-beating. China averaged a growth rate of 10 per cent a year through the 1990s. Yet, at the end of the decade, gross national product per capita was still only $780. As in the 1980s, the dollar value of the economy had been set back by a devaluation, one of more than 40 per cent when China's dual exchange rate system was abolished in 1994. But more important than this was that China's ostensibly high growth was built on a tiny base – an economy worth just $330 per person in 1990.[11] In wealthier emerging economies, lower average growth made for fewer headlines but produced much larger absolute returns. In the Czech Republic, for instance, an average 4.1 per cent growth rate in the 1990s took GDP per capita from $3,600 to $5,060, an increase of $1,500 per person – three times that of China. In the real miracle economy of the 1990s, the United States, average growth of 3.5 per cent per year saw GDP per capita rise from $22,660 to $30,600, or $8,000 per person.[12] It is increases in individual disposable income, not growth rates, that create spending power.

The fastest growth the Chinese economy achieved in the Deng Xiaoping era was 14 per cent in 1992. It was the kind of number that wowed multinational boardrooms. Yet even this growth rate, could it have been reproduced in 1999, would have meant an increase in GNP per capita of only $100. The equivalent amount of additional national income per person would be created in the Czech economy by growth of 2 per cent, in the United States by growth of 0.3 per cent. As it was, China grew only 7 per cent in 1999. The country ended the millennium with a dollar economy slightly larger than those of Spain and Holland combined, with a population more than twenty times as large.

The real perversity of the situation was that two decades of rapid growth were largely made possible because the country's communist leaders had previously dragged the nation down so low. The most remarkable expansion after 1979 was in the area of exports, and in this respect China's performance is genuinely noteworthy. But the base from which exports and imports grew was virtually nothing. By the 1970s, Mao Zedong's government had reduced China's foreign trade to a fraction of its pre-1949 levels. Even with the fastest sustained growth in the world – an average of 15 per cent a year over the past two decades – China's exports and imports as a share of world trade only surpassed their 1928 peak in 1993.[13] After a six-decade hiatus, this performance was celebrated as a miracle.

The same pattern was repeated across different industries. The international insurance executives who fought for tables at Michael Heseltine's dinner in Beijing, who hired George Bush, Brent Scowcroft and Henry Kissinger to do their bidding and who opened 150 representative offices in their quest for licences, were attracted by a vast population and growth in Chinese insurance premiums of 30 per cent a year. But the Communist Party had closed down China's insurance industry between 1959 and 1979. When business restarted, it was beginning at zero – the ideal starting point for high percentage increases. When multinational insurers arrived in the mid 1990s after more than fifteen years of 30 per cent growth, mainland China's insurance market, serving a population of nearly 1.3 billion, was still smaller than that of Taiwan, an island of 20 million people.[14] It was the same story in the automotive sector. Prior to 1979, cars were politically incorrect for all but the most senior government officials. Car sales grew more than 20 per cent a year for two decades, but at the end of the 1990s the Chinese car market was slightly larger than that of Australia, a country of a mere 18 million inhabitants.[15]

Perhaps the most widely reported fast-growth story of the 1990s was China's appetite for commercial aircraft – caused by an increase in passenger traffic of more than 20 per cent per year. Boeing chief executive Frank Stronz was among the most vocal pro-China lobbyists in Washington and hosted a visit to his headquarters by President Jiang Zemin. Momentarily, in 1993 and 1994, Chinese purchases did make up a tenth of Boeing's deliveries.[16] But over time, the real size of the Chinese market showed through. By 1999, after orders had fallen to almost nothing, the total number of aircraft in use among all thirty Chinese airlines was 540 – fewer than in the fleet of American Airlines, which is only one of ten major US carriers.[17] Boeing, which leased large new offices in Beijing on the basis that China would be one of its most important markets, sealed off half the space and left it empty after moving in in 1999.[18] If a mathematical epitaph were to be written for China, it would say that small absolute increases from a low base look deceptively good in percentage terms.

梦

One of the key events that had changed the image of China in the early 1990s, and encouraged companies to rush in, was the World Bank's purchasing power reassessment showing the country to be much richer than it appeared to be. But the purchasing power analysis, just like investors' own wildly optimistic calculations, turned out to be faulty. Even as World Bank economists, led by Larry Summers, were lending their support to unprecedentedly high purchasing power multiples in China, other academics were having their doubts. It was to transpire both that the methodology of purchasing power itself was flawed and that its application in China was doubly flawed. The country was not, as the newspaper headlines of 1992 and 1993 announced, the third biggest economy in the world after all.

The unravelling of the China purchasing power fiasco began when a consultant economist, Albert Keidel, persuaded the World Bank to fund a review of all available data about what China's real purchasing power might be. This led to the publication in December 1994 of a report, incongruously titled *China GNP Per Capita*.[19] The paper was extremely sensitive to the internal politics of the Bank. It offered no estimate of its own for Chinese purchasing power – which would have meant explicitly damning figures that senior officials had published and given in interviews with the press. It said only that a 'reliable estimate' for per capita purchasing power 'would probably be below $2,000'.[20] This left readers to decide for themselves how much less than $2,000 was appropriate. The upper limit was still far more than China's 1994 dollar GNP per capita but, critically, it dismissed the previous World Bank purchasing power estimates that had been five times China's GNP per capita and those of Larrry Summers' father, Robert, which had been seven times higher. Furthermore, Albert Keidel's report quietly but systematically dismantled the methodological foundations on which the calculations that made China one of the world's biggest economies had been built.

There are difficulties with purchasing power methodology everywhere in the world. An assessment of a country's purchasing power requires researchers to find thousands of directly equivalent products and services whose costs can be compared with the same products and services in other countries. Even for a simple item like a pen, product matching issues arise because of quality differences – such as how long the pen will last and whether it writes with the same facility as another pen. With complex products, such as industrial machinery, quality problems multiply. A Chinese tractor is not directly equivalent to an American one, and compensation must be made for this. With services, quality issues can be insurmountable. The simplest example is a service like a haircut. In Beijing, the ambulatory hairdressers who set up shop under the elevated third ringroad cut hair for $1, whereas in New York it is difficult to have a haircut for under $15. Yet to say that Chinese purchasing power for haircuts is fifteen times America's is to imply that the quality of the haircuts is the same. No one who has looked at haircuts in both New York and under Beijing's third ringroad would argue that this is true. For a more telling example, consider the possible difference between a compound fractured leg set by an untrained 'barefoot' doctor in rural China and a leg set in a rural hospital in America.

One way to reduce the margin of error in purchasing power analysis is to have a single agency conduct the research. Most countries in the world participate in United Nations International Comparison Programme (ICP) surveys, which have collated cross-country price data since the 1960s. China has never done so. The data on which estimates of China's purchasing power were based were either ones collected individually by economists like Robert Summers and his colleague Irving Kravis, or inferred from China's own, published data – which in turn are based on a Soviet statistical model and are notoriously unreliable. World Bank economists derived one of their purchasing power estimates from China's educational enrolment statistics, while others were extrapolated from food consumption patterns or industrial output figures. No one worked with reliable primary data. Price information collected by Irving Kravis on trips to China turned out, on inspection, to be wholly inadequate. Not only this, the data were collected in the late 1970s and early 1980s, when the state set almost all prices, and simply extrapolated forward into a different economic environment on the basis of annual growth.[21]

Every purchasing power estimate Albert Keidel looked at for China contained the potential for gross inaccuracy because each one was based on flawed data. The use of secondary school enrolment numbers was dangerous because of the particular emphasis China places on secondary rather than tertiary education – the latter is reserved for a tiny élite – compared with other developing countries.[22] The use of output figures for industrial materials like steel was misleading because Chinese state steel mills produce vast amounts of unsaleable, low-grade steel. The same is true of agricultural commodities, where government purchasing allows Chinese farmers to sell millions of tons of otherwise unsaleable, low-grade grain. And international comparisons with, say, South Korea in the 1960s overlook the fact that quality has risen globally and an $800 per capita economy in 1965 was relatively more advanced than an $800 per capita economy in the 1990s. In short, as 'China GNP Per Capita' pointed out: 'A reliable purchasing power estimate will be available only after China carries out the necessary price and expenditure surveys.'[23]

There was fierce resistance from some World Bank economists to publication of the report, because of the way it questioned – albeit as inoffensively as possible – the work and opinions of some of the world's leading economists. The consensus within the World Bank, however, accepted the validity of Albert Keidel's arguments, and when the report was published it heralded a sea change in the tone of the organisation's dealings with China. There was no press conference, no official admission of error or misjudgement, but from 1994 the World Bank never again referred to purchasing power estimates in media interviews or public pronouncements on China. The institution's own way of admitting it had been wrong was to commission a series of reports and seminars about poverty in China.[24] The story was no longer how rich the country was, but how 270 million people lived below the World Bank's $1-a-day poverty line. One person, however, was not willing to concede publicly that he might have been mistaken. Larry Summers, asked on a trip to Beijing in 1999 in his then capacity as US Treasury secretary if he still stood by his estimates putting China's purchasing power at four to seven times its dollar GNP, evaded a direct answer but stated: 'The suggestion – if they are not already – that China and the US will soon be the largest economies in the world in terms of gross output remains a valid one.'[25] Since the dollar size of the American economy is more than seven times that of China, it is unclear precisely what Mr Summers meant. It is implicit, however, that he still believes that normal statistics are incapable of capturing the importance of the Chinese market.

There was one more quiet retraction to be made before the World Bank fully changed course on China. In 1992, following a mission to the country, the Bank had increased its standard dollar estimate of China's gross national product per capita to compensate for what it said was under-reporting of economic activity. This resulted in a World Bank figure for China's GNP per capita that was 34 per cent higher than the official Chinese one. After allowing for normal growth, the Bank's figures showed a jump from $370 in 1991 to $470 in 1992. Three years later, China conducted a national industrial survey based on sampling – much more accurate than the bureaucratic form-filling which is the basis of most Chinese statistics. Where the World Bank believed there was some under-reporting of services output, the survey uncovered endemic over-reporting of industrial output[26] – the biggest contributor to the overall economy. The case for the World Bank's upward adjustment was impossible to sustain. After a further visit by the institution's chief statistician, the Bank quietly dropped its China inflator in 1998 and went back to using the official Chinese data. Once again there was no press conference or announcement; but on the World Bank's numbers, China shed about a third of its dollar economy overnight.

The China standard

The difficulty of producing accurate research on China is a persistent problem, particularly for non-specialists. The country's half-reformed statistical system measures categories with which westerners are not familiar. Methodologies are weak – leading to frequent double counting[27] – and explanations of how such methodologies are arrived at are either only published in obscure Chinese texts or are non-existent. The American embassy in Beijing has for years sought an explanation of how the Ministry of Foreign Trade and Economic Co-operation (MOFTEC) calculates foreign direct investment returns, but without success. Even the most inconsequential data tend to be treated as state secrets in a society obsessed with secrecy. Furthermore, academic standards are low in an environment where professorships are earned through tenure rather than excellence and criticism is taboo. None of this, however, explains why, when confronted with a lack of reliable information, most foreign companies jumped into China investments anyway. The gap between the little that was known in the 1990s and the vast amount that was expected of the market cannot be put down to bad mathematics and poor research alone. A real understanding of what happened in the China gold rush is arrived at not only through rational analysis but through a psychological leap into the realm of the China Dream: foreign companies invested in China because they wanted to believe that dreams come true.

The story of automotive investment is instructive. In other developing countries, the experience of multinational automotive companies is that private car ownership takes off when economies reach a level of around $6,000 per capita. At such a point – which has been reached in places like Mexico, Chile and Hungary – the pooled resources of families make car ownership an affordable proposition. In the China of the mid 1990s, even if the economy were able to grow at 10 per cent a year indefinitely, and without devaluations, the country's gross national product per capita was not due to reach $6,000 until some time after 2020.[28] Yet in 1994, when annual sales of domestically made cars were 250,000, international car makers were planning to build 2.7 million units of annual manufacturing capacity.[29] General Motors alone wanted the capability to build 900,000 cars across three plants – one and a half times total sales in 2000. As it was, Chinese fears of losing the vast potential market to foreign interests meant that only 1.3 million units of capacity was licensed, and at the end of the decade overcapacity stood at a mere 100 percent.[30]

There was, and is, no logical way to derive from the level of car sales in the mid 1990s, or from China's economic growth rate, the projection of a market of one to three million vehicles a year which both the government and international automakers forecast for 2000. A report in the official *China Daily* in

1996 noted that there were only 50,000 licensed private cars in the country since almost all were bought by government units.[31] But in their pursuit of the China Dream, the hunger of the car makers was blind, sometimes to comic effect. When GM concluded at the height of the frenzy that the company must open components joint ventures to curry favour for vehicle manufacturing licences, the first business it entered was one for a product for which no market in China existed. Wan Yuan–GM Automotive Electronic Control Company was a $30 million joint venture with an arm of China Aerospace, the rocket-launching agency, to manufacture electronic fuel injection systems. But when the venture was signed in January 1994, not a single vehicle made in China used such components. Somehow, GM was oblivious to this. Indeed, Thomas Sheehan, Asia president of the investing GM subsidiary Delco Electronics, told journalists that China was already absorbing a million units of electronic fuel injection systems a year and that there was potential for four to seven million units by 2000. He added that, although total car sales in China in 1993 were only about 300,000, the number was expected to jump to a million in 1995.[32] Even this was less wide of the mark than statements by GM's vice-president for Asia–Pacific operations, Thomas McDaniel, who told reporters several times in 1993 that China would buy one million cars that year.[33] Mr McDaniel appeared to be confused by Chinese statistics for total 'automotive' output, which include not just cars but trucks and agricultural vehicles such as three-wheeled mini tractors. When GM discovered the truth about electronic fuel injection systems – only tiny numbers of which were in use in China even at the end of the decade – the Wan Yuan joint venture was mothballed.

The Sirens of the Chinese market sang to most international auto makers for the first time in the 1990s, but in other industries there was a definite element of *déjà vu*. Carl Crow had written about foreign pharmaceutical companies in China in the 1930s in his book *400 Million Customers*. 'I don't suppose there is a proprietary medicine manufacturer of importance in any part of the world who has not, at one time or another, encouraged his imagination to play with the idea of the prosperous business he might build up, and the wealth he might accumulate, if he could, by some means, convince a reasonable number of Chinese of the efficiency of his remedies,' he wrote. 'The less the manufacturer knows about China, apart from the population figure, the less restricted are his daydreams.' In the 1930s, the drug companies were almost all disappointed; in the 1990s they were back and their market estimations were no more rationally grounded than they had been sixty years before.

By the end of 1995, the State Pharmaceutical Administration registered 1,500 foreign drug joint ventures, with $1 billion invested and another $1.5

billion committed.[34] Three early entrants in the 1980s – Johnson & Johnson, SmithKline Beecham and Bristol-Myers Squibb – had built profitable businesses with factories producing low-cost cold remedies, vitamin supplements and anti-fungal creams for the likes of athlete's foot. The success of these operations was made possible by small investments, an absence of competition and the willingness of the state health system to pay for basic over the counter medicines for government employees. But in the gold rush of the 1990s, international pharmaceutical companies piled into the market with a different proposition – to manufacture expensive, state of the art prescription drugs for the billion-strong market. Almost without exception, the big investments of the decade became lossmakers. Companies like Pfizer, Novartis and Glaxo Wellcome were left with $30 million, $50 million and even $100 million factories which operated at as little as 10–20 per cent of capacity.

In the United States and Europe, premium prescription drugs sold to ageing but wealthy populations are the big money spinners for pharmaceutical companies. In China, a comparable market has never existed, except in the playful imaginations described by Mr Crow. Three-quarters of the Chinese population live in rural areas without medical insurance and on an average cash income of $260 a year.[35] This does not support expenditure on sophisticated medicines costing hundreds or thousands of dollars per course. Another 150 million Chinese live in semi-rural townships and might be able to afford to treat athlete's foot or a vaginal yeast infection, but they are equally out of reach of drugs treating depression, rheumatism or arthritis. The actual prescription drug market is confined to a small number of unusually rich individuals, mostly in big cities, and those state employees whom the government is willing to reimburse for medical expenses; as the 1990s wore on, and pressure on government budgets increased, this latter category was squeezed to keep costs under control. At the end of the decade, a winning prescription drug in the China market was considered to be one that could generate revenues of $5 million a year; in the United States, a drug that produced revenues of less than $250 million a year was considered a dud. Even China's best selling over the counter medicine, SmithKline Beecham's Contac cold cure, generated less than $90 million in 2000.[36]

Corporate Napoleons

Despite the evidence that they should do otherwise, multinational companies kept pushing ahead with investments that were predicated on genuinely large markets. This was only encouraged by the role that chief executives played in shaping business plans. China in the 1990s was *the* place for grand strategy – Jack Smith aiming to use China to increase General Motors' share of the Asian car market from 2 per cent to 10 per cent; Daimler–Benz's Edzard Reuter with his secret 'Megatrends' project plotting straight-line demand graphs; AT&T's Robert Allen looking to reinvent America's most stodgy conventional telecoms company as an emerging market supremo; and Jack Welch of General Electric, normally reckoned so astute, ready to storm Chinese beaches with every one of his twelve operating divisions.

Corporate strategy in China was almost always made at board and chief executive level, and this contributed to the no turning back approach. Removed from day-to-day reality, chief executives were particularly prone to denial when anything went wrong on the ground, and equally likely to blame independent third parties – often politicians – if forecasts were not met. Most of the world's developing countries are small and command no more than passing attention at the board meetings of large corporations. Strategy in the Czech Republic, with a population of 10 million, is not going to land a chief executive on the cover of *Business Week*. China can. Its size and population alone hold out eternal promise. The Chinese market is the means for a successful multinational to close out its global dominance, the magic charm with which a fading multinational can avoid eclipse. At least this is the stuff of the China Dream – and it demands a commitment of resources far beyond that suggested by current sales figures.

At GM, chief executive Jack Smith and head of international operations Louis Hughes invested enormous amounts of personal time and credibility in their China adventure. The closure of the company's Shenyang pick-up truck line and the stagnation of car sales after 1994 had almost no effect on the men's vision. When the Guangzhou Peugeot joint venture was close to insolvency in 1995, GM saw it not as evidence of the weakness of the market, but as an opportunity to acquire the elusive third car plant that boardroom strategy said the company must have. GM built up an office of twenty-one staff in the southern city in an attempt to negotiate a takeover. By 1996, the Peugeot factory was selling less than a hundred cars, and losing a million dollars, a week, but GM wanted it. Whatever had gone wrong was the fault of Peugeot–Citroën, not the market. In May 1997, Louis Hughes thought he had the deal clinched, only for GM to be trumped by Japan's Honda – one of many other international car firms still hungry for a China presence.

In the same vein, AT&T's chief executive Robert Allen and his China chairman William Warwick refused to question China's potential for their company, despite mounting evidence that it was the tiniest fraction of what they had believed. In August 1993, on his first visit to Beijing, Mr Allen met President Jiang Zemin and signed a $500 million memorandum of understanding for a 'comprehensive partnership' in telecommucations development. The piece of paper came to nothing – AT&T was invited to sell equipment in China, but, as was often the case in China, buyers expected to be provided with loans to pay for the purchases.[37] By 1997, the year in which Allen predicted the country would account for $10 billion of AT&T's business, his company was running a series of small joint ventures, most of them lossmakers; AT&T's turnover in China was a few million dollars.[38] But Allen and Warwick would not blame the market; instead, they cursed American politicians for irritating the Chinese government. Robert Allen lobbied furiously in Washington for a more concessionary trade policy toward China. In 1996, when Beijing ordered threatening missile tests off the coast of Taiwan, William Warwick insisted that it was in America's interests not to oppose the action. He told colleagues at the American Chamber of Commerce in Beijing that US companies had created their own problems in China by upsetting its political leaders.[39]

China became a highly emotive issue for many businessmen. When markets failed to materialise, critical enquiry by outsiders was met not just with denial, but outright anger. Chain-smoking before 9 a.m. in an interview in his Beijing office in 1998, Stan Clemens, the second general manager of GM's pick-up truck joint venture, could barely conceal his rage when it was suggested the business was a failure. 'This is a success story and should be presented as such,' he snapped. It was a curious remark to make about a manufacturing line that had produced only a few hundred pick-up trucks in seven years.[40] Mr Clemens insisted GM's accumulated losses were minimal because the 'physical write-off' had to be judged against the 'intangible benefits' of having learned so much about the Chinese market. It became a common justification for businessmen that one had to pay what the Chinese term 'school fees' in order to understand the operating environment. A few people retained a greater perspective. Jack Perkowski, who touted China on Wall Street with more Barnum than most in the early 1990s, had the good humour a few years later to describe the country as 'the Vietnam war of American business' – because so many promising young careers had been lost there.[41]

Those businesses that escaped the jaws of miscalculation did so because they maintained global investment standards. The enthusiasm of General Electric and Daimler–Benz chiefs Jack Welch and Edzard Reuter for China was no less burning than that of their peers. Yet both companies pulled back from the brink. At GE, Mr Welch was saved from misadventure by the very financial systems he had put in place during his thirty years at the helm of the company. GE had transformed itself in that period from a staid engineering business into a lithe manufacturing-to-financial services opportunist through its relentless concentration on investment returns. It was the potential for high returns that Mr Welch thought he spotted in China. After his 1993 visit – at the height of the China frenzy – corporate executives were set scuttling about the country in search of deals. GE Appliances, which makes fridges and other household goods, was one of the most aggressive divisions, scouring dozens of Chinese factories for a partner for a $300 million, pan-Asian manufacturing unit. But the deal never happened. Any investment had to meet an unbreachable GE requirement for a minimum 20 per cent return on investment. No matter how many sets of figures, for however many putative joint ventures, the bean counters at the company's Louisville headquarters tried, they could not achieve the requisite level of profitability. Investment costs were too high, brands too weak, distribution too fraught. The same pattern recurred in other GE divisions, and most units did not invest.

It was just as well. Two of GE Appliances' competitors, Maytag and Whirlpool, leapt into investments and paid a heavy price in the face of cut-throat domestic competition. Whirlpool reported Asian losses of $142 million between 1994 and 1996, most of them in China, and thereafter pulled out of local manufacturing operations.[42] GE went ahead only with a small number of operations where it could plot the road to returns: a successful plastics factory in Guangdong serving export manufacturers; a small business in Beijing assembling medical equipment; a more troubled, larger venture in Shanghai making lighting. In total, and by the end of the decade, the company invested less than half the $1 billion Jack Welch had talked of as GE's initial commitment. Despite this, the wily chief executive – whose celebrity status ensures a meeting with President Jiang Zemin on his visits to China – was careful to stroke the Chinese government's ego by talking up the importance of its market. Invited to speak at a millennial investment conference organised by *Fortune* magazine in Shanghai in September 1999, Mr Welch spoke in glowing terms before the assembled Chinese leaders of his 'very successful' China businesses in which, he said, GE had invested $1.5 billion. This huge number, much to the admiration of GE executives working locally, was concocted by adding to real investment – at most, a third of the total – the value of all aircraft, aircraft engines and other equipment leased to Chinese companies by GE Capital. It was not real investment at all. By the time Mr Welch appeared in Shanghai, his senior strategists had long since been redirected to focus their energies not on China but on real profit opportunities in Japan and eastern and western Europe.[43]

At Daimler–Benz, Germany's biggest industrial company, China investment policy changed because the chairman did. In 1995, the arch-strategist Edzard Reuter gave way to Jurgen Schrempp. The new incumbent announced a GE-like requirement for a minimum return on investment for every corporate division – only his benchmark was a more modest 12 per cent. Any project that could not meet the standard was to be abandoned. The effect in China was immediate. Mr Reuter had beaten off Ford and Chrysler to secure partnership in a $1.1 billion venture making MPVs. He also wanted to invest $800 million in building China's 'family car' and have Daimler–Benz Aerospace be a partner in a European consortium to manufacture a 100-seat passenger jet – the same deal pursued by McDonnell Douglas – that he claimed would generate $40 billion in sales. But the only car plant in China that had made any returns was Volkswagen's in Shanghai, and aircraft orders were drying up. It was impossible – beyond dreaming – to show where profits would come from. Daimler–Benz's MPV and family car plans were put on hold. The company's representatives in the European consortium to build aircraft were told to do nothing that would encourage the project to move forward.[44] The researchers and consultants running Mr Reuter's Megatrends unit were disbanded. When Mr Schrempp travelled to China in December 1997 for an audience with Li Peng, his main concern was that the then-premier would ask why Daimler–Benz had not moved ahead with the MPV project. Mr Schrempp was relieved that the subject did not arise.

The number of companies that held back from China investments, however, was small. The boardroom 'visionaries' almost always triumphed over the sceptics, where they existed at all. Normal standards of assessment were suspended because China was deemed too important. A combination of rudimentary mathematics and 'what if' thinking has long been China's greatest ally. This remained so in the 1990s. In January 1993, Peter Woo, chairman of Hong Kong conglomerate Wharf, could have been selling the China railway bonds of the 1890s or making the case for Lord Macartney's mission of the 1790s when he reasoned: 'Some say that China's GDP will match Japan's in ten years. That assumption is not so far out, because the population base is so huge. Japan only has about 120 million people. China has 1.2 billion. So if every person in China earns one-tenth the GDP per capita of Japan, you've got the Japanese GDP. Is that so unthinkable?'[45] Almost ten years later, China's GDP is still well under a quarter of Japan's, and it is indeed unthinkable. China's economy will not equal Japan's in the next decade, or even in the decade after that. But if history is any guide, this will not stop men like Mr Woo – smart enough to be a billionaire – from dreaming.

8

The socialists' Trojan horse

'We wanted to deceive you, but you wanted to be deceived.'
A Chinese official giving the American sinologist and journalist Jonathan Mirsky
his view as to why Mao Zedong's China of the 1970s was so favourably
misreported in the west[1]

THE BIGGEST MYTH about China in the 1990s was that the country ceased to be socialist. Despite a self-proclaimed communist government, operating through a Politburo, a Central Committee and a national network of 50 million Party members, this myth became received opinion. It was repeated in newspapers and magazines, not to mention boardrooms, around the globe. The official credo of 'socialism with Chinese characteristics', propagandised daily by the official media, was taken by the outside world to be a Chinese formulation for the still politically difficult concept of capitalism. China might not yet be able to use the 'c' word, but it was universally believed that the government was committed to free markets and that opportunity therefore existed for every kind of foreign investor. In ironic fact, China's own description of its economy was entirely accurate. The country in the 1990s was not a free market economy, it was a fundamentally socialist country undergoing some Chinese modifications.

It was the misunderstanding of this reality that cost foreign businesses billions of dollars. They arrived with expectations of rapid deregulation, level playing fields for different actors and a profit-driven culture. What they experienced was fully functioning socialism, involving micro-management of existing economic activity and a determination to plan all future activity. The underlying rationale was the old Maoist one – that China must be as self-sufficient as possible in as many areas of the economy as possible. Nothing could be further from the notions espoused by free trading nations. The Chinese state had no intention of withdrawing from business and would defend the territory of its public companies accordingly. The government maintained a relentlessly bureaucratic environment, in which vast amounts of time had to be expended to perform even the simplest tasks. The Communist

Party retained close control over the legal system, making effective recourse, or protection of intellectual property, extremely difficult, and challenges to its own direct interests unthinkable; in this context, corruption flourished. The Party was also careful to keep a firm grip on education and training, ensuring that the young people who were supposed to lead its economic revolution would be schooled according to socialist rite.

In retrospect, it seems extraordinary that so little of this was foreseen by investors. But such criticism fails to take account of how confusing were the signals that China was sending out to the world. Not only were economists, investment bankers and sections of the media trumpeting a changing nation, but there seemed to be no shortage of hard evidence of this on the ground. Probably the most frequently cited 'proof' of transformation in the 1990s was China's rate of physical construction. Businessmen marvelled at the country's ubiquitous cranes. They looked on approvingly as municipal officials showed them master plans for the forced march of urban construction. But more than this, there were other suggestions that the China Dream was within reach. For foreign companies, business performance was not disastrous in every single case. In a handful of sectors, companies did make money. Mobile telephony and fast food restaurants were the most conspicuous. These successes resulted from gaps in the state's not quite perfect control of the economy. But they suggested to other investors in more tightly controlled industries that profits were around the corner.

There was, in short, a great socialist deception. It was not a planned conspiracy, but it happened all the same. The China Dream of the 1990s was like the Trojan horse of Greek legend. Superficially, it was big, alluring and begging to be seized; the world grabbed it with both hands. Yet the appearance of the gift horse was no guide to what was contained within it or to what it portended. The rate at which tower blocks were thrown up in China was no more a measure of economic reality than purchasing power theory. The pace of building work only revealed the extent to which a socialist state could direct investment without reference to demand. Although a considerable amount of construction was foreign funded, most was ordered and financed by central and local governments. This frenetic endeavour was hailed as a symbol of entrepreneurialism, but as Paul Krugman argued in an Asia-wide context in 'The Myth of Asia's Miracle', it was not the case. By the late 1990s, the most famous living economist of all, Milton Friedman, was exposing the Chinese charade more explicitly. In the 1980s he had praised the country's early reforms, but after visiting Deng Xiaoping's Pudong New Area in Shanghai a decade later Professor Friedman changed his tune: 'The city is not a manifestation of the market economy,' he declared, 'but a statist monument for a dead pharaoh [Mr Deng had died recently in 1997] on the level of the pyramids.'[2] The Nobel prizewinner's hosts were horrified. Yet it is an indication of how little the Chinese knew beyond their socialist ways that they should tour the godfather of monetarist economics around a metropolis built from national debt.

Pudong had become a gargantuan model village – a monument rather more expensive to build than the pyramids – driven by the ego of an individual and paid for almost entirely by public investment. The market proof of this was an occupancy rate for office space in 1998, the year after Mr Deng's death, of just 35 per cent.[3] Across the whole of Shanghai, half of grade A offices were empty and rental prices fell from a peak of $7 per square foot ($75 per square metre) per month in late 1994 to $2 ($25) in 1998. The capacity of bureaucrats to order up – and instruct their banks to pay for – colossal volumes of commercial and industrial construction created a similar situation around the country. It was planning that had put all the cranes there, not market forces, because no market could have sustained them, and this left foreign real estate firms in a nasty fix. Their expectations were unrealistic to begin with and oversupply became endemic. The seven largest Hong Kong developers, which had entered $20 billion of real estate deals nationwide, scrambled to scale back projects. But construction could not be halted because the government enacted regulations in 1994 whereby land that was not used for the purpose for which it was leased reverted to the state. Investors were able only to cut the number of towers they were building or reduce their height. Overseas Chinese billionaires who leased vast tracts of land to create private development zones were similarly afflicted. Henry Fok, Mochtar Riady, Liem Sioe·Liong, as well as the backers of the huge free port area on Hainan island, and others, all cut their plans in half and half again. The pressure on smaller Hong Kong developers led to bankruptcies. Hong Kong newspapers ran regular features about local people who had paid up front for retirement homes or investment properties on the mainland only to be left with half-finished shells.

The only developments that remained unaffected were domestic ones, whose credit lines depended on state backers driven by planning rather than profit. The Golden Trade Building in Pudong, funded by the Ministry of Foreign Trade and Economic Co-operation, was a particularly costly example. This edifice was among the first truly world class skyscrapers in China. Chicago architects designed its eighty-eight floors in the tradition of a Chinese pagoda. It became much the most attractive modern building in Shanghai. Yet it was a socialist monument, and it was structures like the Golden Trade Building that put paid to Minoru Mori's more ambitious 96-

storey, 1,500-foot, chisel-shaped Shanghai World Financial Centre next door. This would have been the highest tower in the world, but it required private financing which, given the state of oversupply, was not forthcoming. [4] Mr Mori piled the site in 1998 and again in 2000 – to comply with government regulations against dormant developments – all the time promising that the building would go ahead. But by 2001, no progress had been made.

The Golden Trade Building, and thousands of smaller state-built towers, should have been seen as giant exclamation marks warning the world of China's excess. Yet this was no more likely than Americans in the late 1920s pointing to the rising Empire State Building – completed in 1931 – and concluding that it heralded the onset of the great depression. What observers saw was the momentous scale of China's construction and, like those who beheld the gift horse of Greek legend, they were awestruck. Equally, those who viewed foreign business activity focused not on the innumerable sectors where companies were losing money, but on the one or two anomalous industries where they were making profits. It was as if there was an intellectual sieve through which only evidence that the China Dream was possible could pass.

梦

Mobile telephony was invariably highlighted by investors because it had made three foreign companies a lot of money in the 1990s. By the end of 2000, China had 70 million mobile telephone subscribers and the rate of increase that year – 27 million new users – was one and a half times that of the United States.[5] The country spent twice as much on mobile telephone infrastructure and handsets as it did on cars or pharmaceuticals.[6] The market was genuinely big and, though the major players – Ericsson, Nokia and Motorola – would not reveal their margins, each conceded privately that it was making tidy profits.[7] Together, the Chinese revenues of these three companies in 2000 were over $10 billion, accounting in each case for more than one-tenth of their global sales. For Ericsson, the market leader, China vied with the United States as its biggest market in the world.[8]

The success of mobile telephony taunted every other business in the country. If it were possible for foreign companies to turn over billions of dollars a year and repatriate profits in this sector, why not in others? In the late 1990s, handset demand so far outstripped domestic licensed production that foreign suppliers – whose legal imports were closely restricted – took to selling millions of phones to Hong Kong middlemen, who in turn arranged for them to be smuggled into the mainland. In a single township in Guangdong province, Panyu (where Clifford Pang built his housing estate), it is estimated that 3 million illegal handsets were wholesaled in 1997.[9] This hardly smacked of the elusive markets of which other investors complained.

Mobile telephony, however, is not the long-sought proof that a Chinese El Dorado exists. Instead, the business is the exception that proves almost every rule about why other investments are unable to turn a profit. Mobile telephones were able to take off in China in the 1990s because they did not face the constraints affecting other businesses. Critically, mobile telephony was a new technology, which was not in competition with existing public sector manufacturing. Unlike cars or expensive pharmaceuticals or infrastructure, demand for mobile phone products and services was driven by private, not public, consumption. With mass demand unleashed, it was a rare instance where large volumes created economies of scale leading to constantly falling prices. The cost of a working mobile telephone fell in the course of the 1990s to no more than the price of a fixed line from the state telecom monopoly, which might take months to arrive.[10] Once the price of a handset is paid, China's user rates are among the lowest in the world – a $6 monthly line rental, with intra-city calls costing $0.07 per minute.[11] For the richest 10 per cent of the population, the portable telephone became the most powerful magnet for their limited disposable income, a symbol both of status and of freedom. The device offers young people living in cramped apartments with extended families otherwise impossible privacy;[12] for those leaving home, it is a means of staying reliably in touch. Finally, because mobile telephones are both complex technical instruments as well as consumer goods which require sophisticated marketing, they are not easy to replace through a state-sponsored localisation programme; nor are they easy to counterfeit.

This did not mean, however, that China's government was happy to see foreigners making money. Far from it. Despite the technical difficulties, the state backed local telecommunication businesses in the 1990s with hundreds of millions of dollars of direct and indirect subsidies and forced orders, in an effort to break the foreign grip on the mobile business. By the end of the decade, public and semi-public companies had cracked the manufacture of a key element of mobile infrastructure – the switches that route calls between base stations – and dominated the market for them.[13] The phones themselves were a trickier target. But, after years of expensive failure, by 2001 Chinese-made handsets were beginning to appear in the shops in significant numbers. Mobile telephony had enjoyed a unique set of advantages for foreign investors in China, but none of the overseas entrants doubted that the state would persist in its efforts to erode their position. In this respect they were less naïve about the intentions of Chinese bureaucrats than companies that would never have a dividend to remit.

Lights out

The international power companies were more stereotypical in both their experiences and their misconceptions. They flocked to China, foreseeing an environment defined by deregulation and opportunity. In August 1994, prior to US commerce secretary Ron Brown's first trip to Beijing, a group of twenty-four American energy corporates wrote a telling letter to their government. The businesses submitted calculations estimating that China would spend $90 billion on power investment in the next decade and forecast that they could claim a market share of not less than 15 per cent, or $13.5 billion.[14] Similarly, a World Bank report of the period, which said China would spend $200 billion on power generation between 1995 and 2004, was seized on by investors as proof of a vast market waiting to be taken.[15] Ron Brown's most memorable soundbite from his first trip referred to 'a quarter of trillion dollars in infrastructure projects in the pipeline', implying that China was a winnable market for American firms. Although such estimates were in themselves grossly exaggerated, the more important point was that the projections sidestepped Chinese reality because they were made without reference to the *modus operandi* of the country's socialist economy. These theoretical, top down forecasts did not consider two, critical variables: whether demand for a product or service was driven by public or private demand; and whether supply of a product or service was already monopolised by the state sector. Without this information it was not possible to say anything useful about investor prospects.

Power generation in China, like most parts of its economy, is a product of socialist planning. Under Mao Zedong, the electricity system was structured to deliver large quantities of artificially cheap power to industry, particularly heavy industry – the backbone of the planned economy. Whereas in developed countries the majority of power is consumed by private households, in China nearly three-quarters has traditionally been used by factories, mainly energy-inefficient state factories. Only a little over one-tenth of electricity is consumed by residential users. When China was in the midst of its credit binge in the early 1990s, state factories were running at full tilt, oblivious to whether markets existed for their products. It was in this period that forecasts for future energy demand were made. But, as with car sales, power consumption was highly susceptible to changes in the government's macro-economic policy. When a period of austerity dampened state sector activity after 1994, electricity consumption growth of over 10 per cent a year fell off to less than 3 per cent a year by 1998.[16] An electricity demand forecast from Peregrine – the Hong Kong investment bank that had won more China listing mandates than any of its international competitors before going spectacularly bankrupt in

1998 – was 50 per cent out by the end of the decade.[17] By 2000 there was not an undersupply of electricity in China, as universally forecast, but an oversupply.

Foreign investors expected that rising private demand for power would more than offset any weakening demand from state industry. Peregrine predicted that residential electricity consumption would grow by 20 per cent a year.[18] But this view missed the point of how modifications to China's state-planned power generation system would play out. As the government added new generating stations, it priced their electricity not at the old subsidised rates, which created infinite demand, but at market rates. By the late 1990s, the price of electricity varied by a factor of up to four times in different parts of the country. The average price rose above levels in many developed countries. Residents of Shanghai, Guangzhou and other cities were paying the same for their power – around 7.5 cents per kilowatt hour – as Americans, and doing so on a fraction of the income. In rural areas, farmers were made to pay the full cost of new electricity infrastructure, while local governments levied power surcharges to fill their coffers. In the most rapacious villages, electricity prices were as high as 40 cents per kilowatt hour, five times the price in New York. Private demand was effectively choked off. Even where affluent Chinese wanted to use more electricity, they were often unable to do so because the government spent almost nothing on residential transmission systems. The state planning bureaucracy focused only on increasing electricity production; it spent a quarter of the proportion of its budget on transmission and distribution facilities as would be the case in a non-planned economy. While new power stations buzzed, ordinary Chinese discovered that the addition of an air-conditioner to their homes was impossible because they lacked the wattage to run it.[19]

Into this curious state of affairs piled scores of international power companies, wanting both to run power stations and to sell generating equipment. The operators signed at least $15 billion in letters of intent in 1994 and 1995 – $6 billion-worth during the infamous trip of US energy secretary Hazel O'Leary alone. Having misunderstood the demand side of electricity in China, the companies went on to misread the supply side of the business as well. The electricity generators were convinced they would secure returns commensurate with the risk of investment. But the Chinese government – with the cancellation of Goldman Sachs' Shandong power financing scheme in December 1993 – had capped maximum returns on foreign investment in power at 12–15 per cent. The international companies signed memoranda anyway, believing it was a matter of time before China accepted the need to offer significantly better returns than those available in the developed world.

Likewise, the sellers of power-generating equipment expected the market to open more fully to international tendering. Both parties were betting that deregulation was inevitable.

It never was. For forty years, China had pursued a policy of self-sufficiency in power, as in other industries. The state plan created three manufacturers of electricity generating equipment – in Harbin, Chengdu and Shanghai – and it was these plants that the government intended to use to meet as much of the nation's demand as possible. In August 1994, the month Ron Brown was in China signing power deals, the State Planning Commission issued a 'hongtou wenjian' or secret memorandum forbidding Harbin – by far the biggest producer – from entering a foreign joint venture. The other two manufacturers were told that they could only consider foreign investment if the outside party had a minority stake and no management control.[20] Domestic power plant developers were ordered to buy local equipment and, with demand growth far slower than anticipated, China never needed to import more than a quarter of its generating units.[21]

Most of the deals initialled by foreign power plant operators were discussed for years and never went ahead. Britain's National Power negotiated for eight years from 1993 for a 2,500 megawatt power station at Jiaxing, in Zhejiang province. After all the planning and specifications had been done, the local government decided to pursue the project without a foreign partner. A smaller deal in Fujian province was also tried. After two years of negotiations, the forecast return on investment had fallen from nearly 20 per cent a year to 10 per cent; National Power pulled out and put its money instead into a plant in Spain with a guaranteed minimum return of 12 per cent a year. In 1997, after four years of equivocation, the State Planning Commission published rules governing build–operate–transfer power stations and National Power won the contract for one of two pilot projects. The company committed to invest $700 million in a plant in Changsha, in Hunan province. After three more years of negotiation, the provincial government cancelled the project, blaming National Power and saying it would keep the UK company's $10 million bid bond. The only investments the firm did make were in four tiny electricity and steam co-generation plants. In each case the local power bureau reneged on agreements stipulating the minimum prices and volumes of electricity it would buy and paid for power it did use up to two years in arrears. As of 2000, National Power was trying to sell out of the plants and expected to close its China office. The company's Chinese adventures cost it tens of millions of dollars.[22]

As demand for electricity eased in the later 1990s, it became standard practice for Chinese power bureaus to disregard the purchase agreements they had signed with producers. Yet even if demand had been greater, there was no mechanism to reward more efficient electricity generators. Instead of drawing more power from the most efficient plants – as happens in market economies – China's regional grid managers despatch electricity for a plan-standard 5,500 hours a year from each power station, representing a load factor of just over 60 per cent.[23] A cost-efficient power plant runs at over 80 per cent of capacity. Further, in cases where one region of China has a power deficit, it rarely draws electricity from a neighbouring area, because regional grids are not connected. Jealous provincial governments prefer to spend public money on new power stations rather than depend on rival provinces for electricity. In the second half of the 1990s, the sliding stock prices of listed Chinese power generators began to reflect the returns in their businesses. Shandong Huaneng Power, which floated American Depositary Receipts at $14.24 in the autumn of 1994, was trading at under $5 in 2000 before being merged with Huaneng Power International, another New York-quoted producer. The US energy company AES, which listed its China Generating Fund on the Nasdaq market in February 1994 and used the money raised to invest in a dozen Chinese power plants, watched its stock slide from $16 at listing, to $9 within two years, to $2 later in the decade. Once rabidly enthusiastic, foreign investors in Chinese stocks were beginning to realise that the country on which they fawned was not one where profit was the main driver of economic activity.[24]

The redundancy of strategy

If it had been easy to predict how adjustments to the Chinese economy would play out in the 1990s, there would have been fewer victims. International power companies came unstuck gambling on the proposition that the electricity industry would deregulate; McDonnell Douglas lost its shirt betting that in the aircraft industry nothing would change. Reality was the mess in the middle – unpredictable change, in a broadly socialist context, with the state determined to keep its hands on the levers of power. The US aircraft maker's approach to business was, if anything, too rational. The company recognised China's socialist obsession with self-sufficiency and played up to it by contracting to build aircraft on the mainland. The reasoning was that the more money state firms spent tooling up factories to make Douglas jets, the more entrenched the US company's market position would become. But the logic was flawed because it presumed logic would triumph. It did not, since principle and conviction do not decide policy in China any more than profitability does. Instead, it was bureaucratic power struggles between competing vested interests that shaped the country's trajectory.

And Douglas, despite a quarter of a century spent trying to crack the market, backed the wrong contestant.

The company had teamed up in the 1970s with Aviation Industries of China (AVIC), the ministry-level organisation in charge of aircraft manufacturing. With 560,000 employees and factories around the country, AVIC looked like the perfect planned-economy bedfellow. The organisation wanted to build a modern aircraft industry and Douglas was ready to co-manufacture planes in China. The inefficiencies of the operation, and AVIC's thirst for cash, meant the aircraft were around 20 per cent more expensive to produce than those made in America,[25] but Douglas assumed AVIC's size and influence – not to mention its backing by central government leaders – meant Chinese airlines would be forced to buy. This was where well-laid plans went awry.

In the 1980s and 1990s, China's provinces and state companies launched more than thirty new airlines. The businesses were started with public money, but the funds were raised at the provincial level or through the state banking system and therefore outside of the national plan. Most airlines were started by better-off coastal provinces which had no interest in paying over the odds for aircraft in order to support AVIC factories in inland cities like Chengdu, Xi'an or Shenyang. The apparatchiks in charge of procurement were also attracted by foreign travel and other inducements offered by Douglas's international rivals, Boeing and Airbus. As Gareth Chang, who was head of McDonnell Douglas in China until 1993, put it: 'If you're buying from Boeing you get fantastic trips to Disneyland.'[26] Douglas was not allowed, under the terms of its deal with AVIC, to solicit orders for US-made aircraft. But Chinese airlines did not want pricey China-made planes whose assembly lines could only be inspected in Shanghai.

The airlines were represented by a formerly unimportant bureaucracy, the Civil Aviation Administration of China (CAAC). However, since regional airlines placed almost all China's orders in the 1980s and 1990s, CAAC began to take on an increasingly important role in the industry. Its senior bureaucrats were rivals to the leaders of AVIC and, in the finest bureaucratic tradition, disliked them with a passion. Such inter-ministry rivalries were common but their ferocity was lost on most foreigners. In one instructive example, when Hazel O'Leary toured the country in February 1995, her department asked the US embassy to arrange an early morning meeting with the leaders of each of China's state energy corporations. What became infamous among American diplomats as the 'oil and gas breakfast' was duly organised. The representatives of China's energy industries answered the summons, but the hostility between them was palpable to everyone present. A US proposal for an open discussion on the future of an integrated industry was met with disbelief and summary rejection. Ms O'Leary waxed lyrical instead about Sino-US relations while hardly a word passed between the other attendees. 'It was,' said Charles Martin, one of the diplomats asked to organise the event, 'one of the stiffest breakfasts I have ever seen.'[27]

The bureaucratic struggle in the middle of which McDonnell Douglas found itself was equally unpleasant. CAAC did not care in the least that AVIC spent hundreds of millions of dollars of taxpayers' money tooling up factories to make Douglas aircraft. The airlines' representative was interested only in asserting its power. While AVIC was promising Douglas new orders, Joe Banko, head of the Shanghai manufacturing operation until 1993, received a very different message at meetings with senior CAAC officials: 'They [CAAC] told me personally that no way did they want to buy McDonnell Douglas aircraft,' he said.[28] It was under pressure from CAAC that AVIC cut the Trunkliner programme from 150 aircraft to forty to just twenty to be assembled in Shanghai and then dropped Douglas from the bidding for China's planned 100-seater Asian Express. CAAC said it would withdraw support for the latter project unless the partner was either Boeing or Airbus Industrie, the manufacturers with which it already had relationships. Finally, in 1998, both the Trunkliner programme and the Asian Express – which had been awarded to the Europeans in 1996 – were abandoned by central government with CAAC's blessing.

The fiasco cost China a huge amount of money, though opinions differ as to how much. Gareth Chang believes around $200 million was spent on tooling for the Trunkliner programme after 1992.[29] John Bruns, a ten-year veteran of Douglas in China, believes the true cost of the failed project to the Chinese taxpayer was in excess of a billion dollars.[30] Estimates of the amount of money lost by McDonnell Douglas vary between similar amounts. When Trunkliner was scrapped, two aircraft were already in production, the factories to make them in Shanghai, Chengdu, Xi'an and Shenyang were operational and there were Douglas staff on the ground in China. Like the three Y-10 aircraft built under Jiang Qing's auspices in the 1970s, the two MD-90s were set to become rare collectors' items, proof that China could build aircraft but not that its lumbering public sector could run a business.

Douglas's returns from more than two decades in China were forty Sino-US marriages among its staff and untold embarrassment. The latter was only highlighted when dual military–civilian machine tools the company sold in 1993 in order to lubricate the Trunkliner deal failed to turn up at their appointed destination in Beijing. A civilian factory had been licensed to accept the instruments by the US Commerce Department, but that factory did not exist. Instead, some of the machine tools ended up in Nanchang, in southern China, at a plant where Silkworm missiles are made. When Douglas discovered the breach, it reported it to the Commerce Department, generating a wave of negative publicity. The incident only added to the pain of the company's financial losses in China which, while they were not sufficient on their own to bring Douglas down, certainly helped. In the second half of the 1990s, the company sold less than half the number of aircraft each year than it had at the start of the decade. Enormous amounts of boardroom time had been wasted pursuing the China Dream. The greatest humiliation came just before the formal cancellation of the Trunkliner programme: in 1997, McDonnell Douglas was taken over by Boeing, the very rival its executives had promised to challenge through their dominance of the Chinese market. Since 1979, despite the fact that all its aircraft were imported, Boeing had outsold Douglas in China by a margin of three to one.[31] Such was the unpredictability of socialism with Chinese characteristics.

梦

Multinationals that invested in China strategised the market a hundred different ways, but ultimately there was only one constant – ubiquitous bureaucracy. The view of China as a non-socialist country implied that the state was in full-scale retreat from the economy. But this was a dubious proposition. The Chinese leviathan actually expanded during the reform period. In 1978, when Deng Xiaoping came to power, there were 4.3 million bureaucrats on the government and Party payrolls; in 1990, the number had risen to more than 9 million and in 1998 almost 11 million.[32] At the onset of reform, the Chinese government spent less than 4 per cent of its budget on administration; at the end of the 1990s the proportion was 15 per cent.[33] The leadership knew its bureaucracy was expanding out of control and periodically launched plans to cut it back. There were retrenchment campaigns in 1982, 1988 and 1993. But the machine has a life of its own. By 1998, when the most recent attempt to downsize the bureaucracy was announced, the apparatus was so bloated that the proposed lay-offs involved 4 million people – the same number as were employed in the entire national bureaucracy in 1978. The chances of achieving such a reduction are low. When pressured to retrench, ministries and local governments variously ignore edicts, shift staff to the payroll of government-owned business units or rehire them on fixed term but infinitely renewable contracts. In the latter two cases, employees are removed from official statistics about bureaucratic employment.[34]

Eleven million apparatchiks – almost one for every 100 Chinese people – have a single justification: control. Although the Chinese state's grip has loosened in some areas of everyday life – the urban street committees are less

Why would companies want to deal w/ such restrictions and tight control?

powerful than two decades ago – in matters new and economic official paranoia leads to farcical invasions into commercial activity. Regulations published in August 1999, for example, required both the questions and answers in any market survey to be approved by a government office in Beijing. A few months later, concern that encrypted communications on channels such as the internet were inhibiting the government's ability to monitor information led to the setting up of the State Encryption Management Commission. This committee, with representatives from the Ministry of Defence, the State Security Bureau, the Public Security Bureau, the Ministry of Information Industry and others, demanded that all users of encryption technologies hand over their codes or be judged illegal. Since even Microsoft software includes some basic encryption, technically this made criminals of almost every computer user in China.[35]

Licensing

With the decision to open the economy to foreign involvement in the 1980s and 1990s, the Chinese government created the biggest commercial licensing regime in the world. No company could operate a factory or open an office without licences. In many sectors, licences are needed not only for the general right to conduct business but to increase production, change products, alter a company's geographic area of activity or adjust pricing.[36] Foreign investors became fixated on the need to obtain licences, yet they rarely delivered the freedom of action necessary to run a profitable business. After seven years of paying American politicians to lobby on its behalf and spending millions of dollars on gestures of goodwill, the American insurer Chubb obtained an operating licence in August 2000. It allowed the company to open an insurance business only in Shanghai, selling only property – not life – insurance products and then only to foreign-invested joint ventures.

If the Chinese insurance market was smaller than expected at the end of the 1990s, Shanghai was a fraction of that and foreign-invested companies in Shanghai a further fraction. Gross premiums for property insurance in the city the year Chubb obtained its licence were $405 million. In theory, the premiums of the 17,000 foreign-invested businesses to which Chubb was entitled to sell might be one-tenth of the total, but most multinationals use global insurance programmes and do not buy cover locally. According to American Insurance Group (AIG), which has been active in Shanghai since 1992, the actual number of foreign-invested companies buying insurance in the city in 2000 was around 1,000.[37] The China Insurance Regulatory Commission put foreign property insurers' share of the Shanghai market at 3–5 per cent, or $12–20 million a year. For the right to target this business, Chubb had to deposit a bond of $24 million with a state bank. After the years of waiting and spending in pursuit of an operating licence, it was a risible deal.

In life insurance, the business pie was larger – $850 million in Shanghai in

1998 – but seven foreign companies had been licensed, so the market was more split. A majority share was held by Chinese companies which, facing serious competition only in one city, slashed prices locally to maintain their positions. Further, foreign insurers were limited to annuity life insurance – not health or pension plans or comprehensive group programmes. With the exception of the first licensee, AIG, the other foreign insurers found themselves losing money. The size of the available market, the cost of expatriate staff and bureaucratic restrictions meant that permission to sell insurance in China was a licence to make not profits but losses. By 2000, the foreign insurers had forgotten the market projections they made in the 1990s and were looking to expand their opportunities instead via China's accession to the World Trade Organisation (which occurred in December 2001). Even after accession, however, market opening under the WTO would be at least three to five years away.[38]

They came like sheep, and they were sheared

The more than sixty private equity funds that assembled nearly $6 billion for direct investment in China in the 1990s were like lambs to the slaughter in the prevailing bureaucratic environment.[39] Their investment strategy was to buy into state companies, increase profitability and sell out via public listings. It was an approach that had been tried and tested in more developed markets, but in China it was totally at odds with what was practicable. Most investors were able to secure only minority stakes in the companies they bought into and so were not in a position to exert any management control. State business managers were less interested in profitability than in investment projects and perks; the expectations of shareholders were wholly unfamiliar. Most important, there was no mechanism for foreign investors to cash out of the public companies into which they had invested. The listing process on the Shanghai and Shenzhen stock exchanges was controlled by central government. Only companies that appeared on a Beijing-sanctioned list were allowed to issue shares.[40] And the government's agenda was to raise money by listing wholly state-owned enterprises; this left no room for foreigners. Even foreign-backed listings in Hong Kong were blocked because the government believed they reduced the pool of capital available to itself.

Most private equity funds were unable to invest all the money they raised for China because they could not find investments to satisfy the criteria they promised their backers. The funds were established on the basis of returns of at least 20 per cent a year and an exit within five to ten years. With no management control and no possibility of listing, this was impossible. More conservative managers redirected as much of their China cash as possible to investments in Hong Kong or other parts of Asia. AIG's $1 billion Asian

Infrastructure Fund – which claimed to be the biggest ever raised for emerging markets – delivered only a fraction of the $500 million it earmarked for China. Mark Mobius, who raised the $800 million Templeton Dragon Fund, changed its terms of incorporation to allow it to invest in Taiwan, helping to secure a modest aggregate return of 3 per cent a year between 1994 and 2000.[41] Most China private equity funds, however, were legally committed to investing most of their money on the mainland. At least $3 billion flowed into projects in the mid 1990s, usually with unpleasant results.[42]

Private equity landed itself in a morass of bureaucratic obfuscation, fraud and corruption. In their hurry to tap the market, international investors unwittingly teamed up with every villain on the block. Wang Baosen, executive vice-mayor of Beijing, hired by ING Baring as 'special adviser' to its $70 million Beijing Investment Fund, was found dead in countryside outside the capital in 1995. Mr Wang – feted on an expenses-paid trip to ING headquarters in Holland – turned out to have been one of the ringleaders in a vast bribery network that extended all the way up to the Beijing Party secretary and Tiananmen apologist Chen Xitong. It was unclear whether Mr Wang committed suicide or was executed by his peers. Whichever, by the end of the decade, ING's Hong Kong-listed fund had lost three-quarters of its value. Venturetech, the princeling-managed firm that ran its own Hong Kong-listed investment fund and acted as a consultant to foreigners on theirs, was closed down by the central government in 1995 under the weight of accumulated debts. The company's China Assets Fund, which was backed by the likes of Standard Chartered, James Capel and the Asian Development Bank, had fallen to a fraction of its listing price, while Venturetech left behind it a trail of aggrieved counter-parties, among them Hong Kong real estate tycoon Ronnie Chan and Wall Street investment bank Goldman Sachs.

Jack Perkowski's ASIMCO seemed to suffer every scam being run in its two automotive private equity funds, but it was not an exceptional case. In a joint venture in Zhuhai in Guangdong province, an employee conspired with staff of a local state bank to defraud the company through a fake letter of credit. ASIMCO took the matter to court, where the judge asked if the firm might help him obtain an American green card. ASIMCO did not oblige and the judge ruled the joint venture was liable for the bank's loss on the letter of credit, despite the collusion of bank personnel. The US company took the case to the local branch of China's anti-corruption bureau, which said it was willing to investigate it but would first require a car and working capital. In 2000, ASIMCO was awaiting a hearing before the Supreme Court. The joint venture employee who had devised the fraud had fled, ironically, to the US, from where he could not be extradited because of China's human rights record. In Jingzhou, in Hubei province, the general manager of another ASIMCO joint venture transferred land belonging to the business to the balance sheet of the Chinese investor's parent company. This was prior to the publicly held parent being listed on the Shanghai stock exchange. The land was being double sold. When ASIMCO announced that the manager was fired, the US firm's president, Tim Clissold, was barricaded in a room for twelve hours by thirty people demanding he sign a document to revoke the sacking. Another eighty protesters and several local policemen milled around outside. Mr Clissold was eventually released, but only having suffered considerable trauma. In five years, ASIMCO faced four serious fraud cases – affecting a quarter of its joint ventures.[43]

If fraud was common, bureaucratic struggles with state companies became the daily staple of the private equity investor. ASIMCO found it necessary to change fifteen out of seventeen general managers at its joint ventures and almost every dismissal involved a protracted fight. In such an environment, it was extremely difficult to improve the operational performance of invested businesses. Six years after making its first China acquisition, not only had ASIMCO been forced to sell out of its breweries at a heavy loss, but the investments in both its automotive funds were carrying accumulated operating losses as well.[44] Despite all this, the tenacity and determination of Jack Perkowski and his colleagues was unbroken. Unable to collect payments or enforce contracts in China's domestic economy, ASIMCO switched its strategy instead to export manufacturing. A new plan was hatched to become an automotive components supplier to vehicle makers overseas. When asked what strength such perseverance drew on, Tim Clissold remarked: 'Jack wants to be a footnote in the pages of history. He wants to be the only guy who made it work in China.'[45]

By the end of the 1990s, the competition was disappearing. Around twenty private equity funds – a third of the total – had cut their losses and dissolved.[46] China Cement Corp., which lost most of its $200 million raised from the likes of Baring and Oppenheimer, was abandoned as early as 1995. China North Industries Investment, the $185 million Dublin- and Singapore-listed fund fronted by Chinese arms trader Norinco, was suspended in February 1999 after auditors PricewaterhouseCoopers refused to sign off its accounts. At suspension the fund was trading at a quarter of its original listing price. Managers who were fired by the board on the grounds of poor performance then refused to hand over the accounts and records of the invested businesses in China; two years later, litigation was unresolved.[4?] Managers Jardine Fleming, Kleinwort Benson, Newbridge Capital, Citi?
Inc., Crosby Asset Management and more all wound down their f?

heavy losses. Others persevered only out of concern for possible legal action. 'If it wasn't for the fear of being sued by their investors, many managers would just walk away and give their shares to their Chinese partner,' said Roger Marshall, who ran Crosby's fund.[48]

Investment bankers also skulked away from what they had thought would be the deal fest of the century. There was no deregulation of their business. Investment banks were allowed to work only on listings of Chinese companies that took place in Hong Kong or overseas as well as token 'B share' offerings in hard currency in Shanghai and Shenzhen. Underwriting of the real market – a thousand domestic 'A share' issues that took place in the course of the 1990s – was off limits, as was trading in the primary bond market.[49] With the exception of the overseas listings of telecoms companies China Mobile and China Unicom, the average Chinese initial public offering in Hong Kong – or the handful which took place in other centres like New York – was both small and bureaucratically fraught. Investment banks charged standard international fees,[50] but the cost of taking a state company to market was far higher than in other countries. Chinese state enterprises typically had no clear ownership structures, no internationally acceptable accounts and carried with them the liabilities of socialist cradle-to-grave welfare – unfunded pension liabilities and company schools, hospitals, housing stock, even fire brigades.

It frequently took more than a year, and the involvement of scores of investment bank staff, to prepare a listing.[51] By the time a business was fit for its initial public offering, the fees on a typical $50–200 million equity sale could not cover the costs of either the investment banks or the international accountancy companies which assisted them. The scale of the listings was small because the Chinese government would sell only minority stakes in its companies. Fees could not be increased because competition was fierce. As Frank Hawke, a veteran of the market at Salomon Brothers, put it at the time of the Asian financial crisis in 1997: 'China's investment banking wallet is the size of Thailand's or Malaysia's when they were healthy. But do they have the same number of investment bankers?'[52] The answer was no – a fraction of the personnel would be committed to south-east Asian countries. Fifty international investment banks were chasing China business in the 1990s – forty-two were in place early enough to apply to be underwriters on China's first Hong Kong listing, Tsingtao, in July 1993.[53]

There was nothing like enough business to go round. Morgan Stanley, which paid a king's ransom to convert the tennis court at Shanghai's Portman Shangri-la hotel into its principal China office, never staffed the building. There was no chief representative and no investment bankers. A lone secretary was left to man the entrance hall and field telephone calls.[54] The firm continued to handle its China operations out of Hong Kong. Merrill Lynch, whose chairman and chief executive Dan Tully declared when opening his mainland offices: 'China's economy is already one of the most important in the world', did send a chief representative to Shanghai.[55] In the mid 1990s, the gentleman was often to be found in his office in the Portman Shanghai Centre playing patience on his desk.[56] This was at the same time as Merrill Lynch was running costly advertisements on the regional television service, Star TV, declaiming its commitment to the vast China market.

Busy doing nothing

The most common memory of businessmen who have worked in China tends to be of the amount of time they wasted. Just before Christmas 1999, a Beijing manager of the Anglo-Australian mining company Rio Tinto was preparing to leave the country. Standing outside his office building on a chilly winter day, he reflected: 'I've been here for three years and I haven't done a thing.'[57] The executive, who arrived in China thinking his predecessor – who also achieved nothing – must have been either lazy or incompetent, tried in vain to advance two coal mining projects. After three years, nothing had progressed. He consoled himself that most of the expatriates he knew had comparable experiences, saying of his friends: 'We don't even talk about work any more. There's nothing to talk about.'

For the average Chinese bureaucrat, time is not money – it is the interval between meals, between going to the office and leaving it, between the end of work on Friday and its start again on Monday. Chinese communist culture teaches that the smartest way to negotiate is to hold out the longest. This is the same in politics – as when Chinese government representatives held seventeen rounds of talks with Hong Kong governor Chris Patten without reaching agreement on election procedures – or in business. The result is that an outside investor's expenditure to set up a deal in China – what economists call the 'transaction cost' – is extraordinarily high. In 1997, the International Finance Corporation, the private lending arm of the World Bank, conducted a review of twenty-five industrial joint ventures in which it had either assisted or invested in China. The organisation found that the average amount of staff time needed to process an investment was twice as much as in its projects in Latin America, South Africa or India, half as much again as in the Russian Federation and more than five times as much as in Turkey. Worldwide, only Vietnam came anywhere close to matching China for bureaucratic inertia.[58]

Alan Smith, chairman of Hong Kong broker and investment bank Jardine Fleming, relates an experience he believes encapsulated the difference between doing business in mainland China and doing business in a free market like Hong Kong. In early 1993, Mr Smith was summoned to a meeting with a senior government official in Shanghai. Like many such meetings attended by foreign executives, it was of no real consequence yet could not be avoided because of the possibility of upsetting a high-ranking bureaucrat. Stuck in Shanghai's then-chaotic traffic on his way to the appointment, Mr Smith decided to call Ronnie Chan, the Hong Kong real estate magnate. He knew that Mr Chan was in the market for a convertible bond issue for his company, Hang Lung. The men talked for fifteen minutes, Mr Chan saying he already had a good offer from Salomon Brothers. Mr Smith hung up and called his Hong Kong office to discuss with colleagues how they might make a better offer. He then called Mr Chan back, spoke for another fifteen minutes and closed the deal for a $120 million convertible bond issue at a 2.5 per cent fee. The fee was the same as investment banks were earning for Hong Kong listings of Chinese state companies. But whereas those listings, which were usually for less than $100 million, took thousands of man hours to complete, Mr Smith – on his way to another dead-end encounter – closed his deal in the space of a cross-town car ride. 'The point,' he says, 'is we did that deal over the phone. To do that deal in China would take a year.'[59]

Mr Chan would agree. Like other Hong Kong property developers accustomed to buying land in the territory, obtaining planning permission and finishing multi-skyscraper projects in three to four years, he was subjected to his own rude awakening on the mainland. Comparable real estate developments in Chinese cities took two to three times as long. Hang Lung entered two large projects in Shanghai in the early 1990s. Land for the first, Grand Gateway, was bought from the army in December 1992. Seven years later, the company was struggling to finish one of five towers and a central shopping mall. It was almost certain the full project would not be completed within a decade.[60] Land for the second project, Plaza 66 on Nanjing Road near the Portman Shanghai Centre, was bought in a Venturetech-brokered deal in December 1993. By 2000, Hang Lung's many times-revised plan was to open the first of two towers in 2001, again after seven years. Delays escalated expenditure on the projects so much that by the end of the decade the company no longer included the cost of capital in its calculations of rental yields. If the cost of financing were included, there would be no return.[61]

As was standard practice, Hang Lung paid up more than 90 per cent of the cost of its land – $331 million – within six months of the contracts being signed. [62] At this point, there was a contractual obligation for the sites to be ready for development. But the contracts were meaningless. The Shanghai district governments with which the firm dealt said they could only relocate residents and begin demolition once they had cash. Site clearance took more than a year. When it was time to install infrastructure, the real bureaucratic battle was joined. The water bureau wanted special fees to connect up water supplies and sewerage, even though such fees had been ruled illegal by the central government. Hang Lung obtained a copy of the original central government directive to this effect, but the water bureau said it had received no direct instruction. And the telephone bureau said it could only provide lines to Grand Gateway if an entire telephone exchange was purchased – a large and unnecessary expenditure. Such gouging was relentless, but there was little the company could do because utility suppliers are state-owned monopolies willing to out-wait those who need their services. The costs of unforeseen expenditure combined with the costs of delay. By the end of the 1990s, Hang Lung reckoned its construction spend in Shanghai was no less than in Hong Kong – around $125 per square foot ($1,350 per square metre).[63] The price of grasping bureaucracy and inefficiency destroyed any savings made from China's $50 per man per month labour costs. And while Hong Kong's real estate market saw only a limited downturn in the later 1990s, Shanghai's crashed by more than two-thirds.

Jurassic Park

If the Chinese government was unable to control its bureaucrats, it was equally unable to contain the broader state sector. Just as the number of apparatchiks grew during the reform period, so did that of employees in state industry. In 1978 the non-administrative state sector had an official payroll of 75 million people; this had risen by the late 1990s to over 112 million. There were millions more people who were not on the official 'state-owned units' payroll but were none the less direct employees of state-controlled companies; it is quite possible, adding in an appropriate portion of collective workers, that in 2000 actual state sector employment was as high as 200 million.[64] The government talked the language of downsizing – and the outside world bought into this – but in reality the majority of urban inhabitants at the end of the decade were public servants.

The government's inability to get to grips with its vast state sector was nowhere more conspicuous than in its antipathy to bankruptcy. China's bankruptcy rate in the late 1990s was at most 0.05 per cent of companies per year – one-twentieth the level of the United States.[65] A decade after the country enacted a bankruptcy law in 1988, only 16,000 businesses had gone to the wall. Most of these were not state-owned enterprises but private firms, collectives and foreign-invested companies. Even when a state company was bankrupted, the process was often a sham. In 1996, the Chinese state media trumpeted the biggest bankruptcy to date, that of the 18,000-worker Shanxi Textile Dyeing Plant. It was reported that in this model insolvency case the assets of the business had found a ready purchaser which had paid $59 million and hired many of the redundant employees. The buyer turned out to be another state company set up specifically for the purpose of the acquisition by the provincial authorities. At other times, central government reached for bankruptcy where it faced claims from foreign creditors. In January 1999, Guangdong International Trust and Investment Corp., which foreign banks had fallen over themselves to lend to in the early 1990s, was put into liquidation. It, and its sister company Guangdong Enterprises, owed creditors – mostly overseas institutions – $10 billion; they were expected to wait years to receive around 20 cents on the dollar.

Throughout the 1990s there was talk in government circles of a new law, one which would facilitate a higher level of bankruptcies by increasing the rights of creditors. The drafting of legislation began in the middle of the decade, but five years later no law had been put before the National People's Congress for ratification.[66] The central government was unnerved by the implications for unemployment and the banking system, which would have to write off huge losses. The state fell back instead on a 'rationalisation' policy that involved few bankruptcies and limited numbers of real redundancies. None the less, the post-1997 premier, Zhu Rongji, claimed in 1998 that he could 'solve' the public sector problem within three years. State enterprises were pressured to send quotas of surplus workers home and pay them only subsistence wages, a condition known as 'xia gang', meaning that a person has 'stepped down' from his post.[67] State companies themselves were allowed to continue in business, albeit with marginally reduced operating costs. Smaller public companies were encouraged to merge with larger ones in a process which resembled the cleaning up of a ubiquitous mess by sweeping it into fewer but larger piles.

At the Anshan Iron & Steel Works in northern Liaoning province, the chairman, Liu Jie, explained how the approach played out.[68] His main businesses employs 180,000 people.[69] But his group company controls more than 400 other local firms, mostly collectives, with another 180,000 employees.[70] Mr Liu named some of his businesses: 'We make machinery. We have a construction company. We have a cement factory. We have a computer company. We have an electronic goods company. There is a transportation company, a drainage systems company, two mining companies. We have a big service company. Then there are other industrial development companies. And we also have milk businesses – it's very good milk, my grandson loves it. We have a fruit farm producing apples. And we have a factory making socks.'[71]

Around the country, forced agglomeration accelerated in the late 1990s. Baoshan Steel in Shanghai, one of China's few profitable steel producers, was required to take over failed local plants with more than ten times its number of employees.[72] There was no problem keeping these businesses open because the large companies selected to become merger conglomerates had guaranteed credit lines. They enjoyed special 'principal bank agreements' with one of the big four state banks, allowing for loans on demand. Few questions were asked about where the loans would end up or how they might be repaid. The result of the merger process was that there was no fundamental change in the economic landscape, merely a tidying up of a failed model. Over capacity was maintained in almost every sector of the economy. Official data showed that one-fifth of steel output in 1998 remained unsold, yet new manufacturing capacity was still being added.[73] A visit to any supermarket in China would have revealed a similar story with household consumer goods. Around the country, there are scores of different detergent powders on sale – thirty in the Carrefour hypermarket in Beijing alone. Almost all are produced by state companies. Many cities have their own local brand, and Shanghai has two – the equivalent of Manhattan having its own washing powder. International manufacturers like Henkel, Unilever and Procter & Gamble – all of which lost money in China in the late 1990s – are adamant the state companies sell at below cost.[74] With guaranteed bank credit, they can afford to do so.

The Chinese government's anti-bankruptcy stance destroyed profit for everybody – foreign and Chinese companies alike. Although state businesses were little interested in profit – status and employment were their driving forces – local as well as foreign private companies were frustrated to find that however hard they worked margins were either razor-thin or negative. The central bank and the Ministry of Finance were conscious of the damage being done to the economy by overcapacity, but the government as a whole was powerless to act. After the prices of cars, trucks and motorcycles – produced by a state sector with 140 automotive makers and 2000 component manufacturers – fell throughout the 1990s, the government's response was to introduce 'price floors' – minimum prices below which producers were not allowed to sell. The policy was repeated in other industries. Anything was preferable to closing down production capacity.[75]

Towards the end of the decade, as the deadline approached for Zhu Rongji's 'solution' to the state sector problem, the government published figures showing that profitability was improving dramatically.[76] But the numbers were not credible. State sector managers knew what Beijing wanted to hear, and when it wanted to hear it. There were many ways to sell output at below cost and use creative accounting to book revenue as profit – there is no such thing as independent auditing for most Chinese state enterprises. If businesses lacked the cashflow to pay workers – and they often did – they took out new bank loans to cover the shortfall. It was no surprise that the reported increases in state sector profitability – and so an alleged reduction in the number of loss-making companies – coincided with a period of looser bank credit and a government fiscal stimulus package in the last three years of the decade which disbursed tens of billions of dollars.[77] By this point, the post-1994 austerity measures were long since forgotten. It was only rising deficit spending that was keeping the economy moving.

梦

Many state companies survived in a condition of industrial limbo, hardly needing to adapt to modern business practice. In the Maoist era of socialist self-sufficiency, China developed its own technologies for everything from oil exploration and chemical processing to tunnelling, bridge building, steel and glass making and cement and gypsum production.[78] The techniques were rudimentary by international standards. Foreign investors regarded the methodologies with barely concealed contempt and expected to drive their state-owned competitors to the wall. But this assumed that bankruptcies would occur, that quality would affect purchasing decisions and that credit would not be given to loss-making enterprises. All these assumptions were wrong, and at the end of the twentieth century the Chinese state sector was still churning out goods made in ways that many foreign managers had not known existed.

In the cement business, four-fifths of Chinese output comes not from modern rotary kilns but from vertical shaft kilns similar to those that produced the first cement in Europe in the early nineteenth century. China makes one-third of all the cement in the world using a process that is nearly 200 years old.[79] The vertical kilns are generally small and housed inside low-rise buildings. Limestone, silica and alumina are shovelled on top of cheap – usually brown – coal, which is ignited. Vast clouds of black smoke fill the air and the chemical process that creates the base for cement begins. When the process is finished, the kiln is cleared and refilled. The output of a vertical kiln is as little as 50 tons a day, compared with 1,000 tons or more in a modern plant. But the costs of building a vertical kiln are as little as $500,000, versus $100 million for a 2,000 ton-a-day rotary kiln. There are 7,000 vertical kilns in China – three for every county in the country.[80]

The quality of Chinese cement is low. In most countries, building regulations and market forces would mean it could not be used. But in China building regulations are either non-existent or unenforced and the private housing market is so small that little consumer pressure is exerted. People who have not paid a market price for their homes rarely enquire into how they were built. Nor do state banks worry about financing construction work that may collapse before their loans are repaid. Roads and buildings with a lifespan of 15–20 years are standard. China is littered with construction that looks as if it took place in the 1950s, but was actually put up in the 1980s or early 1990s. There is often a perverse logic to this in the country's socialist economy. In recent years, for example, the pavements in many cities have been replaced as part of the national fiscal stimulus programme. But instead of using internationally standard 2.5 inch (6cm) paving stones made with high quality cement which last thirty years, local governments usually laid 1.2–1.6 inch (3–4cm) paving stones made with bad cement which begin to break up after two or three years. There is no reason to do otherwise. There is a vast state business making paving stones which would have to downsize if demand fell. Almost every city has its wholly state-owned, or state joint venture, paving company. In Shanghai, every district has its own paving stone company.[81] These 'businesses' rarely make profits, not least because there are too many of them. Their role is simply to exist.

The dream of every local government in China, down to the level of more than 2,000 counties, is to have its own, complete industrial base – a car factory, a steel factory, a cement factory, and so on. This reflects a number of pressures. There is the psychology of the shortage economy which dominated the Maoist era. There is the tradition of fierce local and regional competition. Above all, there is the fact that credit is controlled by the state and is not subject to market pricing. Like a child with a full piggybank in a toy shop, Chinese bureaucrats grab at everything in sight. Possession is all; the larger picture of the national economy is not in view. China's state economy at the end of the 1990s combined the traditional, monolithic enterprises controlled by central government with massive numbers of small state and collective companies controlled by local governments. Despite the official merger policy, local protectionism sustained most of these businesses. By the late 1990s, there were 800 factories making transformers for electricity distribution – nearly thirty for every province. Most supplied only their local utility, which typically had a shareholding in the business.[82]

The attempts of foreign and private Chinese companies to compete with the hydra-like monster of state industry were, to say the least, unrewarding. In the cement business, vertical kiln plants are totally at odds with China's environmental regulations. But those regulations are rarely applied to state companies. They are rigorously applied to non-state companies. Lafarge, a

State-owned businesses can do what they want.

French building materials company which took over a Beijing plant, spent $1 million raising it to international environmental standards. The company was still fined by zealous local officials for dust emissions.[83] At the same time, nearby state-owned vertical kiln plants billowed great clouds of raw smoke directly into the environment, helping to make Beijing one of the ten dirtiest cities in the world.[84]

Due to overcapacity, the price of cement in China halved in the course of the 1990s reaching the lowest level in the world.[85] Lafarge, which ran one of the most efficient plants in the country, scraped an operating profit – excluding the costs of capital as well as those of funding its expatriate-run Beijing office – by producing high grade cement and targeting model national construction projects where quality was an issue. But when the company applied to increase its output, it was stalled. Bureaucrats accepted an application for a new production line in 1997 but by the end of 2000 they had not approved it.[86] While loss-makers could not close, a profitable business was not allowed to expand to reach economies of scale. Like most other foreign investors, Lafarge continued in the hope that the operating environment would improve. If it did not, there was no point in working harder than anywhere else in the world for a negligible return. In 2000, the company estimated it had a less than 5 per cent share of the Beijing cement market but a 50 per cent share of the market's profits; yet the return was still lower than could be obtained by making a deposit with a French high street bank.

梦

The International Finance Corporation (IFC), which invested in and lent to two dozen industrial joint ventures in China in the 1990s, also backed cement plants. These, and most of the other investments, were running at an operating loss by the end of the decade. In an internal note to IFC and World Bank colleagues in 1999, China chief of mission Davin Mackenzie gave an unusually frank summary of the reasons for failure: 'The half-reformed nature of China's economy has structural barriers to achieving fair returns,' he wrote. 'The rules of business in China are fundamentally different from those of most market economies. Until these rules subtantially change, it will continue to be impossible to make a fair return, regardless of China's growth rate or exchange rate. While China's macro-economic condition is of course important, what really matters in the long run is structural reform … How can a large, world-scale plant, with the latest proprietary technology that is built to produce the highest quality with the lowest pollution, and sponsored by an investor who must produce a return for its home country shareholders and must repay its bank debt, how can such an investor get a decent return against competition that need not care about quality, the environment, providing an equity return, or repaying its bank loans?'[87]

The IFC also cited abuse of intellectual property and absence of the rule of law as serious impediments to profitable endeavour. Counterfeiting of branded products in China was so serious by the late 1990s that when Henkel, the German manufacturer of household products, commissioned market research firm A. C. Nielsen to survey its sales, results showed the company was selling 130 per cent of what was leaving its factories. The difference between output and sales was accounted for by fakes.[88] Pfizer, the US manufacturer of Viagra, having been held up by the State Drug Administration for four years before it was allowed to launch its potency drug, did so to discover that there were already fifty products claiming the same effect on the market. All were sold under the product name 'Wei Ge', a transliteration of Viagra meaning 'big man' that is also a slang term for a large penis. Pfizer opted for a different, meaningless transliteration of Viagra – 'Wan ai ke' – but was so late into the market that Wei Ge was already established as Chinese Viagra.[89] Fifty-three multinationals, including Henkel, Volkswagen, Procter & Gamble, Unilever and PepsiCo, joined together to launch an anti-counterfeit lobbying group – the China Anti-Counterfeiting Coalition – in 2000. But the problem is endemic and government units or officials are usually involved in the crime. The state manufacturer of compact disks visited by Deng Xiaoping on his Southern Tour in 1992, Shenfei Laser Optical Systems, turned out to be one of the biggest music and video pirates in China and was closed down only after years of US government pressure.[90] Most consumer goods, chemicals and auto parts companies operating in China in the late 1990s expected a quarter of their branded merchandise on sale in the country to be fakes.

Legal recourse over counterfeiting, or any other issue, was fraught. Just as the government committed itself to the contradiction in terms of a 'socialist market economy', so it promised 'socialist rule of law'. Both these anodyne concepts were enshrined in amendments to the constitution.[91] What socialist rule of law meant in practice was that government talked about its judiciary as being independent, while judges continued to be nominated by municipal and provincial Communist Party committees and formally approved by local people's congresses. The congresses in turn provided the salaries, housing and welfare benefits of judges, who ranked lower than either Party or government officials in the bureaucratic pecking order. Judges, many of whom were ex-military personnel with no formal legal training, were expected to discuss sensitive cases with members of their local Communist Party political–legal committees before making rulings.[92] This was the socialist part of the rule of law. There were improvements in the quality of judicial procedure in the 1990s, as younger, more educated judges came to the bench. But the judiciary remained an administrative tool of the government and the ruling Communist Party.

China offered business investors the alternative of arbitration within the country or, under its 1988 signature of the New York convention, binding hearings before international arbitration tribunals such as those in Stockholm and Paris. The impartiality of domestic arbitration was called into question in the 1990s by accusations of corruption, and the number of cases brought before the China International Economic and Trade Arbitration Commission (CIETAC) declined from 1995.[93] But even when arbitration was undertaken overseas – requiring the prior contractual agreement of a Chinese party – it was plagued by the biggest problem of China's legal system, the failure to enforce verdicts. In the regular court system in the late 1990s, around 40 per cent of rulings went unenforced. The situation was so bad that the Supreme People's Procuratorate launched a campaign to make 1999 'Enforcement Year'.[94] For arbitration rulings, which depended on the regular court system for enforcement whether they were made in China or elsewhere, the chances of satisfaction were even lower. A survey of seventy-two foreign and Chinese arbitration cases by an American lawyer in 2000 revealed that only half the rulings were enforced. The more money that was involved in a case, the less likely were the court enforcers to recover it.[95] With such poor odds of recovery stacked on top of the time and expense of litigation, as well as the possibility of unfair hearings and gerrymandering, socialist rule of law bore only a passing resemblance to international rule of law.

Socialism today, socialism tomorrow

The last and least quantifiable aspect of China's socialist legacy was its education system. That the country has a generation of people who missed out on formal education because of the closure of schools during the Cultural Revolution – from 1966 to 1976 – is well known. Less widely recognised is how long it took to rebuild a system of education after the Cultural Revolution and how flawed that system remains. In 1979, China was short of 3.5 million teachers. In the rush to qualify new ones in the 1980s, many primary level and most secondary level instructors were licensed without meeting the minimum official standards for their posts.[96] There was almost no modernisation of teaching methods, even in the 1990s. The Communist Party maintained a tight grip on educational practice – controlling the content of textbooks and requiring long hours of political indoctrination. Most resources were targeted at a small number of 'key schools' in big cities, monopolised by the children of Party and government officials. In the past decade, spending on education as a proportion of the national economy has fallen significantly, as key schools have been indulged but general education sidelined.[97] In this elitist system, just 3.5 per cent of Chinese children have the chance to go to university within China, compared with 6 per cent in India or 9 per cent in Indonesia.[98]

Those who can afford to go abroad to study do so; few return. Like other authoritarian states, China has paid a high price for its autocracy in terms of a 'brain drain'. Between 1978 and 1999, more than 300,000 of the country's best students left to study in the United States, Britain, Australia and Canada. Estimates of the proportion that came back range between one-tenth and one-third.[99] By 2000, the number of student visas being issued by western embassies in China had risen to 60,000 a year; at Beijing University, one of the best in the country, a third of students left the country upon graduation.[100] The beneficiaries of this flow have been the economies of New York, California, London, Sydney, Vancouver and other favoured destinations where research institutes and businesses alike can recruit the cream of Chinese talent.

Within China, the Party's paranoia about opening up the education system, combined with student flight, has left the nation with a dearth of professional employees. The graduation of certified public accountants (CPAs) began only in 1996; of 38,000 registered CPAs in the second half of the decade, 80 per cent had qualified in the 1940s and 1950s and were over sixty years old.[101] The number of lawyers rose from just over 200 in 1979 to 50,000 in 1995, but many had little formal training.[102] The biggest shortages were for qualified managers. Masters of Business Administration (MBA) courses only started in the mid 1990s. Fudan University's School of Management in Shanghai, the largest in the country, graduated just 270 students in 1997. A joint venture MBA school, China–Europe International Business School (CEIBS), also in Shanghai, turned out 240 graduates that year. This in a city that already had 20,000 foreign-invested enterprises in search of Chinese professionals.[103]

Investors discovered that human resource constraints were no less a problem than a bureaucratic operating environment or overestimated markets. Business survey data through the 1990s showed that multinationals were forced to operate with one expatriate manager for every two to three Chinese managers, such was the difficulty of localisation.[104] Even for the few genuinely successful companies, the average $250,000–350,000 annual cost of expatriates ate up profits.[105] Nokia, which surpassed a billion dollars of China revenue in 1997, had 200 foreigners on the ground.[106] International companies knew that they had to use cheaper local managers to have any chance of making profits, but there was far too much demand chasing precious little supply. In a survey of 229 foreign businesses in 1998, the top three responses as to how profits could be achieved were all to do with personnel: training to increase productivity, localising management, and transferring critical management capabilities to Chinese professionals. Seventy per cent of companies said these were the keys to success; but only one-tenth claimed any progress in implementing the changes.[107]

Foreign executives were flummoxed by the human resource situation because they perceived a paradox. On the one hand, the Chinese work ethic was undeniably strong. In line with reports from individual companies, the 1998 *World Competitiveness Yearbook* ranked the motivation of Chinese workers second only to that of Japan's in Asia.[108] However, when investors tried to harness China's labour for anything more than the simplest manufacturing tasks, they were confounded by a combination of lack of experience, shortage of professional talent and an inability to move beyond the restrictive world view instilled by the Chinese education system. At the end of the century, the most productive and effective human capital in the country was still young women working on the production lines of export processing factories in southern China. Global business had figured out how to shift money, technology and ideas around the world at an unprecedented rate; it was having much less success changing Chinese employees in the face of the Chinese Communist Party's grip on education and the media.

Criticisms of educational practice are common to other parts of Asia. In Japan, the system of instruction by rote – one still more pronounced in China – is said to stifle creativity. In south-east Asia, outsiders point to government interference in the setting of curricula and the writing of text books. But the Chinese situation is far more acute than either, because it combines a traditional prejudice against individual expression with pro-active classroom indoctrination backed up by the largest state propaganda machine in the world. Whatever promises the government may make about other parts of its bureaucracy, it has never once intimated that it will entertain changes to the machinery of thought control. Foreign travel and interchange broaden some minds, but in most respects the intellectual operating environment of international business in China is akin to that of the Soviet Union prior to its disintegration. No one in that period thought of eastern Europe or Russia as a natural context in which capitalists would make money. Logically, the same view should have applied to China in the last two decades of the twentieth century. But it didn't.

9

Other people's money

'Debt is not an issue in China as far as the Bank is concerned'
A senior World Bank economist, interviewed by the author in January 1998[1]

IF THE ONLY thing that had been wasted in China in the 1990s was for-eigners' cash, there would be no cause for concern about the country's future. The Chinese government would be due congratulations for continu-ing to woo tens of billions of dollars of foreign direct investment a year despite evidence that returns on much of that capital were either negative or below bank deposit rates. China, with its population of nearly 1.3 billion,[2] historical sophistication and wealthy overseas diaspora, is the easiest mar-keting job on the planet, but its $350 billion haul of foreign money since 1979 is still a wonder to behold. The country set a record for investment flows into a developing economy that is unlikely to be beaten.

Unfortunately, outsiders' money is not enough to meet the needs of the Chinese state. Foreign investment created numerous revenue streams for the government – including land and property leases, taxation and business fees. But while the sums of money involved are significant, running by the late 1990s to billions of dollars a year, they are nowhere near enough.[3] A vast bureaucracy, a state enterprise sector employing as many as 200 million people and thousands of pet government investment projects create cash demands that cannot be met from foreign inflows. In the period after 1990, between a quarter and a half of industrial state enterprises lost money in any given year.[4] By the late 1990s, official losses – minimised by accounting stan-dards that allow for slow depreciation, few write-offs of bad debt and fre-quent non-inclusion of interest payments on loans – were running at over $10 billion a year; in reality they were far higher.[5] The government's narcis-sistic construction projects, from the gargantuan Three Gorges dam on the Yangzi river, to the creation of a second Shanghai in Pudong, to thousands of lesser undertakings, required billions of dollars of financing. And the state apparatus itself, whose lifestyle in the Deng Xiaoping era became one of champagne communism, needed ever more cash. This was a ruling élite whose paramilitary police force, the Wu Jing – car plates readily identifiable by their distinctive 'WJ' markings – went to work in a mixture of top-of-the-range Cadillacs, Mercedes–Benz saloons and BMWs.

The Chinese government's failure to give up the basic trappings of socialism, and its tendency to take on new excesses, bred a ravenous appetite for cash. In the process of feeding this hunger, the state became hooked not just on 'foreign people's money' but on 'other people's money' in general. This led the government to use its control of the nationalised banking system to make the general population underwrite the costs of its drive for modernisation. It intended to make good on the savings it borrowed from its citizens some day – once economic transition was complete – but as the years wore on it became increasingly difficult to see how. The waste and hubris of the 1990s were therefore likely to have a cost beyond that to foreign investors. Locals would have to pick up a large part of the bill themselves.

梦

Like almost everything in the history of China's reform process, the story of the government's habit of using private savings to pay public bills began not with any conspiracy, but with a half-cocked plan for reform. Until the mid 1980s, the central government funded its projects and paid for much of the fixed investment of state companies from its budget. This was the socialist tradition. In 1984, however, the government informed state enterprises it would no longer make subsidy payments to cover their investment costs; the firms would instead have to borrow money from banks. At face value, this made a lot of sense. Budget funds carried no interest payments and hence created no constraint to produce a return on investments. Bank loans required interest to be paid, which ought to have made managers think twice before expanding their businesses. Subsidy allocations both for investment and for the underwriting of loss-making state enterprises were cut, the latter falling from around one-fifth of the government budget in the later 1980s to just 5 per cent in the mid 1990s.[6]

The problem was that the shift from subsidies to bank credit changed almost nothing. The banks were themselves state-owned and had little idea of what commercial lending involved. Instead of assessing borrowers, they made loans either based on an annual credit plan drawn up between the central bank and the State Planning Commission[7] or as a result of political instruction at a regional level. The central credit plan simply listed the cash needs of the largest state enterprises and infrastructure projects, while, in

the regions, provincial governors and city mayors told state bank loan officers and local central bank representatives which businesses and investments
they believed should be funded. In theory, the central bank, the People's
Bank of China (PBoC), was in charge of the financial system, responsible for
enforcing the government's policy of commercial lending.[8] In reality, the bank
had little power and less independence; it was granted permission to appoint
its own regional representatives only in 1988 and even then was required to
seek the approval of local Party and government leaders.[9] The upshot was
that bank lending grew rapidly because of the move away from subsidies, but
little of it was done on the basis of risk assessment. Almost all lending –
three-quarters of the bank credit outstanding at the end of the 1990s – went
to state enterprises.[10]

The public sector's rapacious appetite for loans was exacerbated by an
unreformed interest rate policy. All rates for loans and deposits were set by
the central bank – or the central government behind it – and no variation was
allowed. This meant that the most fundamental mechanism of a commercial
banking system, the pricing of capital, did not exist. On average, loan rates
were far lower than in a market economy where banks would demand a hefty
premium for the risk of lending to state enterprises with poor records of
profitability. In periods of inflation, like those of 1988–89 and 1993–94, real
interest rates – the nominal interest rate minus the rate of inflation – turned
negative. Public companies borrowed relentlessly at these times. Private or
foreign-invested businesses, meanwhile, were usually denied renminbi
financing because they had no place in the state plan. Chinese entrepreneurs
had to rely on cashflow from their existing operations or usurious lending in
illegal secondary loan markets, part of whose funds were supplied by flush
state enterprises. Foreign businesses were left to bear the exchange risk of
swapping hard currency for renminbi.

From a reform perspective, the situation – whereby almost all credit went
to the least deserving parts of the economy – was indefensible. But the
Chinese government supplied the state sector with the perfect excuse. Public
enterprises had to have preferred access to credit, the argument ran, because
they bore heavy social costs. In the mid 1990s, state firms ran 18,000 of
China's schools, with more than 6 million students, and hospitals that
accounted for one-third of all the beds in the country.[11] These costs ought to
have been transferred to the government's budget. But with budgetary
expenditure already rising to fund a vast national bureaucracy and politically
motivated infrastructure projects, the Ministry of Finance was unwilling to
see a significant deficit. A budget deficit of more than 2–3 per cent of gross
domestic product would damage China's international credit standing and

prevent politicians repeating a favourite mantra that the country's budgetary prudence was such that it could qualify for membership of the European Union.[12] State enterprise welfare costs – estimated by the World Bank at 8 per cent of their revenues – remained on their books.[13] A psychology of victimisation was engendered whereby every time a state firm lost money it blamed the unfair burden placed on it by government. In reality, public companies lost money because they faced no bankruptcy or hard budget constraints and because their access to credit was far too easy. They borrowed and spent with abandon – and not just on investment projects. State enterprises were still building half of all urban apartments for their managers and workers in the mid 1990s, then selling them off cheap to prove their commitment to private home ownership while holding the original, unpayable construction loans on their books.[14]

The government continued with the original, flawed rationale of its financial reforms by licensing more banks. This was supposed to increase both competition and – through more layering and complexity in the system – stability. From the mid 1980s, at least ten new national and regional banks were opened, as well as more than 5,000 urban credit co-operatives.[15] All of these institutions were allowed to take deposits from individuals. In addition, the government licensed hundreds of national and international trust and investment companies (TICs) and enterprise finance firms. These agencies were supposed to raise and invest shareholder funds, not individual deposits. All the new financial entities had one thing in common: they were owned or controlled by the state at either a central or a local level. By 2001, only two regional banks – Shenzhen Development Bank and Pudong Development Bank – had listed shares, and these were minority stakes that gave investors no say in their day-to-day running. Two other small national banks, Huaxia Bank and Everbright Bank, had been trumpeted for their supposed independence in the early 1990s because they were more loosely controlled via state corporations. However, in 1995, after they had made massive illegal loans, they were restructured to turn them into regular state banks.[16] The tiny Minsheng Bank, whose mix of private and state owners are all members of the official All China Federation of Industry and Commerce, continues to claim independence. But in reality, each of China's financial institutions – old and new – remains an arm of the state. They are subject to political direction in their lending and have the price of their loans and deposits dictated. The balance of evidence is that credit quality at financial institutions created after 1980 is, if anything, even worse than at China's original banks.

Tomorrow's problems

For many years, the build-up of bad debt in the banking system was not a pressing issue for the Chinese government. As the country's planned economy was monetised through the 1980s and early 1990s, around a third of bank credit was financed by re-lending from the central bank to the big state commercial banks.[17] In the unique conditions of the time, this proved to be less inflationary than would normally be the case. The economy's need for currency – as what had previously been state-planned barter transactions were replaced by money exchanges – reduced inflation and also produced large, one-off gains for the government. The central bank made a handsome cut from printing money, because cash in circulation – unlike bank deposits – carries no interest; economists call this gain seigniorage. The amount of currency issued each year increased by a factor of six between 1984 and the peak year of 1993.[18] Cash was particularly important because the country had few chequing accounts or other non-cash means of payment. By the end of 1993, however, the monetisation of the economy was largely complete and demand for new currency fell precipitously – from more than 3 per cent of GDP that year to less than 1.5 per cent per year subsequently. It was time for the government to start reckoning with the structural weaknesses of the financial system it had created.

Inflation threatened to spiral out of control in 1994, when it hit an annual rate of 22 per cent nationally and much more in big cities. In the austerity programme put in place to tame rising prices, then vice-premier Zhu Rongji insisted on several changes that made China's financial problems more explicit. First, he decided it was time for the government to stop borrowing money from the central bank to cover its budget deficit, which should instead be funded by domestic debt issues. Treasury bond issuance promptly jumped from an average Rmb40 billion ($4.8bn) a year in the early 1990s to Rmb150 billion ($18bn) in 1994 to 1996 and more than Rmb300 billion ($36bn) a year from 1997. In 2000, the government's debt issue was Rmb488 billion ($59bn),[19] equivalent to roughly 5 per cent of GDP or half the government's annual budget.[20] The trajectory for debt issuance remained upward, with Rmb593 billion ($71bn) budgeted for 2002.

A second, Zhu Rongji-inspired change was that the government created three new 'policy banks', which it said would take over lending to state-sponsored projects that in a commercial banking system might not obtain credit. A Commercial Bank Law was passed making it an offence for loan officers at regular financial institutions to take lending decisions based on political direction. This attempt to remove state-mandated loans from the day-to-day banking system, however, proved to be another fudge. From 1994, the policy banks lent free and fast to government projects whose capacity to repay was at best doubtful; by the end of 1998, they already accounted for 14 per cent of all the assets of the financial system.[21] But the policy banks were either not required – or, often, refused – to take over the large stocks of existing policy loans held by commercial banks. At the same time, the policy banks only lent for capital investment; they left the supposedly commercialised system to provide working capital loans to the state sector, often under political direction and in contravention of the Commercial Bank Law. By the end of the 1990s, such ineffective reforms were drawing widespread attention to some dubious financial practices that had previously been recognised by only a handful of academics.

This was also the case with a 1993 government decree that Chinese banks should begin to conform to international capital adequacy standards, as set by the Basle Committee on Banking Regulations and Supervisory Practice. The Basle standards require banks to have minimum paid-in capital equivalent to 4 per cent of their assets, and net worth – a broader measure of capital – equivalent to 8 per cent of assets. China's banks, however, had expanded their lending in the decade after 1985 by six times as much as they had increased their capital. In 1996, the big four banks had paid-in capital equivalent to just over 2 per cent of their assets and net worth of just over 3 per cent of their assets.[22] This was according to Chinese statistics which showed huge sums of bad debt on the banks' books as 'assets' and involved many other internationally unacceptable accounting practices. When Moody's Investors Service, an international credit rating agency, took a close look at the numbers in 1996, it described them as 'meaningless'.[23] Perversely, China's announcement that it would move to the Basle standards had focused attention on the fact that the country's big banks were insolvent and required government money to refloat them.

In China, as elsewhere, bad news comes in bunches. Just as the world was waking up to the problems of the state-controlled banking system in the mid 1990s, so economists began to point to other mounting liabilities faced by the government. Chief among these were unfunded welfare commitments. The state sector promised its employees pensions and medical benefits in retirement but had put aside almost nothing to pay for this. As of 1995, welfare reserves were the equivalent of only 0.6 per cent of GDP. In the United States, which was also fretting about running out of welfare money, 1995 reserves were 7 per cent of GDP.

China's welfare system had been structured so that those in work paid – via national insurance deductions – for those who had retired. In the first decades after 1949, with a young population and few retirees, the system was self-financing. But by the mid 1990s, China had 30 million public sector retirees and their ranks were growing fast. Meanwhile, the number of new workers able to pay tax was constrained by the one child policy.[24] In the last years of the decade, the pension programmes of most Chinese provinces went into deficit. Worker and employer contributions were insufficient to cover outgoings. A report in 2000 by the Development Research Centre, a government agency, revealed that twenty-one out of thirty provinces were in pension deficit in 1998, rising to twenty-five in 1999.[25]

Calculations by the World Bank in the mid 1990s suggested that even if the state pension system were abandoned or overhauled immediately, the liabilities the government had created for itself would amount to as much as half of one year's gross domestic product.[26] As well as existing retirees, all 110 million employees currently working in the formal state sector were entitled to pensions. By 1994, the Chinese government increased employer–worker welfare contributions to an average 24 per cent of payroll – twice the US rate – in an effort to hold down the deficit. It was subsequently announced that contributions would rise further, to 28 per cent, by 2005. According to the World Bank, contributions would have to hit an untenable 46 per cent of salary to keep the system afloat.[27] The number of retirees was rising every year, while the number of state workers plateaued in the late 1990s. The real solution was to abandon the old, unsustainable pension system and launch a new programme with higher individual contributions and lower pension returns.[28] This, however, would mean the government taking the liabilities of the old system on to its books – something it was loathe to do.

A long bill

When the Chinese state's list of bills pending was estimated, it added up to a lot of money. This came as a surprise to many observers, because the country had traditionally been viewed as one of the developing world's least indebted members. One benefit of Mao Zedong's era of isolation and self-sufficiency was that in 1979 the state had been debt-free – in terms of both domestic and international credit.[29] Compared with Russia and the ex-communist countries of eastern Europe, which carried large debts into the post-Soviet era, it was an extraordinarily fortuitous position from which to begin reform. Yet after twenty years, most independent analyses suggested China had saddled herself with liabilities which would soon make her one of the most indebted nations in the world. This had gone unnoticed because most of the liabilities had built up 'off-budget' – in the country's banking system and in the welfare state.

In fact, there was no shortage of suspect indicators in China, but these were not captured by the standard statistics used to measure a country's financial health. International credit agencies and multilateral institutions like the World Bank, the International Monetary Fund and the Bank for International Settlements tend to focus on ratios such as domestic bonds outstanding as a proportion of gross domestic product or interest and principal payments on external debt as a proportion of export revenues. These formal debt ratios, which make the comparison of countries' indebtedness relatively easy, were quite low in China, even at the end of the 1990s.[30] China's problems were of a different nature. They were reflected instead in a huge build-up in bank credit during the 1990s and increasing evidence that much of that credit was bad. While all other recent financial crises – from Mexico's to those of south-east Asia and South Korea – involved international debt, China's liabilities were almost all domestic.

In 1978, loans outstanding in the financial system were equivalent to half of GDP. By 1998, the proportion had risen to 100 per cent and, by 2001, 120 per cent – or $1.3 trillion.[31] The increase in lending was so fast in the 1990s that from 1992 the annual stock of new loans exceeded the central government budget.[32] Measured by assets – mainly their loans – China's big four banks became among the largest in the world. Industrial and Commercial Bank of China, the leading lender, ranked number five globally.[33] Internationally, there was no significant economy where banks so dominated the financial system – owning 90 per cent of financial assets – and lent so heavily relative to economic output. Even in the eastern European countries that faced banking crises in the 1990s, the ratio of loans to GDP was much lower than in China.[34]

Chinese banks lent their money to the state sector and this was reflected in state enterprise asset–liability ratios, which increased from 10 per cent in 1980 to 85 per cent in 1995. By the later 1990s, half of state firms probably had liabilities in excess of their assets and were only functioning through constant infusions of new bank credit. Many paid no interest on loans, simply rolling their interest and principal outstanding into new, larger loans as necessary. An asset–liability ratio of 85 per cent, as expressed in Chinese statistics, is equivalent to the more commonly used debt–equity ratio of over 500 per cent. When the Asian financial crisis engulfed South Korea in 1997, its largest companies – or *chaebol* – were running debt–equity ratios of 300–400 per cent. The most indebted *chaebol* at the end of 1996, Samsung, had a debt–equity ratio of 473 per cent.[35]

China's banks were able to keep lending only because they held the vast majority of the savings of 1.3 billion people. Every year, lending increased by an ever larger amount, but the deposits of a thrifty population increased by still more. So long as public faith in the banking system was maintained, it was inconsequential that the banks were insolvent – that their liabilities exceeded their capital – because they remained liquid. Household savings deposits rose from just 6 per cent of gross domestic product in 1978 to 70 per cent in 1999.[36] Ostensibly this meant that more than half of deposits in the financial system came from individuals and less than a third from enterprises, mainly state-owned ones.[37] In reality, since most state firm deposits were working capital loans from the banks – sourced from individual deposits – the Chinese people accounted for an even greater share of the country's savings. Unbeknown to themselves, the Chinese masses were underwriting a vast lending programme driven not by commercial gain but by government whim.

The real level of bad debt in the financial system is impossible to gauge, even for the Chinese central bank and Zhu Rongji himself. Non-performing loans are reported by loan officers in individual branches. These officers know what is deemed to be an acceptable level of questionable debt, and their assessments are not subject to third party checks. All banks have internal audit teams which ensure that systems are maintained, reports are filed and that government lending policy is followed. But neither within banks nor across banks are there the teams of credit quality analysts who in international financial institutions would sample loan books to confirm that the status of loans is being accurately reported.[38] Like most Chinese statistics, loan quality numbers are produced by a reporting methodology originally developed in the Soviet Union and exported to China. A lending officer who rolls an unpaid loan and its interest into a new, larger loan and states it is of good quality is almost certain not to be found out.

China published details of an official, three-tier system for classifying non-performing loans in 1995. This featured the categories of 'past due', 'doubtful' and 'bad'. However, the categories were not comparable to international standards. Chinese banks, for example, only classified loans as past due when a repayment of principal was missed; under the guidelines of the Basle Committee, international banks deem a loan to be past due if interest, not principal, is unpaid for between ninety and 180 days. Similarly, banks in China were not allowed to mark a loan as bad – in other words written off – until the borrower had declared bankruptcy or gone through liquidation. Elsewhere, loans are marked bad when interest is not paid for more than 180 days. There were many other discrepancies.[39] But even under China's system, officers of the big four banks and the central bank stated in 1996 and 1997 that non-performing loans were about 20 per cent of the total.[40]

The declared volume of non-performing loans was already higher than officially reported levels in south-east Asian countries and South Korea prior to the Asian financial crisis, but it was not believed by outside observers. By the end of the decade, most informed analysts put China's non-performing loans at 50 per cent of those outstanding. Stu Fulton, a financial systems specialist working with international accountancy firm Pricewaterhouse Coopers, enjoyed rare access to the books of Chinese bank branches in the mid 1990s. (He was one of three partners responsible for a $12 million, World Bank-funded project to assist the Chinese central bank with prudential supervision.) After three years in the field, his conclusion was that half the loans in the system were non-performing: 'I settled on 50 per cent as my personal view,' he said.[41] In some branches he surveyed, Mr Fulton found non-performing loans to be as much as 70–80 per cent of total portfolios. The reason was that risk assessment and cashflow analysis played little part in lending decisions: 'It's not a banking system,' he said. 'It's a state collection system for people's deposits and a state-planned redistribution system of those deposits.'[42]

Even the international credit rating agencies, which in the early 1990s rushed to make China the first transition economy to be granted investment-grade status for its sovereign debt, came to the view that the majority of bank loans might be non-performing. Standard & Poor's annual Sovereign Ratings Service report for China in 2000 stated bluntly: 'Non-performing loans are at least 50 per cent of total loans in the financial system.'[43] More important than the amount of lending on which interest and principal were not being repaid, however, was the sum of money the treasury would have to commit to stabilise and recapitalise the financial system. In 1999, the central government said it would allow the big four state banks to 'sell', at face value, Rmb1.4 trillion ($169 billion) in non-performing loans to specially created asset management companies (AMCs). The AMCs would attempt to recover some of the debt. This, however, addressed only part of the bad debt in those banks, and none of that built up in other banks and financial institutions.[44]

The Rmb1.4 trillion write-off was equivalent to 13 per cent of all loans outstanding at the time. Nicholas Lardy, an American economist who was the most active and influential foreign researcher of China's financial system in the 1990s, estimated that the ultimate write-off would be at least 25 per cent of loans outstanding – some Rmb2.5 trillion ($300bn).[45] This would cover bad debt which still could not be amortised by the big four banks after transfers to the AMCs, plus failed loans from the three policy banks set up in 1994, as well as those of rural credit co-operatives and non-bank financial institutions such as the TICs. Some of the best known TICs were already insolvent by 2000.[46]

In terms of the government's total contingent liabilities at the end of the

1990s, a probable $300 billion bank rescue had to be added to a stock of treasury debt which reached $100 billion, another $100 billion in external sovereign debt,[47] $33 billion dollars issued to the big four banks in 1998 to shore up their capital and more than $60 billion of bonds issued by the policy banks for which central government was ultimately responsible. These liabilities added up to more than half of of China's gross domestic product. If the cost of unfunded pension liabilities turned out to be another half of gross domestic product, China – a country which had been debt-free when it started its reforms – was headed for a debt level associated with Latin American countries of the 1980s or Japan at the end of the 1990s.[48]

梦

When a country becomes highly indebted, its solvency depends on its ability to keep servicing its debts. Leaving aside China's huge unfunded pension liabilities – which will come due over a longer period than other debts – Lardy has shown that without change the Chinese state will likely be insolvent within the first decade of the twenty-first century. On its current trajectory – assuming that the banking system continues to create bad debt at the rate it has in recent years – China's ratio of debt to gross domestic product will be around 110 per cent in 2008.[49] At this level, Chinese citizens are unlikely to want to hold bonds at current levels of interest because of the fear that the government will have to print money to pay the interest on them. Ever higher interest rates will be necessary to offset the increased risk of treasury debt, creating an unbearable burden for the government. By Nicholas Lardy's calculations, interest payments on treasury bonds will take up 80 per cent of central government expenditure in 2008. The likely outcome is a default on state bonds, such as happened in Russia in the autumn of 1998.[50]

In order to avoid this, the government must do two things: increase its tax revenues and end non-commercial lending by its banks. The former may be easier than the latter. China's fiscal revenues as a share of gross domestic product fell to one of the lowest levels in the world – 10.7 per cent – in 1995. The governments of developed countries levy 30–40 per cent of their economies' product in taxes, and even perennially hamstrung Russia manages a quarter.[51] In China, government lost control of its tax base during the reform era. In the second half of the 1990s, tax reforms and a concerted effort at collection – not least from newly arrived foreign enterprises – did lead to some improvement in the situation, with fiscal revenues rising to 14 per cent of gross domestic product by the end of the decade. Yet even if the government sustains this rate of increase, it is unlikely to be able to service its debt.[52] This is particularly so since expenditure is not being held in check; government spending increased from 13.3 per cent of gross domestic product in 1997 to 18 per cent in 1999.[53]

In order to escape the debt trap, central government will have to curtail expenditure and at the same time increase its fiscal revenues dramatically and end the process of bad debt accumulation. Only if the banks are able to write off non-performing loans from their own profits and reserves within a few years will China be out of the woods. But, at the turn of the century, a change to strictly commercial banking is hard to detect. In the wake of the Asian financial crisis that began in 1997, China embarked on a programme of fiscal pump priming and loose credit that made the situation in the banking system even worse than when Nicholas Lardy produced his forecasts. Each year beginning in 1998, the government spent around $18 billion of public money on infrastructure and other investment projects and encouraged banks to lend almost without restraint to state-owned enterprises.[54] The aim was to maintain economic growth of 7–8 per cent. While this was achieved, the policy meant that the public sector's share of fixed investment – which was always high but had been declining – increased again from just over half in the late 1990s to nearly three-quarters in the first six months of 2000. Drunk with bank credit, state businesses added still more capacity and their output rose well ahead of overall growth. The margins of private and foreign companies were further squeezed by public enterprises that would be insolvent but for their access to credit. The likelihood that those companies will be able to repay their loans is no greater than in the past.

There are innumerable pressures working against bank commercialisation in China. The government's fear that lower growth will lead to too much unemployment and social instability encourages it to ease credit to state enterprises, which create short-term growth and jobs by spending national savings. This temporarily helps the Ministry of Finance to collect taxes, more than half of which come from the public sector.[55] (The ministry caps the loan loss reserves state banks are allowed to provide for bad debts because this maximises their taxable income.)[56] Bank managers learn little about commercial behaviour since their activities are being manipulated by outside actors. When banks try to diversify their loan portfolios – as with a recent expansion of mortgage lending – it is on the basis of a political campaign rather than credit quality analysis. Such has been the rush to increase mortgage lending that the central bank had to formally warn lenders in late 2000 against reckless extension of home loans.[57] A supervisor with China Construction Bank, the leading mortgage lender, revealed that less than two years after mortgages and consumer loans became widely available, the default rate for individual borrowers at his bank was running at around 10 per cent.[58] This is extraordinarily high at such an early stage. Ultimately, since their lending is still subject to political interference and they are not allowed to put aside sufficient loan loss reserves, bank directors assume that bad debts will be made good by the state. It is a classic case of what bank regulators call 'moral hazard'.

The money trap

In the short term the Chinese government keeps the lid on its financial woes by trapping money inside China. This requires strict capital controls so that anyone who is nervous of the state's financial health has no alternative place to park their savings. The renminbi is convertible only for international trade and other, closely defined purposes – so-called 'current account convertibility'. Chinese citizens are not allowed to move their money abroad to deposit in offshore banks, to buy foreign stocks or to invest in non-Chinese pension programmes.

It is not easy to hold the savings of 1.3 billion people captive, but through the late 1990s the Chinese government was surprisingly successful. The state's ownership of the financial system allowed it to exert close bureaucratic control. Banks permitted individuals to buy only small sums of foreign currency for overseas travel or study, and at centrally determined rates.[59] Within China, payment for goods and services in foreign exchange was outlawed. Even foreign representative offices were forbidden to withdraw more than $1,000 a day from their hard currency accounts. These measures were backed by an ongoing police campaign against black market moneychangers.

As a result, it is extremely difficult for ordinary people to move savings offshore or hold foreign currency. For the better-connected, or for companies, however, the seal is less hermetic. Government officials or senior employees of foreign companies can request payments into Hong Kong or foreign accounts which they open on trips abroad. Businesses under-invoice for exports and take the balance of their dues offshore. By the late 1990s, China's balance of payments data suggested capital flight was running at somewhere between $20 billion and $30 billion a year.[60] While the country posted huge surpluses from foreign investment and trade, the once breakneck growth of its foreign exchange reserves slowed.[61] None the less, so long as the government held on to the masses' money, it remained in business. As always in developing countries, it was the less well off, less cosmopolitan majority who were bearing the nation's risk.

Full convertibility of the renminbi was announced as a government objective as long ago as 1993. In 2000, after the Asian financial crisis, regulators stated that a freely convertible currency would not be possible before 2010 – nearly twenty years after the policy had been made public.[62] There were those who said the approach was a prudent one, but in reality it reflected only weakness. The government knew that open exchange of the currency would lead to the collapse of its financial system and preferred, by means of isolation, to mortgage current problems into the future. At the end of the 1990s, the leadership had given up talk of deregulation and was focused instead on stricter enforcement of capital controls and on rapid mobilisation of central bank funds to deal with a number of localised bank runs. These panic withdrawals, which began at the time of the first collapses of TICs in 1998, show that despite the best propaganda efforts ordinary people are increasingly nervous about the safety of their savings. In three years from 1998, runs on local banks were reported in cities in Guangdong, Hainan, Henan, Hebei, Beijing and Liaoning provinces, as well as at several rural credit co-operatives.[63] In each case the government's reaction was to provide instant liquidity – with no questions asked – so that depositors could withdraw their funds and confidence was shored up. This was even the case with illegal deposits. At the bankrupt Guangdong International Trust and Investment Corp. people made deposits in high-interest accounts knowing full well that such institutions were not allowed to serve individual savers. They were paid out in full. Such was the government's fear that a local bank run could spread.

梦

The state's one concession to people's wish to diversify their savings was to encourage the rapid expansion of the stock markets in Shanghai and Shenzhen. By the end of 2000, more than 1,100 companies were listed and capitalisation rose to over $500 billion, exceeded in Asia by only Hong Kong and Japan. This total was somewhat misleading, since less than a third of the shares were freely traded, but the growth of the exchanges – which did not exist in 1990 – was none the less startling.[64] As of 2000, Chinese people had opened more than 50 million share trading accounts.

The stock markets, however, proved to be as much of a house of cards as the banking system. Share buying did almost nothing to reduce people's investment exposure to their government and its cosseted companies. Of 1,100 listed businesses at the end of the decade, only half a dozen were privately held.[65] The remainder were state enterprises. The government used its control of the listing process to sell minority positions in struggling public businesses.[66] Despite generally poor records of profitability, investors bought the stocks for want of any others. In this highly artificial environment, the government kept the markets moving upwards through a mixture of official propaganda lauding share buying and downward adjustment of interest rates on bonds and bank deposits.[67] Many listed companies were loss-makers – the proportion reporting losses increased from less than 8 per cent in 1998 to 9 per cent in 1999 and over 10 per cent in 2000 – but share prices continued to rise.[68] Both the Shanghai and Shenzhen market indices doubled in the course of 1999 and 2000. Price-to-corporate earnings ratios of Chinese stocks increased to an average of seventy times by 2001, one of the highest levels in the world and on par with Japan in the late 1980s.

The high ratios reflected paltry profits, but in the closed world of China's financial system profitability had only a marginal influence on the markets. This was starkly apparent from the performance of China's B shares, the only stocks available to foreign buyers who – by contrast with Chinese investors – had a free choice as to what to do with their money. B shares are exactly the same as the A shares sold in mainland China except that their prices are quoted in Hong Kong or American dollars. If foreigners placed the same value on mainland-listed companies as locals, A and B stocks would have the same price. Instead, B shares traded at a discount of up to 85 per cent.[69] Similar evidence of how an open market would value Shanghai and Shenzhen counters was provided by the performance of mainland enterprises that listed part of their equity in Hong Kong – so-called H shares. As of 2000, only one out of fifty such stocks – which had been greeted with euphoria when first launched in 1993 – was trading above the price of its initial public offering.[70] The Shanghai and Shenzhen A share indices, meanwhile, were the world's best performers in 2000.

The Chinese government's use of its stock markets to raise capital for ailing state companies makes some sense. Whereas subsidies and bank loans which will never be repaid create an explicit financial obligation for the state, the sale of stocks does not. The money raised in initial public offerings is not repayable if stock prices fall. However, in order to feed its appetite for cash, the government needs the markets to keep rising so it can sell more equity. As well as lowering interest rates, taxing bank savings and cranking its propaganda machine, the leadership has tolerated tremendous corruption in the markets in order to maintain momentum. Brokerages, all of which are state-owned, indulge in widespread manipulation of share prices by trading on their own accounts. State enterprises use privileged access to bank credit to illegally play the markets. Ultimately, however, there is a limit to what even the Chinese government can do to sustain stratospheric price–earnings ratios. When the leadership proposed in late 1999 to sell down its stakes in already-listed firms to fund pension liabilities, the markets temporarily swooned at the prospect of an oversupply of shares.[71] When the policy was revisited in the summer of 2001 and again at the start of 2002, there was the same effect. Furthermore, the low quality of listed companies makes it difficult to allow profitable private enterprises into the bourses in the future – even though this is what reform, and the need to allocate capital more efficiently, demand.

梦

As of the turn of the century, the three major investment possibilities legally available to the Chinese people all put their money into the hands of their government – via the state banks, in the form of treasury bonds or through investment in state-owned enterprises on the stock markets. This sealed and interconnected financial system ensured the central government a constant supply of other people's money. The question raised by the system is: how long can it last?

The answer is that it is impossible to say. China's banks are technically insolvent, the government's liabilities in the next few years threaten to exceed its ability to pay and, by any normal measure, the Shanghai and Shenzhen stock markets are bubbles ready to burst. Yet the system remains liquid so long as the Chinese people are willing to hold their investments. With the fundamentals shot, everything comes down to psychology. This means the psychology of ordinary Chinese people, not foreigners. Unlike Mexico in 1995 or south-east Asia and Korea in 1997 and 1998, it is unlikely that foreign investors could be a direct trigger for a crisis. The earlier financial collapses were the product of significant dependence on external debt as well as volatile exchange rates. China's external debt is modest and easily serviced by its hard currency export earnings;[72] the exchange rate is fixed. Instead, as has so often been the case, China's problems are internal. A crisis will only occur when Chinese citizens lose faith in their government's ability to manage its – which is to say their – finances. The official state media does nothing to inform them of the dangers they face.

A domestic crisis of confidence could be precipitated by any number of events – a sharp correction in the stock markets, the continued fall of the value of real estate or even, indirectly, by a downturn in the global economy which would reduce demand for Chinese exports. Whichever, a crisis in China would play out through an old-fashioned run on the banks as frightened citizens sought to hold on to their cash themselves or turn it into real, durable goods. Once the contagion starts, it will be almost impossible to stop. Unlike most countries, China has no deposit insurance in its banking system – the population's savings are only as good as the government's promise to repay them. If some people withdraw their money, there will be enormous pressure for everyone else to do the same because no one's funds are insured. Bank branches might close their doors, but this would only add to panic as hundreds of millions of people fought to retrieve their savings before they were lost. It is ironic that today, when the central bank recognises the potential for a crisis of confidence, it dares not introduce partial savings insurance for fear that this itself might trigger bank runs by signalling the precariousness of the financial system.[73]

In the event of a serious crisis, the Chinese government would either have to print money to provide liquidity to the banks – thereby creating a spiral of inflation – or ask for outside help. The latter is unlikely. China has been a member of the International Monetary Fund since 1980, but its government has little truck with foreign organisations that try to tell it what to do. Throughout the 1990s, the IMF was refused permission to station resident advisers inside the Chinese central bank or the Ministry of Finance – a practice that is common in its technical assistance programmes to developing countries.[74] Relations were further soured when a Chinese IMF staff member was jailed in 1997 on allegations of corruption, despite the organisation's diplomatic immunity.[75] There is little to suggest that the current leadership would submit to an IMF structural adjustment programme and request what would have to be the biggest credit line in the institution's – and the world's – history. Moreover, lending scores of billions of dollars to bail out communist China would be a political minefield for the western countries that provide most of the IMF's money. The financial mess that has been created in China will be dealt with from within. The government hopes somehow to muddle through. So long as the financial system remains liquid, it tells itself that economic growth will eventually make its problems go away.

But there is a different argument which says that the longer the current financial trajectory continues, the bigger will be the crisis that ends it. The more debt that is allowed to accrue, in other words, the louder the bang when it can no longer be serviced. In this scenario, Chinese people could experience the kind of wealth destruction associated with the Latin American debt crises of the 1980s rather than the shorter-lived Asian crises of the 1990s. It is worth remembering that not only were savings wiped out in Central and South America in the 1980s, but countries like Argentina, Brazil and Mexico experienced negative annual growth throughout the whole decade.[76] Such would be a particularly ugly end to the China Dream.

Part 3
Reaching for reality

10

Parallel economies

'You must not think that if we have elements of a market economy we shall be taking the capitalist road ... Both a planned economy and a market economy are necessary.'

Deng Xiaoping, *Collected Works Volume III*[1]

CHINA ENTERED the twenty-first century with not one, but two, economies – the result of a reform process that provided space at the margins for new types of private activity but which failed to dismantle the structure of a socialist past. On the one side was an export economy, centred on the southern coastal province of Guangdong and the Yangze river delta.[2] This was backed up by a modest, but rapidly growing, domestic private sector that operated in the cracks between state manufacturing monopolies or, more often, in new service industries. On the other side was the traditional state sector, battered and bruised by assaults from private entrepreneurs, but essentially intact thanks to the rights, privileges, licences and access to credit that protect it. Within this state economy had to be counted probably the majority of the mixed public and private ownership collectives that in the early 1990s were heralded as China's unique economic weapon in her quest for growth. By the end of the decade their performance had collapsed and official media and senior leaders were conceding that most collectives were little better than the state enterprises they were supposed to replace.[3]

China's two economies existed in parallel and dealt with one another only as necessary.[4] Even their business aims were different. State enterprises were motivated by the maintenance of power and patronage – not least the ability to retain large numbers of workers, irrespective of the use to which they could be put – while private enterprises were driven by profit. The differences were most stark in the export sector. The majority of exports at the end of the 1990s were 'processed' by private businesses, meaning that inputs and components were imported, assembled in mainland factories and then re-exported as finished, or more-nearly-finished, products. This type of activity insulated exporters from the vagaries of a state-dominated domestic economy and allowed most of them to be profitable. A processing operation's chief requirement was a steady supply of rural migrant labour, something that was permanently on tap in China and in which the government did not interfere, save to collect small fees to issue worker permits. Private entrepreneurs operating in the domestic market were unable to escape the state sector so completely, but they were also adept at limiting their exposure. Typically, they insisted on cash payments upfront from state units and concentrated on services over which the public sector was unable to exercise monopoly powers – such as running restaurants. The restaurant business boomed, growing by 18 per cent in 2000. Only large-scale foreign investors tried to straddle China's parallel economies. They established joint ventures with state enterprises to target local consumers, but they sought to produce profits rather than exercise patronage. As the experience of corporations from General Motors to Fosters showed, this was usually a recipe for disappointment.

To the outside observer, the key question about China's two economies was how big each of them might be, since the country's future was likely to be determined by the struggle between money-guzzling public activity and profit-making private activity. However, it was hard to answer this question by analysing statistics. Even if official data were to be believed, they painted a blurred ownership picture. A quarter of the country's industrial output was attributed to collectively owned businesses, but there was no way of knowing with any clarity what proportion of these were private firms – which in the past dubbed themselves collectives to avoid suppression – and what part were simply state enterprises by another name.[5] In the service sector, there was precious little ownership data of any nature. Only in agriculture, where the vast majority of farming had been in private hands since the 1980s, was there some certainty about who did what.[6]

Despite the limitations, attempts were made by both local and international organisations to estimate the overall sizes of the public and private economies using a mix of extrapolation and guesswork. A much-publicised report in 2000 by the International Finance Corporation, an arm of the World Bank, put China's non-farm private economy at 33 per cent of gross domestic product and the public at 67 per cent.[7] But the report's methodology was crude. It added 13 per cent of output formally attributed to private domestic firms to 6 per cent from foreign-invested enterprises and simply split collective output down the middle, giving half to the private and half to the public economies. This produced the conclusion of a one-third private non-farm economy – or half private, if the overwhelmingly privatised agricultural sector was included. A more detailed analysis of available numbers by Zhong Jiyin, an economist with the Chinese Academy of Social Sciences, was published in 1999.[8] Mr Zhong used output numbers for the subcategories of industry and construction, and employment data in services, to focus on different sectors of the economy. He concluded that China's agricultural sector was 92 per cent private by output, the construction sector 32 per cent, industry 51 per cent and services only 37 per cent private.[9]

The findings of these two studies were not markedly different although, of course, both operated with the same official statistics – data that may well be badly flawed. None the less, it is reasonable to guess that at the start of the twenty-first century, China's parallel public and private economies were roughly equal in size, but that public ownership predominated outside of agriculture. At face value, this represents tremendous change. When Deng Xiaoping came to power in 1978, everything was state-controlled.[10] The progress of the next twenty years, however, did not imply an inexorable transition to a private economy. The ownership changes of the 1980s – most notably the return to household farming – were the easy ones. Government did not have to force, or even ask, farmers to abandon rural communes and no vested interests lost out in the process. Urban privatisation was a different matter and this was reflected in its far slower pace. For urban privatisation demanded that a communist government proactively dismantle the structure of a public economy in which there were huge vested interests, and which provided the basis of the Party's support. Through the 1990s, the government preferred to throw money at the public sector in a vain belief it would become more market-driven, while expecting a nascent private economy to grow to international scale despite state enterprise privileges. This was wishful thinking. In the absence of radical policy action – the sort that would cause much pain to many people, not least card-carrying members of the Party – economic transition ran up against a brick wall. A one-third private urban economy is a significant achievement, but it is not enough to balance China's books, as an anecdotal tour of her parallel economies makes clear.

Barbie is not American

Although some important caveats are required, the star performer of the last twenty years in China has been the export sector. For two decades, exports grew at an average 13 per cent a year and in 2001 totalled $266 billion. In the ten years prior to 2000, exports nearly quadrupled.[11] Today, Chinese-made goods are available in almost every country, and in developed countries without exception. Anyone who buys a pair of leather shoes or sneakers, an item of clothing, a toy for a child, or a basic electronic product faces a high probability that their purchase was processed in China.[12] The country accounts for more than two-fifths of world output of shoes, more than half of all toys sold internationally and nearly one-fifth of all garments; the latter market share would be much higher but for the Multi-Fibre Agreement, which restricts free trade in clothing.[13] In the United States, the world's biggest economy, the presence of China in everyday life is particularly pronounced: Chinese-made shoes and sneakers – the country makes 7 billion pairs a year – account for 60 per cent of US footwear imports; Chinese-made toys worth $10 billion a year make up two-thirds of toy imports.[14] Products with Chinese country of origin labels fill the shelves of megastores like Wal-Mart, fashion chains such as J. Crew and Tommy Hilfiger and consumer electronics shops like RadioShack. Goods assembled by Chinese hands are also a big part of life's seedier side. The country makes nine-tenths of all the sex toys exported around the world.[15]

China's success in export manufacturing stems from the flexibility of its mostly Asian-owned processing factories. Toymaking, which is a fashion industry in which product cycles can be as short as a few months, is a case in point. Nowhere in the world is as efficient at restyling Barbie for the new season, making toys to go with the launch of a children's movie or bulk manufacturing the latest outlandish Christmas must-have. At the top end, the business is surprisingly sophisticated. International toy firms – most of them American – send ideas for new products and details of acceptable price ranges by e-mail to agents in Hong Kong. The agents prepare a design which, if acceptable, leads to a prototype being made by a Hong Kong model shop. Tenders for production work are sent out to mainland-based factories. The factories are far from the sweatshops of popular imagination: they use 3-D computer modelling, computer-driven milling machines, laser cutters and state-of-the art injection casting, although the workforce is still basically unskilled. Through a finely tuned process, toys – which are increasingly complex products and often involve electronics, memory chips and mechanical innards to make them interactive – pass from drawing board to production line in a matter of weeks. The dominant manufacturers are almost anonymous to the outside world: Hong Kong companies with names like Early Light Industrial, Jetta and V-Tech. But they are huge employers. Early Light alone, which manufactures for Hasbro, Mattel, Playskool, Fisher-Price and Bandai, employs 20,000 Chinese workers in two factories in Shenzhen.[16]

The overseas Chinese connection – in the form of Hong Kong and Taiwanese businessmen – is a critical one in the export economy. The linguistic and cultural affinity of these investors allows them to extract maximum value from China, as they intermediate between the low-cost production potential of the mainland and final demand for consumer products in the developed world. There are major Japanese owned export processing factories in Dalian, Tianjin and Guangdong, and US and European exporters dotted around the country, but it is predominantly Hong Kong and Taiwanese factories that have taken the foreign-manufactured share of China's exports to 51 per cent – and rapidly rising – in 2001. If exports processed by mainland-owned factories for foreign customers are included, the type of activity that accounts for half the world's Nike shoes and all of its Barbie dolls makes up well over 50 per cent of China's exports. The United States, in turn, buys around half of all the processed goods that China produces. American politicians complain about a trade deficit that exceeded $80 billion in 2001, but the reality is that ordinary Americans benefit from ever cheaper consumer goods while American brand-owners capture much of the profit from licensing the production of their toys, sneakers and garments.[17] The problem of the deficit is not how much America imports from China, but how little the country's over-regulated domestic economy buys from the United States. American exports to China today represent an even lower proportion of US foreign trade than they did in the 1930s.[18]

The processing trade has created hundreds of Hong Kong and Taiwanese millionaires in the past twenty years. The greatest number – like the brassière king Frank Lo and Clifford Pang, who made his first millions manufacturing computer disk drive heads – built their businesses in Guangdong. The southern province accounts for nearly half of all foreign-invested exports and 40 per cent of total exports. More specifically, it is not the whole of the large province, but the eight districts and 30 million inhabitants of the Pearl River delta – between Hong Kong and the provincial capital Guangzhou – that account for nine-tenths of Guangdong's shipments. This is the most concentrated export processing region in the world, selling more abroad than Thailand or Malaysia.[19] In one typical town in the Pearl River delta, Dongguan – which used to make shoes but now features largely Taiwan-backed businesses producing electronics – there are 30,000 Taiwanese managers in residence, running 5,000 factories that employ 2 million workers.[20] Most of the labour force is made up of the children of peasant farmers, often young women who – contrary to the claims of international labour unions – are all too happy to escape the greater evils of cashless misery and arranged marriages in the countryside. In the past decade, as many as 100 million peasants left rural areas in search of factory jobs; around 9 million of them work in Guangdong.

Small Hong Kong and Taiwanese firms are the real success story of China investment. Hong Kong's larger conglomerates, like the multinationals, targeted the domestic economy via joint ventures and have had equally miserable returns. 'Among the big companies, you can count the success stories on the fingers of one hand,' said Ian Perkin, economist for the Hong Kong General Chamber of Commerce, the main business association in the territory. But the export manufacturers, he observed: 'are the quiet achievers'.[21] After a decade of training Chinese workers, their factories are beginning to process sophisticated goods that would have been unthinkable a few years ago. Taiwanese firms are assembling computers for the world market; in 2000, mainland exports of computer products exceeded Taiwan's for the first time.[22] IBM expanded its Shenzhen PC plant in 1999 to serve the whole of Asia. In 2000 came the first announcements of investment in low-grade semi-conductor plants, by the Taiwanese companies that dominate the business globally.

The future of export processing in China is assured. The combination of Hong Kong and Taiwanese management and Chinese cheap labour is unbeatable. In the wake of the Asian financial crisis of 1997, when demand in the region plummeted, most economists predicted Chinese exports would fall, too. Sustained by the processing trade with the developed world, they did not. Nor did precipitous drops in south-east Asian exchange rates encourage American and European buyers to switch their orders to Indonesian or Thai factories. Such a move was widely forecast, but there is no equivalent export processing machine in those countries that can guarantee both quality and timely delivery. The insulation of the processing sector from China's domestic economy also means that it is unaffected by events at home. Just as the Tiananmen massacre did not stop the growth of exports in the early 1990s, nor did the central government's austerity programme in the mid 1990s.

The only exporters who suffer by the domestic economy are those unwise enough to meddle in it. Of the thousands of Hong Kong and Taiwanese entrepreneurs who made their millions in the processing trade, not a small part lost their fortunes by investing in Chinese real estate. When the property market crashed after 1996, the country was littered with villas, apartments, shopping malls and office towers constructed by textile makers turned prospective property tycoons. Frank Lo was such a case. In 2000, having spent six years struggling to make his Printemps department store in downtown Shanghai turn a profit, he finally gave in and sold the building to a local company at a heavy loss.[23] Mr Lo had already parted with much of his equity in Top Form, his brassière export business, to pay for the $26 million investment. China, it turned out, could process brassières for France, but was not itself ready for a shopping experience modelled on the Champs-Elysées.

Clifford Pang is a rare exception to the rule that says that successful exporters are best off sticking to exports. He began his private housing project in Guangdong before most foreign developers entered the market and attained critical mass early. By the mid 1990s, Clifford Estates was big enough to sustain its own school, medical services, shops and security. Hong Kong retirees and mainland nouveaux riches snapped up properties because it was clear the project – unlike so many others – would not go bust. At the end of the decade, it was the biggest privately owned housing estate in China, with more than 15,000 homes sold for a total of over $2 billion. In the summer of 1998, Mr Pang stood in the grounds of his own palatial home, under construction on a tree-shrouded hill overlooking the development. As he reviewed the progress of a 100-yard artificial beach and pool, fed by a series of 15-foot waterfalls, ten men behind him struggled to carry a full-grown palm tree to its allotted location. In front of Mr Pang, his 42,000 square foot (4,000 square metre) house filled the horizon, built in pale Xi'an stone and Italian marble and replete with another, indoor swimming pool, massage rooms, sauna and cinema. Below, through the trees, the red roofs of Clifford Estates resembled an aerial view of a Monopoly board. 'Our Chinese tradition,' Mr Pang said, 'is to live in a comfortable place before anything else.' He has recruited a t'ai chi master, who cures the sleeplessness, high blood pressure and ulcers induced by working in China, to live with him and he intends to retire on his hill. 'I am a man of simple tastes,' he declared, somewhat unconvincingly. 'I don't need more money.'[24]

Mr Pang represents a dream that did come true in the 1990s – that of the Hong Kong entrepreneur who achieved his first big break through export processing. There were hundreds, if not thousands, like him and there will be many more. The trajectory for the mainland processing trade is clear – it will move steadily upmarket and the Made in China tag will become as common on computers and palm pilots as it is already on toys and jogging suits. Anything that requires lots of pieces to be put together in an efficient manner at low cost will find an attractive production base in China. This, in the purest sense of the term, is globalisation at work. Hong Kong and Taiwanese firms will continue to dominate manufacturing on the ground and there will be ever more multinational businesses like Nike, Reebok and Adidas – which report sales in the billions of dollars but produce almost nothing themselves. Instead, these companies own brands, design shoes and clothing, employ marketers to promote them and lawyers to defend them. Actual manufacturing is conducted by third-party factories that are supplied with tooling and vast contracts stipulating everything from how products are assembled to the minimum working conditions in a plant. To some, this is a higher form of capitalism; to others, a higher form of first-on-third-world exploitation. Whichever, it is here to stay.

梦

For all its impressive success, and for all the millionaires it has created, however, the export economy will not save China on its own. Apart from the fact that no one part of any economy can be expected to hold up the entire edifice, there are two main reasons. Firstly, the processing trade – accounting for around 60 per cent of total exports – is both confined to a small part of the country and low value-added in nature. In Guangdong, the concentration of processing businesses means exports are equivalent to three-quarters of provincial output, a ratio that exceeds those of richer, export-intensive nations around Asia.[25] But across China as a whole, exports are equivalent to only one-fifth of the economy, a level on a par with Russia.[26] Pockets of the coastline exhibit the Asian prowess for rapid, export-driven growth, but the country as a whole does not. The processing trade separates itself from the rest of the economy geographically and operationally. It depends on easy access to the sea, the means by which components arrive and shoes, toys and computers leave for their predominantly American and European end users. The support services of Hong Kong – from its huge container terminals to its design, banking and legal services – create a particularly strong magnetic pull to the estuary of the Pearl river, which spews out its polluted contents to the south-west of the territory. The Chinese government tries to lure processing factories further inland with offers of tax breaks and other special treatment, but they are rarely tempted. Seventy-one per cent of China's exports, and 82 per cent of those by foreign-invested firms, come from only five of the thirty provinces.[27] Within these provinces, all of them coastal, it is small sub-regions like the Pearl river delta that account for almost all goods produced.

Furthermore, export processing is a low value-added business. In most operations, the difference in price between the components brought into China – the woollen fabric for a suit or the microprocessor for a computer – and that of the products which are re-exported is as little as 25 per cent. Local private and foreign-invested firms profit through economies of scale because their volumes are huge, while multinational retailers capture handsome margins, particularly on branded merchandise, when goods are sold in the shops of developed countries. But the benefit that accrues to the Chinese state – leaving aside much-needed employment creation – is rather less, especially since tax is light on these areas of manufacture. Headline export statistics greatly overstate the contribution of processing to the domestic economy. The data count the final value of goods shipped (around $150 billion of processed items in 2000), not the amount of value added locally.

The difference is enormous and in order to develop China needs to add more value at home. Unfortunately, this is impeded by the country's two-track economic system. A state-dominated industrial base makes it far harder than it should be to replace imported components with local ones because of low quality and poor reliability. Big public companies, with their rigid production systems, are not agile enough to keep up with the processing trade. Furthermore, many have been located by planners in regions hundreds of miles from the coastal areas in which their products might be used. The government is forced to allow tariff-free importation of components to secure export processing investment, but in so doing it rules most state-owned suppliers out of the running. The export processors are the only group in China to have a completely free hand as to whose components they buy.

The second big problem of the export economy relates entirely to the public sector. State enterprises account for some 40 per cent of goods shipped abroad, but there is a real question as to what proportion of these are sold at below the cost of production – what is called 'dumping' – and do not therefore reflect strength in the economy. In the late 1990s, evidence of dumping mounted as China faced an unprecedented amount of international litigation. Some cases, to be fair, were brought by US and European industry associations that perceived Chinese companies as unwilling to defend themselves in international tribunals and which knew they could take advantage of China's 'developing country' status during hearings.[28] But the overall trend was startling. While the Chinese share of world trade was around 4 per cent, the country attracted more than 11 per cent of anti-dumping suits. In the year to June 2000, fifty-three cases were lodged versus a total of 376 in the entire period since 1979; they continued to pile up at a rate of five a month into 2001.[29]

The products at issue ranged from steel and silicon manganese to honey and apple juice. But almost all had one thing in common – they were shipped by state enterprises. As the Asian, and then the global, economies faltered at the end of the decade, and China failed to shake out production capacity, pressure mounted on the government to subsidise exports of surplus production, first in heavy industry sectors, but later in many others. There was considerable official fear that urban unemployment levels could rise to a point where they might cause social instability. But the underwriting of loss-making exports – achieved through tax rebates and bank loans that would never be repaid – was a return to the perversity of the 1970s, when billions of dollars were spent on supporting international sales of coal and other mineral products.

The export economy is China's most obvious success, but its attendant problems recommend a sceptical view of official statistics. The country's position as the sixth biggest trading nation in the world in 2001 does not reflect the value either produced or garnered by the domestic economy.[30] In the medium term, the competitiveness of China's processor operations means that overall shipments can continue to rise at an average of 10 per cent a year. This is no mean feat, but it is not a panacea for the country's ills and nor can exports be relied on to sustain consistent growth. For exports are cyclical because they depend on external demand over which a country has no control. There are periods when there is no increase for a couple of years, followed by rapid expansion. In 2000, China experienced a particularly strong export performance – up more than 30 per cent on the previous year – coinciding with the final period of a decade-long American economic boom. In 2001, with the US and European economies spluttering, export growth in China evaporated. It is in down times like this that the country increasingly feels the frailty of its domestic economy and has to look to its one other hope for sustainable development – private enterprise.

Capitalism, on a leash

Private entrepreneurs, once reviled by the communists, represent China's best chance of escaping a debt trap created by the state sector's failure to reform. Men like Wei Zhonghui, the Qiaotou button factory manager, and Hu Chengzhou, the electrical equipment maker with the enormous diamond ring, are people upon whom the government must depend in order to stave off insolvency. Wenzhou, the city on the south-east coast from where both hail, increased its gross domestic product per capita by a factor of 10 – from $120 a year to more than $1,200 a year – in the two decades after 1978. More important, it did so through private enterprise rather than fiscal expenditure. Hidden from meddling bureaucrats by mountains and sea, Wenzhou today has what is probably the largest private economy – judging by the number of firms – in China.[31] There were 110,000 registered private businesses in the city and its dependant counties in 2000, more than the total for the whole country in 1990.[32] Of state firms, there were almost none.

Wenzhou leads the way but, as with the leading export centres, the place is not typical of the rest of China. Nationwide, firms which are formally registered as Chinese-owned private businesses account for only an eighth of gross domestic product and employ fewer than 20 million people – a small fraction of non-farm employment.[33] Optimism rests with the sector's potential, deduced from its rapid pace of growth, with the number of private firms increasing by 40 per cent a year since 1992 – to 1.3 million in 2000 – and employment in the sector by around 35 per cent a year.[34] The growth, however, like so many statistics in China, is all relative and comes from a tiny base. The percentages are already falling as the base increases. Moreover, there is a dearth of large private businesses. The biggest in the country is the Hope Group, an agricultural supplies conglomerate based in Sichuan, which turns over $600 million a year – small change by international standards. Most private firms are tiny undertakings, like restaurants and shops, although manufacturers are the leading private sector employers.[35]

The achievements of these small businesses are particularly impressive in the light of the obstacles put in their way by the central government. For while the state recognises the need for private business, it is loath to give it much room for manoeuvre. If the sector is to fulfil its potential, it must overcome a daunting array of challenges. At a policy level, the government's unwillingness to bankrupt larger state and collective enterprises limits private companies' room for expansion and helps keep most of them small. The overcapacity created by the public sector reduces or destroys profits for everyone, a problem that only increases as private enterprises become a more significant part of the economy.

At an operational level, the government lays out an impressive set of impediments for the entrepreneur. Registered capital requirements for a private company in China are among the highest in the world – $36,000 in the retail trade and $60,000 in manufacturing or wholesale – and these sums must be paid up in full to the state banking system before business can begin.[36] No company, Chinese or foreign, can operate legally without a series of permits, which require that an investor define precisely the 'scope of business' and location of business. Any activity not mentioned in the licence is thereby made illegal unless it is separately approved. The process of registration, which requires numerous sub-licences, typically takes three to six months for a small concern. A survey of start-up bureaucracy in seventy-five developing nations by Harvard University in 2000 ranked China fifty-first overall for delay and forty-third for cost.[37]

As well as requiring licences, the government maintains both publicly available and 'internal' lists of areas in which private business may and may not operate. A roster issued by the State Bureau of Industry and Commerce Management prohibits investment in fifteen areas, ranging from the specific – like taxis or steel, iron or platinum – to the general, like 'important raw materials'. The more general categories, covering scarce resources, vital national interest and activities entailing public hazard, leave bureaucrats with plenty of scope for interpretation. In addition, unpublished government directives are believed to bar private investment from some thirty industries and seventeen products – including banking, railways, telecommunications and wholesaling – and restrict investment in at least twenty more areas, including automobile manufacture and chemical fibre production. Until 1998, no private firm was allowed to export directly, being forced to pay commission to state-owned import–export agents. As of 2000, only 150 direct export licences had been granted to private companies since the restriction was lifted.[38]

The arm of China's bureaucracy is long indeed. When the International Finance Corporation surveyed 966 private companies in 1999, 80 per cent of those with more than 500 workers and two-fifths of those with more than 100 workers said licences were used to impede their activities. On top of national licensing requirements, local governments also enjoy considerable authority to restrict private sector activity and use this power to protect state and collective units under their control. In other instances, bureaucracies act with contempt for the needs of private enterprise. In Beijing in 2000, the Bureau of Public Health ordered the closure of all restaurants with a floor area of less than 300 square feet on the grounds that they were not hygienic. The same year, the Bureau of Publications ordered the closure of any bookstore smaller than 500 square feet. These regulations should have meant that 3,000 family-run restaurants and numerous private bookshops in the capital were put out of business, without compensation; public sector units invariably have larger premises. In reality, many people ignored the directives, but they live in constant fear of the city government. State expropriation of land for redevelopment also occurs at will. While this ought to entail compensation, it is often not paid and lawyers are unwilling to handle court cases against government at any level.[39]

The most damaging long-term constraint on private business, however, is its lack of access to capital. The government controls the banking system and the stock markets and runs both for the benefit of state enterprises. Central bank data show that as of 1999 less than 1 per cent of working capital loans were extended to private firms.[40] On the Shanghai and Shenzhen stock markets at the end of 2000, under a dozen listed companies were privately held out of 1,100.[41] In 1999, the government promised to create a new board that would be more open to private offerings, in Shenzhen. But as bureaucrats mulled the prospect that this might affect their ability to sell equity in state-owned enterprises – because of a flight to quality – they quietly abandoned the undertaking. In the International Finance Corporation survey, 80 per cent of respondents said access to financing was a constraint. Nine-tenths of the money firms had raised to begin business came from personal savings, friends and family. This compares with research in eastern Europe which indicates that between two-fifths and three-quarters of start-ups are funded by at least one bank loan.[42] While the government touts its commitment to greater private sector lending, Chinese banks know from experience that bad loans to state enterprises will be bailed out, but those to private companies will not. This only adds to the banks' disincentive to lend caused by their unwillingness to value assets like inventory and cashflow as collateral. State enterprises traditionally pledge land and fixed assets, things of which small private businesses have little.[43]

It is a wonder that so many talented entrepreneurs undertake the unequal struggle with their government at all. They face arbitrary taxation and fees and the price of success is ever more attention from rent-seeking authorities. For this reason, many companies set up complex systems of subsidiary businesses and cross-holdings to hide the true extent of their activities. Vast amounts of time are expended heading off a rapacious bureaucracy. It is just as well for China that, despite this, entrepreneurs persist in their endeavours. Since the economy slowed in the second half of the 1990s, and the government began to furlough state workers, the private sector has become the leading creator of new jobs. From 1990 to 1997, private enterprise already accounted for 38 per cent of all new registered employment. Since then, private companies have created more positions each year than all state and collective enterprises combined.[44] Looking into the future, this job creation will have to accelerate exponentially if the private economy is to absorb the scores of millions of surplus workers from the public sector and scores of millions of rural migrants set to arrive in China's cities.

Socialism, asked to behave like capitalism

In the other half of China's parallel economies, nothing exposed the fallacy of the search for 'alternative' solutions to modernisation – ones that, unlike private enterprise, could carry the tag of having 'Chinese characteristics' – quite like the crashing demise of the collective sector. Publicly owned companies that supposedly behaved like private ones were the marvel of the early 1990s. But their promise of a third way, of wealth creation through mixed ownership, turned out to be a neo-socialist utopia. When the dust settled, it was clear there were only two economies in China, communist and capitalist, and the collectives were on the wrong side of the tracks.

In the first few years of the decade, Chinese and foreign observers alike had fawned over the mixed ownership economy, at a time when it was claiming growth rates of over 30 per cent a year.[45] To a large extent, the story turned out to be one of statistical lies. When China conducted a national industrial census – using sampling instead of bureaucratic reporting – in 1994, it was discovered that fully one-third of collective output was imaginary. The situation was worst in the countryside, where township and village enterprises, which account for most collective output, had overstated production by more than 40 per cent. In 1996, the National Bureau of Statistics was forced to wipe $100 billion of industrial output from its national accounts to compensate for the collectives' overreporting.[46]

The exaggerated numbers were an archetypal case of officials in the regions telling government in Beijing what it wanted to hear. The State Planning Commission had declared rural collectives to be 'a miracle'. In 1993 it forecast that township and village enterprises would produce gross output of $1.3 trillion, profits of $130 billion and employ 160 million people by 2000.[47] Just as local administrations in the era of the Great Leap Forward reported to Mao Zedong's government that its ludicrous targets for grain and steel output were being met in full, so the planned growth of the collective sector became an apparently self-fulfilling prophecy.[48] Apparatchiks were motivated both by the potential for their locales to receive larger bank credit allocations and other government support, and by the prospect of personal promotion. The latter phenomenon is known in China as *'guan chu shuzi, shuzi chu guan'*– 'officials produce numbers, numbers produce officials'. In other words, the reporting of positive data is how careers are made. Unfortunately, in the case of the collectives, the gap between plan and reality was shown to be so huge that something had to be done. No announcement was made, no fault was conceded, but historical data in China's statistical yearbooks were quietly rewritten.[49]

False reporting, however, was the lesser of the collectives' two problems. The bigger one was that they did not work – as experience in any number of other countries could have forewarned. It was only the belief that China is somehow different that led both local and international economists and journalists to think otherwise. Mixed public and private ownership – with the state holding at least half the equity – is a messy recipe anywhere.[50] In China, the collectives created a particularly acute form of moral hazard, whereby profits ended up in the pockets of individuals when times were good and debts accrued to the state when business went less well. In the 1980s and early 1990s, the collectives piled into sectors of the economy with low entry barriers where demand exceeded supply – consumer goods, building materials and small-scale mining. The local governments that controlled the businesses were able to secure bank credit, hand themselves planning permission and ignore national pollution standards in toxic industries like leather- and papermaking. A high degree of local protection ensured captive markets for products such as cement and coal. While credit was easy, the collectives diversified relentlessly, chasing into whatever area was the flavour of the month.

In the spirit of Maoist model workers and communes, there were model collectives. The most propagandised was Daqiuzhuang, to the east of Beijing, near Tianjin. Daqiuzhuang was referred to by the state media in the early 1990s as 'the richest village in China', a place of 2,000 inhabitants that grew into a township employing 30,000 industrial workers. The village boss, Yu Zuomin, became a national celebrity. He boasted of having overseen the creation of four large corporations and 200 smaller businesses – all of them collectively owned – which engaged in everything from iron and steel production to agriculture and trading. A second model was the southern part of Jiangsu province, the home of Chinese president Jiang Zemin, where it was claimed that almost the entire economy was controlled by collectives. Among the largest was Jiangsu Zhonggang Group, which combined the production of polyester fibre with the farming of soft-shelled turtles that were said to be a certain cure for cancer. Larger still was Jiangsu Hongbao Group, which began its life as a revolutionary work brigade in the 1970s repairing machinery. In the course of the 1980s and 1990s, Hongbao expanded into medical instruments, stainless steel pipes, handtools, chemical fertiliser, printing materials, household knives and scissors, manicure sets and golf balls.[51]

Each of these model organisations followed the same pattern. The local government that controlled the collective obtained bank loans to finance a new business. When that business ran into trouble, or when a more alluring investment opportunity presented itself, the collective borrowed more money and moved on, while always maintaining its previous activities. In this manner, Jiangsu Hongbao started out with a loan of $720,000 to manufacture stainless steel pipes and by the mid 1990s was looking to borrow $12 million to start its latest enterprise, the manufacture of titanium products.[52] The process, however, could not continue indefinitely. By the mid 1990s, in the absence of bankruptcy and hard budget constraints for state and collective enterprises, most manufacturing businesses were in a state of oversupply. Profits among collectives fell precipitously while the central government ordered its banks to refocus their lending on the largest state enterprises and put more pressure on collectives to pay their own way. The result was that in 1995, for the first time since 1978, the growth of the collective sector dipped below that of the overall economy.[53] Thereafter the collectives entered a period of ongoing recession that saw 10 million jobs shed by township and village enterprises between 1996 and 1998 and as many again at urban collectives.[54] At Daqiuzhuang, the dream had already ended badly. Prestige and power went to the head of Yu Zuomin, who ran his township as a personal fiefdom, ordering the beating and torture of anyone he did not like. After an armed showdown with his local 'protection force', national police entered the township in 1993. Mr Yu was subsequently convicted of conspiracy to murder and numerous lesser crimes and sent to jail for twenty years. Many of his followers accompanied him, while Daqiuzhuang was left to endure a recession and an end to the attentions of the Propaganda Department of the Chinese Communist Party and the state media it controls.

In 2001, the collectives' plight showed no signs of improving. In the first nine months of the year, output increased by 6.9 per cent compared with 2000. At the same time, output from state enterprises – still armed with ready supplies of bank credit – rose by 10.3 per cent, ahead of the overall economy.[55] The collectives' figures are almost certainly much worse than reported, partly because China's industrial output is always overstated and partly because successful private firms masquerading as collectives lift their growth numbers. In March 1998, the central government issued a directive that all private firms that had called themselves collectives in the past in order to avoid suppression – the so-called 'red hat' companies – must re-register to show their private ownership by November.[56] While many did so, making genuinely private companies an ever smaller share of the collective sector, others ignored the ruling.

It is not possible to say in retrospect whether the average government-controlled collective is a better run business than the average acknowledged state enterprise. The point is that the difference is marginal. Both types of company parlayed their access to bureaucratic power and public money – the savings of the Chinese people – to create businesses that look busy but create little or no profit or, more frequently, destroy capital. Once the red hat firms are stripped out – anecdotal evidence suggests that most of these are small, labour-intensive rural enterprises that have created a good part of the 60 million new jobs in township and village enterprises since 1985 – what remains is a net liability for the state. The surprise is that outside observers bought into the collective dream. In 1978, at the start of the reform period, more than a fifth of industrial output already came from collectives set up under Mao Zedong.[57] These companies – the Jiangsu Hongbao Group is a typical example – were created at a time when private enterprise was illegal. Yet twenty years later the world decided that collective enterprises were not state companies by another name, but China's unique contribution to the art of transition from a socialist to a market economy.[58] The improbability of this particular myth was exposed from the mid 1990s when the Chinese government realised that the accumulated savings of the nation would not stretch to underwriting the inefficiencies of both collectives and formal state enterprises. So the government, and the Communist Party, began a staged retreat, preferring instead to indulge the state monoliths they hold most dear.

The heart of the beast

There is never any shortage of official excuses for the performance of China's formal state sector and excuses are useful for the communist leadership because they imply that the country's parallel economies can somehow converge – that progress is possible without fundamental change. In the last years of the 1990s the government and the Party rolled out the latest 'explanation' of the continuing woes of public companies. The argument put forward was that it was small- and medium-sized state enterprises that lost a disproportionate amount of money. Larger public firms were more likely to be profitable.

At face value, there is some evidence to support this. Official statistics touted by the government show that, as of 1997, the 500 largest state enterprises held less than two-fifths of state assets but accounted for nearly two-thirds of profits.[59] The numbers were backed up by the theoretical proposition that large public companies should make money because they often operate in still monopolistic businesses, such as iron and steel or telecommunication services. As a result of its analysis – and pressured by the fact that overall the state sector posted a net loss in 1996 for the first time since 1949 – the government came up with a policy to reform the ownership of small public enterprises while hanging on to large ones. This policy was endorsed by the fifteenth Communist Party Congress in 1997 and, as ever, was blessed with a new slogan: '*zhua da, fang xiao*' – 'grasp the big, release the small'.

The Chinese government's strategy was universally welcomed by agencies like the World Bank and the International Monetary Fund, appearing as it did to herald a new stage in the country's reform process. There was almost no criticism of the notion that big means profitable, something curious given that large state enterprises are also the major consumers of soft bank credit, enabling them to conjure paper profits from thin air. Moreover, little interest was shown in exactly what 'letting go' meant in practice for small and medium-sized state businesses. Attention focused instead on a gratifying annual reduction in the number of officially designated industrial state companies – from 127,000 in 1996 to 61,300 in 1999. Optimism was further bolstered in March 1998 when, assuming the post of prime minister, Zhu Rongji promised at his acceptance press conference a 'three-year solution' to the entire state sector problem.

On the ground, however, *zhua da, fang xiao* raised all manner of concerns about the efficacy of the reform policy. There are no national statistics available, but locally published, regional reports on the progress of ownership reform suggest that in a majority of cases it does not improve enterprise performance or even reduce the state's liabilities. The reason is that very few public firms are sold off to Chinese or foreign private investors, the principals most likely to turn businesses around and least likely to secure soft credit. Instead, most state companies are merged with other state companies, leased to the existing management or turned into joint stock enterprises with a mixture of government and employee ownership. This is the case in two provinces for which comprehensive data exist, Guangxi and Ningxia, as well as in numerous individual cities where reports have been made public.[60] In the provincial studies, less than a fifth of enterprises were either liquidated or sold to private investors.[61] Only in rare, highly localised instances can it be shown that a majority of small and medium-sized state firms have had their state fetters cut.[62]

Mergers, leasing and joint stock reform have marginal impact on state companies. Mergers, which are invariably determined by administrative fiat rather than market pressures, simply reshuffle the state pack. Leasing leaves firms under the control of existing management and repeats the mistakes of profit contracting in the 1980s. The external environment rarely changes and managers' connections to the bureaucracy and state banks remain in place. Indeed, the managers often *are* the bureaucracy. Joint stock ownership, which began in the early 1990s and accelerated as a result of 'letting go the small', does often introduce a new dimension – an infusion of funds through cash raised by the sale of shares to employees. But while this might be expected to mean workers take an active and positive role in the management of their firms, it does not. Even when employees are the majority owners of their companies, they almost never exercise power because company boards – where workers should in theory be represented – exercise no control. The boards exist, but the norm is for a general manager, who is probably also the Party secretary of a business, to concurrently act as chairman of the board of directors and chairman of the advisory board when joint stock reform takes place. The chief alteration that results from the sale of shares to employees – there is often some duress involved, such as the threat of unemployment if they do not accept – is that a new source of cash appears and this encourages rent-seeking from the local bureaucracy as well as straightforward theft by management. Less than a year after the endorsement of *zhua da, fang xiao* by the Communist Party congress, the government launched a national anti-corruption campaign to address crimes committed in the name of joint stock reform.[63]

The model town for joint stock ownership was Zhucheng, in Shandong province. Like all good Chinese models – propagandised by the state media to show how well an idea works – it became a case study of why that idea does not work. In July 1994, Zhucheng sold shares in 210 small and medium-sized state enterprises to managers and employees. Nine-tenths of workers bought stocks and the local government raised $30 million. This was greeted as a triumph in Beijing and most outside observers declared it to be China's first mass privatisation. Even as the model was being celebrated, however, it was already turning ugly. Government and management had written the stock sale rules such that shares could only be sold within companies. In the two years following the initial offering, well-connected local managers secured bank loans and bought up shares from their employees to take control of the companies. The performance of the businesses, meanwhile, did not improve. Money ran out and, by 1997, it was necessary to call for a new share issue of $90 million – three times the original one. In this case, only a quarter of the money was raised from employees. The rest came from state banks and unidentified 'outside investors' – probably other state units – in what amounted to a bail-out. The upshot was badly performing companies controlled by state managers who had bought their equity with borrowed money.[64]

There is plenty more evidence that joint stock reform does not produce desirable results. In the review carried out in Guangxi province, 70 per cent of 'reformed' firms had not improved their performance after five years and a quarter were losing more money than ever.[65] The joint stock adventure followed a familiar pattern of public sector policy in China. In the 1980s, the government borrowed ideas for increased worker bonuses and profit contracting from the former Soviet Union and eastern bloc countries of the 1960s and 1970s. These so-called 'rationalising' reforms failed twenty years earlier in communist Europe and they failed again in China.[66] In the 1990s, the Chinese experiment with joint stock reforms closely paralleled the least successful industrial policies of eastern Europe and Russia in the late 1980s and early 1990s. The Hungarian government, in the period immediately before and after the fall of the Berlin Wall, distributed state enterprise stock to managers and workers in an experiment that led to endemic corruption in the bureaucracy.[67] Likewise, Russia's transfer of shares in 11,000 state enterprises between 1992 and 1994 failed to stem their losses, reduce over-employment or cut wage bills. It was only when eastern European countries began to rein in soft bank credit, allow companies to fold and build functioning judicial systems that ownership changes brought results. Such changes to the external environment in which companies operate, however, have not been entertained in China.

The idea that over 60,000 industrial state enterprises – nearly half the total – have disappeared from government control since 1996 does not withstand scrutiny. More than 14,000 firms showed up in official statistics as joint stock companies by 1999, their ownership and their employees nominally transferred to the non-state sector.[68] In reality, almost all of these businesses remain a state liability. Reports at the provincial and municipal level suggest that, across China, as many as 15,000 state enterprises have been merged with other state enterprises.[69] Of the remaining half of 60,000 companies that have supposedly undergone ownership reform, perhaps half again have genuinely been sold to a third party or, more often, liquidated.[70] The real extent of change among small and middling public firms is likely be a quarter to a third of what is claimed. At an employment level, official statistics show that the number of urban state enterprise workers fell precipitously from 112 million in 1996 to 86 million in 1999. But the same statistics shifted more than 7 million workers into the new categories of 'shareholding units' and 'limited liability corporations'. Meanwhile, 20 million urban workers who appear in the national total have, since 1996, disappeared from China's employment by ownership figures altogether; these employees have made a statistical departure from the public sector but failed to reappear anywhere else.[71] Under such circumstances, the outside observer can use official data with only the greatest circumspection.[72]

梦

To the rationalising reforms of European communists in the 1960s and their stock distribution schemes of the 1980s and early 1990s, China added a third discredited industrial policy borrowed from the outside world. Unlike the first two initiatives, however, the third was lifted from quasi-capitalist Asian countries. This was the state-directed creation and support of key industrial groups, most commonly identified with Japan but more stereotypical of South Korea. It was the 'grasp the big' part of *zhua da, fang xiao*.

Communists like to pick winners, so the policy came naturally to the bureaucracy in Beijing. But it was also a policy that, prior to Japan's decade-long recession in the 1990s and the Asian financial crisis, appeared to have a proven track record. Western and Asian scholars invested Japan's Ministry of International Trade and Investment (MITI) with near-supernatural powers for its supposed ability to allocate credit and determine taxation levels so as to 'guide' the development of key industries. The notion of super-brainy appa-ratchiks planning the minutiae of economic progress was particularly appeal-ing to China, given its insistence that the Communist Party holds a monopoly on political and bureaucratic talent. South Korea, which built up sprawling conglomerates – or *chaebol* – through favoured credit allocation was more appealing still, due to the Chinese state sector's penchant for random diversification. South Korea appeared to prove that bigger is invariably better.

Bureaucrats at the State Planning Commission in Beijing – which was renamed the State Planning and Development Commission in 1998 – were as busy in the 1990s as ever they had been under Mao Zedong. They picked out whole sectors of the economy for special treatment. The first was the automotive industry in 1994. This was followed in 1996 by an industrial policy based around five 'pillar industries': automotive, construction, petrochemicals, electronics and machinery.[73] Soon after, domestic housing construction was given special status. By the end of the decade, much time was being spent nurturing supposedly 'high-tech' state companies. Large firms throughout the economy were guaranteed state support simply by virtue of size.

Across China, provinces and cities issued their own plans for the chaebolisation of state industry, selecting candidates to be pulled together into large enterprise groups. Hebei, the province surrounding Beijing, laid out a plan in 1998 to create two provincial 'mega-groups', five company groups with sales over $1.2bn and thirty companies with sales over $600 million.[74] All of this was to be achieved through administrative fiat. Even before the Asian financial crisis and the collapse of the Korean *chaebol* model, however, China already had evidence of the dangers of trying to 'select' industrial winners. The most widely reported case was that of Capital Iron and Steel, known as Shougang, which had to be rescued from insolvency in 1995.

Shougang's is a remarkable story because the company was in fact one of the few successful examples of profit contracting in the 1980s.[75] Unlike most state enterprises, Shougang's contract had worked because it was closely monitored by a single government agency – the State Council, located just down the road in Beijing – and because in return for the contract the company was genuinely denied access to soft bank loans and subsidies. For eleven years from 1982, the tax Shougang paid to the central government increased at a contracted 7 per cent a year while the steelmaker managed to up its retained profits to a peak of $230 million in 1992.[76] All this hard work, however, came to nought. In May 1992, after his Southern Tour, Deng Xiaoping paid a visit to the company and it was catapulted into the position of a model state enterprise. The firm's general manager and chairman, Zhou Guanwu, created a room-size mural depicting Mr Deng's shopfloor tour and never looked back. With its annointed status, the Ministry of Finance and other state agencies ceased to supervise Shougang and bank credit was suddenly available. Mr Zhou set out to create China's largest steel producer in short order. In the space of two years – 1993 and 1994 – he borrowed $1 billion and poured $1.6 billion into fixed asset investments. He ordered up a new steel works on the coast in Shandong province[77], the so-called Qilu project, and bought the state iron ore mines of Peru to supply its raw material. There were other huge projects for propane processing and diesel oil refining. As well as money from the big state banks, Shougang tapped financing from its proprietary bank, Huaxia, that it had been given permission to open, as well as via back-door listings on the Hong Kong stock market organised by Mr Zhou's son.

It was a veritable spendathon. In 1994, Shougang became China's biggest producer of raw steel, but the company had not yet installed the rolling capacity to turn this into final product. Inventories rose by a million tons. The feasability study for the new Shandong plant revealed that there was no local port deep enough to berth the large ships used to import iron ore. But Mr Zhou determined to press on anyway, arguing that Peruvian ore could be unloaded south of Shanghai and sent up by train. The situation only came to a head because Mr Zhou was spending money so fast that by late 1994 there was not even enough cash to pay workers. When the central government looked into the case, investigators were astonished by how quickly Shougang's once rock solid finances had run out of control. Such is the price of telling a company it is one of the chosen few. The investigators discovered that managers had spent over $20 million on luxury cars and mobile phones alone in the past two years. The Shougang affair ended with huge – but unpublicised – state bail-outs for both the steelmaker and Huaxia bank, the forced retirement of Zhou Guanwu and a suspended death sentence for unspecified 'economic crimes' for his son Zhou Beifang.[78] The Qilu steelworks was abandoned.

Lessons never learned

The idea of concentrating the state's efforts on large public enterprises and nurturing the best of them has been enough to convince the world that reform is alive in China. Government officials point to the most modern of the country's state enterprises – the vaunted computer maker Legend or household appliance manufacturer Haier – and claim they represent tangible progress.[79] With their gleaming new factories and international ambitions, such companies look much more like their South Korean corporate cousins than the state enterprises of old. Yet just as the ubiquitous, state-funded construction work in its cities tells the observer nothing about the sustainability of economic growth in China, so the nation's bell-wether public companies fail to represent a genuine break with the past. It would be a comfort if these firms were on average only as inefficient as South Korea's *chaebol* turned out to be. But in reality they are worse. The reason is that the environment in which Chinese state enterprises operate is far more certain than anything in capitalist Asia to produce waste on the one hand, and false reporting about that waste on the other.

The most fundamental problem of China's public sector is the perversity of the fiscal and financial system of which it is a part. The government, with its public debt – in the form of treasury bonds – accumulating rapidly, still depends for most of its taxation on state companies. Those firms' share of total government revenues fell only from 87 per cent in 1978 to 60 per cent at the end of the 1990s.[80] Most outsiders wonder why it is that such unprofitable companies can pay so much tax. The truth is that large state enterprises can only do so because of their access to a spiral of bank credit. The companies borrow money, increase output, report modest profits – when times are tough they do this by booking more unpaid receivables – and pay high rates of taxation to the central government. The reporting of some profit, and the paying of some tax, guarantees more credit. The only thing that changes is that a company's liabilities – in the form of bank loans – increase.

A close look at large state companies shows why the idea that big is profitable is such a dangerous fallacy. The profitability is for all the wrong reasons, as Edward Steinfeld, an assistant professor at the Massachussetts Institute of Technology, proved in a series of case studies in the Chinese steel industry published in 1998.[81] Each of the three firms he dissected is officially profitable. But each was also generating profits by building liabilities. The Anshan Iron and Steel works – Angang – with the biggest steel sector workforce in the country, is a classic example. Each year that Professor Steinfeld reviewed, Angang reported rising revenue and profits and made large tax payments. Indeed, management made the proud boast that the 400,000-worker conglomerate paid more central government taxation than the whole of Guangdong province.[82] In addition, the business is tapped for numerous local levies by the government of Anshan city. Yet this tale of an apparently successful company falls flat on its face when one sees that each year Angang's current liabilities – mostly short-term bank loans – are greater than its current assets. Furthermore, most of the current assets are receivables generated by giving away steel product on credit that will never be paid. So while Angang delivers its taxes, it remains desperately short of working capital and periodically cannot afford to pay its workers. Management operates in expectation of the next bank loan. As Professor Steinfeld put it: 'Essentially insolvent firms in China today can still appear relatively healthy on paper.'[83]

The economist went on to demonstrate how even overseas listing fails to change the basic behaviour of state enterprises. Ma'anshan Iron and Steel –

Magang – sent the Hong Kong market into a frenzy of excitement with its initial public offering in October 1993. As is the norm with listings outside the mainland, Magang split its best steel-making assets into a company in which shares were sold and left its residual welfare units and less attractive businesses – like iron ore mining – in a holding company that had majority control of the listed vehicle. International accountants and lawyers pored over the books of the listing enterprise – Magang Steel – before it began trading. Yet this was insufficient to bring discipline to the firm. Within a year of its public offering, it had committed most of the $795 million raised to expanding output of products for which there was little demand.[84] Sales were being increased by extension of ever more credit to buyers, and within twelve months the company added receivables of $240 million. The holding company, which technically controlled 62 per cent of Magang Steel, could do nothing to direct its operations because it had no say in the appointment of senior personnel in the listed vehicle. Top management was chosen by the Ministry of Metallurgical Industry in Beijing and the local provincial Party committee.[85] These agencies represented the state, but they had no defined interest in the holding company so they did nothing to assist it. After its first full year of operations, the management of Magang Steel decided to pay a dividend, but refused to pay the share owed to the holding company. Furthermore, Magang Steel failed to pay for a substantial part of the welfare services and iron ore the holding company provided it. Instead, the listed vehicle booked a profit and paid tax to the central and local governments by effectively borrowing from its parent. At the same time, since the tax burden of Magang Steel was now subject to international scrutiny, the provincial and central governments increased the tax burden of the holding company. A year after the Hong Kong listing, the holding company was insolvent and had to be bailed out with bank loans.

梦

This type of behaviour goes a long way towards explaining why, despite ruses like the selective paying of dividends to support share prices, only one out of the fifty mainland companies listed in Hong Kong in 2000 was trading above its initial public offering price. International equity investors might have been suckered by the China Dream in the mid 1990s, but once they wised up they were quick to dump non-performing stocks. The window that public listing provides on to Chinese state companies also gives the lie to the inevitable claim, made at the end of 2000, that the central government's three-year programme to 'solve' the state sector problem had been a success. Despite the absence of any improvement in the performance of the minority of state enterprises that are listed, Sheng Huaren, head of the State Economic and Trade Commission, announced the completion of the turnaround exercise for the sector overall in December 2000.[86] The boast was repeated by premier Zhu Rongji at the annual session of the National People's Congress in March 2001.[87]

The numbers rolled out in support of this transformation were dominated by those of unlisted state enterprises whose accounts are not publicly available. Profits, it was reported, rose a spectacular 130 per cent in the public sector in 2000, to $28 billion. The number of loss-making large- and medium-sized state enterprises, meanwhile, fell by two-thirds between 1997 and 2000, although no figures were published for the actual volume of losses.[88] Not for the first time, official figures painted a picture that could be cause for considerable optimism. Behind the image, however, was the story of massive financial transfers, accountancy changes and cyclical influences needed to produce signs of statistical progress. Between 1998 and 2000, the central government allowed state enterprises to write off $169 billion of bank debt in exchange for shares they issued to state-owned asset management companies. This reduced state companies' annual interest burden by at least $7 billion a year. By 2001, the central bank had also reduced interest rates to their lowest level in a decade, further cutting the expenditure of the state companies that account for most bank loans. And already slow depreciation schedules for public companies were slowed further, allowing additional reporting of short-term profit.[89] Finally, the sudden spike in international oil prices in 2000 led to windfall profits for China's state-owned oil companies. According to one official at the State Economic and Trade Commission, oil production and refining profits accounted for as much as half of all profits in the state sector in 2000.[90] Strip out this windfall and the reduced interest expenses engendered by a $169 billion bail-out and low bank rates, and there is little evidence that much has changed at China's state enterprises. If this were not the case, the performance of listed firms – supposedly the best of the bunch – would be forging ahead as well.

The Chinese Communist Party and government have remained in denial about the depth and seriousness of the problems in the state sector. Lying and obfuscation are such a way of life in the bureaucracy that it is easier to pretend than to confront reality. But pretence changes nothing. Despite consuming most of China's credit, state enterprise profits as a proportion of gross national product fell from 7 per cent in 1987 to close to zero in the late 1990s and only 2.5 per cent in the unusual circumstances of 2000.[91] The state sector's woes may be confined to one part of China's two, parallel economies, but because of their links to the banking system, the whole economy is in danger. As Edward Steinfeld put it in the introduction to his study: 'China today, for all the successes of the past fifteen years, stands at an economic crossroads and at the edge of a monumental economic crisis. The state sector is not simply dying; it also threatens to drag down the nation's entire economy with it.'[92]

Most outsiders believe that in some sense China's reform trajectory is new. But in actual fact every initiative that has been tried out among state enterprises in the past twenty years has already failed somewhere else. Observing China's reform experiments is not like studying an alternative approach to the difficulties of economic transition. It is like re-watching a 1970s socialist B-movie, in which the only thing that has changed is the spin in the preceding trailer. In order to progress, the watching world and the Chinese government must move beyond the idea that there is some fundamental China 'difference'. There is a mountain of evidence from former socialist and national socialist states in eastern Europe, Africa and Latin America about what needs to be done to ensure a successful transition to a market economy, and the requirements vary only minimally between countries.[93] Chief among all these is the necessary political commitment to give up administrative micro-management of the economy, to tolerate an independent judiciary that stands in judgement of government as well as private citizens, and to force financial systems to operate on genuinely commercial terms. These are the developments that determine the environment in which all businesses operate, and allow the good to prosper and the bad to fail – irrespective of whether they are public or private. But these changes also require the state to relinquish economic powers that have been politicised – in the bureaucracy, in the financial system and in the judiciary. The Chinese Communist Party says again and again that politics and economics can and should be separated. This is true. The problem in China is that the dividing line is in the wrong place. The country's economic problems are therefore fundamentally political in nature.

11

Yesterday's politics

'[In Hong Kong] I found that among the government officials corruption was the exception and purity the rule. It was the contrary in China, where corruption among the officials was the rule. I then thought I would try higher up, to the provincial government, but I found that the higher the government the more corrupt were its ways. Finally, I went to Peking, but I found things there one hundred times more corrupt than even in Canton.'

Sun Yat-Sen, founder of the first Chinese republic in 1911, talking about his travels on the mainland in the late 1880s to students of Hong Kong University on 20 February 1923

AT THE START of the twenty-first century, China's unfaded commercial reputation as a potential gold mine stood in stark contrast to her more shadowy political image. A series of incidents in the 1990s – from provocative incursions and military exercises in the South China Sea and the Taiwan Strait to diplomatic showdowns with the United States – convinced an increasing number of outsiders that she posed a genuine threat to the world. This idea was only reinforced by the knowledge that China is a nuclear power. By the end of the decade, the concept of 'China the menace' was helping to pad NATO military and espionage budgets and inspire international bestsellers with doomsday scenarios about conflict with the west.[1]

Yet the notion that China presents a challenge to the global order rests on two improbable arguments. The first is the proposition – similar to but far less credible than the one made by the United States about Japan in the 1980s – that the nation is a rising economic superpower. As this book has shown, nothing could be further from the truth; China's is a rather limited economy facing probable crisis. Second, and superficially more convincing, is the argument that China is an assertive international player determined to project her power outwards. However, while the Chinese government loves nothing more than to see that the world is paying attention, its international image is based largely on what the late sinologist Gerald Segal dubbed its capacity for 'diplomatic theatre'.[2]

Far more serious than any threat posed by China to the wider world is the threat posed to herself by her ossified and stagnant political system. This has come to represent the single biggest obstacle to the country's economic progress. More than a decade after the Berlin Wall was torn down and the Soviet Union collapsed, the ruling Chinese Communist Party is a dinosaur in a changed global environment. The rival Kuomintang in Taiwan accepted the need for political reform in the 1990s, and the people of Hong Kong have struggled for a greater say in the running of their lives, but mainland communists remain unmoved by such currents. The Communist Party bills itself as the only organisation qualified to lead China's modernisation. In reality, however, the Party has continued to impede critical reforms, not least because its membership and constituency stand to lose the most from the dismantling of a socialist economic structure. Instead of instigating fundamental change, the Party delivers a cocktail of intolerance, corruption and secrecy – all of which make such change less likely. The world frets about the possibility of China's geopolitical ambitions, and is unnerved by her bullying diplomacy, but its attentions should be focused instead on the country's domestic political impasse and consequent slow descent towards internal calamity.

梦

The Communist Party's appetite for military adventure overseas was cut down to size almost immediately after it came to power in 1949. In 1950, China annexed Tibet, a nation that proved to be as soft yet resilient a target as East Timor would be for the Indonesian military twenty-five years later. Tibet continues to tie down hundreds of thousands of troops and civilian bureaucrats, costing a small fortune for the maintenance of a pointless occupation and reminding the government of the perils of extraterritorial activity. From 1950 to 1953, China entered the Korean war, a punishing encounter that left it with a million casualties.[3] In the wake of these experiences, the dragon drew in its claws.[4] Already by the late 1960s, the most violent period of the Cultural Revolution, the country's military limitations were sufficiently apparent to its leaders that the most natural outlet for the revolutionary fervour of the era – the retaking of the colonies of Hong Kong and Macau – was not even entertained. Instead, China's politics turned inward and international ambitions have ever since been played out through a low-risk, high-visibility strategy of opportunistic meddling that continues to this day.

In the 1960s and 1970s, the Chinese government armed and backed socialist insurgents and states in Africa and south-east Asia, attempting to assert itself as the leader of the developing world. In time, and at great expense, it discovered that the third world was a more fractious place than it had imagined, and had no desire for Chinese leadership. In the 1980s, the military changed tack again, in line with Deng Xiaoping's call to put business before all else, and made a tidy profit from selling weapons and spare parts to both sides in the Iran–Iraq war. Arms trading relationships were also developed with other middle eastern countries. In the 1990s the end of the Cold War coincided with the running down of Britain's and Portugal's respective leases on Hong Kong and Macau. As it became clear these colonies would return to Chinese sovereignty on schedule,[5] so diplomatic attention turned to Taiwan – China's so-called renegade province, listed in mainland telephone directories as 'temporarily absent'. Here, the pattern was to variously demand that the island engage in talks for reunificiation with the 'motherland' and to threaten violence whenever the Taipei government did anything untoward – such as hold elections or attempt to develop diplomatic ties with other countries. In spring 1996, after Taiwan's president travelled to the United States, Beijing tested medium-range missiles by firing them close to the island. The spectacle received global coverage and appeared to take the developed world by surprise. Yet it was entirely consistent with an established strategy of seeking maximum international impact for minimum tangible risk.[6]

At the turn of the millennium, this strategy was taken to a new level of refinement. With the mistaken US bombing of the Chinese embassy in Belgrade and the collision and forced landing on Hainan island of a US spy plane, Beijing was handed two unmissable opportunities to manipulate domestic opinion and practise the role of indignant victim of western hegemony.[7] In the first instance, the government blacked out news of US apologies for the Belgrade bombing for twenty-four hours, bussed students and workers to demonstrate outside the American and British embassies in Beijing and allowed people to think the attack was a deliberate act. The embassy buildings were pelted with stones and paint. At the United Nations, grandiose threats were made by China, which holds a permanent seat on the Security Council, to block or change the organisation's peace mission in Kosovo, throwing international diplomacy into chaos. No such threat was carried out, but in the midst of Europe's most serious conflict for half a century, China secured top global media billing for a week. The Swiss, who also had their embassy mistakenly bombed, went virtually unmentioned.

In the second incident, full use was again made of press controls. The official media did not report that the collision between a US surveillance plane and a Chinese military jet in April 2001 took place in international air space. Most citizens interpreted the incident as involving an American spy plane that was flying around within China. This aroused justifiable anger. US secretary of state Colin Powell's expression of sorrow for the loss of a Chinese pilot's life was not carried by the media for four days. Meanwhile, without presenting any evidence, the Chinese government sequestered twenty-four US aircrew, trawled through their plane and demanded Washington accept full responsibility and apologise 'to the Chinese people'. This time the result was top global media billing for two weeks until, after twelve days in detention, the crew were released.[8] The plane was only allowed out several weeks later – in pieces.

With such goings-on, it is little surprise that the outside world perceives China as a potential monster. Yet the image is as unhelpful as it is misleading, because it distorts both international and domestic political reality. China's temper tantrums are theatre, nothing more. They hide the country's weakness, but they do not presage any genuine military threat. The People's Liberation Army, which also comprises a navy and an air force, is vast – with around 3 million men and women, 10,000 battle tanks, 5,000 military aircraft and the world's largest fleet – but hardly threatening to the developed world.[9] Most of the personnel are not combat-trained, the army's ground war hardware is similar to that used by Saddam Hussein in the Gulf War (much of which was supplied by China) and the air defence systems are of the same ilk as those that failed to protect Slobodan Milosevic's Serbia from NATO war planes. There is little doubt that – given the capacity for real military projection – the Chinese Communist Party would be tempted to throw its weight around. But it does not have much weight to throw, and the army is aware of this. Since NATO countries provide a modicum of deterrent weaponry to Taiwan, Beijing's bluster about the island's future must remain just that. In the meantime, the fiction of a possible China versus the west Cold War deflects international attention from the domestic political arena and the intolerance and secrecy that threaten the country's own future. The real political point to be grasped, as was the case throughout the twentieth century, is that China is more of a threat to itself than to anyone else. The melodramatic rantings of the senior leadership mirror a brittle and insecure society.

Knowing best

The Chinese state's political problems grow out of its intolerance – the same intolerance that obstructs investors' efforts to open up the market. Whether this is theorised in terms of Confucian tradition or Marxist dogma or, most plausibly, a mixture of the two, the facts of everyday life are the same. Chinese citizens cannot start a fishing club, a self-help group for alcoholics or a community newsletter without official sanction. Even trade associations are required to register and seek approval from the national network of government-run chambers of commerce. Despite twenty years of so-called 'reform and opening up', anything that involves association is deemed a threat to the state. In China, there is the government and Communist Party and their myriad organs on the one hand, and individual people on the other. There is very little in between. Even the five officially approved religions – Buddhism, Taoism, Islam, Catholicism and Protestantism – have their own, government-organised 'patriotic' churches; any other form of worship is illegal. There is no pluralism in ordinary life. If a person is a member of any formally consti-tuted group outside work it must be approved by the state and almost inevitably be a part of the state.[10]

The clearest window on to the intolerance of the Chinese leviathan in recent years was the suppression of the Falun Gong spiritual movement. The group dates from the early 1990s, its followers practising a mix of slow-motion calis-thenics, breathing exercises, meditation and the study of the moralistic writ-ings of its leader, Li Hongzhi. Falun Gong fell through China's cultural police net because it registered not as a religion – no new religion has been registered in China for fifty years – but as an exercise club. As a result, members, unlike adherents of the five recognised churches, could practise their beliefs and exercises wherever they liked – in parks and even, before and between shifts, in their places of work. By the end of the 1990s, the regimen was being fol-lowed by millions of people, some said tens of millions. Li Hongzhi's teachings have their unusual and occasionally racist features – such as a belief in extrater-restrial life and separate-but-equal heavens for people of different races – but the views are no more eccentric than those of the Unification Church, Jehovah's Witnesses and many American TV evangelists. The main moral pre-cepts of Falun Gong are honesty and a requirement to do good for others.

The central government barely even noticed the organisation prior to 1998. The sight of people, particularly the elderly, doing some form of tradi-tional t'ai chi exercises in public spaces in China is entirely normal. But when adherents responded to press criticism from Marxist intellectuals by peace-fully picketing local newspapers and television stations, they came on to the Party's radar screen. Articles written by a handful of critics – branding the group a hive of superstition – continued until, on 25 April 1999, there was a huge sit-down protest by 10,000, mostly middle-aged, followers outside the walled government compound of Zhongnanhai in Beijing. It was the trigger for a savage clampdown. Falun Gong members asked for official recognition. What they received was an announcement that their group was a 'cult'. By the end of the year – contrary to all legal norms – the organisation was outlawed on a retroactive basis. There followed thousands of arrests, widespread use of administrative detention without charge for the purposes of 're-education' and numerous well-documented cases of torture and death in custody.[11]

The two great ironies of Falun Gong were that it originated and prospered in the north-east of China – where the traditional socialist state and economy are strongest – and that the main weapon of the government in suppressing the movement was the honesty of its followers. In a country where political necessity makes lying a way of life, adherents who travelled to Beijing to protest their treatment were often detained because they told police who they were. Falun Gong teaches that lying is wrong. Asked by plain clothes agents outside official Petitions and Appeals Offices and on the approaches to Tiananmen Square if they were Falun Gong members, most said yes, and were carted off for interrogation and beating.[12] Such is the price of honesty. But the larger point confirmed by the Falun Gong story is that intolerance of freedom of personal expression in China outstrips anything seen in other Asian countries like Japan, South Korea and even Indonesia in their early periods of development. Confronted with something it did not like, the Chinese Communist Party did not leave matters to the legal system it talks up so loudly. Instead it launched a programme of eradication. The Ministry of Justice even circulated a directive to lawyers warning them not to take on cases of Falun Gong followers should they attempt legal challenges to the government.[13]

A diagnosis of chronic intolerance for the Chinese state's attitude towards its people is not difficult because its universal symptom – cruelty – is everywhere. In the first comprehensive review of torture in China for a decade, Amnesty International concluded in February 2001 that the practice is expanding, affecting not just political dissidents but criminal defendants and their lawyers, people accused of disobeying the one child policy and alleged tax evaders. Torture by the state is still not illegal *per se*, only in defined instances. The Amnesty International paper presented seventy-five detailed cases of torture from recent years – and 600 more in outline – involving beatings, whippings, electrical shocks, sexual abuse and wrongful commital of victims to secure mental asylums.[14] Capital punishment exists for more than fifty crimes and the country executes more people than the rest of the world put together. There were 27,120 death sentences reported in the official media in the 1990s and 18,000 confirmed executions.[15] This was the publicised use of the death penalty. Among the dead, the politicised, summary nature of the judicial system makes it certain there were many people who were either wholly innocent or at least innocent of the crimes with which they were charged. Despite a raft of new laws passed in the 1990s, and promises to respect the freedoms enshrined in the Chinese constitution and international rights treaties to which China is a signatory, it is still possible to be charged with offences as opaque as 'plotting to split the country and undermine national unity', 'instigating reactionary propaganda' or 'distorting facts and disturbing social order'.[16]

Cruelty is, then, the symptom of the intolerance that makes the Chinese state obsessive in its need to control everything. This is the same in business or in cultural life. The logic that requires a Moslem to join a communist-organised mosque, to worship only at licensed premises and to read only approved religious texts is the logic that requires a businessman to state precisely what business he will conduct, and where, when applying for an operating licence.[17] There is a public commitment to reducing the scale of the bureaucracy, but it is impossible to imagine this happening while control remains the state's defining principle. What actually occurs – as in the case of state enterprises – is a great deal of shuffling that gives the impression of change, but produces no net result. A striking example is the People's Liberation Army (PLA), the ultimate source of the Chinese Communist Party's control. The PLA's full-time employment officially fell from a peak of 4.75 million in 1981 to less than 3 million in the late 1990s. In the same period, however, China established a new paramilitary police force, the People's Armed Police (PAP), which was initially staffed by 600,000 ex-soldiers. Another 1.5 million personnel were added to the PAP by 2000, many of them also former service people. And under president Jiang Zemin, the chief sponsor of the PAP, the Ministry of State Security was expanded to an estimated head count of 2 million. Where once there was the army, now there are thirteen separate agencies dealing with 'security' issues. If anything, the roll call in the state security apparatus has grown in the past twenty years.[18]

A similar trajectory occurs in central government. Despite a much-vaunted reduction in the number of central ministries in 1998, from forty to twenty-nine, lesser agencies proliferate. Most outsiders would expect that a smaller number of ministries would reduce the size of the State Council, China's cabinet. But there are now more non-ministerial agencies than ministries entitled to attend State Council meetings. As well as the twenty-nine ministers, the heads of seven State Council offices, seventeen agencies 'directly under' the State Council and ten other government agencies enjoy access to the cabinet.[19] If everyone turns up, it is a talking shop of more than sixty people. This is only the official Chinese government. The other bureaucratic problem is that there must be two people for every job – one from the formal government and one from the Communist Party – in order to maintain the fiction that there is a separation between Party and state. At every level of government there is a Party apparatus in parallel with the regular administration. From the State Council and the Politburo to the village head and the village Party secretary, this doubling up pervades Chinese life. While the Communist Party claims – in the teeth of the evidence – that formal government is shrinking, it is only too happy to report that the Party itself is growing. The organisation boasted 63 million members by the end of the 1990s, up from 50 million at the start of the decade.

The big cookie jar

The more control there is in an economy, the more likely it is to be afflicted by corruption. Since every significant action requires an approval, the potential for graft is limitless. Until the mid 1990s, most journalists and academics expected to find corruption in the provinces, rather than the capital. There was a presumption that some purity remained at the heart of the Communist Party, a point supported by tales of Deng Xiaoping's humble lifestyle. Many commentators drew a distinction between China, with its supposedly clean senior leadership, and a country like Indonesia, which seemed to be run semi-openly by the Suharto family for its own enrichment. The analysis, however, missed the point. It is not the Communist Party, but the system of control it maintains, that is inherently corrupting. And since more power, licences and approvals emanate from Beijing than anywhere else, it stands to reason that it is the epicentre of corruption. As graft around the country soared in the last decade of the twentieth century, and the Party leadership became ever more desperate to be seen to be doing something about it, a series of high profile cases in the capital gave something of the true flavour of the corruption problem.

The year before Deng Xiaoping died – 1996 – Beijing Party secretary Chen Xitong was sentenced to sixteen years in prison. Chen and his cronies were sent down ostensibly for graft involving $67,000, but investigators conceded off the record that the real scandal was that they had run the capital like a racket for a decade and more than $2 billion of public money was missing. Chen's demise came as a bolt from the blue. He was supposed to be a hardline communist ideologue – one of the strongest supporters of military intervention in the protests of 1989. He turned out to be a mafioso playboy with a huge villa on the shores of Miyun reservoir, north of Beijing. By the end of the decade, Chen's successor as Party secretary, Jia Qinglin, was already tainted by rumours of corruption. His wife was under investigation for allegedly profiting from a gargantuan smuggling operation in Fujian province where Jia had just stepped down as Party secretary. The case was instructive because it showed what can be done through the licence and approvals system.

A privately controlled company in the coastal city of Xiamen had illegally leased the import–export licence and chops of a major state trading house.[20] Armed with the right to import, the firm co-opted and paid off a raft of officials in the city's Communist Party committee, government, customs administration, state banks and different police forces to enable it to bring in everything from luxury cars to crude oil duty free. Since provincial politicians control their local judiciary, police and media, the Party's Beijing-based anti-corruption body, the Central Disciplinary Inspection Committee, was kept in the dark for five years, by which point an officially estimated $6 billion of goods had been smuggled. The case took down a vice-minister of public security, arrested for complicity at the end of 1999, and led to scores of executions. But Beijing Party secretary Jia, a close ally of Jiang Zemin, survived in his post. The investigation into his wife, the improbability that he knew nothing of the case and his incompetence as Fujian Party secretary if he did not know, were all overlooked.

The last years of the 1990s exploded the myth of the purity at the heart of the Chinese Communist Party. As corruption was confirmed to be endemic, China's most senior leaders played a dangerous game. In order to demonstrate they were addressing the problem, they fingered ever more senior officials. Provincial Party secretaries and vice-ministers became fair game. In September 2000, the vice-chairman of the National People's Congress, Cheng Kejie, was executed for graft. The justice minister was sacked.[21] But there had to be a limit. Any attack on the top-most echelon of the leadership threatened to bring the Party crashing down in a storm of allegation and counter-allegation. The Beijing rumour mill churned over the possible activities of Li Xiaolin, daughter of Communist Party number two Li Peng, who has long worked as an energy consultant while her father oversees the electricity industry of which he used to be minister.[22] Mr Li's son runs the largest state power producer, while Mr Li's wife was put in charge of China's first nuclear power plant.[23] The son of Party leader Jiang Zemin, Jiang Mianheng, built one of the largest and the fastest-growing telecommunications businesses in the country in the late 1990s, obtaining an exclusive licence to construct a national fibre optic network.[24] However, such apparent conflicts of interest between the most senior leaders and their offspring remained off-limits to investigators.

The one thing the Communist Party can never accept with respect to corruption is that the problem is born of its system of control – a case of too much regulation and too little independent oversight. Instead of dealing with causes, the Party attacks the evidence of the problem. It does this with increasing ferocity, but no sustainable success. The methodology is called 'yan da' – or 'strike hard' – an ongoing process of campaigns targeting different corrupt activities in turn, from smuggling to vice. Figures are regularly published to show how much is being done: cases investigated, funds recovered, punishment meted out, and so on. The Central Disciplinary Inspection

Committee's report for 1998 claimed the organisation considered 1.6 million possible instances of corruption, investigated 120,000, recovered $560 million and punished 3,970 Party and government officials. The numbers are supposed to impress, but theft and diversion of public funds go on apace. The National Audit Office said that in 1998 more than $13 billion of state property was misappropriated, of which only $3 billion was recovered. In reports in 1998 and 1999 about abuse of public funds allocated for the purchase of grain from peasants and, separately, money provided for poverty relief, resettlement and irrigation, investigators were unable to account for sums of $7 billion and $15 billion respectively.[25]

China's 900 million peasants suffer more than anyone from graft. They are robbed through illegal taxes, see their development funds filched and at the same time have absolutely no claim on the state's social security system, which is reserved for urbanites. Despite brutal official retribution, this has engendered rising levels of rural unrest. In the biggest cities, the situation is more nuanced. Graft is ever present, but registered urban dwellers have learned to milk the system as well as be milked by it. They take advantage of China's parallel public and private economies, grabbing the benefits of both. It is extremely common – in fact, almost certainly the majority case – for families in Beijing or Shanghai to maintain one or two people working in the state sector and have other members in private employment. The former provide low-rental housing and the right to buy at enormous discounts, free medical cover, use of work unit vehicles, mobile telephones and landlines, but little salary.[26] The private economy, by contrast, produces cash. Savvy families can live in a state apartment built within the last five years, have another apartment leased out for rent, make phone calls at a government unit's expense, visit the new out of town superstores in a borrowed state vehicle and still be putting considerable cash earnings into the bank.[27] The government claims that the old 'iron rice bowl' of lifetime employment and cradle-to-grave welfare has been smashed as a result of reform. But in the large metropolises a privileged minority has invented a new iron rice bowl – a combination of public and private economies that delivers a better return than ever. The problem is that this lifestyle is underwritten by a public sector that has amassed unserviceable debts and continues to increase them.

Mum's the word

The landscape of political China, wrought from intolerance, signposted with cruelty and corruption, is darkened by a veil of secrecy. Again, the reasons are a mixture of Leninism and Confucianism, with the proportions depending on the observer's view of the relative potency of each. In pre-1911 China, the emperors of old hid themselves behind the high walls of the Forbidden City and Zhongnanhai compounds. After 1949, Mao Zedong, a new emperor in all but name, headed straight for the latter. There was no obvious difference in their attitude to public exchange. The heart of government remains in Zhongnanhai and, although post-Mao leaders have moved their living quarters out, it is only as far as other traditional, walled-in courtyard houses and apartment complexes in the old city, protected by legions of plain clothes policemen.

The level of contemporary accountability is illustrated by the fact that the Chinese prime minister gives one press conference a year – for which questions must be submitted in advance.[28] The likely successor to Jiang Zemin as president in March 2003 has never given an interview to the foreign media in his life; nor has the putative premier, Wen Jiabao. Little is known about either man from the official state press.[29] Mr Hu built his career on saying as little as possible about anything. If he is quoted in the official media, his remarks are sure to be couched in the most ambiguous terms. The only substantive thing that is known about him is that he was Party secretary in Tibet during a period of violent suppression.[30]

In the 1990s, secrecy produced perverse and extraordinary benefits for China. Had they known the reality of its operating conditions and the true size of its markets, it is impossible to imagine that foreign investors would have poured so much money into the country. Toured about in government limousines and fed an endless diet of spurious statistics, multinational executives lived out their China fantasies. It is telling that India – a nation of a billion people but with a robust free press that reports the country's economic story like it is – amassed one-tenth the direct foreign investment of China. India's headline growth rates were slower, but some of her markets – such as that for cars – proved to be larger. The conclusion that investors knew too little about one country, and too much about the other, is hard to escape.

Beneath the surface, however, secrecy rots away the foundations of the Chinese economy, just as it did in the Soviet Union. Over time, there is a high price to pay for deceit. Not only foreigners are denied accurate information, but the government as well. With no independent means of verification, what passes for knowledge comes from official reports, and official reports are not filled out and fed up the chain of command with truthfulness in mind. Returns are filed to show that official objectives have been met, that growth continues and – critically – to cover up graft and diversion of public funds. When the central government states that the proportion of non-performing loans in the banking system is this, or the losses of state enterprises are that, it cannot possibly know. The whole reporting system makes local bureaucrats the arbiters of truth in their domain, with only the faintest possibility that what they say will ever be cross-checked. It is not so much surprising that there is a great deal of good news in China; it is a wonder that there is any bad news at all.

The word that defines secrecy is 'neibu', meaning 'internal'. It is a two syllable response to any request for information, and is one of the most frequently used terms in the bureaucratic lexicon. Absolutely anything can be neibu – from the identity of an official to the output of coal in a given province. It is only necessary that an apparatchik declares as much. There is no directory of what is or is not covered. The concept is wonderfully evocative, implying as it does that accurate information is available – it is just out of the reach of ordinary people. On the rare occasions where someone is told something deemed to be neibu, he or she will likely feel they have been handed a gem of information. In actual fact, almost all information in China is suspect because of the failings of the system that generates it. But by being made secret, it is invested with tremendous currency. This is the theatre of information that goes hand in hand with China's theatre of diplomacy.

梦

The opacity of government and most of those involved in it is also effective in focusing the attention of foreigners on a minority of supposedly more cosmopolitan front men in Chinese politics. In the 1970s, Henry Kissinger fawned on Mao's premier Zhou Enlai, whom he regarded as an intellectual and an aesthete, like himself.[31] In the 1980s, western politicians and businessmen seized on Zhao Ziyang, the premier who donned western suits and took up golf, as well as Party general secretary Hu Yaobang, whose credentials as a progressive rested largely on his suggestion that the Chinese people should give up wooden chopsticks in favour of more hygienic knives and forks. The 1990s were the decade of Zhu Rongji, first as vice-premier, then as premier. Mr Zhu's no-nonsense manner and his ability to remember the plot outlines of Shakespeare plays were held out as proof of his pro-western sensibilities.[32]

This is curious, since Zhu has been the most authoritarian premier in a generation. Under his leadership, ministers confirmed meetings with persons other than the prime minister no more than a couple of days in advance, because they were expected to be available to Mr Zhu at a moment's notice. His temper is legendary, and even at his annual press conferences his right hand pumped the air in a violent hammering action when conveying a point on a sensitive topic. Subordinates became used to regular table-thumping bawl-outs. The premier, however, tapped into a prejudice shared by some western politicians and many multinational executives. He might have been authoritarian, but his was deemed to be 'the right kind of authoritarianism'.[33] To frustrated foreign businessmen, who all too easily forget the complexity on which prosperous societies are built, Mr Zhu promised quick solutions to the problems of the environment in which they operate. He said he would sort out the state sector, halve the size of the bureaucracy and clean up corruption. But for all the screaming and shouting, his premiership, which ended in March 2003, was an inevitable disappointment. State sector reform was fudged, the bureaucracy was not tamed and corruption remained rampant.

Not just foreigners, but many Chinese as well, spend their time waiting for a charismatic leader to ride to the country's rescue. Political analysis invariably focuses on who is next in line for the top jobs. The death and succession watch over Deng Xiaoping lasted more than three years, beginning with his disappearance from public view in 1994. There was constant speculation that Deng's departure would free up one or more leaders to set the country on a new path of political reform. When this failed to happen, attention turned to the fifteenth Party Congress in October 1997 and Zhu Rongji's elevation to the premiership in 1998. Mr Zhu was billed as the white knight until, with perennial predictability, he turned out not to be so. Two years prior to the 2002 Communist Party congress, there was already passionate interest in the next round of personnel changes. Yet this crystal ball gazing – in which the gazer sees only the dull faces of glum middle-aged men – is a pointless exercise. Charismatic leadership by an individual ended with Deng Xiaoping. China's problem is not who should be the next emperor, but the fact that its whole political system is outmoded and ineffective.

Between Marxism and anarchy

What has happened to Chinese society in the past twenty years is that ordinary life has changed immensely, but the apparatus of political control has barely evolved. Most people – especially city dwellers – lead more private, 'normal' existences than at any time in the previous fifty years. Prosperous Chinese travel to Hong Kong and further afield, watch foreign movies on pirated videos, read pulpy lifestyle magazines and invest in the education of their children. Technology adds a little privacy. Most young urbanites have mobile phones and pagers, and many have internet access.[34] The interfering state is ever present, but people do their best to ignore it until the day it comes looking for them.

On the government side, the leadership pulls at its traditional levers of control and is increasingly frustrated to find that many of them do not work. Official circulars were effective when everybody lived in state housing, the entire working population was employed in state units and all factories of a given type were owned by a single ministry, but there is no longer a clear relationship between instruction and effect. The problem is compounded because China's provinces have discovered they can often ignore directives from the centre with impunity, indulging instead their own regional authoritarianism. National government has become an exasperating business, and this does much to explain the rising level of state violence. Whether the violence is physical – as with beatings and executions in 'strike hard' campaigns – or verbal – as when Zhu Rongji makes an unannounced stop in the provinces to lambaste a local administration and sack recalcitrant officials – it reflects the same inability to think beyond old political standards.

In Beijing, the waning influence of Deng Xiaoping in the mid 1990s, and his death in February 1997, led to the transition to more oligarchical leadership. However, while the end of the pseudo-imperial rule practised by Mao Zedong and Deng was no great loss, this further debilitated the bureaucratic structure by removing its centre of power. Chinese politicians and academics are at a loss when asked where power and policy control is focused in the current system. Among the Standing Committee of the Politburo, the State Council, the prime minister's Working Conference and institutions like the Central Party School, which trains ministers and provincial leaders, there is no definable nerve centre.[35] The state is aggressive but weak. President and Party general secretary Jiang Zemin was a compromise choice at the time of the Tiananmen Square massacre and the new leadership in 2003 is another compromise choice, designed to satisfy as many interest groups as possible in an environment where bureaucratic authority is ever more dispersed and factionalised.[36]

Under these circumstances, it is almost impossible to make pro-active policy decisions. Reform issues are identified, and there is endless debate, but little actually happens. The government knows that the state sector creates an unsustainable drain on its resources, but every department thinks another should act first to address the problem. The creation of a national welfare system has been identified for a decade as a necessary precursor to more state sector bankruptcies, but actual implementation never takes place. The government set 2000 as the date for launching a national pension system, and then retreated to a one-province pilot programme when the deadline arrived.[37] No one can agree on how the costs of the system will be defrayed. The need to open capital markets to private business led to plans for an alternative stock market in 1999, but when details had to be agreed on, bureaucratic bickering scuppered the project.

Until the mid 1990s, government inertia was less of a problem because the loosening of the state plan that induced China's parallel economies created short-term growth. There were easy decisions for central government to make, such as endorsing household farming or private business after they had come into being. In recent years, there have been few such simple decisions to make. Almost everything that needs to be done to set the economy on a course of sustainable growth involves pain, whether in the form of layoffs, bankruptcies or bureaucratic retrenchment. But the government is without a popular constituency of support to take tough measures. It has rejected any move towards democratisation and the formal support base it does have – the membership of the Communist Party – is comprised of state workers and bureaucrats. This ensures that Chinese politics is an unvirtuous circle of endless meetings and endless delays. The only strategies that the government can agree on in order to fend off the three crises it faces – a banking crisis, a fiscal crisis and a bureaucratic crisis – are characterised by a mixture of delusion and vain hope.

Three steps sideways

The solution to a bank meltdown was the creation of four state-owned asset management companies (AMCs) in 1999. These bought up $169 billion worth of non-performing loans from the big four state banks, paying for them in full with bonds and central bank credits guaranteed by the Ministry of Finance.[38] The AMCs then swapped the non-performing loans for shares in the state companies that had taken out the loans. The exercise was a paper shuffle. State-owned banks were allowed to dispose of bad loans equivalent to about one-eighth of all assets in the system, and state-owned AMCs used their claim on the loans to buy equity in already state-owned companies. The point of buying more shares in companies it owned, the government said, was that the AMCs would acquire seats on the companies' boards and have a positive influence on their behaviour. It was a bad omen that all parties to the transaction were happy. The banks swapped bad credit for interest-bearing sovereign bonds, the state companies enjoyed massive debt relief and the AMCs became the focus of propaganda attention.

The official press likened the formation of the AMCs to that of the Resolution Trust Corporation (RTC) in the United States in 1989. The RTC was the vehicle used to clean up America's savings and loans crisis, in which regional financial institutions built up tens of billions of dollars of bad debt through reckless lending in the 1980s. The organisation, empowered by new legislation, moved quickly at the start of the 1990s to sell off loans and other assets of failed finance companies – from office furniture to branch leases – at whatever price the market would pay.[39] The action was brutal and expensive – it cost American taxpayers an estimated $150 billion – but it was effective. The lending practices that caused the US crisis were arrested and the government discovered the full extent of its liability. The operations of the RTC, however, could not be more different than those of the AMCs in China.

Although they have the technical right to do so, the AMCs rarely sell off the equity or assets of the state companies they bought into.[40] There is not the political will for wholesale disposals, which would involve booking huge losses when firms were sold for a fraction of the price the AMCs paid for them. Instead, AMC representatives sit on company advisory boards that are almost powerless. The boards do not appoint management because that right is reserved for local Party committees and industrial bureaus in Beijing. With no ability to sack managers and no credible threat to sell out to a third party, AMC board members can only look on as company officers return to state banks with reduced debt loads asking for new credit. The banks are often willing to lend because their own non-performing loans have been cut, because government is encouraging credit to maintain economic growth, and because the state firms have reduced their debt-to-asset ratios.[41]

The AMC experiment was a straightforward debt amnesty that increased moral hazard. Nothing has occurred to force a change in the behaviour of state enterprise managers, while banks have been shown that bad loans to public companies will ultimately be bailed out.[42] A large chunk of non-performing loans – $169 billion – is warehoused with the AMCs, but much more bad debt remains inside the banking system and the amount is increasing quickly as bank lending rises far ahead of economic growth.[43] The only thing that prevents the banks from collapsing is the deposits of the Chinese people.

梦

The government's response to its looming fiscal crisis smacks even more of wishful thinking. Confronted with an insolvent banking system, a rising budget deficit and unfunded welfare liabilities, the reaction of ministers is to claim that the state owns all kinds of valuable assets that it can sell to cover its expenditures. This view was encouraged in the early 1990s by outside agencies such as the World Bank, which suggested to the Chinese government that it could raise hundreds of billions of dollars through land sales and privatisation of housing stock.[44] A nationwide property crash, and the government's unwillingness, or inability, to sell state apartments for more than nominal prices, put paid to this idea, but it resurfaced as the proposition that great value is locked up in some of China's monopoly state enterprises. In particular, the stratospheric valuations placed on China's telecoms companies during the global technology boom suggested that these businesses alone could be worth $450 billion. In early 2000, the price–earnings ratio of China Mobile, the country's leading mobile telephone operator, soared to 150 times. This gave the company, which handles a third of China's mobile subscribers, a market valuation of $115 billion and implied the national mobile business was worth $345 billion.[45]

It is symptomatic of the fiscal desperation of the government that it should leap on such paper valuations. In the course of the 1990s, one industrial sector after another was talked up – with the aid of international investment bankers – as being worth tens, if not hundreds, of billions of dollars. Aviation, tolled expressways, power generation, iron and steel, shipping and ports – each had their day in the investment sun. But when demand projections proved wildly optimistic, and profits failed to materialise, share prices tumbled and the theoretical valuations of the government's holdings went with them. By 2000, the value of overseas-traded stocks in two Chinese airlines had fallen to less than $400 million, in five expressway companies to less than $500 million and in five power companies to less than $1 billion.[46] Many share prices dropped by eight- or nine-tenths. With the bursting of the technology bubble, China's telecoms companies headed in a similar direction. China Mobile's share price fell by two-thirds by spring 2001 and China Unicom, a second operator that managed to list before the crash, dropped well below its listing price.[47]

Even at reduced valuations, the notion that the government could cash out of businesses it owns is a fallacy. In the extraordinarily favourable conditions between 1997 and 2000, Chinese telecoms companies raised a remarkable $17 billion abroad from listings and placements.[48] But this money was given to the companies to invest in their businesses, not to the Ministry of Finance to balance the budget. State companies have always listed on the basis of issuing new equity to raise cash for development and expansion. Although the government talks about selling down its own holdings, which would mean the revenue was its own, attempts to do so have been disastrous. Trial sales of shares in two mainland-listed companies in December 1999 were both undersubscribed, despite hefty discounts to the market. Second and third attempts at state sell-offs in summer 2001 and early 2002 sent both the Shanghai and Shenzhen bourses into a tailspin.[49] If China's captive investors will not pay for the government's holdings, it is still less likely that foreigners will. Indeed, the whole story of state equity issues is a parable for the psychology of China investment in general. When companies offer new shares in return for investment in new projects, punters buy into the dream of China's future. But when offered a stake in the present – in the form of the government's stock holdings – no one is interested.[50]

The leadership is desperate to keep its international equity pipeline open, even if funds do not flow to the Ministry of Finance. But the returns on the listing of state monopoly assets outside the mainland are diminishing. Encouraged by the early response to its mobile telecom companies, China in 2000 attempted initial public offerings in Hong Kong and New York for three major state oil companies. The listing of the largest oil producer, Petrochina, in April, had to be scaled back from a promised $10 billion to less than $3 billion. The offerings of the country's offshore oil and gas company and its leading refiner were both delayed and the prices cut.[51] Despite a concerted official effort to have overseas-listed firms meet or beat earnings forecasts in 2001, international investors were willing to pay only around five times earnings for Chinese oil companies, a big discount to international norms.[52] In October 2002, the vaunted listing of fixed line telephone operator China Telecom was cut in half and delayed. As years of unfulfilled promise began to tell in international markets, the largest state monopolies turned back to China's stage managed domestic stock markets, still trading at 40–50 times earnings. The telecoms and oil companies requested government permission for additional A share listings, looking to tap a population weened on overpriced and insecure investments.[53]

梦

Of all the strategies presented by the Chinese government in its efforts to avert an economic crisis, the one most widely reported and lauded abroad was the decision to join the World Trade Organisation. From a domestic perspective, this is regarded by reformers as a solution to the nation's bureaucratic impasse – an external pressure to force deregulation and greater competitiveness on a recalcitrant bureaucracy.[54] Like Italians who gave overwhelming support to the political development of the European Union in the hope that it would clean up their own politics, premier Zhu Rongji and his team of authoritarian modernisers turned to the WTO to change the behaviour of an ossified and self-serving administration. On 15 November 1999, after thirteen years of negotiations, a bilateral accord was signed with the United States that paved the way for WTO membership. Over the next two years, the country rumbled slowly down the road to accession, with the terms of China's entry finally settled in September 2001 and accession in December.[55]

To optimists, the WTO commitment was a signal that the government had reached a consensus over the need for open markets, that it was laying its economic cards on the table and that they were no longer marked with nonsense like 'socialist market economy' or 'socialism with Chinese characteristics'. International investors, yearning for any piece of good news, lavished praise on Beijing and spent millions of dollars in Washington to lobby congress to accept the content of the US bilateral agreement.[56] The deal was, on paper, a good one, far better than most businessmen dared hope. China contracted to open almost all markets in which US and other investors were interested – from the internet to financial services – over a period of five years.[57] Foreign direct investment, which a steadily falling volume of contract signings suggested was headed for a steep downturn, held up through 2000 and even began to rise in 2001.[58] Trade bodies, the World Bank and investment banks predicted vastly increased levels of Chinese imports. For the China Dream, the WTO delivered the economic equivalent of lifesaving heart massage.

The rekindled enthusiasm, however, was once again based on dubious analysis. The inference that the government's decision to pursue WTO membership reflected a new willpower to enact change had nothing to substantiate it. In fact, most of the evidence was to the contrary. China began to negotiate seriously with the United States at just the moment when foreign investment levels were set to fall, pulling another cornerstone from the foundations of a weak economy in which only public expenditure can maintain growth. The government's chances of doing a deal with the Clinton administration were also far greater than with a new incumbent who would be looking forward to re-election. China policy has a history of making American presidents look bad rather than good. Critically, at the end of what would become George W. Bush's presidency in January 2005, China faced an unmovable deadline. That year the Multi-Fibre Agreement, which governs world trade in textiles and apparel, the country's leading exports, would expire. If China was not within the WTO by then, thereby ensuring quota-free access to foreign markets, she would have to tour the world negotiating new bilateral deals on a country by country basis. This was never an attractive prospect. Finally, by the time Zhu Rongji came seriously to the negotiating table in the spring of 1999, he had had a year as premier to discover just how intransigent China's bureaucracy can be.[59] The lure of the WTO – a new stick with which to beat those who defied the schoolmasterly premier – was suddenly powerful. Mr Zhu had sworn to change China within a single, five-year term in office.

The government committed to the WTO from a position of weakness, not strength, because of quiet desperation, not unified political resolve.[60] It reached for an outside force to do a job it was failing to do itself – the deregulation and de-bureaucratisation of China's economy. But the capacity of the

WTO to complete this task is vastly overestimated, both by China's would-be reformers and by foreign investors. Although greatly strengthened by internationally agreed changes made to its rules in 1995, the WTO is not equipped to tackle the domestic economic constraints that make China – and countries like it – so impermeable to profitable international trade and investment. The WTO has not solved the bureaucratic problems of member countries like Japan and India, and it has even less chance of solving China's. What the organisation does is to set tariff levels for imports, lay down principles of equal treatment for local and foreign businesses and set out timeframes for the opening – at a legislative level – of different markets. What the WTO does not do, however, is become involved in issues of how a domestic economy is run. It will not – unlike an International Monetary Fund assistance programme – require that a currency is made convertible, that approval processes are simplified, that a central bank allow the market to set interest rates or that commercial banks not take lending orders from ministers. Yet it is precisely these kinds of bureaucratic controls – part of what are known as non-tariff barriers – that close out competition. What is promised on paper at the WTO headquarters in Geneva matters little when a country's bureaucratic system is unable to deliver it.

Amid the euphoria surrounding WTO entry, much was made of China's offer to cut its average import tariff from 17.5 per cent to 10 per cent by 2005. It was this proposed change that induced heady forecasts of swelling imports. Yet China had already cut average tariffs from 43 per cent in 1992 to 17.5 per cent in 1998 without any resulting import boom.[61] Tariff reductions have only a marginal impact for a range of bureaucratic reasons. Most important, China's currency is not freely convertible and all imports require a foreign currency allocation to pay for them. The government can turn the import tap on and off as its likes. Even were this not the case, since there is no fundamental deregulation taking place in the economy, the rate of imports depends almost entirely on the rate of overall economic expansion. The story of the past fifteen years is that imports from the US and Europe rise and fall about three times as fast as the annual change in economic growth. If China's growth drops below 6 per cent, import growth ceases or turns negative – irrespective of tariff levels.[62]

The same disjuncture between theory and practice occurs with investment regulation. As a WTO member, China promises to treat all businesses equally and not to impose requirements for minimum levels of exports, local content, technology transfer and so on. But the whole bureaucratic structure is set up to treat companies differently, not equally. China will retain its ubiquitous licensing regime – a domestic issue over which the WTO has no power. The organisation forbids many explicit, contractual investment requirements, and stipulates a free choice of a partner where joint ventures are necessary but these guarantees are rendered meaningless when an official can withhold or delay an operating licence until his interests are satisfied. The licensing authorities will still be departments and ministries connected with state enterprises in the same sector where foreign entrants wish to operate. In the wake of the Sino-US accord, the heads of bureaucracies including the Ministry of Information Industries and the China Insurance Regulatory Commission made it abundantly clear they foresaw no reduction in licensing requirements as a result of WTO accession.[63]

The armoury of a Chinese bureaucrat is a large and diverse one. The state is not just a licenser, it is a major buyer of goods and services. The manner in which public procurement is conducted will not be touched on by China's WTO agreement, but most investors will remain beholden in some way to state purchasing agencies. China – like many other countries – is also a practised employer of technical standards to impede trade. One typical case in the 1990s concerned US citrus fruit and medfly, a bug that attacks fruit. Although the insect lives for only a month, and is unlikely to survive transcontinental shipment, China blocked all US citrus fruit imports on the basis that America had localised medfly cases. Beijing demanded three-year, 12,000-square mile quarantine zones in every instance where medfly occurred in the US before it would open its market. Yet at the same time, the country was awash with smuggled US citrus fruit that was being bought at street markets around the capital by – among millions of others – government officials. No medfly ever crossed the Pacific alive.[64] When the bilateral Sino-US accord on WTO was signed in November 1999, one of the first legal shipments of fruit was allowed to sail from Florida to Tianjin. In an incident that was never reported, the fruit was left rotting in port. Chinese customs ruled that, although the produce did not originate in a US county that had suffered medfly – as had been agreed – it had been transported through and shipped from a Florida county that had had a medfly outbreak.

The WTO does have a binding dispute resolution mechanism, but it is slow and costly and mainly of use to large industry organisations with patience and generous budgets. Moreover, China will pose unique problems for parties wishing to challenge its record of enforcement of WTO obligations. The granting of bank loans, for instance, to tens of thousands of insolvent state enterprises constitutes systematic unequal treatment of businesses in China. Yet to prove before a panel in Geneva that a bank loan should not have been made would be all but impossible. China has few explicit subsidies, but myriad hidden ones – via the banking system, internal memoranda from ministries about procurement preferences,

ment of environmental rules against private and foreign,
terprises, and so on. These types of subsidy almost never
...all on which a legal case can be built.

...ne context of China's entry into the WTO – because of the failure, not the success, of domestic economic policy – makes doubtful the government's ability to comply with the terms of membership. The WTO is not going to solve China's problems because ultimately change must come from within. A country that will not enforce its bankruptcy laws, that cannot commercialise its banking sector, that vacillates for a decade over the need for welfare reform and that brazenly manipulates its judicial system is not going to be transformed because it signs another international treaty.[65] Yet just when investor expectations were coming in line with reality, the prospect of WTO accession once more catapulted them into the clouds. Such is the durability of the China Dream.

Strange, even for politicians

The simplest way to grasp the lack of direction, absence of conviction and general listlessness of Chinese politics, is to reflect on what the senior leaders talk about at their interminable meetings and the statements they release to the public. Most politicians have a tendency to vague and ambiguous language, but what passes for political dialectic in China is often jibberish:

Beijing 7 July 2000 (Xinhua) – The Eighth Plenary Meeting of the Central Guidance Committee on Ethical and Cultural Construction was held today to conscientiously study and put into effect the spirit of General Secretary Jiang Zemin's important speech at the Central Ideological and Political Work Meeting, and to study and arrange the work of ethical and cultural construction ...

The meeting maintained that the Central Ideological and Political Work Meeting is an important meeting held at the historic moment of our party in its advance toward the new century, and also a major move of the party's central committee with Comrade Jiang Zemin at the core which adheres to the strategic principle of 'doing two jobs at once and attaching equal importance to both' for promoting the cause of reform, opening up, and modernisation in a comprehensive way. General Secretary Jiang Zemin's important speech shows great foresight, has the overall situation in view, contains rich and profound ideas, possesses the distinct features of the times, and aims at very definite objectives, which is of momentous practical significance as well as far-reaching historical significance to intensifying and improving the party's ideological and political work oriented to the new century. We must study the gist of the speech and put it into practice in a conscientious manner ...

As an example of the Party's and government's activities, this release, which carries on for a couple of thousand words, could be subsituted by a report from any day in the past fifty years. China in the 1990s was presented as a country of change, but the language of its politics demonstrates how shallow the changes can be. At an economic level, the government mobilised the population's savings through the banking system and spent much of them in an extremely wasteful manner. While there were important developments in the private economy, such state spending was no more proof of progress than the investment-led boom of the Soviet Union in the 1950s and 1960s. At a political level, the Communist Party rejected all forms of change – whether a degree of independent oversight from the media, non-governmental organisations or judiciary, or an extension of the popular franchise beyond elections of some village committees.[66]

The excuse for political stasis – employed almost as often by international businessmen as by mainland politicians – is that the Chinese are somehow genetically indisposed to political modernisation and pluralism. Any reduction in the Communist Party's power, it is said, will inevitably lead to total chaos – what the Chinese call 'da luan'. But the truth is that all the da luan of the past half century was created by the Chinese Communist Party, whether through cruel political adventures like the Cultural Revolution or the bombastic economic mismanagement that gave rise to the Great Leap Forward and is today shunting an industrious people toward a new crisis. Through murder, avoidable starvation and harassment, the Party has been responsible during its tenure of office for perhaps 50 million deaths – a million a year.[67] Yet the organisation claims to have a monopoly on good sense.

The excuses for the mainland's political inertia contrast with the genuine, profound changes that took place in another Chinese society in the 1990s – that of Taiwan. For a long time after the end of the Chinese civil war in 1949, there was little to choose between the rival Chinese governments in Beijing and Taipei. Both Mao Zedong and the Kuomintang leader, Chiang Kai-shek, reached at the slightest provocation for brutality and repression as a means of governance; both men specialised in the mass murder of intellectuals and professionals.[68] The difference was only that one man acted in the name of communism and the other in the name of anti-communism. Chiang and Mao died a year apart, in 1975 and 1976 respectively. Thereafter, however, the regimes they bequeathed followed different courses. While the communists in Beijing refused to entertain any possibility of political change, in the course of the 1980s Chiang Kai-shek's son, Chiang Ching-kuo, ended martial law, legalised opposition parties and eased press restrictions. This paved the way for parliamentary elections. In the 1990s, under President Lee Teng-hui, Taiwan held the first fully democratic ballot to its Legislative Assembly in 1995, and a presidential vote the following year. At the next election, in 2000, the population chose a non-Kuomintang president, Chen Shui-bian of the Democratic Progressive Party (DPP). Taiwan's political transformation was complete.

Change was just as profound in the economy. Through the 1980s and 1990s Taiwan reinvented itself, ditching the low valued added manufacturing of toys and clothing to become one of the world's leading centres of high-tech production. The island is the dominant global player in notebook computers, the world's third largest manufacturer of semi-conductor wafers and a regional force in petrochemicals. This modernisation was not achieved through central planning and government largesse. Taiwanese companies prospered through their own endeavours; they have the lowest debt-to-equity ratios in Asia while Taiwanese banks boast the lowest bad debt ratios.[69] The degree of openness of the Taiwanese economy, compared with that of the mainland, is shown by the remarkable fact that through the 1990s Taiwan imported more goods from the United States than did the whole of mainland China. An island of 22 million people was a bigger US export market than a continent-size country of 1.3 billion people.[70]

Beijing's reaction to a changing Taiwan is as sad as it is predictable. The more free and the more prosperous the island's people become, the angrier is the Chinese Communist Party. The bad guys of communist folklore – the Kuomintang – turned out better than the mainland government that over-threw them and were even willing to cede power peacefully to another party. This makes the leadership in Beijing livid. At his March 2000 annual press conference – just before the presidential election in Taiwan – the supposedly liberal premier Zhu Rongji railed against Taiwanese politicians, threatening that the People's Liberation Army would 'spill blood' if there was any move towards a declaration of independence. The people of Taiwan were not cowed and elected the pro-independence lawyer Chen Shui-bian as their president. Immediately after Mr Zhu's tirade, many Beijing-based correspondents headed straight to Taipei for the election. The atmosphere could not have been more different. Tens of thousands of people were celebrating in the streets. Taxi drivers refused to take money from foreign journalists. There was an ambience of tolerance and goodwill that has been witnessed on the mainland only by those who were present in Beijing in the last weeks prior to the 4 June massacre of 1989.

Hong Kong is less fortunate than Taiwan, at least in the sense that its people do not control their own destiny. A British imperial government that waited 150 years to introduce a degree of political pluralism left behind a semi-democratic legislature that can be bullied by Beijing. Despite endless verbal and written promises to the contrary, the temptation for China's monolithic state to interfere in Hong Kong's affairs has proved irresistible.

After resuming sovereignty in 1997, Beijing reversed democratic reforms introduced by the last governor, Chris Patten, reducing the role of the popular franchise from the maximum to the minimum allowed under Hong Kong's constitution.[71] The central government made explicit its right to remove the Hong Kong chief executive at will and showed no intention of allowing popular opinion to play a role in his selection – despite previous acceptance of this as an objective.[72]

A hardening of attitudes to the media was slow but perceptible. Hong Kong's best-known political columnist, Willy Wo-lap Lam, was demoted and subsequently resigned after writing a series of exposés of the new political order in the main English language daily, the *South China Morning Post*. One of Lam's articles had described a meeting hosted by the Chinese government at which Hong Kong tycoons, who are allowed to 'vote' as members of a 400-person panel for the chief executive, were told to back the post's first incumbent, Tung Chee-hwa, for a second term. One of those alleged to be present at the meeting was Robert Kuok, the billionaire owner of the *South China Morning Post*. When the Chinese president was asked on a trip to Hong Kong in October 2000 if Beijing's endorsement of Tung Chee-hwa amounted to an 'imperial instruction' for his continuation as chief executive, he flew into a rage before the assembled media. Jiang warned Hong Kong journalists they would be held responsible for 'errors' in their reports, and twice returned from a walkabout to lambast them.[73]

The first serious constitutional clash between Beijing and Hong Kong occurred in 1999 when the Standing Committee of China's National People's Congress asserted that it is the final arbiter of Hong Kong law. In January that year, the territory's own Court of Final Appeal struck down mainland supported legislation on immigration and the right of abode, saying it was contrary to Hong Kong's constitution.[74] In May, the chief executive and the Hong Kong government asked Beijing for its 'interpretation' and the National People's Congress overruled the Hong Kong court. The precedent set was that a mainland appointed chief executive can request a Beijing review of any court decision that irks him. In reality, Beijing and its appointees have to tread carefully since there is organised opposition to the erosion of Hong Kong's autonomy, from the public and lawyers alike. But the sense of a gradual, inexorable reduction of freedom and judicial independence in Hong Kong is hard to escape.

At an economic level – and although it was hard hit by the Asian financial crisis – Hong Kong's outlook is more positive. Despite the attentions of Beijing, the administration remains one of the cleanest in Asia, the judiciary is still an efficient enforcer of commercial contracts and the principles of low taxation and small government are intact. Hong Kong's trajectory of development is unlikely to change for some time. As it becomes richer, it manufactures less and less within its borders, instead providing management and other services to the economy of southern China, centred on Guangdong province. This region, which is the least regulated in China, produces the most dynamic mainland companies and is home to the most successful Hong Kong ones. As more and more Hong Kong residents buy property in Guangdong and cross the border every week for cheap shopping, mainland Cantonese gain more than anyone from their integration with the outside world. Guangdong natives even have a sense of global reality since they pick up Hong Kong television with their aerials and illegal satellite dishes.

Throughout China's 'reform and opening' period it has been Hong Kong and Taiwan – the two outposts of freedom in the Chinese empire – that have provided the majority of direct investment entering the mainland. The failings of Chinese statistics make it impossible to say exactly how much, but the sum total is certainly in excess of $150 billion.[75] Much of the money has been invested more sensibly and productively than that coming from multinationals, focused as it usually is on the possibilities for low-cost export processing. Without Hong Kong and Taiwanese money, and the jobs that it creates in labour-intensive industries, the mainland would be in a sorry state. It is therefore the final irony of contemporary communist China that its economy is kept afloat by the historical legacy of its sworn enemies – the Kuomintang and western imperialism. If Mao Zedong had overrun Taiwan in 1950 and forced the British out of Hong Kong at the same time, there would have been no one to pay for the excesses of the Communist Party of China.

12

The longest dream

'So long as people of one country make goods to sell to others, so long as ships cross the ocean and international trade exists, the golden illusion of the sales which may be made to China's industrious millions will always be an intriguing one. No matter what you may be selling, your business in China should be enormous, if the Chinese who should buy your goods would only do so.'

Carl Crow, *400 Million Customers*[1]

FOR ALL THE difference between expectation and reality in the Chinese marketplace, for all the millions of dollars lost in the pursuit of an age-old fantasy, it does not pay to count China out. The China Dream is too resilient, and the world's determination to see it come true too great. Like adventurers in the quest for some fabled relic, investors press unendingly forward – if only on the basis that the legend may one day prove real. In 1998 and 1999, when officially reported growth sank to its lowest level since the 1989 Tiananmen Square massacre, and actual growth was reckoned by some economists to be close to zero,[2] investor patience did show signs of wearing thin. Foreign direct investment fell in 1999 for the first time since the start of the reform era.[3] But the flirtation with reticence was short-lived. Within two years the bulls were back, their morale shored up by fresh Chinese promises to integrate into the world community just as other investment prospects were being dashed by international terrorism and economic downturn in the developed world. By 2002, foreign investment was rising again and China was being referred to not as the disappointment it had been for so many companies, but as a 'safe haven' in a world destabilised both politically and economically.[4]

In this context, China's accession to the World Trade Organisation (WTO) – finally effected on 11 December 2001 – was invested with tremendous expectation. A five-year phase-in of her commitments notwithstanding, China's membership traded, in the words of one sceptical foreign investor, 'at a very high p/e'.[5] In the 2001–2 China member questionnaire of the American Chamber of Commerce, the largest foreign business association in the country, 83 per cent of respondents predicted WTO accession would increase demand for their products and services, and a similar proportion said their investment plans were being adjusted accordingly.[6] For those who wanted to believe, there was other evidence available – albeit circumstantial – that China might be entering a new era. Beijing's victory in the contest to host the 2008 Olympic Games, and the national soccer team's first qualification for a World Cup finals, in 2002, provided foreigners as well as Chinese with a renewed sense of optimism. In October 2001, President Jiang Zemin played host to US president George W. Bush and the other twenty leaders of the Asia–Pacific Economic Co-operation (APEC) forum in Shanghai, against a backdrop of terrorist atrocities in New York and Washington. As in the politically tumultuous years after the dissolution of the Soviet empire, 'stability' was back in fashion, even where it equated to dictatorship. China's sequestration of a US surveillance plane and its crew six months earlier was forgotten. Instead, in a further parallel with the early 1990s, politicians and investors contrasted China's headline growth (even though it was half the rate of 1993) with the fact that by the end of 2001 the economies of North America, the Eurozone and Japan were simultaneously contracting.[7] The old addendum, 'fastest growing economy in the world', was reattached to China's name.

It was not an environment in which much time was given to thoughts of China's long-term economic outlook or the recent performance of her reform initiatives. Indeed, both growth and reform were slowing through 2001. The government promised a fifth successive year of heavy fiscal stimulus to pump up the growth rate in 2002 – with more again expected in 2003. In late January 2002, the government formally announced a suspension of its plans to sell down stakes in state enterprises while the Supreme Court ordered provincial courts not to take on bankruptcy cases of companies with assets more than Rmb50 million ($6 million).[8] None the less, though these developments worsened the government's budget outlook and promised the accumulation of further bad debt in the banking system, few people in 2002 were focused on problems that would play out several years hence. When investors looked around for growth they saw a developed world facing recession, south-east Asia – still reeling from the Asian financial crisis – dropping to its knees before the prospect of harder times to come, and Latin America generating news only because of economic chaos in Argentina.

Without any real change at home, China suddenly looked quite good. Walled in behind her non-convertible currency and comforted by aggressive public spending, the country enjoyed a definite upswing in investor senti-

ment. This was assisted in the course of 2001 by a series of foreign investment deals in telecommunications and television media that were hailed as
groundbreaking. At the start of the year, Goldman Sachs and Rupert
Murdoch's News Corporation were the lead investors in what was billed as
the first direct investment in a Chinese telecommunications service. The two
firms, together with lesser investors, were authorised by the State Council to
pay $325 million for a 12 per cent share of Netcom, a broadband internet
media company connected with Jiang Mianheng, son of President Jiang
Zemin.[9] In June 2001, AOL Time Warner announced a $200 million joint
venture with China's leading computer manufacturer, Legend, to develop
mainland internet services. In October, both News Corporation and AOL Time
Warner revealed that they had been granted permission to operate Mandarin
Chinese cable television channels in the far southern province of Guangdong
in return for carrying Chinese state television programming on their networks in North America.

At first sight, these deals looked revolutionary and suggested that the
investment environment might really be changing for the better. On closer
inspection – a step that wishful investors did not take – the deals contained
many of the ambiguities of earlier 'experimental' contracts. The Netcom
investment led by News Corporation and Goldman Sachs was not, in fact, an
immediate purchase of shares in the mainland operations of the Chinese
carrier. Instead, money was being paid into a Hong Kong company that was
to be granted a 'call on equity' in China Netcom once foreign investment in
mainland telecommunications was legalised under the WTO, more than three
years hence.[10] Less than a year after the investment was made, the central
government announced its intention to merge Netcom with a part of the
national fixed line carrier, China Telecom, threatening to dilute the foreign
investment to a minuscule portion of a business the investors had never con-
templated. Similarly, the AOL Time Warner–Legend deal was predicated on a
market opening that WTO membership would only require after several
years. The small print of the agreement referred to AOL Time Warner providing 'technical support ... pending regulatory changes'. The $200 million joint
investment was only a theoretical investment and, six months after signing,
little was happening.[11] The Guangdong cable television deals were more
immediately substantive, coming into effect in 2002. But both News Corporation and AOL Time Warner were restricted to one free-to-user Mandarin
language channel in different parts of a single province.[12] That province,
though boasting a relatively wealthly audience, is unusual in its viewing
habits. Most Guangdong natives are used to watching Cantonese television,
picked up from signals in nearby Hong Kong. Only advertising revenues – not

subscription fees – would be available to the foreign companies, but most possible advertising income is already firmly in the grip of the Hong Kong television companies. And, unlike the Hong Kong broadcasters, the foreign companies licensed in China would be subject to mainland censorship.

梦

Despite the caveats, the changes to the global economic outlook and the talk of new deals were enough to produce a subtle but profound shift in the China investment debate coming into 2002. In a climate of low expectations, claims of miracle markets and exponential growth were replaced by discussions of the fact that it is possible to make positive returns in China. Deflation and over-supply reduced foreign companies' costs in the late 1990s, experience taught most to look before they leapt and a market that was small and diffused was none the less slowly growing. Having left behind their more egregious invest-ment follies, and supported by accounting practices that sometimes billed substantial costs to headquarters, many investors in the domestic market could manage a small operating surplus. The difficulty was that such returns did not justify the deployment of money and resources on the scale committed to China. As Teresa Woodland, a McKinsey consultant who for several years col-lated returns in American Chamber of Commerce surveys, said of the average investor: 'Companies are profitable but they are not earning their cost of capital.'[13] The China Dream was not dead, but it was far, far from being realised.

The American Chamber surveys began asking members more detailed questions about margins and profitability in 1999. That year, an extraordi-narily low 12 per cent of respondents said that their China operations gener-ated returns above what the companies considered their cost of capital for China. Well over half had returns on investment below their cost of capital, and nearly a third significantly below.[14] This performance was not only poor from a normal business perspective, it was particularly weak given the 20–30 per cent returns on capital invested – considered a standard expectation in higher-risk emerging markets – that companies envisaged when they arrived in China. Looked at another way, such returns should mean a company making back its investment in three to four years. But, as American Chamber and other surveys show, most entrants in China take more than three years just to produce an operating surplus.[15] It was only in the context of global recession, and with enduring belief in China's future, that not making oper-ating losses could be redefined as a measure of success.

In line with this more upbeat spin, there was a strong vogue at the start of the twenty-first century for case studies of the minority of multinationals that had already performed particularly well in China. The mobile telephone companies and fast food chains like McDonald's and Kentucky Fried Chicken were becoming increasingly recognised for having succeeded in sectors where Chinese state companies had not previously operated. But there were a few other companies that had made money in competition with state enterprises – and their bureaucratic protectors – where most foreign entrants had lost. One of the most widely reported cases was Carrefour, the French retailing giant that built the second largest retail group in China in only five years. Rivals had spent far longer building smaller businesses that had made either meagre returns or, more often, none at all. Carrefour, which turned over nearly $1 billion in China in 2000, became a celebrated market leader, not least among its European peer group.[16] There were other recognised stars in businesses where it was notoriously difficult to operate. International Data Group (IDG), a privately held, Boston-based technology publishing and consulting firm, attracted the jealous attention of larger rivals for having launched twenty-two magazines and thirty internet sites in China. The firm's most successful title, *China Computerworld*, boasted 170,000 paid subscribers and, together with another IDG technology magazine, captured half of all the technology advertising pages in the country.[17]

The problem, however, was that these companies were not only strategically and operationally exceptional in their performance, they were also serial breakers of China's foreign investment rules. It was a striking comment on the Chinese operating environment that a disregard for the letter of the law was both a prerequisite of success and a source of admiration from other foreign investors. Carrefour opened its twenty-eight mainland discount stores without ever applying to Beijing for a 'joint venture retail investment licence' – despite a well-known requirement for this. The company's representatives instead tore around China negotiating store openings with local governments that were hungry for its tax revenue and employment until, in 2001, the State Economic and Trade Commission announced that the French firm was under investigation for illegal activities.[18] Likewise, IDG entered its first magazine business in 1980 when publishing joint ventures were not only illegal – as they still are – but China had not even passed its original joint venture law. But, as a privately held firm, IDG found ways and means to operate in an ostensibly closed market and subsequently started to publish well-known titles like *Cosmopolitan* and *Esquire* for bigger media groups.[19]

Both Carrefour and IDG were aggressive risk takers who highlighted an increasingly clear rule of China investment: that given the state's determination to micromanage economic activity, there was almost no strictly legal way for foreign investors to make money. Even then, those who risked retribution by skirting round or breaking the rules reaped limited dividends in what is a limited market. Although Carrefour's high-risk strategy gave it a China market share greater than its three main rivals – America's Wal-Mart, Holland's Makro and Germany's Metro – combined, its 2000 China revenues were still only 1.2 per cent of its global turnover.[20] There was nothing else in China that compared with the exceptional mobile phone business, in which Ericsson, Nokia and Motorola each derived more than a tenth of their worldwide revenues from the country.[21] In media, while IDG led the pack, with China its second biggest market worldwide, the private Boston firm's China revenues were only $150 million in 2000.[22] And since IDG operated in territory that was at best grey legally, the firm found it difficult to obtain foreign exchange, which depends on official approval. For twenty years, most of its profits have been reinvested in new Chinese businesses while viable exit strategies are awaited.

Two crises in search of a victim

The reality for most companies at the start of the new millennium was that adherence to regulations constrained investors' profitability, but the majority of multinationals regarded rule breaking as unacceptably risky. As a result, they settled for low near-term returns in the belief that developments like WTO accession would translate into more business and improved margins. The China investment proposition came down – as it always had – to hopes for the future. All the evidence was that confidence remained strong. Whatever present operating conditions might be, each year business surveys showed that the great majority of investors believed their margins would improve the next year – even when this failed to happen in previous years.[23] The performance of listed companies did not improve, but there was never any shortage of buyers for fresh equity in Chinese corporations launching new projects. It was only when investors were asked to buy stakes – particularly those held by the government – in existing operations that they balked. Future earnings remained credible because of the common belief that the China Dream must eventually come to fruition.

In order for the dream to pass, however, investors had to believe that China would avoid two potentially ruinous scenarios. The first was a situation in which structural reform failed to materialise, government debt piled up and growth slowed to a snail's pace. A trend in this direction had been apparent from the mid 1990s, as growth dropped from its double digit pace to around 7 per cent. The economy recovered temporarily in 2000 under the influence of government spending, but dipped again in 2001 and was pumped up still more fiercely with public funds in 2002. There were uncomfortable similarities with the Japanese experience in the 1990s. For a decade, Japan had skirted the need for deregulation in its economy, relying instead on public expenditure to maintain ever slower economic expansion.[24] In China, the year 2002 was the country's fifth in a row for heavy economic stimulus.[25] The only parts of the Japanese domestic economy that were dynamic in the late 1990s were a few sectors where deregulation actually occurred: it was striking that Japan, like China, had a vibrant mobile telephony business.[26] Powerful state relationships with the construction industry, by contrast, had led to massive overbuilding in both countries followed by collapsing real estate prices.[27] Across the overall economies of Japan and China, a failure to close down excess capacity engendered years of persistent deflation. The prospect that prices would continue to fall, and fears about the security of future income, dampened consumption irrespective of the level at which interest rates were set.[28]

Although Japan had been exhibiting these symptoms for longer than China – the whole of the 1990s became, in economic terms, a lost decade for the country in the way the 1980s were for Latin America – to the outside investor the Chinese situation offered at least as much cause for concern. Japan ran into growth stagnation and debt accumulation when she already enjoyed a per capita GNP of more than $25,000 a year.[29] China appeared to be encountering these problems while she had a GNP per capita of under $1,000 a year. Although China's headline growth rate of 7 per cent at the end of the 1990s was presented as respectable, in fact it was already slower than the growth of other Asian nations when they were far more wealthy in per capita terms than China is today. Japan had expanded by over 8 per cent a year throughout the 1950s and 1960s even though, as of 1968, the country was already the second biggest economy in the world in dollar terms.[30] Taiwan, in the same era, grew at 10 per cent a year while, prior to 1997, South Korea managed average growth of 9 per cent for thirty years.[31] The comparisons are more stark when it is remembered that most non-partisan China economists – including those at the World Bank and the International Monetary Fund – believe that Chinese growth rates are perpetually overstated by one or two percentage points because of systematic overreporting of industrial output.[32] Even without the special massaging of data that appears to have taken place in the wake of the Asian financial crisis in 1998 and 1999, real Chinese growth in 2001 was likely to be of the order of 5 or 6 – not 7 – per cent.[33] It is debatable whether the Chinese government would ever find it politically acceptable to publish a growth figure below 7 per cent.

The second dream-ending scenario for China would be far more brutal – for investors and citizens alike – than a condition of stagnant low growth. It is a threat that also confronts Japan, having, in the course of the 1990s, built up the highest debt level of any industrialised country. Japan, like China, has traditionally been a low debt nation.[34] Yet in the first decade of the twenty-first century, both face the possibility of a debt crisis. In China, with its sealed and nationalised financial system, this would be triggered by a loss of confidence in and run on the country's state-owned banks, or by a stock market crash – which, in turn, might lead to a bank run. A crisis of confidence is almost certainly several years away, since government liabilities are still piling up and popular consciousness of them is limited. But the potential is certainly there. When the first projections of Chinese fiscal unsustainability were made at the time of the Asian financial crisis in 1998, the government's annual debt issue was around Rmb300 billion ($36 billion). By 2002 it was Rmb593 billion ($71 billion) and rising. With the government guaranteeing tens of billions of dollars of other bonds to be swapped for bad bank debt, to shore up the banks' capital and to raise money outside the state budget for investment,[35] it will not take long – as Japan has demonstrated – to build a debt load that challenges the country's ability to pay.

A debt crisis would likely mean a long period of economic and political instability. Latin America has still not escaped the debt trap it fell into in the 1980s, as Argentina's continued woes with international creditors attest. For the weakest victims of Asia's financial crisis, like Indonesia, the fall-out looks set to continue for many years. China could suffer at least as great a setback, not least because its closed financial system means there is no market mechanism to restrain the government's borrowing. Debt can grow to levels that would be impossible in an even partially open financial structure. If public confidence does one day crumble, and crisis ensues, the present regime is likely to be finished. The one indignity the Chinese people will not tolerate is the destruction of their savings. The population's unspoken truce with the country's autocratic leaders has long been that they must continue to deliver improved living standards in return for maintaining power. Yet, in the event of crisis, China's history of persecuting political opposition means that there are no immediate political alternatives to the Communist Party, just uncertainty.

Some foreign investors would find opportunity in crisis – as they have in south-east Asia and South Korea since 1998 buying up distressed assets. But the vast majority – who have already made their investments – would prefer that China avoids a debt trap and the inflation and unrest that would follow in its wake. The country is already experiencing a rapid widening of the wealth gap between successful urbanites and underemployed farmers; such income disparities would only be exacerbated by a crisis. Unmanageable debt

might make China look like a poorer version of Latin America
wealth and poverty, seesaw growth, perennial bouts of savir
inflation and shattered investment dreams. It is often forgotten that many
investors of the 1970s had the same ambitions for Brazil as they had for
China in the 1990s.

In terms of probability, the China debt crisis is less likely than the long-
term low growth scenario, if only because the government has such a tight
grip on the financial system. Nowhere else in the world are a population's
savings so closely managed by the state – through banks, stock markets and
bond issues – as in China. As a result, a failure to conduct structural reform of
the economy is more likely to translate into falling growth, as government
borrows from the banking system to make low-return investments and forces
savers in turn to accept low returns on savings deposits and stock and bond
purchases. This would be a hopeless environment for most outside investors
looking to turn a profit, because consumption would be permanently
depressed. The companies that have caused China's contracted foreign
investment levels to rise strongly in the wake of WTO accession therefore
must assume that deregulation of the economy is about to take off.[36] Based
on previous experience of promised reforms that have failed to materialise,
this is a bold prediction.

What works today will work tomorrow

Something far easier to forecast in the next ten years is China's continued
rise as a global manufacturing base for exporters. As the world sank into
recession in 2001–2, it was notable that the downturn only accelerated the
transfer of export processing operations to the country. Many Asian governments were aghast that this should be happening during a recession –
though it is at just such times that multinational manufacturers pay most
attention to their costs. South Korea's economic and finance minister, Jin
Nyum, lamented at the end of 2001 that China was 'turning itself into the
world's manufacturing plant, which will suck all manufacturing facilities into
it like a black hole'.[37] Newspapers from Japan to Singapore fretted that the
Chinese export economy was 'hollowing out' local manufacturing bases.[38] All
that the manufacturers themselves were concerned with was the ability of
China's export processing economy to cope with more complex products
than previously and deliver cost savings – and hence improved margins.

Japanese consumer electronics companies were typical in their reaction to
a tougher international operating environment. Matsushita, the parent
company of brands such as Panasonic and Technics, posted a worldwide loss
in the first half of 2001. The company, which already had thirty-six Chinese

factories, promptly announced it was going to spend $160 million relocating other unprofitable production facilities from western Europe and the US to China. Toshiba, which had held off moving lower-value added production to China in the early 1990s, said at the beginning of the year that it would close all its colour television plants in Japan and move them to mainland China. Similarly, Hitatchi announced plans to invest $826 million in increasing the share of its worldwide production processed in China from 2.5 per cent to 7 per cent.[39] A few years previously, Japanese multinationals would not have made such announcements for fear of upsetting domestic opinion. But by the start of the twenty-first century, the need to conduct basic manufacturing tasks offshore was a given.

The process of shifting export manufacturing to mainland China was complete by the turn of the century for Hong Kong and far advanced for Taiwan. According to mainland statistics, Taiwanese investment in the mainland exceeded $22 billion by the end of 2000, with the same amount again contracted. Taiwan's central bank, in a report released in 2000, however, claimed this was a gross underestimate and that Taiwanese investment paid up and promised on the mainland was more like $100 billion.[40] Some Taipei government officials projected there would soon be nothing manufactured at home. Industry estimates showed that half of Taiwanese high-tech goods were already assembled on the mainland, including most of the output of digital cameras and monitors and a rapidly rising share of other computer hardware.[41]

The fears aroused about the pace at which manufacturing operations were being moved to mainland China had much to do with delayed economic restructuring in developed Asian countries. Corporations were leading the way by shifting processing operations to China, but governments had not yet come to terms with the need to find other sources of domestic growth and employment. Throughout the 1990s, countries like Singapore and Malaysia assumed that multinational companies would maintain local processing operations indefinitely. The Japanese government preferred not to dwell on the pressures for its consumer electronics sector to move production offshore. Ultimately, however, the relocation of processing factories into the functioning half of China's two parallel economies – the private, export-oriented part – is inevitable. At a regional level, it should restore or improve profitability for Japanese, Taiwanese and south-east Asian manufacturers and finally focus the governments of those countries on the need to deregulate their service sectors. Rich Asian countries can no more afford to hang on to assembly of consumer electronics products and avert deregulation than the United States in the 1980s could afford to maintain a garment industry and leave its telecommunications monopoly intact.

China as a global manufacturing base for multinational companies – Asian, European and American – is unavoidable. The trend towards this is only accelerated by the fact that the China Dream in the domestic market has not materialised. Many investors in the mainland who arrived with ideas of tapping what they predicted would be limitless local demand subsequently switched to exports. Jack Perkowski, who raised $418 million on Wall Street to brew beer and make cars for Chinese consumers, is today running a slimmed down car components business that is focused almost exclusively on exporting.[42] Likewise, Gruppo Finanziario Tessile, an upscale Italian garment manufacturer that produces clothing for many Italian designers, built up a factory in Tianjin in the early 1990s capable of producing a million suits a year. The plan was to sell 80 per cent of output in the domestic market and to export 20 per cent. By the end of the decade, the company was exporting four-fifths of its output and selling only one-fifth locally, for want of a sufficiently affluent indigenous market.[43] There are similar examples from around the world, including many Asian plants producing industrial inputs from chemicals to cement that have been switched to exports. Home country export capacity is often being closed down in the context of global recession because factories in China that were originally planned for local sales are newer as well as cheaper to run.

China's export economy is a force to be reckoned with, but its success is hardly proof that the China Dream is around the corner. The exporters are succeeding because they have access to an industrious population without being involved in China's troubled domestic economy. The export sector is also one that ought to be growing because it is not only competitive but also immature. China's exports are still only a quarter of GNP – low by developing country standards. When she moved up to become the seventh biggest exporter in the world in 2000, it was notable that one of the two countries she overtook was the Netherlands, population a mere 15 million.[44] Within a few years, China will rise to become the world's number four exporter, behind the United States, Germany and Japan. But this will be based on headline figures that do not reflect relatively low levels of Chinese value-added and it will mainly be the achievement of foreign-invested enterprises.

'No' is the hardest word to say

Given the proven success of export processing in China, the lowest risk – and perhaps most rational – approach for investors would be to manufacture for export where appropriate and sell into the domestic market as and when demand develops. Many small foreign businesses have learnt this lesson, but multinationals – with their long-term strategic outlook – are unable to escape a fixation on the theoretical potential of domestic sales. Their predicament is summed up by Alan Smith, the former chairman of Hong Kong investment bank Jardine Fleming: 'China is too big to ignore,' he says, 'and too difficult to make any money.'[45] This is the point on which the China Dream impales its many victims.

In 2002, General Motors was still as good an allegory as any for the trials of the China market and investors' inability to look reality in the face. The company had invested more than $2 billion in auto parts and vehicle manufacturing businesses. Some $750 million of that went in 1995 on a half share in Shanghai General Motors, a venture designed to produce Buick saloons. By 2001, with sales of this $35,000 luxury sedan appearing to have peaked the previous year at 30,000 units, the company was seeking new markets by adding a minivan and retraining its workforce to make a $12,000 compact car, the Buick Sail.[46]

With early 1990s forecasts of required China capacity of up to a million units, it was hardly a success story.[47] GM insisted it was making an operating profit at sales of 30,000 vehicles, but it was inconceivable that such revenues were covering its vast cost of capital. Yet for all the setbacks on the ground – the company's Shenyang pick-up truck venture was closed for six years before restarting small-scale production in summer 2001[48] – GM's China Dream was unaffected. The company, obsessed with market share irrespective of the present size of the market, was still negotiating for new ventures.[49] Unchastened by the flawed projections of the 1990s, its forecasts of future sales remained enormous – the company simply pushed the forecasts back as deadlines came and went. In the early 1990s, GM's then managing director for Asia, Jerry Wang, stated that China was going to be one of the world's biggest auto markets by 2000. 'This is not a dream and it is going to happen,' he insisted.[50] By 1999, the date offered by GM's new chief executive officer, Richard Wagoner, was 2020, by which time, he said, China would be the largest auto market in the world.[51] In 2001, Wagoner – who seized on China as the only bright spot in a world where global car sales were forecast to fall in both 2002 and 2003 – had shifted the date to 2025. But by this point his target had also been redefined – for China to exceed the current size of the US market.[52]

When launching the Buick Sail in 2001, GM spokesman Alan Adler repeated the corporate mantra: 'China is the largest developing market in the world in terms of untapped demand for cars,' he said.[53] That was all that mattered. Here was the market that could – in the dream scenario – change the fortunes of his company, one which had a turnover of $180 billion a year but margins of barely 2 per cent, keeping its stock price forever in the doldrums.

China was the magic bullet, just as it had been for McDonnell Douglas, AT&T and countless other multinationals in search of big profits and new direction. As Richard Wagoner put it in June 2001: 'This [China] is a once in a lifetime bet.'[54]

People have been betting on China for centuries and will continue to do so. Despite all the evidence that only the tiniest minority strikes it rich in the Chinese domestic market, there is never any shortage of corporate gamblers. The reasons why most fail to make a decent return are entirely intelligible, but the potential rewards of success are deemed to be so great that companies are compelled to participate. As Carl Crow intimated in the 1930s, the invention of the calculating machine – not to mention more recent creations such as the business consultant – have only encouraged the ancient art of speculation on what sales a company might achieve if only a large part of the Chinese population would buy its goods or services.[55] At times when the economies of developed countries are weak, as during the great depression, the early 1990s and the first years of the new millennium, the China Dream has a particular potency because it stands out in starkest relief from the mundane reality of normal business life. It is at just these times that gamblers place their biggest bets on the propositions with the longest odds and the largest potential returns. As a result, the next few years will likely see both investment and expectations rise to unprecedented levels. Should those expecations be met, in spite of the limitations of the market, the political state of China and the mismanagement of the nation's finances, it would indeed be a dream come true.

Epilogue

'THE CHINESE GOVERNMENT is transparent! Your China Dream concept is wrong!' said Xiang Huaicheng, the Chinese finance minister, raising an admonitory forefinger. His opinion was as expected, but it is a tribute to him that in September 2002, six months after this book was originally published, he was willing to sit down with its author for nearly two hours at his office in Beijing to talk about China's problems. Unfortunately, despite a year of record exports in which China would likely be the world's leading destination for direct foreign investment, there was little Mr Xiang could point out to demonstrate that the country's financial health was improving. The dichotomy between China's powerful export processing sector and her sickly, indebted domestic economy became starker than ever in 2002. A theoretical change in leadership at the quinquennial Communist Party Congress in November did nothing to gloss over this. Even Mr Xiang, repeating a word he first used in the spring, described the fiscal outlook as *yanjun* – 'grim'.

This was the year the international press stopped saying that China might face serious financial problems and began instead to report those problems as fact. In January 2002, under an agreement with the Basle-based Bank for International Settlements (BIS), for the first time the Chinese banking system used international standards to publish figures for non-performing loans. The country's big four commercial banks revealed that more than 28 per cent of their loans outstanding were not being serviced by borrowers. This after the banks were allowed to clean from their books Rmb1.4 trillion ($169bn) in failed loans – equivalent to more than 13 per cent of their portfolios – in 1999. It was confirmed – as had long been suspected by outsiders, and equally vehemently denied by Chinese officials – that more than two-fifths of bank loans at the end of the 'miracle' decade of the 1990s were duds. Much of China's growth in those years had been paid for with borrowings that would never be honoured. Jiang Jianqing, president of the country's largest bank, the Industrial and Commercial Bank of China, admitted in an interview in September 2002 that he already knew in 1999 that non-performing loans at his bank made up an astonishing 47 per cent of the total.[1]

Until 2002, the government claimed that the special asset management companies (AMCs) it set up would be able to recover much of the banking system's bad debts through work-outs and negotiation. But that summer, figures were published which showed that, after more than three years of operations, the AMCs had tackled less than a fifth of loans handed to them, while the cash recovery rate was just 22 per cent. The first distressed asset sale to foreign investors – to a consortium led by American investment bank Morgan Stanley – yielded 9 cents on the dollar. The more difficult non-performing loans had not been addressed. Yet Xiang Huaicheng – roughing out calculations on a sheet of A4 in the Finance Ministry – still wanted the world to believe that an overall recovery rate of 30 per cent was achievable.

In the course of the year, both the Ministry of Finance and the central bank conceded that there were likely to be further bad debt write-offs for state lenders. At the time of the 1999 debt amnesty Dai Xianglong, the governor of the central bank, said the banks 'should not expect either a midnight feast or a breakfast' at the public trough again. But that resolution has since evaporated, as the Finance Minister confirmed: 'It is true that originally it was said that it was the last free lunch,' said Mr Xiang. 'But, speaking frankly, I think there are more to come. The transition of China's economy is going to take a long, long time. I cannot say that the institutional and individual reasons that generate non-performing loans have disappeared.'

China's debts are accruing at a startling rate. The state's ability to service those debts has become increasingly questionable. In January 2002, less than a month after more reliable bank data were published, the government abandoned a third attempt to sell down shareholdings in listed companies to fund its liabilities. Beijing has insisted for several years that it owns billions of dollars of equity in public companies that can be sold to prop up a welfare system in which twenty-six out of thirty provinces are now in deficit. But each time it tries to sell its shares, the markets swoon at the threat of oversupply and the government backs away. On 31 January, with the Shanghai and Shenzhen bourses down 40 per cent in six months, the state share sale was put on indefinite hold. There is no alternative scheme – bar debt creation – for paying for pensions and unemployment benefits.

Political will was similarly lacking when it came to the enactment of measures announced in 2001 to liberalise bank interest rates. The failure to price capital according to risk is the most salient characteristic of China's financial system – one which allows profitless state enterprises to absorb the bulk of credit. But when the time came for floating deposit and loan interest rates in spring 2002, the reform was put off. The reason was fears that free-market competition for deposits might precipitate a banking crisis in an environment where each of the major banks is insolvent by normal accounting measures. In September, a revised Bankruptcy Law, which would facilitate the liquidation of companies that owe unserviced debts to the banks, was also shelved. Under discussion for seven years, the new law was supposed to be ratified by China's National People's Congress in March 2003.

In the short run, China's economy is kept moving by infusions of deficit financing and bank lending that runs at twice the pace of overall growth. In the five years to the end of 2002 the Ministry of Finance sold Rmb 660 billion ($80bn) of special public bonds to finance infrastructure projects. The budget deficit increased seven-fold in the lifetime of the last parliament, from $5.5 billion in 1998 to $37 billion in 2002. And while central government revenue went up – by 11 per cent in the first nine months of 2002 – expenditure went up by more – 18 per cent in the same period.

Each year, deficit spending adds a couple of percentage points to growth, keeping China above the 7 per cent level its leaders believe is essential for social stability. But the public expenditure is unsustainable – hence Mr Xiang's references to a grim future. At some point in the next five years, without fundamental change, the country will face a financial crisis. The state's indebtedness will reach a point where people are unwilling to buy its bonds or put their money in its banks.

One country, two economies

To many outsiders who do business with China, the notion that the country could be close to crisis seems risible. When the returns for 2002 are confirmed, it is probable that China will have attracted more than $50 billion in foreign direct investment, outstripping even the United States. Exports will have risen by a fifth to more than $300 billion, making China the sixth largest trading nation in the world. How is it possible that success like this can be associated with fiscal meltdown?

The section of this book that provides the answer is Chapter 10, Parallel Economies. The reform approach of the Chinese government has failed to tackle the inefficiencies, waste and corruption of the old socialist economy, and it is these which are bleeding the country dry. But reform has opened up space at the margins, where an entirely new economy has taken root. The most potent symbol of this second, parallel economy is the export processing sector that supplies the world's sneakers, clothing, electrical appliances and, increasingly, more sophisticated goods such as computers as well.

Data published in 2002 show just how far exporting companies have come in making China a manufacturing centre for the world. Starting in May, China began to outstrip long-berated Japan as an exporter to the US; on Washington's numbers, the Sino-US trade surplus in 2001 was already $83 billion. Wal-Mart, America's biggest retailer, confirmed that it alone bought $14 billion of merchandise for its stores from suppliers in China that year. In some sectors, like shoes or bicycles, almost every product sold in the US now comes from China. The country makes half the world's cameras, a third of its air-conditioners and televisions and a quarter of its washing machines. Increasingly, it also assembles higher-tech products. Taiwanese, American and Japanese companies are shifting semiconductor and laptop computer production to China; one company, Toshiba, is building a factory in Hangzhou, south of Shanghai, that will turn out 2.5 million portable computers a year by 2004.

The common factor that runs through all China's export industries is cheap and productive labour. With 150 million migrant workers and another 200 million who are probably surplus to requirements in agriculture, there is little upward pressure on factory wages, which average less than $100 per month. Each year the vast assembly workforce becomes a little more skilled and the export components base expands. This in turn encourages more manufacturers to relocate production capacity to China to be close to downstream suppliers. More than half of China's exports – up from next to nothing fifteen years ago – are produced by non-mainland companies, among whom Hong Kong and Taiwanese investors lead the way. They come to China not for her mythical markets, but for her 40 cents an hour labour; they make their profits in the rich countries to which their products are sent.

The rise of Chinese manufacturing, coming in the wake of the Asian financial crisis of the late 1990s, is breeding fervent paranoia among the governments of the region. Politicians in south-east Asia, Korea and Japan talk of the Chinese 'hollowing out' their economies. But while China's export sector is strong, propaganda about the nation's relative economic might runs, as usual, far ahead of reality. In constant price terms, China's export performance in the past twenty years is considerably less impressive than that of either Japan or the south-east Asian nations in their periods of rapid development. The country's share of world trade is still less than 5 per cent, compared with around 8 per cent each for Japan and south-east Asia; and – critically – most of China's trade is conducted by foreign corporations using the mainland as a platform. The fact that so many exports are assembled from imported components holds down the Chinese trade surplus at less than 0.5 per cent of world trade compared with 1.5 per cent for Japan, which originates most of what it manufactures. It is instructive that the people who do not fret about Chinese export prowess are the foreign businessmen who have opened factories there, cut costs and are thereby increasing their global profitability. Hon Hai Precision Industries, for example, the high-tech electronics maker that recently became the biggest company in Taiwan, attributes its success squarely to having relocated capacity to China faster than its rivals.

In a perverse twist to the story of China's parallel economies, the exporters are now being helped by the Beijing government's failed domestic policies. In the past few years, deficit-financed spending has improved infrastructure far beyond the standards of comparable developing nations and helped push down the price of real estate in east coast cities by as much as four-fifths. Mr Xiang, the Finance Minister, confirmed that more special bond issues, raising more money for projects with no cashflow and no ability to produce returns on investment, will go ahead in 2003. The government is hooked on the steroids of public financing. Fixed investment in China, most of it state-mandated via banks or bond issues, rose an incredible 24 per cent in the first ten months of 2002. The government's largesse makes the operating environment for export processors still more attractive. For investors in the domestic economy, by contrast, deficit spending and the absence of bankruptcy continue to guarantee oversupply and meagre profits in markets that loom far larger in the imagination than in practice.

In late 2002, almost a year after China acceded to the World Trade Organisation (WTO), the development that four-fifths of surveyed American firms said would increase demand for their products and services appeared to be the dampest of squibs. The WTO, as explained at length in this book, cannot change the realities of China's closely controlled domestic economy or promote a sudden increase in her demand for imports. Some multinational companies appear to have grasped this. Despite wild projections twelve months before about a first opening of telecommunications services to foreign investment, Minister of Information Industries Wu Jichuan told the author in September 2002 that he had yet to receive a single application. Likewise, there had been very few requests for licences in the stockbroking and fund management industries. But perhaps the most telling story of the post-WTO experience was that of agriculture, the sector where American politicians promised that the WTO terms accepted by China would lead to its receiving a flood of grain, fruit and other foodstuff imports. In the event, in the first eight months of 2002, US agricultural exports to China fell in value by $200 million, while Chinese agricultural exports to America increased in value by $100 million. Beijing also promised new regulations to restrict future purchases of a key US import commodity, soybeans, citing a need to control more closely genetically-modified produce. Membership of the WTO has not revolutionised the

Chinese marketplace, where change will have to come from within when China herself decides to implement it.

At a corporate level, there were the usual disappointment colour stories in 2002. AOL Time Warner, the world's biggest media company that was hugely feted in 2001 when it claimed to have made the first licensed inroads into both internet services and cable television in China, spent a year doing very little. A $200-million internet joint venture with mainland computer maker Legend failed to secure necessary government approvals, while it became apparent that the outlook for the cable business – restricted to less than 1 per cent of Chinese cable viewers – is one of long-term losses. In April, soft drinks giant PepsiCo made the extraordinary admission that after twenty years in China it had still not made any money. The frustrated announcement was followed by legal proceedings to dissolve a 1993 bottling joint venture in which the American company alleged its Chinese partner looted the business to pay for executive vacations in the United States and Europe and luxury cars. In an editorial about multinational misfires in China, the *Asian Wall Street Journal* commented: 'Pepsi's China story is another classic of the genre. It has invested $500 million in the country over the past twenty years, and has yet to make a dime of profit – the company says it hopes to break even in the next few years. Elsewhere that would be called madness, but in China it's known as "long-term investing".'[2] As if to reassure the world that ethnicity and local connections are not the keys to profit, Hong Kong's wealthiest tycoon, Li Ka-shing, notified shareholders in the spring that one of his main companies was taking a $64-million write-off against failed infrastructure projects on the mainland, not least in his own home town in Guangdong province where he had lavished millions on charitable causes.

This anecdotal evidence of continuing woes in the domestic market was borne out by the annual business survey of the American Chamber of Commerce, China's largest foreign business association, in which only a minority of members reported improving profit margins. Among those under siege in 2002 were the mobile telephone companies – for a decade the exception of success that proved the general rule of disappointment in China. Motorola, a corporation frequently cited as proof of what is possible in the market, posted China revenues of $5.7 billion in 2001 – 13 per cent of global turnover. But competition from domestic manufacturers, carefully nurtured through cheap credit and government orders, was beginning to erode the foreign share of the mobile market, just as had happened in less sophisticated consumer goods businesses during the 1990s. Having already learned to make the backbone infrastructure for wireless communications, state-backed companies were conquering the handset business through cut-throat pricing. Domestic businesses grabbed 18 per cent of the market in only two years to mid-2002 and targeted 30 per cent by year-end.

Perhaps the most interesting industrial story of 2002 occurred in the auto-mobile market where, after a decade of undershooting investor forecasts, car sales suddenly took off. Soaring purchases – up by half in the first nine months of 2002 – only expanded the Chinese car market from the size of Australia's (with 19 million people) to Spain's (with 39 million, poorer people), but the performance was striking and took long-suffering foreign investors by sur-prise. International auto-makers pronounced that at last the sun was rising on their promised land. The reasons for the sales spurt and the reaction of multi-national investors, however, provide much more telling insights into the workings of the Chinese marketplace. Faster sales in 2002 were attributable to four factors. First, WTO accession did not produce a forecast import surge as tariffs fell but government was slow to distribute import licences; instead foreign-invested car plants in China slashed prices by around one-fifth to hold off the expected import challenge. Second, foreign factories afflicted for years with over-capacity rolled out many new models to tempt their Chinese cus-tomers and utilise more of their production facilities. There are now thirty dif-ferent models of car made in China. Third, the three richest areas of the country – the Beijing, Shanghai and Guangzhou regions – reached income levels where private car ownership was possible, given falling prices, even though most cars were still bought by government and taxi fleets. Fourth, car loans finally became available through the state banking system.

But what was truly revealing in 2002 was that the two star performers among new car models were both made by wholly domestic companies. Their success was based on undercutting the foreign competition while – to the chagrin of international auto-makers – borrowing their basic designs from foreign cars already manufactured in China. The Zhejiang province-made Geely and Shanghai-produced Chery may carry off-kilter English lan-guage names, but they came from nowhere to take nearly a tenth of the market in the first three-quarters of 2002. Both cost under Rmb100,000 ($12,000). The Geely is based on the Daihatsu Charade, manufactured under licence from the Japanese company in Tianjin, while the Chery closely resem-bles the Volkswagen Jetta, produced at a joint venture car plant in north-east China. Indeed, many of the components in the Chery are original Jetta parts, procured in breach of written contracts from Volkswagen's own Chinese sup-pliers. One of the owners of the Chery factory is Volkswagen's joint venture partner, Shanghai Automotive Industry Corp. The German company, the only foreign auto-maker to have profited in China's car market, has decided it must grin and bear the situation.

As has repeatedly been the case in other industries in China over the past fifteen years, the car market looks set to become a race to the bottom in terms of price, a race in which foreign companies are competing with local ones that possess often insuperable advantages because of state support. The first victim of such competition is any profit that may be accruing to foreign companies. Yet the multinationals' reaction to auto market growth in 2002 was the traditional one of the China Dream. Between August and October, Toyota, Nissan and Hyundai, three auto-makers not yet manufacturing in China, committed to $3.4 billion dollars-worth of joint ventures with capacity to make 1.6 million cars – more than 1.5 times that year's market. There were other investment announcements from Ford, Mazda and Russia's Sok, as well as the existing foreign car makers. Unless China becomes an assembly centre for exported cars, just as it has for furniture or household electronics, this new rush of investment merely guarantees that the car business will remain where it has been for twenty years, with very few winners and a large number of losers.

The political watershed that wasn't

The crowning event of the year 2002 in China was supposedly the 16th Communist Party Congress. For the previous two years political analysts had billed this quinquennial forum as a watershed for Chinese politics. It was to have been the first time since 1949 that an institutionalised transfer of power had taken place, as the leadership of General Secretary Jiang Zemin gave way gracefully to the next generation of leaders – a group of men ten to fifteen years younger than Jiang. By the summer, however, it was clear that Mr Jiang was having second thoughts. Rumours flew that the 76-year-old elder statesman was concerned that national 'stability' required his continued presence at the helm. A propaganda campaign was launched in the official media to promote Jiang's contribution to socialist ideology, a formula he calls the 'Three Represents'. This otiose theory contends that the contemporary Communist Party of China represents not just peasants and the proletarian masses, but 'advanced culture' and 'advanced productive forces' – code for entrepreneurs and private business – as well. In other words, the Party can be all things to all people and is therefore justified in its continued tenure of power.

In the run-up to the 8 November opening of the congress, Sinologists and journalists split into competing camps: the one that said Jiang would hang on and the one that said he would go. The only sure conclusion to be drawn from a general reading of the commentators' analysis is that Chinese politics remains as opaque as ever. No outsider has a reliable idea of anything that is going on because there is no due process.

The shenanigans ended in a political compromise that begged more questions than it answered. Jiang Zemin was not able to hang on to the Party general secretaryship, which passed to the younger Hu Jintao, 59, a man originally fingered for leadership by Deng Xiaoping in the early 1990s. But Jiang's name and his Three Represents theory went into the Party constitution and he was allowed to pack the all-powerful Standing Committee of the Politburo with his acolytes and allies. Among these are several members of his so-called 'Shanghai faction', including Zeng Qinghong, Mr Jiang's long-time aide and political hatchet man. The horse-trading was so fierce that the Standing Committee had to be expanded from seven to nine members to accommodate all factions.

When the National People's Congress, China's tame parliament, meets in March 2003 the top government posts will be divvied up among these nine men. Hu Jintao is set to become president, Zeng Qinghong will probably be vice-president and Wen Jiabao, deputy to current premier Zhu Rongji, should succeed his boss. The extent to which Mr Jiang will be able to pull strings from behind the political curtain is impossible to say, but there is no doubt he will try. It was already clear at the end of 2002 that he had manoeuvered to hang on to the chairmanship of the top army body, the Central Military Commission, for at least a couple of years. The late Deng Xiaoping used the same position to maintain his influence over civilian politics after he gave up other posts in 1987. Above all, the political fudge that overtook the 2002 transition makes strong policy-making and determined enforcement of policy decisions unlikely in a period when it is most needed. It is difficult to see how the 2003–8 government will achieve more in the tasks of banking reform, bankruptcy legislation and deregulation than did its more unified predecessor, which stalled on each of these issues. The slow slide towards financial crisis continues.

梦

The symptoms of China's political and bureaucratic malaise were inescapable in 2002. Corruption cases showed once again that the system is so rotten that it co-opts even those who profess to be cleaning it up. Two protégés of premier Zhu Rongji, who was billed at the last congress in 1997 as the man to end corruption and rescue the Communist Party, went down in major scandals. In January, Wang Xuebing was dismissed as one of China's top state bankers pending charges relating to illegal loans made while he worked at the Bank of China. In August, the official Xinhua News Agency alleged that Zhu Xiaohua, formerly chairman of China Everbright Group, a financial services conglomerate that controls the mainland's number six bank, had taken 'huge amounts of bribes'. The two cases followed the earlier suicide of another key Zhu Rongji acolyte rumoured to be under investigation – Li Fuxiang, formerly head of the foreign exchange regulator. The pattern of 'new broom' hotshots who are supposed to cleanse and modernise state industry and government being caught with their hands in the till is hard to miss. It was revealed in 2002 that when Mu Suixin – sent by Beijing to fight corruption and speed up privatisation in the north-eastern city of Shenyang – came under investigation for graft, police found $6 million-worth of gold bars hidden in the walls of his country villas; 150 Rolex watches were secreted elsewhere. When interviewed by the author soon after he became Shenyang's 'turnaround' mayor in 1998, Mu stressed at length how he was a graduate of China's top university, Qinghua, and uniquely qualified to sort out the complex problems of a rustbelt city in need of radical, original thinking.

The Shenyang-based Chinese corporation that features several times in this book was also much in the news in 2002. One of the men who set up New York-listed Brilliance China Automotive (BCA), a subsidiary of local state company Jinbei Automotive, was accused by the government of stripping hundreds of millions of dollars of state assets. Officials alleged that Yang Rong, who formerly worked with the already-disgraced Jinbei chairman Zhao Xiyou, operated a web of 300 on- and offshore companies into which he siphoned public money. As chairman of BCA, Mr Yang had been named by the press in 2001 as the third-richest tycoon in China. In the summer of 2002 he fled to the United States when Chinese state security closed in on him. As a result of these events, the latest in a long line of jilted Brilliance and Jinbei foreign investment partners are likely to be British black-cab maker Manganese Bronze and tottering car manufacturer MG Rover. The former this year licensed BCA to make its taxis but failed to receive a contracted £600,000 fee. The latter had been told by Yang Rong that a co-manufacturing deal announced in March was going to secure thousands of British jobs. Not for the first time, China was to provide the magic bullet for a foreign business in trouble. The episode recalls once more Lord Elgin's warning to the British merchants of Shanghai in 1858 that China was not going to make them all millionaires. Speaking during the Second Opium War (being fought to force China to open treaty ports up and down its coast for the hungry Western entrepreneurs) he reminded them of their expectations after the first Opium War, which ended sixteen years earlier, in 1842:

> The expectations held out to British manufacturers at the close of the last war between Great Britain and China, when they were told that a new world was

opened to their trade, so vast that all the mills in Lancashire could not make stocking-stuff sufficient for one of its provinces, have not been realized; and I am of opinion that when force and diplomacy shall have done all that they can legitimately effect, the work which has to be accomplished in China will be but at its commencement.[3]

Joe Studwell
December 2002

Notes

Preface

1   The main Nasdaq index peaked at 5,048 on 10 March 2000 before falling to a low of under 2,000 within a year and under 1,400 in September 2001.

2   By the late 1990s, more than half of American households owned stocks, this explosion of popular share ownership being closely associated with the rise of the Nasdaq market. Trading volume on the technology-heavy Nasdaq exceeded that of the New York stock exchange for the first time in 1994, while in 1997 the market became the first in the world to trade a billion shares in a day; by 2000, the capitalisation of the Nasdaq was around $6 trillion.

3   This figure includes an estimated 30 million overseas Chinese living in Asia, Europe, Australasia and the Americas, as well as 30 million Chinese who live in the 'Special Administrative Regions' of Hong Kong and Macau, and on Taiwan. The latter group are claimed by the Chinese government as regular citizens, but in reality have different status and levels of freedom from ordinary mainland citizens.

4   *Crouching Tiger, Hidden Dragon*, it should be pointed out, is a Taiwanese, not a mainland Chinese, movie, though it is often perceived as the latter. The film was far more popular among western audiences than with mainland China's educated élite, who tended to see the work as lightweight and myth-sustaining.

5   The curiosity of Chinese character tattoos in Europe and America leaves Chinese observers baffled and somewhat amused. The tattoos are often done by non-Chinese artists and are frequently misdrawn. The sight of Caucasians with 'Butterfly' or 'Enemy' or some such incongruous word scrawled on them is a strange one.

Chapter 1   The Dream through history

1   See Jonathan D. Spence, *The Chan's Great Continent*, W. W. Norton & Co, 1998, p. 18.

2   S. A. M. Adshead, *China in World History*, 2nd edition (Macmillan, 1995) and Seneca, *De Beneficiis*, VII 9, 5.

3   Had there been heavy traffic on the silk routes, it might also be expected that plague would have migrated from Asia to Europe earlier than it actually did so in the sixth century.

4   'Golden' refers to the period prior to the An Lu-shan rebellion in 755.

5   Adshead, *n*. 2 above. The author quotes Abu Zayd of Siraf estimating the foreign population of Guangzhou (Canton) at 120,000.

6   Anne of Kabudhan.

7   The general ban of 845 on foreign religions was subsequently lifted, but the damage was never undone in the wake of widespread persecution.

8   Adshead puts it better than anyone: 'For all its manifest splendours,' he writes, 'Sung China was a cut-flower civilisation' (Adshead, *n.* 2 above, p. 110). The Southern Song dynasty (1127–1279), fabulously wealthy as it was, was still forced to retreat south of the Yangtze by Mongol invaders. Although Europe in this period was typified by civil wars, plague and economic depression, it was also a time when territorial states, capitalist cities, a supranational church, parliamentiary government, legal systems, independent banking and competing educational establishments took root. Though as yet it had little to show for it, Europe was developing pluralistic societies while China was politically, institutionally and culturally static. At another level, the intellectual liberation represented by Peter Abelard and Thomas Aquinas can be compared with the Song's reinforced authoritarian Confucianism.

9   The debate about whether Marco Polo really went to China is unending. At the heart of the argument is the fact that *The Travels* discusses some aspects of every-day Chinese life in minute detail yet completely omits to mention three defining features: the character-based nature of the language, the footbinding of women and tea drinking. These omissions lead some scholars to speculate that Polo pulled together *The Travels* second-hand from the accounts of others.

10 Sir Henry Yule, *Cathy and the Way Thither*, vol. 2, (Hakluyt Society, 1915), p. 179.

11 Yule above, vol. 4, p. 137. Ibn-Batuta travelled around Africa and Asia between 1325 and 1354 and wrote the *Rihlah*, an account of what he saw.

12 Chinese printing dates back to the first millennium but it was under the Song dynasties (AD960–1279) that wood block printing of books and money developed to a new level. Moveable type printing in earthenware, metal and wood appeared simultaneously in the Chinese, Korean and Uighur languages as the technology spread around the periphery of the Chinese empire.

13 See Spence, *n.* 1 above, p. 17.

14 Zhu Yuanzhang, whose power base was around Nanjing, founded the Ming as the Hung-wu emperor.

15 See Adshead, *n.* 2 above, p. 206. Another measure of the trade is the '*almojarifazgo*', or tax on silver exported from Acapulco to Manila, largely to pay for purchases from China. This ran at a hefty 8,000 pesos a year in the first three decades of the seventeenth century before falling to 3,000 pesos a year in the late 1630s. The China–Manila–Acapulco trade tailed off thereafter with the decline of the Spanish empire in the seventeenth century.

16 This estimate of trade volume is made by Huguette Chaunu and Pierre Chaunu in *Seville et L'Atlantique (1504–1650)*, vol. 8 (Sevpen, 1959), p. 386.

17 Rhubarb root was used for the treatment of, among other things, dysentery. The first commercial tea shipment was to Holland in 1610.

18 Or, as Adshead puts it: 'The springs of Chinese creativity, already choked and desic-cated in the transition from Tang to Song, were further dammed' (*n.* 2 above, p. 179).

19 This limited trade deal continued for 150 years but, from 1728, was amended so

that exchanges of goods took place on the Sino-Russian border. From a Chinese perspective, this had the benefit of keeping the Russian barbarians out of Beijing.

20 Note from Emperor Qian Long to Macartney, 1793.

21 From the most literate society in the world, China became a nation of perhaps 30 per cent literacy by 1800; the English literacy rate would soon be double this. A high Chinese birth rate contributed to both falling literacy and falling productivity as small and medium-sized market towns multiplied and the largest cities shrank. The population of Nanjing, for instance, reduced from 7 million in the sixteenth century to less than one million by the nineteenth century. Europe, meanwhile, had made huge breakthroughs in physics and astronomy by the late eighteenth century, and was headed for new discoveries in electromagnetism and chemistry. Qian Long, by contrast, sought to freeze the achievements of the Chinese mind with what had gone before and refused to tolerate new works in his imperial library. A war junk in the reign of Qian Long carried 13 guns; a standard British ship of the line carried 74. See Adshead, *n*. 2 above, p. 243, for a full comparison of the England of George III and China of Qian Long.

22 Adshead, *n*. 2 above, p. 263.

23 Quoted in Spence, *n*. 1 above, pp. 69, 91.

24 As of the mid-nineteenth century, China would already be growing most of the opium her people smoked within her borders.

25 Akira Iriye, *Across the Pacific: An Inner History of American–East Asia Relations* (Harbinger, 1967), p. 14.

26 The tonnage of American shipping entering Chinese ports declined from 2.6 million tons in 1864 to 1.3 million tons in 1905 (Adshead, *n*. 2 above, p. 345).

27 The first four cities were Shanghai, Ningbo, Fuzhou, Xiamen. The treaty of Tianjin opened up coastal cities further north, like Tianjin itself, as well as upstream on the Yangzi river.

28 Adshead, *n*. 2 above, p. 339.

29 Adshead, *n*. 2 above, p. 288.

30 Opium imports peaked in 1879 at 100,000 piculs (6,000 tonnes); tea exports peaked in 1886 at 2 million piculs (120,000 tonnes); at the end of the nineteenth century, Manchester cotton exports to China were worth about £16 million (the pound in 1900 had the purchasing power of about £61 or $81 in 2000; see *n*. 42 below). See Adshead, *n*. 2 above p. 366 and Carl Crow, *400 Million Customers* (Harpers, 1937), p. 277.

31 Quoted by, among others, James Mann in *Beijing Jeep: A Case Study of Western Business in China* (Westview Press, 1997), p. 24.

32 Duke, from North Carolina, created the American Tobacco Company, the original high-volume, mechanised manufacturer of cigarettes. See John Kennedy Winkler, *Tobacco Tycoon: The Story of James Buchanan Duke* (Random House, 1942) and Sherman Cochrane, *Big Business in China: Sino-Foreign Rivalry in the Cigarette Industry: 1890 to 1930* (Harvard University Press, 1980). Duke's atlas story is also repeated at http://www.essential.org/monitor/hyper/issues/1992/01/mm0192_06.html.

33 See Iriye, *n*. 25 above, pp. 204–5 and John A. Garraty, *Henry Cabot Lodge* (Alfred A. Knopf, 1953). Lodge's sentiment was widely held. 'Multiply your ships and send them forth to the East,' was how William Seward, another US senator, exhorted American businessmen.

34 Protestant US missionaries probably made up half the total missionary force working in China in the 1930s.

35 Charles S. Campbell, *Special Business Interests and the Open Door* (Yale University Press, 1951), p. 111.

36 Crow, *n*. 30 above, p. 22.

37 A few examples of buildings completed in the 1920s and 1930s Shanghai real estate boom are the Hong Kong Bank Building (started 1923); the French Club, or *Cercle Sportif Français* (opened 1926, now the old part of the Garden Hotel); the Park Hotel (opened 1934, at twenty-two storeys the tallest contemporary building in China) and Cathay Mansions (opened in 1929, now the old Jin Jiang hotel).

38 Crow, *n*. 30 above, p. 286.

39 According to the Public Security Bureau (PSB) in 2001, there are 150,000 long-term foreign residents in China holding residents' permits. There may be the same number again living and working in China on short-term business and tourist visas. The PSB estimates there are 400,000 Hong Kong residents living and working on the mainland and another 400,000 holders of Taiwan passports. The author is indebted to the journalist and author Jasper Becker for this information.

40 See Adshead, *n*. 2 above, p. 355.

41 Adshead, *n*. 2 above, p. 365. China's total tea exports hit a record 2 million piculs (120,000 tonnes) in 1886. Between 1867 and 1905, China's tea exports to England – its key market – fell from 1.25 million piculs (72,000 tonnes) to just 40,000 piculs (2,400 tonnes). Exports from India to England in the same period increased from 50,000 piculs (3,000 tonnes) to 1.1 million piculs (66,000 tonnes). The contemporary unit for measurement of tea and opium in the Far East, the picul, derives from a Malay word meaning the heaviest thing that a man can carry. The picul was equivalent to 60 kilograms or 133.3 imperial pounds.

42 See Crow, *n*. 30 above, pp. 264 and 283. He gives the figures for manufactured cotton imports as around £16 million a year in 1900, falling to £2 million in 1935. These values have been updated using calculations from Economic History Resources (see eh.net) that equate one pound of purchasing power in 1900 to £61, or $81, today and £1 from 1935 to £53, or $75, today. These historical purchasing power calculations are far from a perfect science – as the failure of the respective sterling and dollar updates to reflect today's exchange rate illustrates – but they do give a sense of China's past market sizes in current terms.

43 Adshead, *n*. 2 above, p. 368.

44 Crow, *n*. 30 above, p. 23. By the 1930s, actual manufacturers of razors had begun to break into the market, but only after a long struggle with the established horse shoe alternative.

45 This point has been noted by other authors, including Mann, *n*. 31 above, p. 31.

46 Iriye, *n*. 25 above, p. 109.

47 Crow, *n*. 30 above, p. 203.

48 Crow, *n*. 30 above, p. 203. Crow gives 1935 values for the foreign pharmaceutical and cosmetics markets of £400,000 and £125,000 respectively (see *n*. 42 above).

49 Crow, *n*. 30 above, p. 62.

50 Crow, *n*. 30 above, p. 91.

51 Crow, *n*. 30 above, p. 96.

52 Even George Curzon, British arch-imperialist and viceroy of India, had the sense to say of the rail project that 'the prolific literature to which it has given birth' would be best used for 'a bonfire'.

53 Population data released by China in 1979 show that at least 30 million people died as a result of famine in the late 1950s and early 1960s. See Jasper Becker, *Hungry Ghosts: China's Secret Famine* (John Murray, 1996).

54 Paul A. Varg, 'The Myth of the China Market, 1890–1914', published in the *American Historical Review*, February 1968.

55 Crow, *n*. 30 above, p. 286.

56 Europeans, Japanese and overseas Chinese had visited the Canton Trade Fair since its inception in 1957, even though – during the Cultural Revolution – this could involve listening to mandatory readings from Mao Zedong's *Little Red Book*. The arrival of the Americans, who had been banned from trade contacts with the mainland, however, put the fair on the global map.

57 Mann, *n*. 31 above, p. 31.

58 *Ladies Home Journal*, February 1972.

59 'From a China Traveler', *The New York Times*, 10 August 1973.

60 Randal A. Stross, *Bulls in the China Shop and Other Sino-American Business Encounters* (University of Hawaii Press, 1990), p. 61. Needless to say, China today is a major net oil importer.

61 Stross, above, p. 61. Almost fifty test wells were drilled by foreign companies in the South China Sea between 1979 and 1985, at a cost of around $10 million per well. Prices were inflated because all support services had to be purchased from China at rates well above international market levels. The results of seismic surveys also had to be turned over, at no charge, to the Chinese government. The one significant gas find was by Atlantic Richfield (Arco), which the company was allowed to develop in a joint venture with Chinese partners.

62 Stross, *n*. 60 above, p. 72.

63 It was a nice piece of Potemkinisation, since the backs of the buildings – unseen by the Queen – were left as black as soot. The author is grateful for this observation to long-time Shanghai resident Norman Givant.

64 The expression was coined by Paul Hollander, author of *Political Pilgrims: Travels of Western Intellectuals to the Soviet Union, China, and Cuba, 1928–1978* (Oxford University Press, 1981).

65 Stross, *n*. 60 above, p. 60.

66 Mann, *n*. 31 above, p. 54.

67 *Detroit Free Press*, 7 May 1983.

Chapter 2   A man called Deng

1   See 'Excerpts from talks given in Wuchang, Shenzhen, Zhuhai and Shanghai, 18 January to 21 February *1992*', in *Selected Works of Deng Xiaoping*, vol. 3 *(1982–1992)* (People's Publishing House, 1993).

2   Fourteen families were moved out of the house so it could be opened to the public in 1987 (interviews of Tiffany Bown and the author in Paifang, August 1994). When Rewi Alley, a left-wing New Zealand sinologist and friend of New China, was allowed an early post-reform visit to the Deng family home in 1981, fifty-one people comprising nine familes were living in it.

3   The Dengs' land would yield about 10 tonnes of grain a year.

4   According to Harrison Salisbury in *The New Emperors: China in the Era of Mao and Deng* (Avon Books, 1993), Deng's actual passage was paid for by the Chamber of Commerce of Chongqing, the capital of Deng's home province of Sichuan.

5   Liu Shaoqi, China's head of state from 1959 to 1968, could perhaps be added as a third 'internationalist'. However, since Liu was stripped of power in October 1968 and driven to his death in prison a year later, he played no part in China's opening to the outside world.

6   Normalisation of diplomatic relations with Beijing was announced in Washington on 15 December 1978.

7   This is the story as told by Armand Hammer himelf in his autobiography, *Hammer* (Putnam, 1987).

8   The American diplomat Winston Lord, who met Deng Xiaoping on numerous occasions between 1974 and 1989, asserts he was four feet ten inches tall.

9   Recently it has been suggested that Deng may have remained in Beijing during this period, under house arrest. See Richard Baum, *Burying Mao* (Princeton University Press, 1996). The author has stuck to the previous version of events since the new version has not been substantiated.

10   See Barry Naughton, *Growing Out of the Plan: Chinese Economic Reform, 1978–1993* (Cambridge University Press, 1993).

11   Most importantly, Zhou Enlai and Chen Yun.

12   See Li Zhisui's account of the Chairman's visits in *The Private Life of Chairman Mao: The Memoirs of Mao's Personal Physician* (Chatto & Windus, 1994).

13   China has just 0.2 acres (0.08 hectares) of cultivable land per person compared with, for example, 0.5 acres (0.2 hectares) in India. See the author in *The Dragon and the Tiger, Business China* special report (Economist Intelligence Unit, summer 1995).

14   Richard Evans, *Deng Xiaoping and the Making of Modern China* (Penguin, 1995).

15   Naughton, *n*. 10 above, p. 139.

16   Extrapolated from figures in Naughton, *n*. 10 above, p. 47.

17   *China Statistical Yearbook 1997* (National Bureau of Statistics), pp. 399–400.

18   Author interview with Ma Jinglong, director of the Wenzhou branch of the State Commission for Restructuring the Economic System, April 1998.

19   Communist China maintained an artificially high exchange rate against the dollar and other foreign currencies until the 1980s, when a series of managed devalua-

tions was used to improve export competitiveness. The most complete discussion of Chinese exchange rate policy is contained in Nicholas R. Lardy, *Foreign Trade and Economic Reform in China, 1978–1990* (Cambridge University Press, 1992).

20 Author interview with Ma Jinglong, as *n*. 18 above. These family businesses are the category known in China as '*getihu*' – literally, 'individual business registration'.

21 Author interview with Yu Xunsheng of the *Wenzhou Geti Laodong Xiehui*, April 1998.

22 Author interview with Huang Jiuquan, of the Wenzhou State Administration of Industry and Commerce, April 1998.

23 Rmb50,000 at the 1984 exchange rate. Author interview with Hu Chengzhan, April 1998.

24 Author interview with Yu Xunsheng, as *n*. 21 above. Mr Yu recalled how on a trip to Los Angeles in 1996 he bought what he thought were superior quality foreign ball pens as gifts for colleagues in Wenzhou. On his return, he was embarrassed to discover the pens had been made in the city.

25 Average GNP growth, 1978 to 1991, based on numbers supplied by the National Bureau of Statistics.

26 State Council Circular no. 29, 1990.

27 China's State Council passed the so-called 'Tentative Stipulations on Private Enterprises' in June 1988.

28 *Selected Works of Deng Xiaoping*, vol. 3 *(1982–1992)*, *n*. 1 above, p. 370.

29 See Naughton, *n*. 10 above, p. 97.

30 Naughton, *n*. 10 above, p. 100.

31 Refers to SOEs included in the state budget.

32 Naughton, *n*. 10 above, pp. 202–3.

33 *China Statistical Yearbook 1995* (National Bureau of Statistics), p. 84.

34 See Naughton, *n*. 10 above, for details of research into total factor productivity (TFP) improvements in the state sector in the 1980s. It has to be remembered, of course, that any improvement came off an extremely low productivity base – far lower than that of eastern Europe at the start of the 1980s. Furthermore, while state enterprise TFP may have risen in China in the 1980s, TFP elsewhere in the world was also rising. So it is a moot question as to whether Chinese enterprises made relative gains.

35 Data extrapolated from annual household survey returns published in the *China Statistical Yearbook*, various years.

36 *China Economic Quarterly*, Q2, 1997, p. 34.

37 *Ownership structure of industrial production, 1978–93, %*

Ownership category	1978	1985	1990	1993
State-owned	78	65	55	42
Collectively owned	22	32	36	40
Private	–	2	5	9
Foreign-invested	–	–	2	7

Source: National Bureau of Statistics

38 A leaked copy of the report, 'Some Problems in Accelerating Industrial Development',

was published in Hong Kong in 1977. See Lardy, *n*. 19 above, p. 37.

39 See Lardy, *n*. 19 above, p. 27.

40 China's share of global trade in 1928 was 2.3 per cent; at its nadir, in 1977, the share fell to just 0.6 per cent. See, 'China's Place in the World Economy', *China Economic Quarterly*, Q3, 1999. Data drawn from original research by Nicholas Lardy.

41 See Lardy, *n*. 19 above, p. 135.

42 This is the local Cantonese spelling of the name. The village is located close to Foshan township, which is in turn 17 miles (27 kilometres) from the Guangdong provincial capital, Guangzhou.

43 The importation of more than 1 million trade units of any garment allows for a quota to be imposed. The trade unit for brassieres is one dozen, so it was the importation of 12 million, i.e. 1 million units, that triggered the US quota. In December 1983 China applied to join the Multi-Fibre Agreement (MFA), which then operated under the auspices of the General Agreement on Tariffs and Trade (GATT); it was admitted in January 1984.

44 See chapter 5.

45 Author interview with Victor Fung.

46 Estimates of the number of people killed by Chinese troops and police in early June 1989 vary widely. A conservative estimate, based on contemporary reports from Beijing hospitals, is around 500 deaths. (See Michael Fathers and Andrew Higgins, *Tiananmen: The rape of Peking* (*Independent* in association with Doubleday, 1989). Thousands more people were arrested after the 4 June crackdown, of whom most were jailed and some were executed.

47 See Naughton, *n*. 10 above, p. 253.

48 Naughton, *n*. 10 above, p. 264. Bank debt as a share of state enterprises' book value increased from 11 per cent in 1979 to 45 per cent by 1988. Book value represents depreciated fixed assets plus inventories.

49 For an extended excerpt from the meeting on 19 May 1988, see 'We must rationalize prices and accelerate reform' in *Selected Works of Deng Xiaoping,* vol. 3, *n*. 1 above.

50 For details of data quality problems relating to Hong Kong foreign direct investment in mainland China, see the Author Note at the beginning of this book.

51 Egon Krenz replaced Erich Honecker as East German head of state on 18 October 1989 in a last ditch effort by the politburo to appease rising popular protests. Mr Krenz held the position, however, only until 6 December, when he resigned, paving the way for democratic elections in March 1990.

52 Zou Jiahua is the son of Zou Taofen and the son-in-law of Marshal Ye Jianying, both first generation communist revolutionaries.

53 Although the details of how the plan for the Southern Tour came about are still far from clear it is the belief of the author – based on interviews with a source close to the Deng family – that Deng Xiaoping's children were important in convincing him to travel to Guangdong. The children, in particular Deng Rong, Deng's youngest daughter, were anxious he should do something to blur the memory of the Tiananmen massacre before he was incapacitated by old age and failing health.

54   See *Selected Works of Deng Xiaoping*, vol. 3, *n.* 1 above.

55   See *Selected Works of Deng Xiaoping*, vol. 3, *n.* 1 above.

56   See *Selected Works of Deng Xiaoping*, vol. 3, *n.* 1 above. There is no logic to support Mr Deng's contention that Special Economic Zones are socialist. The first such foreign investment zone was opened in Shannon, on the west coast of the Republic of Ireland, in 1959. Taiwan opened its first export-oriented foreign investment zone in 1965 and many other developing countries followed suit in the late 1960s, encouraged by the United Nations Industrial Development Organisation (UNIDO). Marxist economists around the world have consistently opposed such zones. For a discussion, see George T. Crane, *The Political Economy of China's Special Economic Zones* (ME Sharpe Inc., 1990). A typically Shenzhen twist to Deng's visit to the compact disc factory is that it subsequently turned out to be a major counterfeiter of western films and music.

57   He called for a twenty-year 'development plan' to be drawn up.

58   The video was shown at the fourteenth Congress of the Chinese Communist Party in October and subsequently released for public sale.

59   Reference News operates on a graduated access system, with the most sensitive foreign news and analysis – all translated into mainland Chinese characters – available only to the most senior leaders. At the other end of the scale, some Reference News publications with minimal controversial content now find their way on to public newsstands.

60   The rule of collective leadership was formally adopted by the Central Committee of the Chinese Communist Party (CCP) in 1981.

61   A perennial problem in China for economic planners is the limitations of the country's Soviet-style statistical reporting system. In 1992 and 1993, Chinese leaders did not know quite how fast the economy had grown in 1991. Growth was initially given as around 7 per cent, a figure revised up to 7.7 per cent in the course of 1992 (see Reuters, 8 January 1993). Not until the second half of 1993 was economic growth for 1991 stated as 9 per cent.

62   See Baum, *n.* 9 above, p. 319 on the Deng–Chen relationship.

63   Since 1989, the Communist Party's Propaganda Department and key organs of the state media – notably Central Television and the *People's Daily* – had been in the hands of orthodox Marxists.

64   See *Selected Works of Deng Xiaoping*, vol. 3, *n.* 1 above.

65   The leading propaganda leftists of the day were nicknamed by their enemies 'the Gang of Five'. They were He Jingzhi, acting minister of culture; Wang Renzhi, director of the Propaganda Department of the Central Committee of the CCP; Xu Weicheng, propaganda director in Beijing municipality; Gao Di, editor of the *People's Daily*; and Deng Liqun, the prolific leftist writer and ideologue often referred to as 'Little Deng'.

66   At the bottom of the billboard was Mr Deng's pronouncement: 'Without adhering to socialism, without reform and opening up, without developing the economy, without improving the people's livelihood, there will only be a blind alley.'

67 The Central Party School in Beijing not only trains undergraduate cadres for important posts around the country, it also offers refresher courses and retraining classes
to Communist Party officials in mid career.

Chapter 3 Frenzy

1 James Mann, *Beijing Jeep: A Case Study of Western Business in China* (Westview Press,
1997), p. 55.

2 Report by the Ministry of Agriculture, March 1993. The ministry, highlighting the
amount of productive land being given over to investment zones, said there were
117 foreign investment zones in China at the end of 1991 versus 8,700 at the end
of 1992. The ministry claimed as much as 7 per cent of China's farmland would be
lost if all the zones were developed as planned. Those investment zones already in
existence in 1992 included the four original SEZs, fourteen zones opened in other,
major coastal cities in 1984, a fifth SEZ added on Hainan island in 1988, more than
thirty high technology zones opened in university cities either in 1988 or, after the
Tiananmen delay, in 1991, four zones in Pudong in Shanghai inaugurated in 1990
and miscellaneous others. See the author in *Unlocking China: A Key to Investment
Regions* (Economist Intelligence Unit, 1993).

3 China consists of thirty provinces, plus the annexed province of Tibet and the so-
called renegade province of Taiwan. Below this level there are 331 prefectures and
below that 2,109 counties (the number has been reduced since the early 1990s).
Hong Kong and Macau have a unique status based on their own mini constitutions
and are known as Special Administrative Regions (SARs).

4 Visit by the author, August 1993.

5 Visit by the author, March 1993.

6 At average official exchange rates of Rmb5.3 : $1 in 1991, Rmb5.5 : $1 in 1992 and
Rmb5.76 : $1 in 1993. Renminbi turnover in the two exchanges was Rmb43bn in
1991, Rmb 681bn in 1992 and Rmb3,667bn in 1993.

7 Haikou's airport, which was less than five minutes from the city centre, has since
relocated outside the urban area.

8 Author interview with Feng Lun, April 1999.

9 See Kathy Chen in the *Asian Wall Street Journal*, 13 July 1993. The leading mainland
provinces investing in Hainan island were Beijing, Sichuan, Guangdong, Jiangsu and
Hunan. The US dollar conversion is made at the prevailing official rate of $1 :
Rmb5.3.

10 Local officials tried to finesse their gambling proposal by presenting the casino as
a venture open only to foreigners – most obviously, overseas Chinese. This is why
the island location was chosen, since it could be secured. The small island,
however, was already allocated as the foundation for a leg of a new bridge over the
Haikou river which would link the city centre to a seven square mile (eighteen
square kilometre) real estate development invested by an international consortium
called Washington Investment. When the casino proposal was in full flight the

Haikou government informed foreign investors that they would have to find another location for their bridge. Author interview with Robert Choy, chairman of Washington Investment, August 1993.

11 The figure for nominal growth in fixed asset investment for 1992 given by the National Bureau of Statistics in January 1993 was 32.5 per cent, with an estimate that real growth was 'over 20 per cent'. The figure for nominal growth in fixed asset investment for 1993 given by the SSB in January 1994 was 47 per cent. The nominal figures were subsequently revised and are given in the 1998 *China Statistical Yearbook* as 44 per cent for 1992 and 62 per cent for 1993.

12 *China Daily*, 20 September 1993. TVE gross industrial output was reported as Rmb2,900 billion in 1993; the plan published at the Working Conference called for this to rise to Rmb7,600 billion by 2000.

13 See Geoff Hiscock, *Asia's Wealth Club* (Nicholas Brealey Publishing, 1997). Hiscock lists fifty Asian billionaires with estimated net worth of more than $2 billion, of whom thirty-one are ethnic Chinese. The methodology by which the net worth estimates are arrived at is far from scientific and the figures therefore need to be treated with scepticism. Asian billionaires hold much of their wealth within private companies, or through nominee shareholders in their public companies, so it is impossible to state with accuracy who is worth what. Hiscock's book, however, confirms one basic point: that most Asian billionaires are ethnic Chinese. Of fifteen families Hiscock reckons are worth more than $5 billion, only six are non-ethnic Chinese and two of these – the Sultan of Brunei and the Suhartos – can be considered the beneficiaries of wealth derived from positions of state power rather than from business interests.

14 Eka Tjipta Widjaja has at least eight wives with separate homes around Jakarta and has fathered more than forty children.

15 See author and Stephen Stine, 'Homeward Bound', *Asia Inc.*, August 1993.

16 See author and Stine, above.

17 See *South China Morning Post*, 12 July 1992. This was just one of several such demonstrations.

18 Author interview with Ben Fok, one of Henry Fok's sons. The elder Fok has at least three wives and at least ten children. Ben is in charge of infrastructure development and a boat yard making high-speed inshore passenger catamarans at Nansha.

19 Announced by the company on 14 July 1992.

20 Signed August 1992.

21 Signed in December 1992.

22 *Business Times* (Singapore), 14 May 1993.

23 Signed by Li Ka-shing's company, Hutchison Whampoa, in September 1992.

24 Hong Kong's GNP was $116 billion in 1993.

25 See author in the *China Economic Quarterly*, Q3, 1998, where the mainland exposure of Hong Kong's seven biggest real estate companies is discussed in detail.

26 Robert Thomson in the *Financial Times*, 18 November, 1993.

27 Kerry Wong in the *South China Morning Post*, 21 February 1993.

28 *China's first six initial public offerings of 'H' shares (mainland incorporated companies listed in Hong Kong), 1993*

Offer date	Company	Main business	Capital sought	Application funds received	Times over-subscribed
12/07/93	Tsingtao Brewery	Beer	$96.6m	$10.70bn	110
23/07/93	Shanghai Petrochemical	Diversified petrochemical	$343.0m	$0.60bn	1.77
02/08/93	Guangzhou Shipyard	Shipbuilder	$40.0m	$3.04bn	76
02/08/93	Beiren Printing	Offset printing machinery	$26.9m	$0.65bn	24
01/11/93	Maanshan Iron & Steel	Iron and steel	$510.0m	$35.2bn	69
07/12/93	Kunming Machine Tool	Machine tools	$20.0m	$12.56bn	628
		TOTAL	$1.04bn	$62.75bn	

Source: author's compilation from financial wire service reports

29 *Selected initial public offerings of 'red chips' (listed Hong Kong subsidiaries of mainland corporations)*

Offer date	Company	Main business	Capital sought	Application funds received	Times over-subscribed
08/92	China Overseas Land	Real estate and construction	$110.0m	$11bn	100
08/92	Hai Hong	Paint maker	$11.6m	$4bn	373
02/93	Denway Investment	Car maker	$51.6m	$31bn	657
11/11/93	China Travel International	Travel agent	$51.6m	$21bn	411
		TOTAL	$225m	$67bn	

Source: author's compilation from financial wire service reports

30 At the height of the bull run of the 1990s, US stock market capitalisation was a little over two times GDP; the highest such multiple in Europe is Britain's, at around 1.5 times. Ratios in developing countries tend to be much lower; in Africa, for example, they average around one-third of GDP.

31 When the US congress began to seriously address the issue of the budget deficit in 1993, it was forecast to rise to $455 billion by 2000 (White House press briefing, 17 July 2000). In the event, America's booming economy of the 1990s would turn the deficit positive.

32 The parlous state of Russian government finances and the precariousness of the rouble meant most state level Sino-Russian business in the 1990s was conducted in the form of barter. China had already bought twenty-four Su-27 aircraft in 1992 and, according to Russian press reports, paid two-thirds of the price with consignments of down jackets, sneakers and tinned stew. (See Andrew Higgins in the *Independent*,

17 December 1992.) At the time of writing, a 2,000 megawatt Russian nuclear power station ordered during Yeltsin's visit was still being paid for with a similar roster of consumer goods and food.

33 Li Zhisui, Mao's personal physician from 1955 to 1976, provides a first-hand account of the incident in *The Private Life of Chairman Mao: The Memoirs of Mao's Personal Physician* (Chatto & Windus, 1994).

34 The last Soviet technical advisers left in 1960.

35 Author interviews, June 1998 and 21 February 2000.

36 Prospectus, Brilliance China Automotive Holdings Limited, pp. 4 and 20.

37 China National Automotive Industry Corporation (CNAIC).

38 Earnings per share (eps) at Brilliance were $0.40 in 1992. CSFB forecast eps of $1.25 in 1993 and $1.50 in 1994.

39 One thing of which Carl Walter was not aware at the time was that the karaoke bar of the Zhongshan hotel was part-owned by another American entrepreneur, arms dealer Warren E. Sessler. This explained the presence of a comprehensive playlist of classic American rock songs, allowing Mr Walter to introduce his communist hosts to the likes of Steppenwolf.

40 This anecdote was told to the author by a long-time Boeing employee. Official Boeing records confirm that conversations did take place between the Chinese and the US secret services on the ramp but do not indicate a direct cause-and-effect relationship between these and the sale of the aircraft.

41 In its pursuit of foreign aviation technology in the 1970s, Maoist China also took out an option to purchase Concordes; it was never exercised.

42 Author interviews with Richard Swando and Jay Hunt, GM China director of marketing, 22 February 1999.

43 Until his death, just before the onset of the Cultural Revolution in 1965, Ke was also secretary of the East China Party Bureau.

44 Cathay Mansions today forms part of the Jin Jiang hotel, while the former French Club is the old, low-rise element of the Garden hotel. Although Ke Qingshi died before the start of the Cultural Revolution in 1966, he was instrumental in introducing Jiang Qing to two other members of the Gang of Four, Zhang Chunqiao and Wen Wenyuan.

45 Sun Yat-sen (1866–1925) was instrumental in the overthrow of the Manchu dynasty and became China's first president, in 1911.

46 Work on the main, 16 mile (25 kilometre) section began in November 1993 and was completed in December 1994. A trial 4 mile (6 kilometre) section had already been built in 1992–3.

47 The claim is usually attributed to the Shanghai government, in the form of its mayor and vice-mayors, and is repeated almost without exception by China guide books. The original provenance of the claim, however, is unclear.

48 Henceforth, the city government retained one portion of its tax revenues and passed the remainder to Beijing. The proportions involved are subject to periodic renegotiation.

49   *China Economic Quarterly*, Q3, 1998, p. 36, extrapolated from company reports.
50   In the London real estate boom between 1955 and 1965, an estimated 50–60 million square feet (4.5–5.6 million square metres) of office space was put up. The author is grateful to Sam Crispin of First Pacific Davies, an international real estate agent, for this comparison.
51   First Pacific Davies, *Pudong Property Focus*, August 1997.
52   This structure is the cover image of this book.
53   The Shanghai Golden Trade Building is 1,379 feet (420 metres) tall. The Sears Tower remained the tallest building in the world until 1996, when it was overtaken by the twin Petronas Towers in Kuala Lumpur, which rise 1,483 feet (452 metres).
54   The Shanghai government would subsequently decide to create a small park in Little Lujiazui – the Central Green Area – close by the plots of land bought by Mr Mori. Three and a half thousand families were cleared from the land required in only three months.
55   Hong Kong press reports in 1993 asserted that Lao Yuanyi is the son of Lao Sun, director of China's intelligence service, but this has not been independently verified by the author.
56   The others were Sincere, Wing On and Xin Xin.
57   The retail space is greater than that of Harrods in London but, as noted above, less than the 2 million square feet (186,000 square metres) occupied by the Herald Square Macy's in New York, which takes up an entire city block.
58   Author interview with Tom Gibbian, Goldman's lead negotiator on the Shandong deal, 11 October 2001.
59   Author interview with Tom Gibbian, above, also covering his conversations with Liu Erfei on the subject. Details corroborated by other sources.

Chapter 4   All roads lead to Beijing

1   There were many different requirements for central government approval. One of the most important was, and still is, a ruling that any foreign investment over $30 million must be approved in Beijing. Other regulations stipulate that investments in so-called 'restricted' sectors – which include almost all service businesses – require central sanction.
2   Author interview with a former US diplomat who was a senior Beijing embassy official at the time of the *Economist* article.
3   *Renmin Ribao,* 15 December 1993.
4   Robert Summers, along with Irving Kravis, did pioneering work on purchasing power measures at Pennsylvania University in the 1960s. This led to the creation of what became known as the 'Penn Tables' of international purchasing power comparisons.
5   $370 is the World Bank's *World Development Report* figure for Chinese GNP per capita, following the Bank's 'Atlas' reporting method (which uses an average three-year exchange rate), for 1990. China's National Bureau of Statistics gave a 1990 GNP

per capita figure which converts to US dollars at an even lower $300 per capita at the prevailing commercial exchange rate, or $330 at the official exchange rate. See World Bank Report No. 13580-CHA, *China GNP Per Capita*, 15 December 1994.

6   Summers joined the Treasury as under-secretary for international affairs on 5 April 1993 when Lloyd Bentsen was Treasury secretary. On 10 January 1995 he became deputy secretary of the Treasury under Robert Rubin.

7   See Steven Greenhouse, *The New York Times*, 30 May 1993.

8   See the World Bank's 1993 *World Development Report*.

9   William H. Overholt, *China: The Next Economic Superpower* (Weidenfeld & Nicolson, 1993). The book was published by W. W. Norton in the US under the title *The Rise of China: How Economic Reform is Creating a New Superpower.*

10   Overholt, above, pp. 20–21.

11   Overholt, *n.* 9 above, p. 1: 'Even today about 40 million people live in caves in China's north-east'. This author, despite numerous trips to China's north-east, has never met any of these Flintstones. There are small numbers of people in China's north-central areas who have traditionally hewn their homes from the faces of hillsides, notably in Shaanxi province, but they are not counted in millions.

12   The author's copy of this report is as reproduced in *Business Times* (Singapore) by permission of *Business Week* on 27 October 1993.

13   See John Micklethwait and Adrian Wooldridge in *The Witch Doctors: Making Sense of the Management Gurus* (Times Books, 1998), for a discussion of AT&T's consultancy habit.

14   *South China Morning Post*, 24 August 1993.

15   Author interviews with GE executives and others who met with Mr Welch on his Shanghai trip.

16   *China Daily*, 3 June 1994.

17   Mr Allen first made this forecast public in his August 1993 trip to China and repeated it in a keynote speech to the Asia Society in New York in April 1994.

18   Reuters, 11 November 1994.

19   It should have been the Italians, not the Germans, who were the first beneficiaries in this era of trade diplomacy. Italian foreign minister Gianni de Michaelis made the first European opening to China post-Tiananmen with a visit in May 1991. Italian premier Giulio Andreotti followed in September, just days after British prime minister John Major, and Li Peng travelled to Rome in January 1992. The Chinese were keen to reciprocate for this reintegration into the global diplomatic club. Beijing offered the Italian government potentially huge contracts to supply infrastructure for the development of Pudong New Area in Shanghai, so long as some concessionary financing was available. The Andreotti government agreed but was soon subsumed in the Italian anti-graft movement of the early 1990s known as 'Clean Hands'. With Gianni de Michaelis and the soft loans department of the Foreign Ministry as prime suspects of Italian magistrates, government to government commercial co-operation with China was frozen. Between 1993 and October 1996, when Foreign Minister Lamberto Dini travelled to Beijing, there were no top level

exchanges. The Chinese government delayed many Pudong infrastructure projects waiting for the Italian government to put its financing package in place, but could eventually wait no longer and the business went elsewhere.

20 James Mann, *About Face: A History of America's Curious Relationship with China, from Nixon to Clinton* (Alfred A. Knopf, 1999), p. 293.

21 Major trade missions to and from China between 1991 and 1997 are summarised by country of exchange in the following table. The countries are ordered according to their earliest trade mission during the decade.

Visit	Date	Reported contract signings, report sources, highlights	Executives accompanying politicians
ITALY			
Foreign minister Gianni de Michaelis & PM Giulio Andreotti	May & Sep 1991	De Michaelis set up Andreotti's September visit, when Chinese premier Li Peng was invited to Italy. The pay-off was a Chinese promise to buy Italian infrastructure equipment for Shanghai's Pudong New Area – potentially worth billions of dollars. Italy was to support sales with $500 million of concessionary finance between 1991 and 1993, at interest rates as low as 1.5 per cent over twenty years. See *n*. 19 above.	
Li Peng to Italy	Jan 1992	An undisclosed deal total included a letter of intent by engineering giant Snamprogetti and a contract for a $150 million Technimont ethylene plant. See *n*. 19 above.	
Paulo Baratta, trade minister	Sep 1993 & Nov 1993	$470 million of deals done according to the Italian government on the first visit, including Snamprogetti fertiliser plant. No details of signings on second visit.	30 on second visit
	1994 to 1996	Clean Hands leads to a suspension of high-level Italian visits to China.	
Foreign minister Lamberto Dini	Oct 1996	First senior level visit for nearly three years was an icebreaker.	150
PM Romano Prodi & foreign trade minister Augusto Fantozzzi	Jun 1997	Prodi made a brief visit to coincide with the signing of major deals involving Italian companies Agip and Volani. Fantozzi overlapped on a trip accompanied by 150 Italian executives.	
Totals		N/a	**180**

Visit	Date	Reported contract signings, report sources, highlights	Executives accompanying politicians
GERMANY			
Chancellor Helmut Kohl 1	Nov 1993	$1.8 billion of deals itemised by German side. Kohl himself said $4.1bn. Included six Airbus A340s, Guangzhou subway equipment and ships.	35 (very senior)
Li Peng to Germany	Jul 1994	$4.45 billion of signings reported in the *China Daily*, of which $4 billion to Siemens for four power plants and industrial equipment.	
Jiang Zemin to Germany	Jul 1995	$3.1 billion of deals claimed by Chinese Foreign Minister Qian Qichen. The German Foreign Ministry reported 'more than $1.4 billion'. The biggest deal was a $1billion-plus Daimler-Benz minivan plant.	
Chancellor Helmut Kohl 2	Nov 1995	$1.4 billion according to German TV station ARD. Included two Siemens power stations.	40
Totals (range)		**$9.05 billion to $13.05 billion**	**75**
FRANCE			
PM Edouard Balladur & Gerard Longuet, minister of posts & telecoms and foreign trade	Apr & Jul 1994	$1 billion of deals claimed in the *China Daily*. No details.	100
Jiang Zemin to France	Sep 1994	$3 billion according to the French government. The biggest deal was a $2 billion Elf Aquitaine petrochemicals plant.	
Jose Rossi, Industry Minister	Jan 1995	$2.8 billion, according to the French, for phase 2 of the Daya Bay nuclear power station in Guangdong.	
Li Peng to France	Apr 1996	$2.3 billion according to the French government, including thirty Airbus planes.	
President Jacques Chirac	May 1997	$1.8 billion according to the French government, including $1.5 billion for thirty Airbus A320/321s and ten small ATR-72s.	60
Totals		**$10.9 billion**	**160**

Visit	Date	Reported contract signings, report sources, highlights	Executives accompanying politicians
UNITED STATES			
Wu Yi, minister of foreign trade and economic co-operation, to US	April 1994	Biggest Chinese government delegation to the US since 1979 introduces 800 prospective sale and investment projects including sixty power stations, 100 transport projects, 500 industrial projects.	
Commerce secretary Ron Brown 1	Aug 1994	$6 billion of deals reported by Ron Brown and the US Commerce Department.	24 (very senior)
Hazel O'Leary, energy secretary	Feb 1995	$6 billion reported by Hazel O'Leary and the Department of Energy.	60
Commerce secretary Ron Brown 2	Oct 1995	No details disclosed although Brown said he had discussed a $20 billion list of projects.	4
Jiang Zemin to US	Oct 1997	No deal total released. China signed to purchase fifty Boeing planes. White House had opposed signing the deal on the trip until the Chinese government said it would give half the order to Airbus if this did not happen.	
Totals		**At least $12 billion**	**88**
CANADA			
Prime minister Jean Chrétien 1	Nov 1994	$6 billion (C$8.6 billion) of export sales according to the Canadian government, including two nuclear reactors for the Qinshan plant in Zhejiang province.	375
Li Peng to Canada	1995	Deals were signed but no details released.	
Prime minister Jean Chrétien 2	Nov 1996	Deals signed included Manulife insurance joint venture but no financial details released. Chrétien signed the Canadian government loan package for Qinshan.	
Totals		**At least $6 billion**	**375**
UNITED KINGDOM			
Michael Heseltine 1 (as president of the Board of Trade)	May 1995	$1.6 billion of contracts signed according to Heseltine and the British Foreign Office.	130

Visit	Date	Reported contract signings, report sources, highlights	Executives accompanying politicians
Wu Yi, Minister of foreign trade and economic co-operation, to UK	Feb 1996	$2.7 billion according to *Wen Wei Po*, an official mainland newspaper published in Hong Kong.	
Michael Heseltine 2 (as deputy prime minister)	May 1996	Only project disclosed was an $80 million paraquat joint venture by Zeneca.	280
Totals		**At least $4.3 billion**	**410**

22 See table in *n.* 21 above.

23 Lindsay Griffiths, Reuters, 27 August 1994.

24 *Financial Times*, 30 August 1994.

25 Now Labour MP for Wirral South and chair of the House of Commons' All Party Country Group on China. He is also a member of the UK/China Forum.

26 *Manchester Evening News*, 5 June 1995.

27 Reuters, 30 August 1994.

28 *Sunday Times*, 25 May 1996.

29 Theresa Poole in the *Independent on Sunday*, 26 May 1996.

30 See Mann, *n.* 20 above, p. 262.

31 Mann, *n.* 20 above, p. 294.

32 According to Boeing, total commercial aircraft orders at the company fell to just 124 in 1994, the lowest figure since 1963.

33 Boeing delivered 409 airplanes in 1993. The author is grateful to Steve Hendrickson, director of Strategic Planning for Communications at Boeing in Tulsa, for company data.

34 Mann, *n.* 20 above, p. 292.

35 *Business Week*, for example, was able to describe the policy in some detail as early as October, based on 'administration sources'.

36 Mann, *n.* 20 above, p. 296.

37 Mr Friedmann, the 'special envoy' and a political confidant of French prime minister Edouard Balladur, made at least two secret visits to Beijing in 1993, in July and December. He met with, among others, Chinese premier Li Peng and foreign minister Qian Qichen.

38 Reuters, 29 November 1993.

39 Jonathan Dimbleby, *The Last Governor: Chris Patten and the Handover of Hong Kong* (Little, Brown & Co, 1997), p. 227.

40 Dimbleby, above, p. 226.

41 Dimbleby, *n.* 39 above, p. 278.

42 Global cross-border direct investment was $219 billion in 1993. All figures relating

to foreign direct investment (FDI) in this section come from the United Nations Conference on Trade and Development (UNCTAD), the principal global source for such data. UNCTAD publishes its *World Investment Report* annually.

43 The data for China's GNP in this section are calculated from a 1993 figure of Rmb350 billion converted to US dollars at a rate of 8.3 – the unified national exchange rate introduced as of 1 January 1994. As noted earlier in this chapter, the World Bank by this point had decided to revise upwards its estimates of Chinese GNP and quoted $450 per capita for 1993.

44 Utilised foreign direct investment in China, 1993–6, was $137 billion, versus $421 billion for all developing countries, $269 billion for all Asia, $131 billion for Latin America and the Caribbean and $40 billion for central and eastern Europe. US inward FDI during the period was $224 billion.

Chapter 5   Demand and supply

1 Two sets of data have been used here which show that around $130 billion of foreign investment was committed to non-manufacturing businesses by the end of the 1990s, with $55 billion of that going into real estate. An undefined proportion of manufacturing investment was also targeting domestic consumption. The first source is the State Administration of Industry and Commerce (SAIC), which issues business licences in China and publishes statistics based on the type of licences received by foreign investors. The second source is the Ministry of Foreign Trade and Economic Co-operation (MOFTEC), which publishes other statistics for the utilisation of foreign capital across sectors which are similar to – but not the same as – those used by the SAIC. Both sets of data contain worrying inconsistencies, not least that they fail to tally with national totals for foreign direct investment. However, the data do provide a guide to investment trends and can be found, in abbreviated form, in recent issues of the *China Statistical Yearbook*.

2 Only thirty-four Shanghai-listed companies had issued dollar denominated B shares by this point; in Shenzhen, only twenty-four companies had issued shares available to foreign investors.

3 This figure represents fund equity earmarked for investments in mainland China.

4 The AIG fund completed two rounds of fund raising, in February and May 1994.

5 Author interview with Ian Perkin, chief economist at the Hong Kong General Chamber of Commerce, 6 October 1997.

6 Author interview, September 1997.

7 *South China Morning Post*, 25 February 1994.

8 Author interview in Shanghai, notes undated, and exchange of e-mail 21 February 2000. The actual sum raised was $795 million.

9 See Mark Mobius's 1996 book, *Mobius on Emerging Markets*, in which he writes: 'Of the markets which lead the pack in one year, few appear even in the top five in subsequent years … Clearer evidence of the benefits of diversification would be difficult to find.'

10 China North Industries Investment Fund was listed in Singapore and Dublin in October 1994. Its major investors included Hambrecht & Quist (Asia), ABN Amro, Swiss Bank Corp. and a group of Singaporean backers.

11 Known in Chinese as *Biao Zhun*, the firm's Beijing offices are located within Zhongshan Park, just west of Tiananmen Square. Mr Chen's partner is He Di, an academic from the Chinese Academy of Sciences.

12 One example of this is the huge Plaza 66 development on Shanghai's Nanjing road, where Venturetech was retained to help secure the site and received a 10 per cent equity stake in the development.

13 This is not a uniquely American phenomenon; however, in no other western country have so many senior former government ministers gone on to do China consultancy work. In Britain the most notable case is Sir Edward Heath, former Conservative prime minister and sinophile, who is a regular China lobbyist and closely connected with the China consultancy Batey Burn (now Apco Batey Burn). For Canadian corporations, an important link to premier and China enthusiast Jean Chrétien existed in the 1990s through his son-in-law Paul Desmarais, a member of one of Canada's wealthiest families and long-time chairman of the China–Canada Business Council.

14 James Mann, *About Face: A History of America's Curious Relationship with China, from Nixon to Clinton* (Alfred A. Knopf, 1999), pp. 123 and 133. Richard Holbrooke visited China on behalf of Lehman Brothers in the early 1980s and was a consultant to Nike and Seagram, both big investors in China. Alexander Haig's major clients include United Technologies, the makers of Sikorsky helicopters, on whose behalf he lobbied for the sale of military aircraft to mainland China.

15 Bush's secretary of state, Lawrence Eagleburger, joined Kissinger Associates (see below) but the author has no knowledge that he was closely involved in Mr Kissinger's many China projects.

16 See Steven Mufson in the *Washington Post*, 25 November 1999. The *Post* quoted the figure of $250,000 in reference to George Bush's work for Chubb. Interviews by the author with Chubb executives, however, indicate Mr Bush's total payments were considerably higher than $250,000.

17 Brant Free is a vice-president of Chubb Insurance.

18 Interviews with Chubb executives, 1997 and 2000. Bush came to China for the first time for Chubb in April 1996 and reappeared on behalf of Hancock in October. He returned to Beijing for both companies in 1998.

19 Interviews with representatives of two Kissinger Associates clients, 1997 and 26 February 2000.

20 AIG paid $515,000 for the windows according to Maurice Greenberg.

21 For example, the UK's Royal Sun Alliance paid for the Royal Opera to come to China, Commercial General Union (CGU) paid for the Royal Shakespeare Company to perform *Othello* there and Prudential sponsored the Royal Ballet, while a US insurer paid for the Philadelphia Orchestra to perform. Senior leaders did not always respond to their invites. Jiang Zemin did attend the Royal Ballet but the most senior people to turn up to *Othello* were vice-ministers; Jiang sent a message.

22 AIG in 1992 and Tokio Marine and Fire in 1993. Steven Mufson, writing in the *Washington Post* on 25 November 1999, quoted an unnamed foreign insurance executive in China who had estimated the insurance industry was spending $300 million a year in the pursuit of licences. Given the number of offices opened to show commitment to the market, educational and public relations spending, charitable gifts and so on, such a sum is not impossible when spread across nearly a hundred insurance companies.

23 Brooke Hillier Parker Research, 1995.

24 *Business China*, 23 July 1993.

25 Various author interviews with an officer at the US consulate in Shanghai, including 6 March 2000.

26 According to Cushman & Wakefield, a US real estate agent, prime midtown Manhattan office space was leasing for $2.88 per square foot ($31 per square metre) at the end of 1994. According to FPD Savills, a UK real estate agent, prime London office space in the City and elsewhere was leasing for $5 per square foot ($54 per square metre) at the end of 1994 at the prevailing exchange rate.

27 FESCO frequently justified its charges to foreign companies by saying it trained staff and provided them with housing. In reality, the organisation provided apartments to only 400 of its 7,000 staff in 1994 and had not run a training course in Beijing since the late 1980s. See *Business China*, 21 February 1994.

28 *Business China*, 16 May 1994. This includes expatriate salary and accommodation costs.

29 This included a 'capital levy' of $5,000 per year.

30 Commercial real estate in mid-city Los Angeles or the San Gabriel Valley was considerably cheaper than in Shanghai's Pudong New Area. The San Gabriel Valley is home to much of LA's Chinese community as well as scores of industrial parks. All price comparisons from Cushman & Wakefield.

31 Author interview with Ben Fok.

32 See the author in *China Economic Quarterly*, Q3 1998.

33 Rmb200,000 at the prevailing official exchange rate of Rmb5.2 : $1.

34 Shanghai is the richest city in China. Average annual per capita disposable income in 1995 was Rmb7,699 ($930). *China Statistical Yearbook 1997* (National Bureau of Statistics, 1997).

35 Government policies on the automotive industry, issued by the State Planning Commission 19 February 1994, approved by the State Council 3 July 1994.

36 Although the joint venture's total production was only 60,000 units in 1992, Chrysler executives predicted this would rise to 300,000 units in three to five years.

37 Many official projections for car sales in 2000 were higher than 1.3 million. This figure was quoted publicly on several occasions by He Guangyuan, minister of machine industry.

38 Author interviews with one contemporary and one former Daimler–Benz executive, 10 February and 3 March 1998.

39 *Asia Inc.*, November 1995.

40 Quoted by Jeffrey Parker, Reuters, 14 November 1994.

41 *Los Angeles Times*, 2 December 1995.

42 The poll was originally published in *China Business*, a weekly publication of the State Technology Supervision Administration. The poll findings were in turn publicised by GM's China public relations firm Hill & Knowlton.

43 For example, GM invested $365 million (DM530m at the contemporary exchange rate) to acquire 100 per cent of its production plant at Gliwice, Poland and $350 million for 100 per cent of the Chevrolet Industrial Complex at Rosario, Santa Fe, Argentina.

44 *Wall Street Journal*, 24 October 1995.

45 *Asian Wall Street Journal*, 17 November 1994 and *Asia Inc.*, November 1995.

46 The 'International Seminar and Exhibition on Family Car Industry Development', 14–19 November 1994, held at the International Trade Centre Exhibition Hall in Beijing.

47 Author interview with a senior Daimler–Benz executive responsible for China operations, 10 February 1998. The prototype was a hybrid of what would later become Mercedes's A-class and Swatch vehicles with unique modifications for China.

48 *Asian Wall Street Journal*, 17 November 1994.

49 Author interview, 21 September 1997.

50 See author's report *Multinational Companies in China: Winners and Losers*, Economist Intelligence Unit, January 1997.

51 All figures supplied to the author by the United Nations Conference on Trade and Development. Foreign direct investment inflows into all developing countries were $35.3 billion in 1990.

Chapter 6   The mornings after

1 Paul Krugman's article 'The Myth of Asia's Miracle' was published in the November–December 1994 issue of *Foreign Affairs*.

2 See Krugman above.

3 Notable among the economists studying Russian growth was Yale professor Raymond Powell.

4 The most important new research had been conducted by Professor Alwyn Young at the Massachusetts Institute of Technology.

5 Importantly, Japan was not among the countries whose economic credentials were questioned by 'The Myth of Asia's Miracle'. The Japanese economy, argued professor Krugman, had made substantial gains in total factor productivity, allowing it to become the most developed country in the region.

6 *China Statistical Yearbook 1997*.

7 China's cost of living index is its broadest inflation measure. Nationally, the retail price index, which is China's traditional headline inflation indicator, rose 5.4 per cent in 1992.

8 Since China's currency is not freely convertible, its black market value is the best proxy for its real value.

9 *People's Daily*, 30 January 1994.

10 See Lincoln Kaye in the *Far Eastern Economic Review*, 27 May 1993. Mr Zhao forecast sales of 50,000 deluxe Toyota minibuses alone by 1995.

11 Analyst Nick Colas forecast earnings per share of $1.25 in 1993 and $1.50 in 1994. Actual earnings per share were $0.73 in 1993, $0.20 in 1994 and $0.20 in 1995. For the original forecasts, see Reuters, 23 June 1993.

12 See the author, 'Sob Story with a Happy Ending?', *Business China*, 22 August 1994, and *Financial Times*, 18 November 1993.

13 A week before Denway's listing, Peugeot managers contacted by phone from Hong Kong refused to believe the listing was happening until a journalist faxed them twenty pages from the prospectus. The prospectus used Peugeot's name 636 times. *South China Morning Post*, 12 February 1993.

14 See the author, 'Entente Uncordiale', *Business China,* 9 August 1993.

15 *Asian Wall Street Journal*, 11 December 1995.

16 Reuters report of AGM highlights, 20 May 1994.

17 Xinhua, 28 July 1993. Interestingly, Louis Hughes also told Xinhua that GM had exported at least 9,000 vehicles to China in 1992, whereas the actual number was less than 3,000.

18 Author interview with Tom Gibbian, Goldman's lead negotiator on the Shandong deal, 11 October 2001.

19 This information was conveyed to Goldman Sachs by the chairman of the China Securities Regulatory Commission. Author interview with Gibbian, above.

20 One of the power companies, Huaneng Power International, made Lehman Brothers its lead underwriter on the basis that the US firm would achieve a price of thirty to forty-five times earnings; in the event, Lehman barely got the issue away at fifteen times earnings. See the *Economist*, 11 February 1995.

21 The SIPD listing was first delayed in 1994, then again in 1997, 1998 and February 1999 before actually taking place in Hong Kong on 30 June 1999.

22 Author interview, March 1999.

23 See Joe Kahn in the *Asian Wall Street Journal*, 23 May 1996.

24 See Kahn above.

25 The renegotiated deal was signed in November 1994.

26 Author interview, 8 October 1997.

27 Original CNN interview as reported by Agence France Presse, 10 June 1999.

28 As reported by Donna Smith for Reuters USA, 13 October 1995.

29 The delayed power projects had been signed up by Wing Group, Entergy Corp and Community Energy Alternatives.

30 Theresa Poole in the *Independent*, 19 October 1995.

31 *South China Morning Post,* 20 October 1995.

32 Author interview with US embassy officers involved with the trip.

33 Reuters, 12 June 1996.

34 The BBC's Carrie Gracie received a particularly harsh tongue-lashing at a Heseltine press conference.

35 Author interview with a German embassy officer who worked on Mr Kohl's trips. The types of direct subsidy used by the Germans in China in the early 1990s are now illegal under European Union rules.

36 *Financial Times*, 16 January 1995.

37 Hazel O'Leary left office at the end of Bill Clinton's first term in 1996 with her China deals still 'pending'. She and her department were censured for overstating the return on overseas export promotion trips around the world. Ms O'Leary was further criticised for using public money to pay consultants to monitor journalists' coverage of her department and identify 'problem reporters'. In April 1996, Ron Brown died in a plane crash and it was not until well after his death that a fuller story of his China adventures emerged. In 1997, when the world came to know the name of Deputy Assistant Secretary of Commerce John Huang in connection with a campaign finance scandal, it was revealed that Mr Huang had travelled to China with Mr Brown on his first visit. He subsequently received donations to the Democratic Party from three corporations which believed they had signed lucrative deals on the trip. Entergy Corp. gave $156,500, AT&T gave $325,000 and GE gave $125,000. See *National Review*, vol. 49, no. 5, 27 March 1997 as well as various reports in early March 1997 in the *Washington Times* and the *Washington Post*.

38 Author interview with one of the US embassy officers cited above.

Chapter 7 Suspect numbers and the perils of projection

1 W. H. Auden and Christopher Isherwood, *Journey to a War* (Faber & Faber, revised edition, 1973)

2 Retail sales of consumer goods rose 6.8 per cent in 1998 and 1999 according to official statistics. They rebounded to around 10 per cent in 2000 and 2001 in the context of heavy fiscal stimulus. One problem with China's numbers for supposedly 'retail' sales is that they also include various purchases by government, such as office furnishings and computers, which rise dramatically in periods of high government expenditure such as 2000 and 2001. The figures are therefore only an approximate guide to real retail demand. Furthermore, official retail sales statistics – gathered through bureaucratic reporting – are almost always higher than returns from household surveys, compiled from random sampling, would suggest. The implication is that official retail sales growth is consistently overstated.

3 *South China Morning Post*, 14 March 1996.

4 *Asahi Shimbun*, 19 September 1997.

5 Author interview, 2 February 1999.

6 Author interview with Clinton Dines, China chief representative of Broken Hill Proprietary (BHP), 30 August 2000. At the time of Fosters' China investments, BHP held a 38 per cent stake in the company.

7 Author interview with Tim Clissold, president of Asimco, 7 September 2000.

8 *Global Companies in China: The Quest for Profitability* (A. T. Kearney, 1998).

9 Author interview with Jay Hunt, GM Marketing Manager (China), 2 February 1999.

A further sixty GM expatriates were paid by the joint venture. In a separate interview, Marcus Chow, head of the GM components business Delphi, in 1996, confirmed that the same pattern was repeated in his joint ventures. The components business, which had thirteen China ventures in operation at the time, was employing expatriates paid for by headquarters in every case.

10 To the derision of other foreign auto makers, GM's Shanghai joint venture also claimed to have made an operating profit in its first year. The plant put out a press release in January 2000 claiming the company made Rmb600 million ($73m) 'profit' in 1999. An unidentified Chinese manager at the joint venture was quoted in *Homeway Financial News* saying that profits rolled in 'so fast that the partners had no time to discuss what to do with them'; see *Hexun Caijing*, 24 January 2000.

11 This is the National Bureau of Statistics' figure for 1990 GNP per capita at the official dollar exchange rate. The World Bank's adjusted Atlas figure for 1990, as used in its annual *World Development Reports*, was $370.

12 Figures for GDP per capita in the Czech Republic and the US are World Bank numbers using the Bank's Atlas conversion method.

13 See Nicholas Lardy, *China in the World Economy* (Institute for International Economics, 1994). China's foreign trade in 1928 accounted for 2.3 per cent of world trade, slightly less than in 1993.

14 See the *Far Eastern Economic Review*, November 1993. Taiwan's total life and non-life premia amounted to $10.1 billion in 1992. China did not surpass this figure until the late 1990s.

15 Sales of domestically made cars in China in 1999 were 565,000 according to Automotive Resources Asia, a research and consultancy company. Because of high tariff barriers there was only a small number of legal imports; smuggled imports were probably also negligible due to an ongoing anti-smuggling campaign in which smugglers faced severe punishments including the death penalty. Car sales in Australia in 1999 were 548,000 units according to the *Black and White Data Book* of the Federal Chamber of Automotive Industries of Australia.

16 Thirty-two aircraft delivered to China in 1994 accounted for 10.2 per cent of the 312 planes delivered by Boeing worldwide. This total was the lowest for thirty years. In 2000, nineteen deliveries represented 3.9 per cent of a Boeing total of 488 deliveries.

17 American Airlines operated 720 jet aircraft as of 2000; Delta and United operated similar size fleets, the other seven major US carriers somewhat smaller fleets, but all in the hundreds of aircraft. The US also has more than twenty minor carriers. Author interview with John Bruns, Boeing China, 4 December 1998 and confirmation from American Airlines.

18 The Boeing office is located in the Pacific Century building in Beijing's Sanlitun district.

19 World Bank report no. 13580-CHA, 15 December 1994.

20 World Bank report, above, p. 41.

21 Author interview with Albert Keidel, September 1997.

22 China's education statistics are also major suspects for misreporting. The central government sets enrolment targets which tend to become self-fulfilling when local statistics bureaus return their data forms to Beijing.

23 World Bank report, *n.* 19 above, Executive summary.

24 This process built up to the release, in September 1997, of a 7-volume series of reports – *China 2020* – focusing on poverty, environmental degradation and social welfare issues. Yukon Huang, the China country director for the World Bank, opened a press conference about the reports by stating that one-fifth of the world's poor live in China – a resonant change in tone compared with the 1992–3 period.

25 Response to a question posed by the author at a press conference at the Diaoyutai state guesthouse, Beijing, 25 October 1999.

26 The worst of this was among township and village enterprises (TVEs); see chapter 10.

27 The usual reason for double counting in China is that most statistics are collected through reporting rather than sampling. This leads to the same product being recounted at different points in its manufacturing process. In the pharmaceutical industry, for example, imported raw materials for drugs are counted at the point of import and then recounted once the raw materials have been processed. This is one of many statistical flaws that explains why, in 1999, Chinese data showed the country's drug market to be worth around $15 billion a year, while sampling by international polling companies suggested it was more like $7 billion – on a par with the market in South Korea.

28 At 10 per cent growth without devaluations, China's GNP per capita would reach $870 in 2000, $2,261 in 2010 and $5,864 in 2020. The prospect of sustained 10 per cent growth is remote, as is the prospect of no further devaluations.

29 Car sales for 1994 from Automotive Resources Asia. The figure of 2.7 million units of planned production excludes some smaller car factories. The planned capacity of major plants and the 1999 sales of those in operation are contained in the following table.

Planned car manufacturing capacity, 1994

Auto maker/plant	Planned capacity, (1,000 units)	Actual sales, 1999, (1,000 units)	Status, 2001
GM Shenyang	300	–	Original S10 pick-up truck abandoned. GM introducing a new line to make the Blazer 4-wheel drive
GM Shanghai	300	20	In production
GM mini car	300	–	Did not receive licence
Daimler–Benz MPV	60	–	Licensed but abandoned
Daimler–Benz Family Car China	250	–	Abandoned prior to licence
VW Shanghai	300	231	In production. The only genuinely successful car plant in China

Auto maker/plant	Planned capacity, (1,000 units)	Actual sales, 1999, (1,000 units)	Status, 2001
VW & Audi Changchun	240 + 50	81 +15	In production
Peugeot–Citroën Guangzhou	150	–	Abandoned by Peugeot in 1997. Joint venture taken over by Honda, which sold 10,000 units of its Accord model in 1999
Peugeot–Citroën Wuhan	300	40	In production
Chrysler Beijing Jeep	150	9	In production, but line expected to close. Daimler Chrysler to decide whether to invest in a new line for the Grand Cherokee
Daihatsu Tianjin	150	102	In production but the future of this Charade outdated model is uncertain. Sales fell 45 per cent year on year in Q1 2000
Toyota Tianjin Corolla	100	–	Did not receive licence
Suzuki Chang'an Alto	100	45	In production
Total	**2750**	**565***	

*Total includes some sales by small plants not covered in this table
Sources: Planned capacity as announced by auto makers; 1999 car sales data from Automotive Resources Asia

30 According to Automotive Resources Asia, installed car capacity in 2000 in China is 1.3 million units versus forecast sales of around 600,000 units. Overcapacity for car engines was much more than 100 per cent because the Chinese government required many auto makers to build additional engine capacity as a requirement for a vehicle manufacturing licence.

31 'Car craze cruising our streets', *China Daily,* 13 February 1996. The report still confidently predicted output of 4 million sedans a year by 2000.

32 See *Business Times* (Singapore) 8 February 1994. At the time Mr Sheehan was based in Singapore.

33 See, for example, an interview with Mr McDaniel by Barry Porter, published in the *South China Morning Post* on 24 July 1993. At a time when GM's Shenyang joint venture had already ceased production, Mr McDaniel asserted it was producing 30,000 vehicles a year. Similar statements were made in an interview with Juliette Walker carried in *Business Times* (Singapore) on 8 July 1993.

34 See the author, *Multinationals in China: Winners and Losers* (Economist Intelligence Unit, January 1997).

35 Cash incomes of Chinese peasants derive from sales of surplus crops and sideline commercial activities. Most 'income' in rural areas is in the form of food grown and consumed by the peasants themselves. According to the National Bureau of Statis-

tics, average per capita cash income in 1999 was Rmb2,205 ($266).

36 Data in this paragraph were supplied by Micah Zimmerman of Strategic Marketing Asia, a pharmaceutical research firm.

37 See, for example, *South China Morning Post,* 27 November 1994.

38 Lucent Technologies, the equipment business that was formerly part of AT&T, fared somewhat better. By 2000, the company was turning over around $600 million a year in China, through a commanding share of the market for high-capacity digital transmission equipment and sales of internet-related hardware, for both of which China is dependent on foreign suppliers. Mr Allen, however, had envisaged billions of dollars of revenue from telecommunications services, whereas, by the end of the decade, AT&T's only inroad was a small trial venture in Shanghai's Pudong New Area to manage network services.

39 Author interview with Bob Nichols. Mr Nichols was one of many American Chamber members in Beijing who was regaled with what he called William Warwick's 'pet theme' of 1996.

40 Author interview, June 1998. Mr Clemens insisted 1,200 pick-up trucks had been produced over seven years. Another senior GM executive said on a non-attributable basis that the line had produced only 660. These figures are higher than the 300 S-10 trucks produced when the line first closed – see earlier in the chapter – because there was a short-lived effort to restart production. Of all the GM staff interviewed by the author, only Stan Clemens claimed that all the trucks produced were sold; others said that many of them were given away or sold for token prices.

41 Jack Perkowski made this remark during a presentation to a World Economic Forum meeting in Beijing in April 1998.

42 See *Fortune,* 21 July 1997.

43 Interviews with three senior GE executives, each of whom demanded anonymity, contributed to this section. In the author's experience the company has been one of the most difficult to speak to, on an on- or off-the-record basis, in China.

44 When the author interviewed Norbert Graeber, Daimler–Benz's chief representative in China, on 10 February 1998, Mr Graeber had not met the Italian president of the European consortium despite the fact that both men had worked out of the same office building in Beijing for the previous nine months. See 'Stalling in China', *The Economist,* 18 April 1998.

45 *Institutional Investor,* US edition. January 1993.

Chapter 8 The socialists' Trojan horse

1 Mirsky was a member of the first post-reconciliation US 'friendship tour' of China in 1972, which was shown a collection of carefully prepared Potemkin villages. Years later, Mirsky met his Chinese guide again, at a point when it was clear that he and the world had been completely misled about conditions in the country. See Jonathan Mirsky, 'Message from Mao', *New York Review of Books,* 16 February 1989, p. 17.

2 Quoted by, among others, Pierre Nebel, Anne Gaudard and Sybille Oetliker in an article of 4 January 2001 entitled 'La Ruée des Nouveaux Chercheurs d'Or', which can be found at www.webdo.com. Professor Friedman made his point on several occasions, also referring to Pudong – in another historical analogy – as an enormous 'Potemkin's village', after the model villages built for Catherine the Great on the orders of her minister and lover Grigori Potemkin, to show her how well ordinary people lived in her empire.

3 The vacancy rate in Pudong was a subject of some debate, but almost all estimates ranged between 50 per cent and 75 per cent of available office space. The figure given here is based on research by First Pacific Davies, a property agent and consultant.

4 The Golden Trade Building stands 1,379 feet (420m), exceeded in height only by the Sears tower in Chicago at 1,450 feet (442m) and the Petronas twin towers in Kuala Lumpur at 1,483 feet (452m). These are the internationally accepted measurements for total height of architectural structures. In terms of highest occupied, or usable floor space, the Sears tower is the tallest building in the world; it has 110 occupied storeys. The Golden Trade Building and the Sears tower were both designed by the Chicago firm Skidmore Owings Merrill.

5 Net new mobile phone subscribers in the United States in 2000 were 16.5 million. In fact, the number of mobile subscribers added in China surpassed the United States for the first time in 1999; the respective figures that year were 20 million in China and 14 million in the US. The cumulative total of Chinese subscribers was forecast to exceed that in the United States by late 2001; the respective cumulative totals in 2000 were 70 million in China and 86 million in the United States. Data from Ross O'Brien, director of information technology research at Strategic Intelligence, an Asian research company.

6 Data from O'Brien, as above. Strategic Intelligence estimates China's annual spend on mobile infrastructure in the late 1990s at $12–15 billion a year. Sales of 27 million handsets in 2000 grossed more than $10 billion. By contrast, at an average retail price of no more than $15,000, the 600,000-unit Chinese car market was worth around $9 billion in 2000. According to international pharmaceutical research company IMS Health, the Chinese pharmaceutical market in 2000 amounted to some $7 billion.

7 A senior executive at Ericsson, for example, explained to the author that while different lines of business in China had different margins compared with other countries, overall profitability was not less than in Europe or the United States. In China, profits on handsets tend to be higher than in developed country markets because the business is not built around low-cost phones given away free by network operators. Domestic call charges are low in China and relatively more profit is concentrated in the sale of the handset itself.

8 China was Ericsson's biggest worldwide market in 1998 but slipped to second behind the US in 1999. Ericsson expected China to regain the number one position in 2001.

9 Estimate contained in an internal 1998 Motorola research report of which the author obtained a copy. Panyu is China's leading smuggling centre for mobile phones as well as other types of electronic goods. Before an anti-smuggling clampdown at the end of the decade the merchandise was sold openly in a large market in the centre of town.

10 A working mobile phone, with its SIM card, cost less than $400 in 2000, down from several thousand dollars at the start of the decade. It takes no more than fifteen minutes to purchase one, complete with service contract, in China.

11 Author interviews with Ericsson, Nokia, Motorola, April 1998.

12 Italy, where the extended family living under one roof remains more common than in any other large western European country, is also Europe's biggest mobile telephone market.

13 For more, see 'Silicon Valley, PRC', *Economist*, 27 June 1998, co-written by the author.

14 See Reuters, 1 September 1993. The companies claimed that a 15 per cent market share would create 270,000 American jobs.

15 *Infrastructure Development in East Asia and Pacific: Towards a New Public–Private Partnership* (World Bank, 1996).

16 In 1993, electricity consumption grew by more than 15 per cent; in 1998, it increased just 2.8 per cent. By 2001, electricity consumption was again rising strongly because the government was spending heavily on state industry to maintain economic growth.

17 Peregrine forecast China's power demand by 2000 would be 1,600 billion kilowatt hours, versus 900 billion kilowatt hours in 1994. Actual consumption in 1999 was just over 1,200 billion kilowatt hours. *China Statistical Yearbook*, various years, and *China Power Sector: Demanding* (Peregrine, 1995).

18 *China Power Sector*, above. Peregrine forecast residential consumption growth of 20 per cent a year, and service sector growth of 16 per cent a year, from 1994 to 2000.

19 Author interview with Paul Chan, ABB China, 28 August 2000.

20 In Shanghai, Westinghouse accepted these terms; in Chengdu, Siemens balked.

21 Author interview with Paul Chan as *n*. 19, above. Mr Chan maintained an extensive database of Chinese power equipment purchases from foreign suppliers.

22 Author interview with Vince Harris, China chief representative of National Power, 12 September 2000.

23 Author interview with Vince Harris, above.

24 The only things AES had to offer investors at the time of the initial public offering were memoranda of understanding for Chinese power projects and the company's own profit forecasts. Despite this, the issue was heavily oversubscribed.

25 Author interview with Bill Young, former Douglas field representative in north China, 7 December 1998.

26 Author interview, 22 January 1999.

27 Author interviews with Charles Martin, a former US embassy staffer in Beijing, August 1998, and Bob Tansy, another US embassy officer involved in the O'Leary

trip, 15 September 1998. The heads of Sinochem, China National Petroleum Corp., Sinopec, China National Offshore Oil Corp. and the minister of geology all attended the 'oil and gas breakfast'.

28 Author interview, 21 January 1999.

29 As above.

30 Author interview, 4 December 1998.

31 By the time of the Boeing takeover of Douglas in 1997, the former had sold more than 250 aircraft in China, the latter less than ninety.

32 *China Statistical Yearbook* 1999 (National Bureau of Statistics, 1999), employment and wages chapter. These figures include a fairly constant number of Party positions – just over half a million. Also included are staff of so-called 'social organisations' such as official trade unions. The number of positions in this category fell from 1.5 million in 1990 to around 300,000 at the end of the decade. The number of jobs in the regular government bureaucracy increased to 10 million. See *China Economic Quarterly*, Q2, 1998.

33 *China Economic Quarterly*, Q2, 1998.

34 As above.

35 The demand that all encryption codes be handed over to the State Encryption Management Commission was quietly abandoned in 2000 after an unprecedented combined protest from European, US and Japanese governments.

36 Among businesses discussed earlier, cement, cars and mobile phones are all examples of sectors where production 'targets' are set by bureaucratic fiat. In the automotive industry, China set minimum prices below which manufacturers could not sell until 2001. In many industries – for instance, beer – national distribution is impossible because of licences which sustain local protectionism. Bass, the UK brewer operating in north-eastern Liaoning province, was unable to obtain permission to sell its bottled beer in Dalian, the most prosperous city in the province.

37 Author interview with a senior AIG executive responsible for property insurance, 29 August 2000. AIG is the only foreign company allowed to sell both property and life insurance and the only company not required to operate as a joint venture with a Chinese state company.

38 Under the terms of its WTO accession protocols, China promised to end geographic restrictions on foreign insurers after three years and to allow them to sell a complete range of products after five years.

39 As in chapter 5, these figures are drawn from a database maintained by the *Asia–Pacific Private Equity Bulletin*, a Hong Kong-based industry newsletter. The publication recorded sixty-two private equity funds set up for China by 1996 with $5.6 billion of available funds.

40 The regulatory authority which issues permissions for initial public offerings is the China Securities Regulatory Commission (CSRC), although in the course of the 1990s the State Council, China's cabinet, took a close interest in listing rosters.

41 The return of 3 per cent a year is calculated with the inclusion of dividends paid

out. Mr Mobius described the China market as 'disastrous'. E-mail exchange between the author and Mark Mobius, February 2000.

42 Author interview with Cathy Ng, editor, *Asia–Pacific Private Equity Bulletin*, 14 February 2000. David Mahon, founder of CMG Mahon, a Beijing-based fund manager, concurs that actual private equity investment into mainland China reached a cumulative total of $3–4 billion by 2000. Mr Mahon maintains his own database of investments. Author interview 27 November 2000.

43 Author interview with a senior ASIMCO executive, 7 September 2000.

44 Author interview with a senior ASIMCO executive, as above.

45 Author interview, September 2000.

46 Author interview with Cathy Ng, as *n*. 41 above.

47 Author interview with one of the new managers the fund's board attempted to introduce, 27 November 2000. See also *South China Morning Post*, 26 May and 2 July 1999. The fund listed at $1 per share and was suspended at $0.25 per share.

48 See Henny Sender in the *Asian Wall Street Journal*, 10 November 1999.

49 The only exception was one pilot investment banking joint venture, China International Capital Corporation, in which Morgan Stanley Dean Witter holds a 35 per cent stake.

50 The standard fee for Hong Kong listings of mainland companies was 2.5 per cent of proceeds, the same as would be earned for a Hong Kong company.

51 This point has been confirmed in numerous interviews with executives at Jardine Fleming, Morgan Stanley, Salomon Brothers, Goldman Sachs and others.

52 Author interview, 8 September 1997.

53 See Hugo Gordon in the *Daily Telegraph*, 13 February 1993.

54 Andrew Browne, the Reuters bureau chief in Shanghai in the mid 1990s, was located in an office nearby. After several attempts to reach Morgan Stanley executives by phone to arrange an interview, he went round to the tennis court office one day. There, all alone, was the secretary.

55 *South China Morning Post*, 8 March 1994.

56 Andrew Browne, as *n*. 54, was in the habit of stopping by for a chat.

57 Conversation with the author, 14 December 1999.

58 Author interview with Davin Mackenzie, chief of Beijing mission at the International Finance Corp. (IFC), September 1997. The IFC's findings for staff time, expressed in years, taken to process an investment in different developing countries in which it operates are: China: 1.63; Vietnam: 1.37; Philippines: 0.91; Brazil: 0.80; Argentina: 0.73; Mexico: 0.97; Egypt: 0.51; Ghana: 0.92; India: 0.77; Pakistan: 0.39; Russian Federation: 1.02; South Africa: 0.73; Turkey: 0.29.

59 Author interview, notes undated.

60 Author site visit and interviews with Charlie Lin, Hang Lung's director responsible for China, in October 1997 and July 1998.

61 As above.

62 As *n*. 60. Hang Lung paid $164 million for the Grand Gateway site and $167 million for Plaza 66.

63 As *n*. 60.

64 All figures from the employment and wages chapter of *China Statistical Yearbook*, various years. Among workers who do not appear as employees of state units in official data are 30 million staff in 'urban collective' units. A significant, but unquantifiable, proportion of 135 million workers at rural township and village enterprises should also be considered state employees because the state effectively owns most of these companies. For a fuller discussion of this issue, see chapter 10.

65 Based on statistics from the People's High Court. See *China Economic Quarterly*, Q4, 1998. In 1997, for instance, there were 5,396 bankruptcies, of which just over 3,000 were state companies. This compares with 7.9 million registered industrial enterprises that year (see *China Statistical Yearbook 2000* (National Bureau of Statistics, 2000), p. 407). Taking into account service sector businesses, for which no reliable numbers exist, the bankruptcy rate must be much lower than 0.05 per cent.

66 See Nicholas R. Lardy, *China's Unfinished Economic Revolution* (Brookings Institution, *c*. 1998), pp. 142–3. Interestingly, Lardy points out that the passage of a new bankruptcy law may be something of a red herrring. The State Economic and Trade Commission (SETC) had already overridden the pro-creditor provisions of the old bankruptcy law when it issued SETC Circular no. 492 in 1996, stating that proceeds from all bankruptcies must first be used to settle pension and other worker welfare liabilities. Given the government's willingness to interfere in the legal process, it is unclear what effect any revised bankruptcy law might have.

67 The subsistence wage varies from place to place, but in coastal provinces it is around Rmb200 ($25) per month – usually one-third to one-quarter of the regular wage.

68 Author interview, October 1997.

69 This comprises 70,000 people in the core steel business and 110,000 in sister companies.

70 Anshan Iron & Steel began investing in collective enterprises in the 1980s as a strategy to provide future employment for children of existing workers. By 1998, the company controlled 400 collectives, businesses which are described by the Chinese government as being of 'non-state ownership'.

71 Author interview, as *n*. 68.

72 *Asian Wall Street Journal*, 5 May 1998.

73 As above.

74 Author interview with Dr Michael Zipp, China country manager of Henkel, September 2000. Henkel's washing powder brands include Persil and Dixan.

75 Another government policy of the late 1990s was to ban new investment in specified industries. In every case, however, this was done in industries already suffering massive overcapacity, which was not reduced. As of 1 September 1999, the SETC banned investment in 201 products, including VCD players, refrigerators, air conditioners, bicycles, microwave ovens, toothpaste, sweets, salt, apple juice and alcoholic beverages. See *China Daily*, 27 August 1999 and *Wen Wei Po*, 28 August 1999.

76 Official figures from the National Bureau of Statistics for the first eleven months of

2000 showed a 40 per cent increase in profits from profitable SOEs, to $25 billion, versus the same period in 1999. Losses from loss-making SOEs fell by 16 per cent to $12 billion.

77 The most obvious indicator that SOE profit figures are suspect is that they increase in tandem with companies' current liabilities as they borrow more money from banks. This credit allows for expanded output which is often 'sold' in return for IOUs rather than cash. The receivables are booked as revenue with no allowance for possible non-payment, permitting increased paper profits to be reported. There is little chance the profits will ever be collected in full. For an excellent introduction to creative accounting at SOEs, see Edward S. Steinfeld's study of the steel industry, *Forging Reform in China* (Cambridge University Press, 1998).

78 As examples: most float glass in China is made by the 'Luoyang' or 'farmers' glass' process rather than the Pilkington process. Tunnels are often built by digging holes rather than boring (as was the case with the massively over-budget Guangzhou subway). Cable-stayed bridge construction employs both domestic methodologies and hybrid techniques adapted from international practice.

79 Author interview with Dung Van Ahn, China chief executive officer of French building materials company Lafarge. Official statistics show that China produces 650 million tons of cement a year, more than a third of global output of 1.5 billion tons. The Chinese figures are believed by Lafarge to be overstated by around 20 per cent.

80 Author interview with Dung Van Ahn, as above. This compares with less than a hundred rotary cement kilns with a capacity of more than 300,000 tons per year.

81 Author interview with Emory Williams, general manager of Sureblock China, a US manufacturer of paving stones with joint ventures in Shanghai and Tianjin, 1 September 2000.

82 Author interview with Paul Chan, as *n*. 19 above.

83 Author interviews with Toby Littlewood, Lafarge China, various dates.

84 The UN Environmental Protection Bureau ranked Beijing the eighth most polluted city in the world in 1998.

85 Author interview with Dung Van Ahn, as *n*. 79 above.

86 Author interview with Dung Van Ahn, as *n*. 79 above.

87 International Finance Corporation memo obtained by the author.

88 Author interview with Dr Michael Zipp, as *n*. 74 above.

89 Various author interviews with Micah Zimmerman, founder of Strategic Marketing Asia, a pharmaceutical market research firm. There is no shortage of equivalent anecdotes. Calum Macleod, a consultant to condom manufacturer Durex, was embarrassed to find that when he introduced the company to a possible state-owned joint venture partner in Guangzhou, it was already producing Durex-branded condoms. During their first visit to the factory, executives of the UK company were confronted with replicas of their products spewing out from the production line. The Chinese venture subsequently became Durex's partner. Author interview, notes undated.

90 Shenfei was a subsidiary of state-owned Advanced Science and Technology

Laservideo Company. To be fair to Mr Deng, company chairman Ye Huaming told the *South China Morning Post* that the patriarch had warned him to comply with international copyright standards during his visit. See *South China Morning Post*, 2 December 1993. Shenfei was one of twenty-nine compact disc pirates named by the US government in 1995, whom it claimed had cost the US music and movie industries $900 million in the past five years. China promised to shut the pirates down, but movie and music piracy remains rampant. According to annual estimates of software piracy published by US software companies, 91 per cent of desktop software programmes being run in China in 2000 were pirated. This compares with 59 per cent in a comparable developing country like India. See *China Economic Quarterly*, Q1, 2001.

91 Jiang Zemin promised 'socialist rule of law' in his report to the quinquennial Party congress on 23 September 1997. The phrase was incorporated into the constitution by amendment in 1999.

92 For lengthy discussion of recent developments in the Chinese judicial system, see 'Justice and Debt Recovery', *China Economic Quarterly*, Q4, 1999, and Randall Peerenboom's study of China's arbitration courts, 'Seek Truth from Facts', to be published in the *American Journal of Comparative Law*.

93 See *China Economic Quarterly*, above. The publication related several allegations of corruption. CIETAC was founded in 1956, on a Soviet model, to arbitrate international trade disputes. Uniquely in China, the tribunal allows foreign lawyers and other professionals to become registered panellists. Corruption allegations, however, tend to arise from the behaviour of the CIETAC bureaucracy.

94 See *China Economic Quarterly*, above. In June 1999 the Supreme People's Procuratorate said there were 850,000 oustanding unenforced court verdicts at the end of 1998 involving $31 billion of claims.

95 Peerenboom, *n*. 92 above. The only other extant research into enforcement of arbitral awards was published by the Beijing-based Arbitration Research Institute (ARI) in 1997. While this organisation claims to be independent, it is in fact a subsidiary of the China Council for Promotion of International Trade (CCPIT), which is in turn the parent unit of CIETAC. The director of ARI is concurrently a senior offical at CIETAC. ARI's research claimed that more than three-quarters of CIETAC awards were enforced; in order to ascertain enforcement, the ARI survey asked local courts to report if they had rejected any cases.

96 See *China Economic Quarterly*, Q4, 1998. According to a report in the official *Education Daily* (*Jiaoyu Bao*) in 1987, only 29 per cent of secondary school teachers and 63 per cent of primary school teachers met the formal requirements for their posts.

97 See *China Economic Quarterly*, *n*. 92 above. China's spending on education as a proportion of GNP is around 2.5 per cent, one-third less than India and half the world average.

98 See *China Economic Quarterly*, *n*. 96 above. Original data from UNESCO.

99 The official Ministry of Education line is that 340,000 Chinese students travelled abroad to study between 1979 and 1999 and 120,000 returned. Author interviews

with consular officials at the American, Canadian, Australian and British embassies in Beijing produced estimates of the return rate for Chinese students ranging between 5 per cent and 35 per cent. The lowest estimates came from the US embassy. The actual return rate is impossible to quantify because host countries do not issue exit visas.

100 *China Economic Quarterly*, Q4, 2000.

101 *China Economic Quarterly*, n. 96 above.

102 Many figures, all of them low, have been given for the number of Chinese lawyers registered at the start of the reform process. This was the number published at ' Chinese Lawyers in the Tide of Reform and Opening-Up', an officially sanctioned exhibition held in Beijing in June 1998.

103 *China Economic Quarterly*, n. 96 above.

104 See, for example, the survey conducted for the Economist Intelligence Unit report, *Multinationals in China: Winners and Losers*, January 1997, or published research from Shanghai by Keith Goodall of the Judge Institute of Management Studies at Cambridge University.

105 Despite crashing real estate prices, China remained the second most expensive country in Asia after Japan to which to post expatriates in the late 1990s. Oil multinational Shell, which maintains an expatriate cost index in the region, uses Malaysia as a base of 100. In mid 1998, when the index was recalculated, South Korea scored 135, Singapore 160, Thailand 160, Hong Kong 185 and China 230. Author interview with Rick Brown, human resource manager for Shell China, November 1998.

106 *China Economic Quarterly*, n. 96 above.

107 *Global Companies in China: The Quest for Profitability* (A. T. Kearney, 1998).

108 *World Competitiveness Yearbook* survey, 1998.

Chapter 9 Other people's money

1 The basis of the interview was that it would not be attributed to the staff member concerned.

2 The official population of China at year end 2000 was 1.27 billion. In reality, the population is higher: because of the one child policy, a lot of 'illegal' children are hidden during censuses.

3 According to the Xinhua news service of 19 January 2001, China's gross tax take from foreign-invested enterprises rose 40 per cent in 2000 to $28 billion. This represents about one-fifth of all fiscal revenues at central and local levels.

4 See Nicholas R. Lardy, *China's Unfinished Economic Revolution* (Brookings Institution, c. 1998), p. 34. The incidence of loss-making industrial state-owned enterprises (SOEs) had first declined in the mid 1980s to a 1985 low of 10 per cent before rising sharply from 1988. In 1990 the level was 28 per cent and, in 1993, 30 per cent. At this point the National Bureau of Statistics stopped publishing regular data. A figure for state enterprises under the central government budget, an indicative

subset of all SOEs, revealed 44 per cent lost money in 1995. The proportion continued to rise until the launch of the government's fiscal stimulus policy – which provided orders for many SOEs – in 1998. There are no useful data for losses by service sector state enterprises.

5   Lardy, above, p. 38. On creative SOE accountancy see also Edward S. Steinfeld's study of the steel industry, *Forging Reform in China* (Cambridge University Press, 1998). Officially reported SOE losses in the first eleven months of 2000 were Rmb101 billion ($12bn).

6   Lardy, *n*. 4 above, p. 37.

7   Known since 1998 as the State Planning and Development Commission (SPDC).

8   The PBoC, formerly China's principal commercial bank, was made the central bank in September 1983 and took over responsibility for managing credit, issuing currency, setting interest rates and so forth in 1985.

9   Lardy, *n*. 4 above, p. 172.

10 There was a modest decline in the second half of the 1990s – from a high of 83 per cent at the end of 1995 – in the proportion of total credit outstanding to state enterprises.

11 Lardy, *n*. 4 above, p. 50.

12 This implausible refrain was heard by the author from central bank and National Bureau of Statistics officials on several occasions in the course of the 1990s. The European Union sets a target budget deficit for members of the Eurozone of not more than 3 per cent of GDP.

13 *China: Reform of State-owned Enterprises* (World Bank, 1994).

14 Lardy, *n*. 4 above, p. 50. State enterprises built 1.9 billion square feet (177 million square metres) of urban residential housing in 1995, compared with 1.2 billion square feet (116 million square metres) in 1985. When the author visited the Anshan Iron & Steel Works in October 1997, the company was selling off old apartments for Rmb30 ($3.60) per square foot ($39 per square metre) and newly built apartments for Rmb80 ($9.60) per square foot ($103 per square metre) – a fraction of replacement cost.

15 China already had rural credit co-operatives, which predated the reform era.

16 Huaxia Bank was originally 100 per cent owned by Beijing-based Capital Iron & Steel (Group) Co., a model state enterprise visited by Deng Xiaoping after his Southern Tour in 1992. In 1995, following the forced retirement of Shougang chairman Zhou Guanwu and the handing down to his son Zhou Beifang of a suspended death sentence for corruption connected with Shougang's operations in Hong Kong, the company's stake in Huaxia was reduced to 20 per cent. The change in ownership was effectively a bail-out, with new capital supplied by other state entities. Everbright Bank, started by the Everbright Group, was also restructured as a joint stock bank in 1995 following irregular lending to group companies. See Lardy, *n*. 4 above, p. 66.

17 Lardy, *n*. 4 above, p. 83.

18 Lardy, *n*. 4 above, p. 13.

19 In March 2000, the National People's Congress approved an annual domestic debt issue of Rmb438 billion ($53 billion). In August, finance minister Xiang Huaicheng requested approval for an additional Rmb50 billion ($6 billion) in long-term bonds to fund infrastructure development.

20 In 1998, for instance, bond issues were equivalent to 46 per cent of total central government expenditure based on the following calculation: total debt issued is net of debt redeemed; expenditures refer to central government expenditures excluding transfers to local governments but including net interest payments (China does not count interest payments in central government expenditures). The author is grateful to Nick Lardy for these data.

21 See 'Policy Banks: The New Black Hole' in *China Economic Quarterly*, Q4, 2000.

22 Lardy, *n*. 4 above, p. 92.

23 Lardy, *n*. 4 above, p. 96.

24 The one child policy, which is most rigorously enforced in Chinese cities, dates from the late 1970s. It therefore began to affect the supply of new labour in the job market in the late 1990s.

25 See *China Daily Business Weekly*, 2–9 September 2000.

26 *China: Pension System Reform* (World Bank, 1996).

27 *China: Pension System Reform*, above.

28 Average individual pension contributions in the state sector are less than 3 per cent of salary versus more than 20 per cent for employers.

29 In the 1950s, the Chinese government issued domestic debt and accepted industri-alisation loans from the USSR. With the Sino-Soviet split, Mao Zedong decreed that from 1959 the country would endeavour to become debt-free. By 1968, all external and internal loans were repaid. China recommenced external borrowing in 1979 and domestic bond issuance in 1981. See Chen Jingyao in the *China Economic Quarterly*, Q1, 1998, p. 25.

30 China's interest and principal payments on external debt as a proportion of export revenues – the debt–service ratio – for example, have been under 10 per cent in every year since 1987. The ratio is not normally deemed unsafe until it exceeds 30 per cent.

31 Loans outstanding at the end of 1999 were Rmb9.38 trillion ($1.13 trillion) versus 1999 GDP of Rmb8.04 trillion ($969 billion). *China Statistical Yearbook 2000* (National Bureau of Statistics, 2000), pp. 53 and 640.

32 New loans in 1992 were Rmb498 billion ($60 billion) versus a government budget of Rmb439 billion ($53 billion). By 1996 the figures were Rmb1.1 trillion ($133 billion) for new loans and Rmb791 billion ($95 billion) for the budget. See Lardy, *n*. 4 above, p. 76.

33 Calculated for 1997. Lardy, *n*. 4 above, p. 80.

34 The Czech Republic had the biggest loan stock relative to its economy at 75 per cent of output; more typically, the ratio in Poland was only 20 per cent. See Lardy, *n*. 4 above, p. 160.

35 See Lardy, *n*. 4 above, p. 38. At year end 1996, debt–equity ratios among Korean

chaebol ranged from 262 per cent at Sunkyong to 473 per cent at Samsung.

36 At the end of 1999, urban and rural savings deposits were Rmb5.96 trillion ($718 billion) versus 1999 GDP of Rmb8.04 trillion ($969 billion). *China Statistical Yearbook 2000*, *n*. 31 above, pp. 53 and 639.

37 At the end of 1999, individual urban and rural savings deposits were Rmb5.96 trillion ($718 billion), enterprise deposits Rmb3.7 trillion ($445 billion) and total deposits Rmb10.9 trillion ($1.3 trillion) (the balance being made up by treasury, government and other deposits).

38 Author interviews with John Campbell, 2 December 2000, and Stu Fulton, 22 November 2000, both partners in the international accountancy firm Pricewater-houseCoopers (PWC). PWC has done more consultancy work, mostly funded by the World Bank and the Asian Development Bank, with China's central bank and commercial banks than any other accountancy firm. Mr Campbell heads PWC's international banking practice.

39 See Lardy, *n*. 4 above, p. 116.

40 In early 1996, a senior officer with the Industrial and Commercial Bank of China stated that non-performing loans at the big four banks as of year end 1995 were 12 per cent 'past due', 8 per cent 'doubtful' and 2 per cent 'bad'. Lardy, *n*. 4 above, p. 119. In 1998, the central bank promised to move to a new classification system in line with international standards by 2000, but no further data had been published by 2001.

41 Author interview, 1 February 1999.

42 Author interview, 22 November, 2000.

43 S&P Sovereign Risk Service, August 2000.

44 The AMC issue is discussed in detail in chapter 11.

45 Lardy, *n*. 4 above, and Nicholas Lardy, 'Fiscal Sustainability: Between a Rock and a Hard Place', published in the *China Economic Quarterly*, Q2, 2000. Lardy points out that in international bank failures a good rule of thumb has been that external auditors' estimates of non-performing loans (NPLs) are double those of bank staff, estimates by bank inspectors are double those of auditors and final liquidation has cost double the estimates of external auditors. If this holds true in China, the price of bank recapitalisation will be much more than 25 per cent of GDP.

46 The bankruptcies of Guangdong International Trust and Investment Corp. (GITIC) and Guangdong Enterprises (GDE), the twin investment vehicles of the Guangdong provincial government, left debts outstanding of $10 billion. In 2000, another insolvent 'ITIC', Guangzhou International Trust and Investment Corp. (GZITIC), offered to repay creditors 40 per cent of its $3.6 billion debt in order to stave off bankruptcy, while Dalian International Trust and Investment Corp (DITIC) signed to pay back 60 per cent of principal and no interest to mostly Japanese creditors on a debt of $150 million. See *Wall Street Journal*, 31 August 2000.

47 Total external debt, according to official figures, was $152 billion at the end of 1999. The estimate of $100 billion is for the portion of the debt which is guaranteed by the Chinese government. This includes loans from international financial

institutions like the World Bank ($25bn) and foreign governments ($27bn), as well as commercial loans guaranteed by the government. Total debt outstanding from *China Statistical Yearbook 2000*, *n*. 31 above, p. 280.

48   The gross – external and domestic – debt of Japan, the most indebted rich country in the world, was forecast by the OECD to reach 118 per cent of GNP in 2001. The external debts of Latin American countries – the borrowings that led to their debt crises – were lower as a percentage of GNP than is sometimes imagined. It was high interest rates in the 1980s that pushed the countries into the abyss. Brazil's external debt as a proportion of GNP was 32 per cent in 1980; Argentina's was 46 per cent in 1990 while Chile's was 67 per cent; Mexico's was 49 per cent when its most recent crisis occurred in 1996. See Frederick Stirton Weaver, *Latin America in the World Economy* (Westview Press, 2000), p. 172.

49   See Lardy's 'Fiscal Sustainability', *n*. 45 above. His projection of fiscal unsustainability by 2008 is based on the following scenario: 1) That government revenue as a share of GDP does not increase; 2) that budgetary expenditures as a share of GDP do not increase; 3) that interest on government debt averages 6 per cent; 4) that the budget deficit is financed entirely by an increase in treasury debt; 5) that net issuance of bonds by China's policy banks continues at the 1996–8 average rate and that interest costs are borne by the issuers, not the government budget; 6) that the cost of bank recapitalisation is 25 per cent of loans outstanding in 1998 plus 20 per cent of new loans; 7) that the annual GDP growth rate averages 6 per cent; 8) that the growth of loans relative to GDP maintains the 1995–8 average. Obviously, some factors can be above and some below these assumptions and still produce fiscal meltdown. In 2001, for example, fiscal revenues rose as a share of GDP, but so did budgetary expenditures.

50   On 17 August 1998, the Russian government declared a 90-day moratorium on $43 billion of rouble-denominated treasury bills and bonds. Short-term debts the government was unable to pay were subsequently exchanged, in a unilateral 'debt swap', for longer-term, bills bearing fixed interest rates. The market price of the bonds plummeted. The government denied its actions represented a default, but the savings of many middle-class Russians who owned short-term bonds were decimated. Foreigners, who held around one-third of the rouble bonds, fared even worse since the rouble–dollar exchange rate fell from six to around twenty within three weeks of the moratorium.

51   The Russian government's fiscal revenues as a share of GDP were 25 per cent in 1998. See *Interfax Statistical Report*, 13–19 March, 1999.

52   Lardy, 'Fiscal Sustainability', *n*. 45 above. Lardy calculates that if the government is able to maintain its rate of tax take increase relative to GDP, and use half the gain to reduce its deficit, the ratio of debt to GDP will still reach 90 per cent in 2008 with 50 per cent of the government's budget devoted to interest expenditure. The other forecast assumptions listed above apply.

53   S&P Sovereign Risk Service, August 2000.

54   Additional public expenditure financed by bond sales was $37 billion across the

two years 1998 and 1999, and $18 billion in 2000. A further $18 billion was spent in 2001, with at least as much slated for 2002.

55 The Ministry of Finance's dependance on taxes from state-owned enterprises lies at the heart of a perverse financial system. The SOEs are often only able to pay taxes because they receive a constant stream of credit from state banks.

56 Formal data on loan loss reserves are not published in China, but in the late 1990s it was reported that the Ministry of Finance allowed banks to maintain a maximum 1 per cent of their outstanding loans as reserves. Patchy data included in Lardy, n. 4 above, show China Construction Bank and Agricultural Bank of China loan loss reserves in 1996 at just 0.58 per cent and 0.47 per cent of outstanding loans respectively.

57 In a speech carried by *China Securities News*, in November 2000, Dai Genyou, director of the central bank's monetary policy committee, warned against 'sacificing lending principles' and 'wasteful competition'.

58 Bloomberg, November 2000.

59 As of 2000, Chinese people were allowed to exchange renminbi to the value of $1,000 for trips of two or more days to Hong Kong and Macau, and $2,000 for trips overseas. The State Administration of Foreign Exchange said at the end of the year that it was looking at ways to tighten foreign exchange regulations for travellers because of concern about capital flight.

60 See *China Economic Quarterly*, Q4, 1998, p. 47. It is interesting to note that Latin American countries in the 1970s also faced huge outflows of domestic capital but were able to ignore them because of the easy availability of credit – in that case, from international banks. For more on this comparison, see Weaver, *n*. 48 above.

61 In 1998, for instance, China recorded a trade surplus of $40 billion and foreign direct investment inflows of $45 billion, yet foreign exchange reserves rose only $5 billion. In 2000, the trade surplus was $24 billion and foreign direct investment $40 billion, while foreign exchange reserves increased $11 billion to $165 billion.

62 Liu Minkang, president of the central bank, was quoted in the Hong Kong paper *Ming Pao* on 1 November 2001 saying that capital account convertibility is not realistic before 2010. At the Sixth Financial Symposium across the Straits in late October 2000, deputy secretary-general of the central bank's monetary policy committee Yi Gang said free convertibility 'may' be possible by 2015. See ChinaOnline, 1 November 2000.

63 Bank runs in Guangdong were triggered by the collapse of GITIC in October 1998. The closure of Hainan Development Bank in the summer of 1998 led to runs on other financial institutions on Hainan island. In the winter of 1998–9, there was a run on Merchants Bank in Shenyang, capital of Liaoning province. A run on branches of the Bank of Communications in Zhengzhou, Henan province, in 1998 was started by rumours, posted on the internet, of corruption among the bank's senior personnel. In June 2000, a decision by the local government in Luan county – 100 miles (160 kilometres) east of Beijing in Hebei province – to shift its deposits from the Construction Bank of China to another state bank led to a run by individ-

ual depositors at six out of seven Construction Bank branches in the county. In the second half of 2000, temporary closure of bank branches in order to test software for year 2000 compliance led to several reported bank runs around the country. It is likely there have been many more localised bank runs which have not been reported, since the state media are not encouraged to do so.

64 As of 2000, 68 per cent of the shares in listed companies in Shanghai and Shenzhen were owned by either the government or state companies. Market capitalisation of the combined Shanghai and Shenzhen bourses, which includes all shares outstanding – traded and untraded – rose from $42 billion in December 1995 to $211 billion in December 1997 and more than $500 billion in December 2000. In the aftermath of the Asian financial crisis, the capitalisation of China's markets exceeded that of Bombay, Seoul, Manila, Bangkok and Jakarta combined. See *China Economic Quarterly*, Q1, 1999, p. 42.

65 *China Economic Quarterly*, above.

66 The listing process is almost entirely bureaucratic, with the central government often giving out the right to list on the basis of a certain number of state enterprises per province or per industry. The China Securities Regulatory Commission promised this practice would cease in 2001, but there has been no upsurge in listings of private enterprises.

67 In addition, from August 1999, a 20 per cent tax on interest earned on bank deposits came into force.

68 These figures are for the proportion of listed companies officially reporting losses. Many analysts believe that the actual proportion of loss-making listed companies would be more like one-fifth, were many not able to avoid reporting losses by periodic restructuring exercises and other balance sheet manipulation which is counter to internationally accepted accountancy principles.

69 See *China Economic Quarterly*, n. 64 above. The B share to A share discount increased from only 10 per cent in 1994 to over 80 per cent by 1999. However, in 2001, the government changed B share regulations to allow Chinese investors to use their hard currency savings to buy B shares. By mid 2001, the discount dropped to around 40 per cent.

70 The stock was Guangdong-based Kelon, China's leading refrigerator maker and also an important manufacturer of air conditioners.

71 In the fourth quarter of 1999, the government said it would gradually reduce its average holding in state enterprises from 68 per cent to 51 per cent. When the markets fell sharply, however, the government retreated and said this was only a long-term objective. Two sell-downs of existing listed businesses did occur as an experiment in December 1999 – Guizhou Tyre and motorcycle maker China Jialing Industry. Both were undersubscribed despite hefty discounts to market price–earnings ratios. A second attempt to sell down state shareholding in summer 2001 saw the markets drop 30 per cent before the exercise was abandoned. See *China Economic Quarterly*, Q1, 2000, p. 45.

72 Indeed China's foreign debt is no larger than its foreign exchange reserves, an

unusual situation for a developing country. All the government's problems stem from its domestic liabilities.

73 The central bank has looked at the possibility of introducing a deposit insurance scheme similar to that run by the Federal Deposit Insurance Corp. in the United States. Investors would be given a choice as to whether to take lower interest on insured funds or higher interest on uninsured funds. Nothing has been done as a result of the study because of the concern that partial deposit insurance, which would replace the government's implicit guarantee of all funds, would lead to an outflow from the banking system. Author interview with John Campbell, *n*. 38 above.

74 Author interviews with IMF staff members. Placement of IMF advisers inside central banks and key ministries is standard practice in developing countries such as Russia. China has consistently refused this and insisted instead that the IMF's technical assistance work be conducted through seminars.

75 The individual in question, Hong Yang, was accused of accepting a bribe from China Construction Bank prior to joining the IMF. Since Mr Hong was working at the IMF's Washington headquarters, the Chinese government requested he join a mission to Beijing in December 1995, at which point he was arrested. Mr Hong was sentenced to ten years in prison at a trial in 1997, despite the IMF's diplomatic status. The IMF protested the action as an infringement of diplomatic immunity and refused to replace its chief of mission in Beijing until Mr Hong was released, which occurred after he had served three and a half years.

76 Average GDP per capita growth in Argentina in the 1980s was –2.2 per cent, in Brazil –0.6 per cent and in Mexico –0.6 per cent. See Weaver, *n*. 48 above, p. 175.

Chapter 10 Parallel economies

1 Original remarks from a speech to senior members of the Communist Party Central Committee, entitled 'Seize the Opportunity and Develop the Economy', delivered on 24 December 1990.

2 Guangdong province and the three provinces of the Yangzi delta – Zhejiang, Jiangsu and Shanghai – account for two-thirds of China's exports.

3 Recent Chinese press coverage of rural industry, where most collectives are concentrated, is strikingly downbeat. An article in the *China Daily* of 3 April 2000, for example, stated that rural industry, 'once the nation's economic locomotive, continues to fade into oblivion'. Another article in the same paper of 24 October 2000 referred to the condition of rural collective enterprises as one of 'stagnation'.

4 The first truly independent survey of China's private economy, conducted by the World Bank's International Finance Corp. with funding from the Australian government, polled 966 private Chinese companies in the summer of 1999. In the survey, only 12 per cent of respondents said they compete head-to-head with state-owned enterprises; most private firms compete among themselves in market niches vacated by the state sector. See *China's Emerging Private Enterprises: Prospects for the New Century* (International Finance Corp., 2000).

5 The technical definition of a collective is that the more than 50 per cent of shares are in the hands of the state, but so-called 'red hat' collectives – in which private businesses masquerade as collectives – evade this requirement.

6 Recent reporting changes on the part of China's National Bureau of Statistics (NBS) have made the ownership issue more, not less, opaque. Since 1997, the NBS has reduced the proportion of economic activity it attributes to state-owned enterprises by shifting units which have been corporatised or listed on domestic or foreign stock markets to new categories called 'joint stock' companies and 'shareholding' companies. The effect is that the share of state-owned enterprise output appears to be falling precipitously. However, since corporatisation or listing almost never ends state control, the change in ownership is only taking place on paper. (The government, for instance, retains an average 70 per cent interest in listed companies.) Any attempt to construct an ownership picture for the Chinese economy is now more difficult than ever.

7 *China's Emerging Private Enterprises*, n. 4 above.

8 See *China Economic Quarterly*, Q2, 1999, or the *Economist*, 19 June 1999, and *Business Week*, 27 September 1999, where Mr Zhong's findings were subsequently reported.

9 See *China Economic Quarterly*, the *Economist* and *Business Week* above. Although there is a considerable black economy in China's service sector, the relatively low figure for private output in services from Zhong Jiyin reflects the dominance of state businesses in areas such as distribution, telecommunications, utility supply and financial services.

10 Official Chinese statistics for 1978 indicated that the economy was four-fifths state-owned and one-fifth collective. All collectives in that period, however, were state businesses.

11 From $72 billion in 1991 to $249 billion in 2000.

12 The author speaks from experience. Each year that he was permanently resident in mainland China, from 1993 to 1999, he would receive gifts of clothing for birthday and Christmas purchased by his mother at the UK department store Marks & Spencer. In every single case, the label of origin showed that the presents, mailed from Britain to China, were made in China; they had undergone a 10,000 mile round trip.

13 Chinese shoe exports were 43 per cent of global shoe exports in 1999, reported *Zhongguo Maoyi Bao* (*China Trade News*), a publication affiliated with the Ministry of Foreign Trade and Economic Co-operation, on 27 February 2001. Chinese toy exports – both from the mainland and via Hong Kong – were $18 billion in 1998 out of a global total of $31 billion; see the *Economist*, 17 December 1998. Total Chinese exports of 'mechanical and electronic products', a category which includes consumer electronics, were $105 billion in 2000.

14 US shoe imports from China reported in *Zhongguo Maoyi Bao*, 27 February 2001. The Mexico Shoe Manufacturing Association, which says its members are being put out of business by Chinese competition, was reported by ChinaOnline on 2 March 2001 as forecasting that China will soon produce more than half the world's

exported shoes. US toy import data from Toy Manufacturers of America reports that China accounted for $9.8 billion of $14.6 billion total US toy imports in 1999.

15 Dildo shops have proliferated in large Chinese cities in recent years in the hope of expanding the domestic market.

16 For an excellent article about the top end of the Chinese toy industry, see Chris Anderson, 'Where the Furbies Come From', the *Economist*, 17 December 1998.

17 The US trade deficit is based on US customs data. China claims the deficit is much lower because it does not count most goods exported via Hong Kong to the United States.

18 According to the US Census Bureau, American exports to China in 2000 were $16.2 billion, or about 0.75 per cent of total foreign trade of $2.2 trillion. At their peak in the 1930s, American exports to China were around 1 per cent of US foreign trade.

19 Thailand's 1998 exports totalled $53bn and Malaysia's $74bn versus $76bn from Guangdong.

20 See 'Guangdong: Another Country?', *China Economic Quarterly*, Q2, 2000.

21 Author interview, notes undated.

22 Asia regional export analysis provided to the author by Credit Lyonnais Securities Asia. China's high-tech exports tripled as a proportion of total exports between 1995 and 2000, to a level of 15 per cent.

23 The buyer was Mr Lo's mainland Chinese partner, a department store company called Shanghai Yimin. The deal was concluded in May 2000. Printemps had posted an overall loss each year since opening in 1995. Sources in Shanghai indicated that Mr Lo had recouped around two-thirds of the original Top Form investment through the sale.

24 Author interview, 1998.

25 In 1999, Guangdong's exports were equivalent to 76 per cent of the province's GDP. By way of comparison, IMF data show that in 1997 the ratio in Thailand was 36 per cent, in Taiwan 42 per cent and in Malaysia 100 per cent. A ratio of 100 per cent or more is possible because GDP measures value-added, whereas exports do not.

26 Based on IMF data, Russia's 1997 exports were 21 per cent of its GNP; China's in 1999 were 20 per cent.

27 The provinces are Guangdong, Fujian, Jiangsu, Shanghai and Shandong. *China Statistical Yearbook 2000* (National Bureau of Statistics, 2000), pp. 602–3.

28 'Developing country' status means that developed country complainants in anti-dumping suits can pick a so-called 'comparable' developing country to ascertain what the market price of a given product in China should be. The Chinese government argues that in many cases the supposedly 'comparable' countries chosen have higher cost structures. None the less, China will continue to have developing country status in trade disputes even after it joins the World Trade Organisation, having conceded this in bilateral negotiations with the United States.

29 In 1997, for instance, China's share of world trade was 3.8 per cent, whereas it was the subject of 11.25 per cent of international anti-dumping suits. Figures for suits against China in the year to June 2000 are taken from China's State Economic and Trade Commission (SETC).

30 Exports by the world's leading export nations in 2000, according to World Bank figures, were United States, $782 billion; Germany, $551 billion; Japan, $479 billion; France, $298 billion; United Kingdom, $280 billion; Canada, $277 billion; China, $249 billion.

31 See *China's Emerging Private Enterprises*, *n*. 4 above. The fieldwork for this study focused on four cities that are leaders in developing private enterprise: Wenzhou, Shunde in the Pearl river delta, Chengdu and Beijing. The number of registered private domestic businesses in each in 1998 was 110,000, 4,000, 12,000 and 61,000 respectively. The ultimate source of this data was the Bureau of Industry and Commerce Management.

32 There were 89,000 registered private enterprises in China at the start of 1990.

33 Figures from the State Bureau of Industry and Commerce Management show that by June 1999 there were 1.3 million registered private enterprises (*siying qiye*), employing 17.8 million people.

34 These percentages are compounded growth rates; in other words, the sum of annual percentage increases divided by the number of years.

35 *China's Emerging Private Enterprises*, *n*. 4 above. Of 1.3 million private enterprises registered by the State Bureau of Industry and Commerce Management at June 1999, 30,000 were in primary industry (mostly agriculture), 530,000 in manufacturing and 722,000 in services. In terms of employment, manufacturing accounted for half of 17.8 million private sector workers.

36 These minimums are for a limited liability joint stock company. Minimums vary by type of registration but these are typical. *Getihu* – individually registered business people – do not face such high registered capital requirements, but they can employ no more than seven people.

37 Simeon Djankov, Rafael de la Porta, Florencio Lopez de Salinas and André Shleifer, *The Regulation of Entry* (Department of Economics, Harvard University, mimeograph 2000). China's registration procedures can be compared with those of Hong Kong, where incorporation need take no more than a week, or the United States, where, in Delaware, article 102 of the state's company registration procedures says that it is enough for a business to affirm that it is 'engaged in any lawful activity'.

38 The contents of this paragraph are based on *China's Emerging Private Enterprises*, *n*. 4 above, p. 37.

39 *China's Emerging Private Enterprises*, *n*. 4 above, p. 40.

40 *China Financial Outlook* (People's Bank of China, 1999, p. 92), and *Almanac of China's Finance and Banking* (People's Bank of China, 1999). The central bank only publishes data for loans by ownership of recipient for working capital lending, which accounts for about three-quarters of all loans outstanding. It is even less likely that a private company will receive a long-term loan than a short-term working capital one. According to official figures, lending to private companies increased from 0.3 per cent of all outstanding working capital loans in 1991 to 0.9 per cent at the end of 1999. However, it is probable that in reality lending to private firms is more than 1 per cent of outstanding working capital loans because the central bank classifies

some lending to private firms in its 'other' category, which mostly comprises lending to foreign-invested companies. None the less, private enterprise lending is extremely limited.

41 See Gao Shiji and Gung Xu, *Sources of Private Equity Capital for Non-State Firms in China* (World Bank mimeograph, 2000). The authors identified eleven listed private companies in their paper, five listed in Shenzhen and six in Shanghai.

42 See Leila Webster, *The Emergence of Private Sector Manufacturing in Hungary*, World Bank technical paper no. 229, 1993; Leila Webster, *The Emergence of Private Sector Manufacturing in St Petersburg*, World Bank technical paper no. 228, 1993; Leila Webster and Dan Swanson, *The Emergence of Private Sector Manufacturing in the Former Czech and Slovak Republic*, World Bank technical paper no. 230, 1993. The researchers found that 75 per cent of Czech and Slovak private businesses, 43 per cent of Hungarian ones, 68 per cent of Polish ones and 47 per cent of those in St Petersburg received at least one bank loan to finance their early operations.

43 Only in exceptional locations like Wenzhou have banks become used to dealing with private businessmen. In the city, the local branches of the Agricultural Bank of China – which has the lowest quality loan portfolio of any bank at a national level – make 70 per cent of their loans to private companies and have a non-performing loan ratio far below the bank's nationwide average. See *China's Emerging Private enterprises*, *n*. 4 above.

44 *China Statistical Yearbook*, various years, and Thomas Rawski, 'The Political Economy of China's Declining Growth', paper presented at the eleventh Annual International Conference of the Association for Chinese Economic Studies, July 1999.

45 Official figures published in or prior to 1995 showed that township and village enterprises (TVEs), the main component of the collective sector, increased output by an average 33.7 per cent a year at current prices between 1980 and 1994. See *China Economic Quarterly*, Q2, 1997, p. 34.

46 The originally published data showed TVE output in 1994 was Rmb2.89 trillion ($348 billion). After the results of the decennial national industrial survey were published in 1995, the 1994 figure for TVE output was revised to Rmb2.04 trillion ($245 billion), a difference of Rmb850 billion ($102 billion). *China Statistical Yearbook*, various years.

47 It was Chen Yaobang, vice-minister of the State Planning Commission, who presented the growth forecasts for township and village enterprises to a National Working Conference on Rural Enterprises in autumn 1993 and called the collectives a 'miracle'. The renminbi targets for TVEs were output of Rmb7.6 trillion ($1.3 trillion at the prevailing exchange rate) and Rmb750 billion ($129 billion) in pre-tax profits by 2000. See *China Daily*, 20 September 1993.

48 The 1959 target for steel output – 30 million tonnes – was finally achieved in 1978. The 1959 target for grain output – 407 million tonnes – was achieved in 1984. On current trends, the 1993 target for TVE output in 2000 may be achieved as soon as 2010.

49 *China Economic Quarterly*, *n*. 45 above.

50 The author is grateful to one of China's best-known economists, Wu Jinglian of the State Council's Development Research Centre, for clarifying that the original, technical definition of a collective is that more than 50 per cent of the equity must be 'inseparable public assets'. Obviously, so-called 'red hat' firms evade this requirement.

51 See *China Economic Quarterly*, Q4, 1997, p. 17.

52 *China Economic Quarterly*, above. The State Planning Commission supported this latest diversification on the grounds that China was deficient in titanium products.

53 Collective sector growth declined from 13 per cent in 1994 to 8 per cent in 1995, while growth of the overall economy slowed from 12.6 per cent to 10.5 per cent.

54 Employment at township and village enterprises declined from 135 million in 1996 to 125 million in 1998. Employment at urban collectives reportedly declined from 30 million to 20 million in the same period, but some of this reduction may be due to statistical reclassification of urban collectives as other types of enterprise. Data from *China Statistical Yearbook*, *2000*, *n*. 27 above.

55 National Bureau of Statistics data released 16 October 2001.

56 *China's Emerging Private Enterprises*, *n*. 4 above, p. 14.

57 The collective share of industrial output in 1978 was 22 per cent, while 78 per cent came from formal state enterprises.

58 China's collectives enjoyed their own sub-field within sinology in the 1990s. The concept of 'local state corporatism' (LSC) was developed by foreign academics to explain a process in which fiscal reform in the 1980s that allowed local governments to retain some taxes supposedly engendered an environment of property rights in which local governments naturally set up businesses and created economic growth. LSC was supposedly a superior development model to both state ownership and private ownership. Yet the model did nothing to explain why the most successful collectives – small township and village enterprises – blossomed in southern coastal China but failed to appear in many parts of the interior and north. In fact, successful collectives demonstrate a regional correlation not with state intervention but with relatively less state intervention and relatively less soft bank credit. See Edward S. Steinfeld, *Forging Reform in China: the Fate of State-owned Industry* (Cambridge University Press, 1998), p. 235.

59 In 1997, according to official data, the 500 largest SOEs held 37 per cent of all state-enterprises' assets, contributed 46 per cent of state enterprises' taxes and accounted for 63 per cent of state enterprises' reported profit.

60 The best review of available regional data, backed up by additional field work, was conducted by Jean-François Huchet in 2000. See *China Perspectives* no. 32, November–December 2000.

61 Huchet, above. In Guangxi, of 1,205 state enterprises undergoing 'ownership reform' between 1993 and 1998, 2 per cent were sold to a non-state third party and 2 per cent were liquidated. In Ningxia, of 603 companies reformed after 1996, 10 per cent were sold to a non-state third party and 8 per cent were liquidated. In both provinces, the remaining state enterprises were leased to management, turned into joint stock companies or merged.

62 The best-known example is Shunde in the Pearl river delta, a town famed for its commitment to private enterprise. In Shunde as of 2000, only 16 per cent of 1,001 former state enterprises continued to have state investment. Shunde, however, is atypical in the extreme.

63 Huchet, *n*. 60 above.

64 Huchet, *n*. 60 above.

65 Huchet, *n*. 60 above.

66 As discussed in chapter 2.

67 See David Stark, 'Recombinant Property in East European Capitalism', in G. Grabher and D. Stark (eds.), *Restructuring Networks in Post-Socialism* (Oxford University Press, 1997), pp. 36–69.

68 The National Bureau of Statistics listed 14,200 joint stock companies as of 1999.

69 See Huchet, *n*. 60 above.

70 According to the State Economic and Trade Commission, 11,270 state enterprises were liquidated between 1988 and the end of 1996. Since this time, no further national data have been published. Huchet estimates 3–4,000 small state enterprises were liquidated each year from 1997 to 1999.

71 *China Statistical Yearbook 2000*, *n*. 27 above, p. 118. Column entries for urban employment by ownership sector summed to 175.41 million in 1996, 23 million less than the stated national total of 198 million. In 1999, the column entries summed to only 155.76 million, while the stated national total for urban employment had risen to 210 million and state enterprise employment had fallen 27 million to 85.7 million.

72 One other guide to the real level of lay-offs in state enterprises in recent years is the official total for '*xia gang*' workers. These are state employees who have been 'stood down' from their formal posts and are awaiting new employment. Workers remain in this condition for up to three years, receiving a basic monthly living allowance while they seek new jobs. Qiu Xiaohua, deputy director of the National Bureau of Statistics, said in December 2000 that by the end of that year the number of *xia gang* workers would be 7 million, covering those stood down between 1998 and 2000. This implies that a total of 10–12 million workers have been stood down since state sector lay-offs began in earnest in 1996. The total is a more credible sum for the reduction in state enterprise employment than the figure of 26 million since 1996 given in the *China Statistical Yearbook*.

73 *A National Programme for the Automotive Industry* was published by the State Planning Commission in 1994. The five pillar industries were defined by the *Long-term Programme to 2010 for the National Economic and Social Development of China*, published by the State Planning Commission and ratified by the National People's Congress in March 1996.

74 Huchet, *n*. 60 above.

75 The following section draws on the work of Steinfeld, *n*. 58 above.

76 Steinfeld, *n*. 58 above.

77 Zhou's enthusiasm for Shandong had much to do with the fact that it was his home

province and he wanted to be seen as a prodigal father.

78 Zhou Beifang was detained in Beijing on 13 February 1995, and his father resigned the next day.

79 Haier, based in Qingdao in Shandong province, is technically a collective, but its close government support and access to bank credit make it indistiguishable, for practical purposes, from a formal state enterprise.

80 See Steinfeld, *n.* 58 above, p. 17, and Standard & Poor's annual China report, August 2000.

81 Steinfeld, *n.* 58 above.

82 Steinfeld, *n.* 58 above, p. 91.

83 Steinfeld, *n.* 58 above, p. 111.

84 Magang Steel raised a total Rmb6.6 billion through the sale of 26.85 per cent of its stock in Hong Kong and 9.29 per cent of its stock as A shares in Shanghai. China's unified 1994 exchange rate has been used to calculate the dollar total.

85 The Hong Kong prospectus for Magang Steel failed to point out that the Party would control senior management appointments. The Shanghai prospectus, in Chinese, made this explicit. Steinfeld, *n.* 58 above, p. 124.

86 Sheng Huaren first announced the 'successful' completion of the three-year campaign at a government conference on trade and the economy on 11 December 2000. See *Shanghai Zhengquan Bao* (*Shanghai Securities News*) of that day and Zhongguo Xinwen She (China News Service) of 12 December 2000.

87 According to a Reuters report of 6 March 2001, Zeng Peiyan, head of the State Development and Planning Commission, was rather more candid during the NPC meeting, saying: 'There has still not been a fundamental change in the way [SOEs] operate.' Sheng Huaren was moved out of his post as head of the State Economic and Trade Commission three months after declaring the success of the three-year reform programme.

88 The profit figure for 2000 represents profits by all profitable state enterprises. It is not a net profit figure for the sector because losses by loss-makers have not been deducted. The number of large- and medium-sized state companies reporting losses in 1997 was 6,599; preliminary figures from the State Economic and Trade Commission suggest the number in 2000 was around 2,300.

89 Tom Rawski, of the University of Pittsburgh, pointed out the changes to depreciation schedules during an exchange of e-mail with the author in February 2001.

90 Author interview, February 2001. The idea that Chinese oil companies could have made $14 billion in 2000 after crude oil prices tripled is put into perspective if one considers that Royal Dutch Shell, a single international oil company, reported profits of $13 billion in 2000.

91 The 1987 figure was calculated by Nicholas Lardy in *China's Unfinished Economic Revolution* (Brookings Institution, *c.* 1998), p. 33. The 2000 figure is calculated by the author based on preliminary statistics. In both cases, the profits are not net for the whole state sector because they include only profits of profitable state enterprises, not losses of loss-makers.

92 Steinfeld, *n*. 58 above, p. 3.

93 A joint programme of International Finance Corporation (IFC) and World Bank assessments of the private sector development of thirty states during the 1990s produced strikingly similar conclusions about what inhibits private enterprise in different countries. A summary of these obstacles – all of which come down to political commitment – was included in the draft version of the IFC's 2000 private economy study in China, but excised from the printed version.

Chapter 11 Yesterday's politics

1 See, for example, the remarkable success in the United States of Samuel P. Huntington's *The Clash of Civilisations and the Remaking of World Order* (Simon & Schuster, 1997) (in which China is only one of the civilisations with which the 'West' is forecast to clash) and *The Coming Conflict with China*, by Richard Bernstein and Ross H. Munro (Alfred A. Knopf, 1997).

2 See Gerald Segal, 'Does China Matter?', *Foreign Affairs*, September–October 1999.

3 China took around twenty casualties for every one on the United Nations side.

4 In 1958, Mao Zedong did order the bombing of the Taiwanese frontier island of Quemoy – an act of bravado rather than invasion – and China also sent troops to support the forces of North Vietnam during the Vietnam war. Ironically, in 1979 China ended up in a short-lived but brutal border conflict with Vietnam in which the People's Liberation Army was easily repulsed by Vietnamese militia units; Vietnam did not even need to mobilise its regular army.

5 Doubt existed in particular about the return of Hong Kong because only the New Territories were held by lease. Hong Kong island and the Kowloon peninsula were seized earlier as a crown colony.

6 The same point can be made about China's repeated, and strident, assertions that the whole of the South China Sea – as far south as Malaysia and as far east as the Philippines – is its territorial waters. In 1992, the National People's Congress passed a highly provocative piece of legislation asserting Chinese sovereignty and requiring any non-Chinese military vessel to seek China's permission before entering the South China Sea. There has been no effort to enforce this legislation, although China continues to assert its claims in other ways – most often by construction of what it insists are 'fishermen's lodges' on coral reefs hundreds, even thousands, of miles from its shores.

7 The Belgrade embassy bombing took place in May 1999, the spy plane collision in April 2001.

8 China had refused to free the crew from a military guest house on Hainan island when the US government said it was 'sorry' about the incident, but changed its mind when the United States put in writing that it was 'very sorry'. Washington did not, however, accept any liability for the incident.

9 See Jasper Becker, *The Chinese* (John Murray, 2000), pp. 270 and 283. The Chinese navy and air force are included as subsidiary units of the People's Liberation Army.

10 This situation does not apply in the the Special Administrative Regions of Hong Kong and Macau, which have their own legal systems, but the Beijing government does attempt to exert influence to curtail personal freedom beyond what was tolerated in the colonial era.

11 A person can be administratively detained without charge in China for up to three years and, potentially, indefinitely if the authorities decide to renew the detention. The best journalistic coverage of torture and death in captivity cases related to Falun Gong was Ian Johnson's reports in the *Wall Street Journal* in 2000, for which he won a Pulitzer Prize. Johnson's detailed investigation of the death of Chen Zixiu, a 58-year-old retiree from Shandong province who was beaten by police with batons and electrocuted with cattle prods until dead, was taken up by both the United Nations Committee against Torture (CAT) and the US government. See also annual Amnesty International and Human Rights Watch reports.

12 China's Petitions and Appeals Offices date back to imperial times but were maintained by the communist government after 1949 as a form of social safety valve. The offices, which are not listed in telephone directories and are separate from the formal court system, provide a forum for citizens to petition for redress of wrongs. Plain clothes police at the entrances to the offices, however, turn away or detain anyone with an unacceptable grievance, such as political dissidents or Falun Gong members. Tiananmen Square is the traditional focus for anti-government protest and swarms with plain clothes security personnel.

13 Johnson, *n.* 11 above. Freedom of expression is enshrined both in the Chinese constitution and in the International Covenant on Civil and Political Rights, signed by the Chinese government in October 1998.

14 Amnesty International, report index 17/22/2000, 4 May 2000.

15 Amnesty International, China annual report, 2000. A well-connected Chinese defector in the United States who writes under the pseudonym Zong Hairen claimed in 2002 that there were 15,000 executions each year between 1998 and 2001. If true, this would mean China in 2001 accounted for more than 95 per cent of the world's state executions.

16 Amnesty International report above and Ian Johnson, *n.* 11 above. One crime that has, since 1997, been removed from the statute books is that of 'counter-revolution'. This charge was frequently employed against those involved in the 1989 protests and attracted widespread international attention. People already jailed as 'counter-revolutionaries', however, have not had their cases reopened.

17 The State Administration of Industry and Commerce (SAIC) requires businessmen to explain in detail all aspects of the business they will conduct and then assigns them to one of thousands of business licence categories. A small restaurant, for example, might be given a licence for 'Chinese hot service', 'Chinese cold service', 'western hot service' or 'western cold service'. These categories are mutually exclusive, while business can only be conducted at a specified location and only on a retail basis.

18 See Becker, *n.* 9 above, pp. 278 and 329 and Yitzhak Shichor, 'Demobilisation: The

Dialectics of PLA Troop Reduction', *China Quarterly*, no. 146, June 1996. Becker guesses that the current security apparatus includes 3 million PLA soldiers, 2 million PAP (*wu jing*), 2 million regular police (*gong an*), 2 million Ministry of State Security employees and up to 12 million people working full or part time for local public order committees and street committees.

19 Author interview with a senior official at the State Council Office for Restructuring the Economic System (*tigaiban*) who works closely with the prime minister's office, February 2001. The ten 'other government agencies' entitled to attend State Council meetings include institutions like the Development Research Centre, the Chinese Academy of Social Sciences and the China Securities Regulatory Commission. The source rejected the notion that the machinations of central government are unfathomable. 'I could explain the Chinese administration to you, but I would need two or three days,' he quipped. Another senior government source told the author in 2002 that 86 government units currently answer directly to the State Council.

20 The company at the centre of the scandal is called Yuanhua; it leased its chops and licences from Xiamen Dongfang Group, a large state enterprise. According to official media reports, Yuanhua smuggled a total of $6.4 billion of goods over a period of more than five years and evaded $3.6 billion in import duty. See *Far Eastern Economic Review*, 30 November 2000.

21 The minister was Gao Changli. The Party did nothing to counter widespread reports that the sacking was because of corruption.

22 Li Peng was minister of electric power and then deputy premier responsible for electric power in the 1980s. When he rose to the position of premier, his interest in the industry did not abate. Mr Li became the greatest champion of the controversial Three Gorges hydropower project on the Yangzi river, which has been plagued by corruption cases. Li Xiaolin runs China Power Investment Corp., which often helps western firms lobby China's monopoly State Power Corp. and other agencies for projects. See John Pomfret in the *Washington Post*, 26 January 2001.

23 Li Xiaopeng was already vice-president of Hong Kong- and New York-listed China Huaneng Enterprise Group at the age of 34; he subsequently became chairman. Li Peng's wife, Zhu Lin, took charge of the Daya Bay nuclear facility in Guangdong province, which was built with French reactors.

24 Jiang Mianheng, a graduate of Drexel University in the United States, came to prominence in 1999 with a spate of huge telecommunications deals, mostly via his main business, China Netcom Corporation. Mr Jiang's ability to do deals, and win licences, in the most closely guarded and heavily state-controlled sector of the economy is striking.

25 See Becker, *n.* 9 above, p. 360, with respect to the grain funds investigation. The report into diversion of money allocated for poverty relief and other rural development work was published by the National Audit Office in 1999. Both reports focused on the mid and late 1990s.

26 One indicator of how many urban dwellers tap their work units for all they can get

is returns from sample surveys that are sometimes permitted by the government. In 1994, the Gallup Organisation conducted China's first national consumer survey and was surprised to discover that the number of private households claiming to have a fixed-line telephone was not much less than the total number of telephone lines the then Ministry of Posts and Telecommunication said were in existence. When Gallup made spot checks with respondents, many explained that their telephones were installed by their work units but used privately. The percentage of households in Beijing and Shanghai claiming to have a private telephone at this stage was already 40 per cent. See the author, 'Among the Tea Leaves', *Business China*, 6 March 1995.

27   As an example of the lengths people go to to maintain their state sector entitlements, a friend of the author who is a successful rock musician still plays concerts in state-owned factories because this is the 'job' of the official work unit of which he has remained a member. In return for a day's work every couple of months, the musician is in line for a new two-bedroom apartment in Beijing. He will either lease the apartment at a low rent or buy it at a fraction of its construction cost.

28   This takes place after the annual meeting of the National People's Congress and lasts about half an hour.

29   At the start of 2001, the author, the Beijing bureau chief of the *Wall Street Journal* and the Beijing bureau chief of the *Financial Times* all tried to find evidence that these gentlemen had given an interview – or even answered a question – from the non-state media during their careers; nothing was uncovered.

30   Hu was Tibet Party secretary from 1988 to 1992. Following rioting and renewed calls for independence in 1988, martial law was declared in Tibet in March 1989.

31   See James Mann, *About Face: A History of America's Curious Relationship with China from Nixon to Clinton* (Alfred A. Knopf, 1999), p. 32, for more on the Kissinger–Zhou love affair. Most Chinese still regard Zhou as a kind and benign force in recent history, although this is hard to square with the known facts. In 1931, for instance, after Zhou's security chief Gu Shunzhang was arrested by the Kuomintang and gave away the names of hundreds of Communist Party members, the future prime minister reacted by ordering the murder of almost all Gu's known relatives – around thirty people, including his wife and three children. This was not the act of a mild-mannered individual. Unfortunately, the world awaits a really good biography of Zhou.

32   At his annual press conference on 15 March 1999, for instance, Mr Zhu answered a question about international banks' lending in China by mentioning that he had read *The Merchant of Venice* in middle school. Although the plot of the play involves a loan, it was unclear what point Mr Zhu was trying to make – other than that he had read the play – and he quickly changed tack. A little while later he was telling his audience how he had recently explained to US secretary of state Madeleine Albright that he had studied Rousseau in school and that they therefore had many views in common.

33   In the year after he took up the premiership in March 1998, western governments

fell over themselves to invite Zhu Rongji to their capitals, in stark contrast to his predecessor, Li Peng. Zhu travelled to London and Paris in 1998 and Washington in April 1999 – the first visit to the latter city by a Chinese premier since 1984. After the British prime minister met the Chinese premier in London, his spokesman gushed that Tony Blair was 'fascinated' by Mr Zhu and 'in no doubt he was in the presence of a fellow moderniser'. Mr Zhu also enjoyed an audience with the Queen.

34 The use of pagers and the internet has been critical in sustaining the Falun Gong. Members with net access use encryption software available free on the web – most frequently Pretty Good Protection (PGP) freeware – to insulate themselves against the attentions of state security. Mobile telephones are usually not used because they are too easily monitored.

35 The prime minister's Working Conference is the group referred to in Chinese as the *zongli bangonghui*. A Chinese friend of the author who has translated for many of China's most senior leaders and studied the country's political system for two decades, asks rhetorically: 'What is the nerve centre? I always try to find this out from insiders but I am mystified.' The source draws a distinction between central government since the mid 1990s, where it is impossible to identify the leading forum of power, and cities and provinces where the Party boss is always clearly the person in charge.

36 Chinese politics has begun to resemble Russian politics in the pre-reform Soviet Union, when the most faceless leaders – like Yuri Andropov and Konstantin Chernenko – rose to the highest levels.

37 The original plan was for a national pension fund that could make a range of investments, including ones in stock markets. The revised plan is for a pilot pension fund, restricted to Liaoning province in the north-east, that invests only in government debt.

38 The bonds pay the same interest as 10-year treasury bonds.

39 The new law was the Financial Institutions Reform, Recovery and Enforcement Act.

40 The first case of an equity sale by an AMC took place in December 2000, nearly two years after the institutions came into being. *Shanghai Securities News* reported on 11 December 2000 that Huarong AMC would sell its holding in Xinjiang Shiyue Tractor Manufacturing to a private enterprise for $13.9 million. A larger equity sale by Huarong took place in December 2001. The book value of the assets offered was $1.31 billion but bidders offered just 9 per cent of this figure. It was expected this would further delay subsequent offerings. See *Financial Times*, 29 November 2001. In the US, by contrast, the Resolution Trust Corp. in its second full year of operation, 1991, resolved 268 savings and loan institutions involving $88 billion in assets.

41 Edward Steinfeld, the MIT economist, published a telling case study of Central China Non-Ferrous Metals (CCNFM) in October 2000. The 9,500-worker state company, which has lost money every year for a decade, was allowed to swap $337 million of bank loans for nearly 90 per cent of its equity, making two AMCs its nominal owners. The AMCs obtained the right to appoint seven out of nine advi-

sory board members, but not the chairman. The AMCs did not obtain a presence on site, and control over management appointments remained with the local Party Committee. The net result was that the AMCs – on paper owners of nine-tenths of CCNFM's stock – exercised no real control. Management, meanwhile, was taking new loans from state banks and dreaming of an initial public offering whose proceeds would be used to buy back equity from the AMCs. Steinfeld's paper was published in Asia by Credit Lyonnais Securities Asia, *Greater China Research*, October 2000.

42 Naturally, the government claimed the $144 billion transfer of non-performing loans would be the last of its kind, but without the commercialisation of the banking system it is unlikely to be the case.

43 Lending by all financial institutions increased by 13.4 per cent in 2000 versus GDP growth of 8 per cent.

44 In a 1993 report, 'China: Urban Land Management in an Emerging Market Economy', the World Bank valued the Chinese government's real estate holdings at Rmb2–5 trillion ($350–850 billion at the contemporary exchange rate).

45 China Mobile listed in 1997 as China Telecom (Hong Kong) and changed its name on 5 July 2000. A valuation of $115 billion was based on a peak price of HK$80 per share. A total $450 billion valuation for all state telecoms companies was arrived at by adding $100 billion for fixed-line operations to a theoretical $345 billion for all mobile operations (only one-third of which are listed through China Mobile). See 'On the Block: What is the Family Silver Worth?', *China Economic Quarterly*, Q2, 2000, p. 42.

46 ABN AMRO China research, May 2000, quoted in the *China Economic Quarterly*, as above. Aviation: the foreign traded market capitalisation of China Eastern Airlines was $160m, that of China Southern Airlines $231m. Expressways: the foreign traded market capitalisation of Jiangsu Expressway was $127m, that of Shenzhen Expressway $78m, that of Zhejiang Expressway $171m, that of Anhui Expressway $35m, that of Sichuan Expressway $49m. Power: the foreign traded market capitalisation of Beijing Datang Power was $195m, that of Guangdong Electric $150m, that of Huaneng Power $320m, that of Shandong International Power $138m, that of Zhejiang SE Power $167m. The total market capitalisations of the companies are higher because they include domestic Chinese A share capitalisations that trade at prices often ten or twenty times those which foreign investors are willing to pay.

47 China Mobile was trading in Hong Kong at HK$25 in April 2001, down from a peak of HK$80. China Unicom listed in 2000 at HK$19.99, fell below HK$10 and recovered to HK$15 by April 2001.

48 In its initial public offering in 1997, and a subsequent placement, China Mobile raised almost $5 billion in return for 24 per cent of its issued shares. A further, record placement at the end of 2000 – just before the technology bubble burst – raised $6.6bn. China Unicom's initial public offering in 2000 was the largest ever by an Asian company outside Japan, raising $5.6 billion.

49 The companies were motorcycle maker China Jialing Industry and Guizhou Tyre. They were chosen as model candidates after a long selection process. The government aimed to raise only $65 million, but could not find the investors to take up the stock. The second attempt to sell down state holdings in summer 2001 lasted only three months before it was put on indefinite hold in October. Even if the state does manage to sell down its holdings in the future, the idea that the money will go to the treasury – the Ministry of Finance – is at best theoretical. Many other players, such as local and provincial governments, industrial bureaus in Beijing and the Ministry of Labour and Social Security all have claims on the ownership of state shares and any funds raised by their sale. Which agencies own what part of state companies is almost never clearly defined.

50 For a discussion of this phenomenon see *China Economic Quarterly*, as *n*. 45 above.

51 The listing of China Petroleum and Chemical Corp., known as Sinopec, was delayed from April to November 2000. At a reduced price, international oil majors Exxon, Shell and BP, as well as several Hong Kong congomerates, put up nearly $2 billion. BP also took up a large part of Petrochina's offering at a reduced price and with undisclosed agreements about future co-operation. The listing of China National Offshore Oil Corp. was delayed from October 1999 until 2001; the pricing was reduced to a price–earnings ratio of less than five.

52 The government has many means to massage the reported profit figures of listed state monopolies and, with international interest waning, the oil and telecom companies all reported figures at or ahead of earnings forecasts through late 2000 and 2001. None the less, foreign markets were underwhelmed. Petrochina reported a $6.7 billion profit for 2000, off the back of high oil prices, yet its stock price valued the company in April 2001 at only $35 billion.

53 Among New York- and Hong Kong-listed companies requesting mainland offerings in 2001 were Sinopec, China Unicom, Huaneng Power, China Shipping, Yanzhou Coal, and Tsingtao. China Mobile said an A share listing was under consideration.

54 The US-educated director of a State Council office who works regularly with the premier presents a frequently heard argument as follows: 'We can use WTO as an external pressure to go forward. We have no choice.' Author interview, February 2001.

55 China's accession occurred on 11 December 2001 following ratification by the National People's Congress.

56 Congress does not vote on approval of China's WTO accession, which is an executive decision of the president, but congress did have to grant Permanent Normal Trade Relations (PNTR) status to China, which happened in June 2000.

57 The opening of markets will in many sectors mean the legalisation of joint ventures, not wholly foreign-owned investments.

58 The annual volume of contracted foreign direct investment peaked in 1993 at $111 billion and fell steadily to a level of $41 billion in 1999. Since some contracted investment never materialises, it was widely expected that in 2000 the actual volume of foreign direct investment delivered would drop well below $40 billion,

the level at which it held since 1996. In the event, China reported foreign direct investment of just over $40 billion for 2000 and $32 billion in the first nine months of 2001. There are, however, innumerable questions hanging over the reliability of China's foreign investment data, which are issued by the Ministry of Foreign Trade and Economic Co-operation without any clear explanation of how the statistics are gathered and collated.

59   At his 15 March 1999 press conference, Mr Zhu's frustration was already palpable: 'I am disatisfied that I have not done a good job [in the last year],' he told reporters. 'But some individual departments and localities have failed to fully implement the decisions of the Central Committee and the State Council.' It was in the same press conference that Mr Zhu went on to make his famous remark that in thirteen fruitless years of WTO talks 'black hair has turned white, now it is time to complete the negotiations'. Quotations from author's notes.

60   The most telling evidence of China's weakness was its acceptance, in the bilateral discussion with the United States, of so-called 'special safeguard' rules with respect to Chinese exports. Under the terms of the deal signed in November 1999, China agreed that for a period of twelve years Washington could block Chinese exports of any goods that it deemed to be 'surging', or rising too fast. China will have no recourse at the WTO in Geneva against these unilateral US decisions. The only precedents for such an arrangement are anti-surge rules enforced by the US against Poland, Hungary and Romania when they joined the WTO's predecessor, the General Agreement on Tariffs and Trade (GATT), at the height of the Cold War thirty years ago. Officials at the World Bank, International Monetary Fund and US embassy in Beijing who spoke off the record with the author at the time expressed disbelief and embarrassment that China had accepted the anti-surge mechanism over so long a period.

61   There is no direct correlation between tariff rates and import levels in China; the correlation that exists is between imports and the overall rate of economic growth. See Mark Frazier, 'Coming to Terms with the "WTO effect" on US–China Trade and China's Economic Growth', National Bureau of Asian Research, 2000, and 'Life after the WTO Honeymoon: Theory and Practice', China Economic Quarterly, Q1, 2000. Average tariff figures calculated by the World Bank.

62   Frazier, above. From 1984 to 1999, for every one percentage point change in China's GDP growth – up or down – there was a 2.94 percentage point change in imports from the US and a 3.68 percentage point change in imports from the European Union. This is called the elasticity of demand for imports.

63   The minister of information industries, Wu Jichuan, said in an interview with the foreign editor of the Wall Street Journal shortly after the Sino-US accord was signed: 'I believe that once China joins the WTO, China will allow foreign investors to have a 50 per cent interest in telecom joint ventures. I think that for any country, companies must be registered with the national telecom authority.' When it was put to Mr Wu that in the United States anyone could become, for example, an internet content provider (ICP) without a registration or licence, he appeared genuinely

flummoxed by the possibility. 'If you operate without a licence, there's a tax collection problem,' he attempted, going on to say that in China ICPs would continue to require subsidiary licences to carry advertisements, hold auctions and conduct other normal business activities. (From the original interview transcript.) Only four days after the Sino-US accord was signed, the head of the China Insurance Regulatory Commission, Ma Yongwei, had told a press conference that China would still block new insurance licences after WTO accession if they were deemed not to be 'prudent' from the perspective of monetary, financial or credit policy. See *China Economic Quarterly*, Q1, 2000.

64 China promised to resolve the medfly stand-off, along with another technical standards dispute about TCK smut in wheat, as part of the Sino-US WTO accord of November 1999.

65 It is a slightly churlish comparison to make, but it is interesting to see how the Italians' love affair with the European Union as a vehicle for domestic political change turned out. The EU commissioners themselves proved to so be bureaucratic and corrupt in the late 1990s that, in an ironic twist, an upstanding Italian – Romano Prodi – was brought in to restore the institution's credibility. Italian politics was cleaned up considerably in the 1990s, but all the change came from popular pressure and from within the country.

66 By 2001, direct elections to some of China's 800,000 village committees had taken place in each of the country's thirty provinces. There is not always a free choice of candidates – in many instances the candidates are selected by the Party – and 70 per cent of village leaders are Party members. Senior Chinese leaders have held out the prospect for a decade of extending direct elections to the leaders of China's townships and counties – Zhu Rongji reiterated that this would happen 'as soon as possible' at his annual National People's Congress press conference in 2000 – but no progress actually occurs.

67 Population data released by China in 1979 show that at least 30 million people died as a result of famine following the Great Leap Forward. Add to this the millions-long death toll from the killing of landlords and other 'anti-revolutionaries' between 1948 and 1955 (Mao Zedong claimed only 700,000 died, former minister of public security Luo Ruiqing reportedly estimated 4 million), those who died during the anti-rightist campaign of 1957 (there were 553,000 officially recorded denunciations) and in the Cultural Revolution of the 1960s and 1970s, and other extra-judicial killings that continue to this day, and a total of 50 million is far from fanciful. See Nicholas D. Kristof and Sheryl WuDunn, *China Wakes: The Struggle for the Soul of a Rising Power*, revised edition (Nicholas Brealey, 1998), p. 65, Jasper Becker's *Hungry Ghosts: China's Secret Famine* (John Murray, 1996), and *The Chinese*, *n*. 9 above, p. 24.

68 Chiang Kai-shek is most infamously remembered, in the wake of civil unrest on Taiwan in 1947, for the massacre of an estimated 25,000 professionals and intellectuals on 28 February that year. The incident is known in Taiwan by the numbers of its date, '28-2', just as the Tiananmen massacre of 1989 is known to mainlanders as '6-4'.

69 See Chris Anderson, 'A Survey of Taiwan', *Economist*, 5 November 1998.

70 By the fairest reckoning available, US exports to China from 1990 to 1999 inclusive totalled $140 billion. This figure takes account of the deficiencies of US official statistics, which exclude US exports to mainland China via Hong Kong. See K. C. Fung and Lawrence J. Lau, *New Estimates of the United States–China Bilateral Trade Balances* (Institute for International Studies, Stanford University, April 1999). US exports to Taiwan from 1990 to 1999 inclusive totalled $169 billion, according to data published by the US Census Bureau. In the late 1990s, the Asian financial crisis heavily impacted Taiwanese imports from the US, which totalled $22.5 billion in 2000. The latest year for which adjusted Chinese import numbers are available is 1999, when purchases from the US totalled $20.4 billion.

71 China effected numerous changes to election procedures after 1 July 1997, all of which make it harder for pro-democracy politicians to be elected. These included a switch from single to multiple seat constituencies for popular elections, reduction in the number of voters in so-called 'functional', or industry and profession-based, constituencies and the reintroduction of appointed politicians. Most of these changes reversed ones introduced by Chris Patten.

72 The principle is enshrined in Article 45 of Hong Kong's Basic Law.

73 Lam, who had been China editor at the *South China Morning Post*, resigned on 4 November 2000, a week after this incident took place, having been told that he was being reassigned to a general reporting job about China and that his articles would have to be reviewed by the paper's editor, Robert Keatley, prior to publication.

74 In January 1999, the Court of Final Appeal struck down elements of the immigration law passed by the Beijing appointed Provisional Legislation Council in July 1997.

75 The proportion fell to just under half in the aftermath of the Asian financial crisis. On official Chinese figures, Hong Kong and Taiwan accounted for 47 per cent of China's foreign direct investment in 1999 ($16.3 billion and $2.6 billion respectively) and 47 per cent in 1998, down from 58 per cent in 1996 and 62 per cent in 1995. The official figures should be treated with caution. Those for Taiwan are probably too low since many Taiwanese firms use companies incorporated in Hong Kong and elsewhere as their mainland investment vehicles. The figures for Hong Kong are overstated since they include investment from Hong Kong-registered, but not Hong Kong-owned, businesses, not least mainland investments which 'round-trip' through Hong Kong to take advantage of tax breaks for 'foreign' investors.

Chapter 12 The longest dream

1 Carl Crow, *400 Million Customers* (Harpers, 1937), p. 304.

2 Many secondary indicators failed to tally with reported overall growth rates of 7.8 per cent and 7.2 per cent in 1998 and 1999 respectively. Energy consumption, domestic freight and air passenger traffic barely increased during the period, while sales of clothing, for instance, fell heavily. Tom Rawski, a US economist at

the University of Pittsburgh who compared China's reported GDP growth with a range of 'proxy' indicators, concluded that real growth in both 1998 and 1999 was somewhere between −2.5 per cent and +2 per cent each year. See 'Numbers That Suck (And Some That Don't)', *China Economic Quarterly*, Q1 2001. Privately, World Bank economists agreed that Chinese growth was significantly overstated in 1998 and 1999, though perhaps not by as much as Professor Rawski claimed.

3   Utilised foreign direct investment, as officially reported, fell 11 per cent from $45.2 billion in 1998 to $40.3 billion in 1999 and $40.8 billion in 2000.

4   Contracted, which is to say promised, foreign direct investment, having fallen 20 per cent in 1999 to $41 billion, bounced back by 50 per cent in 2000 to $63 billion and rose another 32 per cent, year-on-year, in the first eight months of 2001 to $44 billion.

5   Remark made to the author by Stefan Ogden of Glencore, a multinational minerals mining company, at a meeting of business executives in Beijing, 31 November 2001.

6   Preliminary results of the 2001–2 survey obtained by the author, for which returns were collected in September 2001 for publication in March 2002, showed that 83 per cent of respondents believed WTO membership would increase demand for their products and services, 81 per cent said it would increase their investment options and 86 per cent said it would increase legal and commercial transparency in China. Separately, 82 per cent of members said their five-year business plan was being affected by the prospect of WTO accession benefits. The survey covered around 150 American companies.

7   US GDP shrank around 1 per cent in the third quarter of 2001 on an annualised basis, according to initial returns. It was the first quarterly contraction since 1993. A recession is defined as two successive quarters of contraction, which last occurred in the fourth quarter of 1990 and the first quarter of 1991. At the time of writing (November 2001), official growth figures for Japan and the Eurozone for the third quarter of 2001 were not published, but the forecasts of many economists were that both would be negative.

8   See the *Financial Times*, 26 October 2001. The suspension of the government's sale of state shareholdings came only four months after the announcement, in June 2001, that it would push ahead with the plans which have been mooted for several years.

9   The deal was confirmed by Netcom CEO Edward Tian in February 2001. See FT.com, 20 February 2001. Individual stakes in the investment were not broken out, but News Corporation and Goldman Sachs were stated to be the two largest investors. It was subsequently reported that the News Corporation share was $60 million. See Reuters, 5 September 2001.

10   Author interview with one of the lead negotiators in the deal, 6 November 2001. Also, the Netcom deal was not the first direct investment by foreign companies in a Chinese telecommunications service, since AT&T already operated a small 'experimental' joint venture in Shanghai's Pudong New Area. This had been China's sop to AT&T after its plans to build a multibillion dollar business in the country did not receive the necessary licences.

11 The partners had opened a small office in Hong Kong.

12 News Corporation was granted permission to distribute its Phoenix Mandarin language general entertainment channel, part of the loss-making Star television satellite service, through Guangdong cable television, which has a maximum potential audience of about six million homes. AOL Time Warner was granted permission to broadcast approved programming from a Mandarin language network called China Entertainment Television (CETV), which it acquired in June 2000, in selected parts of Guangdong province. Both foreign companies agreed to broadcast similar volumes of Chinese state television on their North American networks in return.

13 Author interview, 6 November 2001.

14 American Chamber China member questionnaire 1999. The question about China operating margins and cost of capital was answered by 108 companies. Twenty nine per cent of respondents said margins were 'significantly lower' than their cost of capital, 27 per cent said 'slightly lower', 32 per cent said 'comparable', 9 per cent said 'slightly higher' and 3 per cent said 'significantly higher'. Companies' cost of capital in China is more than that in developed economies because of the risk of emerging markets and is usually reckoned internally by multinational companies at 10–15 per cent. This rate, higher than headline global borrowing rates, is sometimes referred to as the 'hurdle rate', meaning the rate of return that must be exceeded to produce a genuine profit in the market.

15 In the 1999 Amercan Chamber survey, for instance, 60 per cent of eighty responding companies said they took more than three years to achieve profitability in their first China venture. Of forty-nine companies that had started further ventures, 71 per cent said profitability took more than three years in those cases.

16 See 'The Best Multinationals in China', *China Econonomic Quarterly*, Q2 2001. Carrefour's China revenues in 2000 were Rmb8.1 billion ($976 million). The performance of Carrefour's low-cost hypermarkets is particularly striking in a retail sector where so many upmarket department stores have failed and where foreign entrants have been unable to build a single national supermarket chain.

17 See *China Economic Quarterly*, above.

18 The scheduled openings of ten more stores were suspended. At the time of writing, it was unclear what would happen to Carrefour. Closure of its business was highly unlikely given strong European Commission support for the company and backing from Chinese municipal governments that benefit from taxes paid by Carrefour. It was more likely that the company would be fined by the State Economic and Trade Commission and required to apply for national licences before opening new branches. This latter sanction would slow the company's expansion, which could pose a serious problem. Economies of scale are critical to discount retailing and Carrefour only turned an operating profit in China after opening its twentieth store.

19 These titles are owned by Hearst Corp., for which IDG also publishes *Modern Bride* and *Good Housekeeping* in China.

20 See *China Economic Quarterly*, n. 17 above.

21 See the discussion of the mobile telephony phenomenon in chapter 8.

22   This includes revenues from IDG's consulting business. See *China Economic Quarterly, n.* 17 above.

23   In the 2000 American Chamber survey, 75 per cent of respondents forecast better margins in 2001. When the 2001 survey came, only 46 per cent reported that this had happened while a similar proportion said margins were the same or worse. With a gloomy macro outlook for 2002, 63 per cent of companies still forecast margins would get better in 2002. In the 1999 American Chamber survey, which contained additional questions about global investment comparisons, only 14 per cent of respondents said China margins were better than their world averages, and 58 per cent said margins were worse.

24   Between 1992 and the end of 2000, Japan launched ten fiscal stimulus packages involving total expenditure of ¥130 trillion ($1.2 trillion), or more than one-quarter of GDP. Average GDP growth in the 1990s was just 1.3 per cent.

25   The budgeted fiscal stimulus over the five years from 1998 to 2002 came to Rmb750 billion ($90 billion), or about 9 per cent of GDP. This was superficially slower than the pace of Japan's public investment programme (which committed over a quarter of GDP in 10 years), but when Chinese investment paid for via state policy banks and the regular nationalised banks is included, China's rate of fiscal stimulus is higher.

26   China was the biggest mobile telephone market in the world by 2002 and Japan the most advanced. The latter had over 25 million third-generation mobile internet subscribers in 2001, before such services had been launched anywhere else in the world.

27   In China, most of the construction industry is state-owned; in Japan, it is in private hands but enjoys very close relations with the bureaucracy and the dominant Liberal Democratic Party. In both countries the construction industry is the main beneficiary of state investment.

28   In China, despite repeated interest rate cuts, retail price deflation had been continuing for four years by the end of 2001. In Japan, where interest rates were cut close to zero, there were persistent bouts of deflation from 1993, with prices falling almost every month between 1999 and 2002.

29   Japan's 2000 per capita GNP was more than $34,000, according to World Bank data.

30   Japan Information Network/Ministry of Foreign Affairs.

31   IMF data. Singapore managed a similar feat, growing an average 8.7 per cent a year from 1965 to 1995.

32   As Albert Keidel, until 2001 the World Bank Senior Economist for China, writes: 'It is virtually certain that official growth data overstate actual growth by varying degrees and that the overstatement became more serious in the latter 1990s ... GDP growth rates must be used with some care, especially when making comparisons with other countries in their high-growth periods.' See analysis of Chinese GDP figures in *CEQ Statistics*, a statistical service provided by the *China Economic Quarterly*.

33   See *ns*. 2 and 8, above.

34 Japan's budget was in balance or in surplus through the 1980s and early 1990s. Thereafter the government began to run large budget deficits – around 6 per cent of GDP – as it attempted to reignite the economy. By 2001, government debt had risen to 120 per cent of GDP.

35 The government said in 2000 it would guarantee Rmb1.2 trillion ($144 billion) in interest bearing bonds to be given to the four largest state banks in exchange for non-performing loans. In 1998, the government already guaranteed a Rmb270 billion ($33 billion) bond issue to replenish the banks' capital. By 2000, state policy banks had issued Rmb500 billion ($60 billion) of state guaranteed bonds and the rate of issuance accelerated in 2001. See chapter 9.

36 After falling 20 per cent in 1999 to $41 billion, contracted foreign direct investment in China rose 50 per cent in 2000 (following the November 1999 Sino-US bilateral accord on WTO accession) to $61 billion and a further 32 per cent in the first eight months of 2001, compared with the same period in 2000, to $44 billion.

37 See *South China Morning Post*, 30 October 2001.

38 An article about 'hollowing out' in Singapore's *Straits Times* on 15 September 2001, for example, began with the words: 'The economic ascent of China is casting a lengthening shadow on the region.' Singapore's exports were experiencing heavy falls at the time.

39 See *South China Morning Post*, 30 October 2001.

40 See Andy Rothman, 'Economic Solutions to the China–Taiwan Conflict', a Credit Lyonnais Securities Asia research report published in May 2001.

41 See Rothman, above.

42 The breweries of Mr Perkowski's company, ASIMCO, were sold off at a large loss. The reorganised, export-oriented car components factories were, by 2000, producing a modest operating profit, though nothing like what Mr Perkowski had projected to Wall Street investors. Author interview with Tim Clissold, ASIMCO president, 7 September 2000.

43 The author visited the factory twice in the course of the 1990s. The company acquired several second-tier European labels in order to give European branding to its exports from China.

44 Exports by the world's leading export nations in 2000, based on World Bank data, were: United States, $782 billion; Germany, $551 billion; Japan, $479 billion; France, $298 billion; United Kingdom, $280 billion; Canada, $277 billion; China, $249 billion; Italy, $235 billion; Netherlands, $212 billion. Between 1999 and 2000, China overtook both Italy and the Netherlands.

45 Author interview, notes undated.

46 Data from Automotive Resources Asia. Shanghai GM's 2000 sales of 30,000 units were 20,000 units less than the company had forecast. In the first ten months of 2001, sales of the Buick saloon fell further to 15,814 units, implying a total of around 20,000 for the year. Sales in late 1999 and 2000 had been helped by the fact that GM invested considerable effort in winning pre-orders before beginning production. Also, car sales are booked in China when vehicles are shipped to retailers

and retailers held no stock of Buicks in 1999. GM managed to sell 7,655 GL8 mini-vans – known in North America as the Pontiac Montana – in the first ten months of 2001. The Buick Sail compact car launched in May 2001 and around 16,000 units were sold by the end of October. However, because of pre-orders and retailer stock requirements, it was again far from clear whether the company could maintain this rate of sales.

47 See chapter 3.

48 The Shenyang joint venture was originally signed in 1991, began production in 1992, ceased in 1993, revived briefly in 1994–5 and thereafter shut down for six years. Under a deal signed in June 1998, GM put more cash into the venture and in return increased its equity from 30 per cent to 50 per cent. The factory was retooled to make an S-10 pick-up truck with a double cabin as well as GM's Chevrolet Blazer sports utility vehicle. Production was supposed to start in 2000, but actually began in 2001. Target sales for the first year of operations were just 4,000 units.

49 Car sales in China in 2000 were around 600,000 units. As noted in chapter 7, this is only slightly more than in Australia, a country of 19 million people. In late 2000 and 2001, GM re-entered negotiations for a joint venture to make a sub-compact car with Chang'an Automobile Group, formerly part of the Norinco military industrial conglomerate, that manufactures Suzuki Alto minicars under licence. GM had already spent long periods in negotiation with the company in the 1990s as part of its strategy to have three separate China production centres with three different product ranges.

50 As quoted in the epigraph at the beginning of chapter 3.

51 This prediction was made at the Fortune Shanghai Global Forum in September 1999 and widely reported. See *Nikkei Weekly*, 6 December 1999.

52 This latest prediction was repeated several times to journalists in 2001. See, for instance, *China Daily Business Weekly* of 7 August 2001. Mr Wagoner said his forecast was based around average 17 per cent growth per year in the Chinese automotive market for a decade, followed by somewhat slower growth for another fifteen years.

53 *Asiaweek*, 4 April 2001.

54 *Barron's*, 18 June 2001. Wagoner granted the publication's editors a two-hour inter-view that dealt at length with GM's global strategy.

55 Crow observed: 'Any time an export manager wants to enjoy a pleasant day-dream of the future, in which fame and prosperity will unite to banish daily cares, all he has to do is to take a pencil and a pad of paper and start figuring out what sales he could make if he only found an advertising agent clever enough to induce a reasonable proportion of China's 400 million customers to buy his goods. Merchants wore out quill-pens on the same pleasant speculations long before graphite pencils, calculating machines and advertising agents began to play an important part in the affairs of the business world.' See Crow, *n.* 1 above.

Epilogue

1 Author interview, September 2002.

2 *Asian Wall Street Journal*, 22 August 2002.

3 Quoted in George Wingrove Cook, *China; being 'The Times' special correspondence from China in the years 1857–58*, (G. Routledge & Co., 1859), p.xxii.

Selected bibliography

The following is a list of books that were particularly useful in researching *The China Dream*. There are short descriptive notes after each entry.

Foreigners and foreign businesses in China

Carl Crow, *400 Million Customers* (Harper,1937) The classic tale of business in inter-war Shanghai

James Mann, *Beijing Jeep: A Case Study of Western Business in China* (Simon & Schuster, 1989; updated version, Westview Press, 1997). One 1980s joint venture becomes an allegory for the woes of others.

James Mann, *About Face: A History of America's Curious Relationship with China from Nixon to Clinton* (Alfred A. Knopf, 1998). The bizarre twists and turns of the US's China policy since Nixon and the influence of the US business lobby.

Alain Peyrefitte, *L'empire immobile, ou, Le Chos des mondes*, translated as *The Collision of Two Civilisations: The British Expedition to China in 1792–4* (Harvill, 1993), Lord Macartney's 1792–4 mission to China.

Jonathan D. Spence, *The Chan's Great Continent: China in Western Minds* (W. W. Norton, 1998). A history of foreign perceptions of China, particularly as expressed in literature.

Randall E. Stross, *Bulls in the China Shop and Other Sino-American Business Encounters* (Pantheon, 1990). Broader ranging than *Beijing Jeep*, with many more strands to it; follows the foreign investment story into the early 1990s.

Joe Studwell, *Multinationals in China: Winners and Losers* (Economist Intelligence Unit, 1997) An industry by industry review of multinationals' performance in the mid 1990s.

History

S. A. M. Adshead, *China in World History* (Macmillan, 1987). China by comparison with her peers through the last 3,000 years; dense, erudite.

W. H. Auden and Christopher Isherwood, *Journey to a War* (Faber & Faber, 1939). A highly readable tale of two Englishmen wandering around China during the Sino-Japanese war.

Ray Huang, *1587: A Year of No Significance: The Ming Dynasty in Decline* (Yale University Press, 1981). The story of the reign of Wan Li, but equally a parable for the perennial problems of Chinese politics.

Edward H. Schafer, *The Golden Peaches of Samarkand: A Study of T'ang Exotics* (Cambridge

University Press, 1963). An eclectic and entertaining view of the Tang dynasty.
Jonathan D. Spence, *The Search for Modern China* (Hutchinson, 1990; second edition, W. W. Norton, 1999). Perhaps the best regular history of China.

Economics

George T. Crane The Political Economy of China's Special Economic Zones (Studies on Contemporary China) (M.E Sharpe, April 1990). Academic treatise on the genesis of China's special economic zones.

China's Emerging Private Enterprises: Prospects for the New Century (International Finance Corporation, September 2000). The fullest survey to date of the development of China's private economy.

Nicholas R. Lardy, *Foreign Trade and Economic Reform in China, 1978–90* (Cambridge University Press, 1992). The first decade of market opening reforms.

Nicholas R. Lardy, *China in the World Economy* (Institute for International Economics, 1994). Development of China's foreign trade in the 1980s.

Nicholas R. Lardy, *China's Unfinished Economic Revolution (Brookings Institution Press, 1998).* The emerging problems of the nationalised banking system in the 1990s.

Barry Naughton, *Growing out of the Plan: Chinese Economic Reform 1978–93* (Cambridge University Press, 1995). Key textbook for economic and policy developments in the 1980s.

Edward S. Steinfeld, *Forging Reform in China: From Party Line to Bottom Line in the State-owned Enterprise* (Cambridge University Press, 1998). The best available study of the plight of state enterprises.

Politics/Contemporary China

Richard Baum, *Burying Mao: Chinese Politics in the Age of Deng Xiaoping* (Princeton University Press, 1996). Well written political history of China in the Deng Xiaoping era.

Jasper Becker, *The Chinese* (John Murray, 2000). Useful contemporary survey.

Deng Xiaoping, *Selected Works of Deng Xiaoping, vol. 3 (1982–92)* (Beijing Foreign Languages Press, 1994). Turgid, ugly prose, but a key source for 1980s China.

Richard Evans, *Deng Xiaoping and the Making of Modern China* (Hamish Hamilton, 1993; new edition, Penguin, 1995). Highly readable biography.

W. E. F. Jenner, *The Tyranny of History: The Roots of China's Crisis* (Allen Lane, 1992). Classic study that traces the links between China's history and her current social and political problems.

Nicholas D. Kristof and Sheryl WuDunn, *China Wakes: The Struggle for the Soul of a Rising Power* (Nicholas Brealey, 1994). Two journalists' reflections on early 1990s China; the social observations are stronger than the economic ones.

Willy Wo-Lap Lam, *China after Deng Xiaoping:The Power Struggle in Beijing since Tiananmen* (J. Wiley & Sons, 1995) and *The Era of Jiang Zemin* (Prentice Hall, 1999). A born conspiracy theorist, Willy Wo-Lap Lam is Hong Kong's leading follower of Chinese politics; he is also a man who often turns out to be right.

Li Zhisui, *The Private Life of Chairman Mao: The Memoirs of Mao's Personal Physician, Dr Li Zhisui* (Chatto & Windus, 1994). The inside story of Mao's household and the machinations of Chinese palace politics.

Perry Link, *Evening Chats in Beijing: Probing China's Predicament* (W. W. Norton, 1992). Perceptive commentary on contemporary China, based on interviews with Chinese intellectuals.

Jan Wong, *Red China Blues: My Long March from Mao to Now* (Bantam, 1997). Evocative journalistic potboiler that brings early 1990s China to life.

Zhang Liang, edited by Andrew J. Nathan and Perry E. Link, afterword by Orville Schell, *The Tiananmen Papers : The Chinese Leadership's Decision to Use Force against Their Own People – In Their Own Words* (Little, Brown, 2001). Leaked documents that allegedly record key conversations between senior leaders in the run-up to and aftermath of the 1989 Tiananmen massacre.

Acknowledgements

A LONG LIST OF thanks is due to those who made this book possible. First, to the editorial teams in London and New York which improved on everything I did: publishers Andrew Franklin and Morgan Entrekin and editors Martin Liu, Penny Daniel, Brendan Cahill and, especially, Sally Holloway. The gentle criticism and unpaid endeavours of Ian Johnson and my wife, Tiffany Bown, were invaluable. I am embarrassed to have consumed so many people's time. Second, I am indebted to a group of economists who variously explained to, argued and disagreed with me in the course of my research: Albert Keidel, Nicholas Lardy, Paul Heytens, Davin Mackenzie and Robin Bordie are some, but not all, of them. May their patience be rewarded. I would also like to thank all those businessmen and women – Chinese and not – who granted me interviews during my years living in China. The tyranny of multinationals' press officers is often no less than that of China's media managers, and there were many who risked the censure of their corporate and state handlers to speak openly. They were the makings of this book. Thirdly, thank you to Joe Spieler for selling this book in New York, to Edward Young for research that contributed to chapter 1, to Jeanne-Marie Gescher for providing office space and other support in Beijing and, once again, to my wife, whose list of indulgences is too long to recount. Finally, a word of thanks for the inspiration provided by those who write with humour and humanity about business and economics. The likes of John Maynard Keynes and Milton Friedman, and in the case of China Carl Crow, were a constant reminder that books about these subjects do not have to be dull.

Index